COLONIZING THE PAST

COLONIZING THE PAST

Mythmaking and Pre-Columbian Whites in Nineteenth-Century American Writing

EDWARD WATTS

University of Virginia Press

CHARLOTTESVILLE AND LONDON

University of Virginia Press
© 2020 by the Rector and Visitors of the University of Virginia
All rights reserved
Printed in the United States of America on acid-free paper

First published 2020

1 3 5 7 9 8 6 4 2

Library of Congress Cataloging-in-Publication Data

Names: Watts, Edward, 1964– author.
Title: Colonizing the past : mythmaking and pre-Columbian whites in nineteenth-
century American writing / Edward Watts.
Description: Charlottesville : University of Virginia Press, 2020. | Includes
bibliographical references and index.
Identifiers: LCCN 2019037204 (print) | LCCN 2019037205 (ebook) |
ISBN 9780813943862 (hardcover) | ISBN 9780813943879 (paperback) |
ISBN 9780813943886 (epub)
Subjects: LCSH: American literature—19th century—History and criticism. |
Imperialism in literature. | National characteristics, American, in literature. | Whites in
literature. | Colonies in literature. | Mythology in literature. | America—In literature.
Classification: LCC PS217.I47 W38 2020 (print) |
LCC PS217.I47 (ebook) | DDC 810.9/3587001—dc23
LC record available at https://lccn.loc.gov/2019037204.
LC ebook record available at https://lccn.loc.gov/2019037205.

Cover art: "St. Brendan and His Monks Set Sail For a Western Land," from
Our Country In Story, Franciscan Sisters of the Perpetual Adoration, 1917 (New York
Public Library); additional elements from Shutterstock (therealtakeone/Santi S/Celig)

To Stephanie, Tony, and Alex

It is curious that time and again, when people create alternate histories, they are largely replicating a history we already know, and intimately. They are replicating histories where whiteness thrives, and people of color remain oppressed.

—Roxane Gay, *New York Times*, 25 July 2017

CONTENTS

ACKNOWLEDGMENTS

Primary thanks are to the editors, readers, and other participants at the University of Virginia Press. I especially thank Eric Brandt for his patience in finding readers who truly understood the project. Sections of this book were presented at the Newberry Library's D'Arcy McNickle Seminar in American Indian Studies and at Michigan State University's English Departmental Speaker Series. Conference papers drawn from it were presented at various Society of Early Americanists, Charles Brockden Brown Society, Western American Literature, Native American Literature, and Society for the Study of American Women Writers meetings. At every stage and venue, I thank my friends and participants for their insights. Sections were read and feedback provided by Malini Johar Schueller and Keri Holt at different stages of its development. My colleagues at Michigan State, especially Steve Arch and Steve Rachman, provided moral support. Pat O'Donnell helped me secure research leave in fall 2014 as I set the work in motion. Ultimately, though, my most deeply felt thanks are to my family. I lost my parents and my brothers in recent years, but always there to help me through—each in their own ways—were my wife, Stephanie Wengert Watts, and my sons, Anton Peter Watts and Alexander Wengert Watts.

An earlier version of chapter 1 was published in *Mapping Region in Early American Writing*, edited by Edward Watts, Keri Holt, and John Funchion (Athens: University of Georgia Press, 2015). It is reprinted here with permission.

COLONIZING THE PAST

Introduction

The Primordial Nation

It is astonishing how intimate historians do daily become with the
patriarchs and other great men of antiquity. . . . I shall not therefore, stop
to inquire, whether America was first discovered by a wandering vessel
of that celebrated Phoenician fleet . . . ; nor by the Norwegians in 1002,
under Biorn. . . . Nor shall I investigate the more modern claims of the
Welsh, founded on the voyage of Prince Madoc in the eleventh century
who, having never returned, it must have been wisely concluded that he
must have gone to America.

—Washington Irving, *The History of New York by Diedrich Knickerbocker*, 1809

Washington Irving saw it coming. He discouraged it with satire and parody, yet his countrymen persisted. He perceived that, after the Revolution, Americans lacked the common, deep, or meaningful history that, according to the new romantic nationalism, could bind a loose confederation of communities into a genuine nation.[1] The facts of the colonial past—from European discovery to the Revolution—were well documented and may have inspired the required heroic narratives of conquest and settlement. Early republic historians and poets tried to work with existing resources: tomes and epics were written, all of which, to Irving, amounted to pretentious hyperbole, a meaningless slog through tedium reenacted by his own fictive historian's attempt to convert the rather dreary history of New Amsterdam into an epic of transformational significance and community-building meaning.

Most basically, Knickerbocker and his fellow would-be Homers lacked the homegrown, undocumentable legends developed through centuries of telling and retelling in an oral culture needed for events to be transformed into nation-building myths and legends. Of course, such legends and tales about the geographical space of their nation were available; however, they celebrated the peoples whose place they were taking: indigenous Americans.

As such, they were unavailable to the white settlers; in fact, such memorials only reminded them of their late coming and illegitimacy. Whatever epic events the continent had witnessed only diminished their ancestors' connection to America and reminded them of their Old World roots. To transform from political coalition to the "imagined community" of modern nationalism, the new nation needed legends from a premodern, predocumented past that transcended the prior indigenous claim. Moreover, those stories had to be about white people.

To fill this gap, by 1809, early republic writers had already started to fantasize about whites occupying the territory claimed by the nation for centuries before 1492: Phoenician, Norse, and Welsh, as suggested by Knickerbocker, to name only a few. Moreover, their interest transcended sensation or historical happenstance: the adventures and fates of their archaic whites most often prefigured the nation the republic wanted to become.[2] Irving mocked these efforts at creating a foundation for an autonomous and authentic American culture as inherently derivative: each relies upon secondhand Old World legends to tell a new country's story. For him, and for other skeptics of celebratory literary re-creations of pre-Columbian whites, such efforts only mimic Old World quests for exclusionary foundational pasts, subverting rather than authenticating the settler nation's claims to a distinct national identity.[3] Settlers—descendants of the founders of European colonies in spaces previously occupied by conquered and colonized indigenous populations—struggle to reconcile their recent arrival with their need to declare themselves as the land's "natural" inhabitants.[4]

Colonizing the Past explores the many texts produced between 1780 and 1915 that engaged pre-Columbian whites in ways that reflect and express anxieties and ambitions peculiar to settler nations. If sheer numbers are indicative of public interest, pre-Columbian whites drew significant readerly interest throughout the era in question. In the long nineteenth century American settlers consistently sought out any and all potential pre-Columbian whites, upon whom they cast the anxieties and conflicts of the settler nation's growth. Some of these were either salaciously sensational or amateurishly scientific. However, a significant minority brought to bear literary devices and trenchant social and intellectual commentary to compel their readers to make meaningful thematic connections between the prehistorical and the modern. In these texts, anxieties about race and nation, for example, were openly disputed. These pre-1492 prehistories celebrated, critiqued, and problematized these transmutations in the larger context of settler nationalism.

By contrast, profit-driven American print culture throughout the long nineteenth century was peppered with fantasies of pre-Columbian whites, just as Irving had feared, that allowed the settlers to disavow the moral complexities of both the colonial past and their own ongoing colonization of the continent. For example, Josiah Priest's best-selling *American Antiquities* (1834), William Pigeon's *Traditions of De-Coo-Dah* (1858), John Delafield's *An Inquiry into the Origins of the Antiquities of America* (1839), and Alexander Warfield Bradford's *American Antiquities and Researches into the Origin and History of the Red Race* (1843), as well as shorter volumes such as John B. Newman's *The Early Peopling of America* (1848), all depict ancient America as a site of ancient global crossings.[5] Even in the genre of local history, mythic ancient whites are used to evade and erase Indian history: for example, the subtitle of George Atkinson's *History of Kanawha County (West Virginia): From Its Organization to the Present* (1876) would seem to justify the exclusion of all events before 1800. However, a chapter appears on white "Ancient Civilization," yet Indians feature only as the antagonists of settlers. More recently, in *Fantastic Archaeology*, Stephen Williams links these texts and their claims to other sensational aspects of nineteenth-century American culture that were motivated primarily by the commercial potentials of tapping into Americans' hunger for a pre-Columbian past defined by the same interracial violence and bloodied white conquerors that characterized the emerging pulp and dime novel genres.

The quest for pre-Columbian whiteness also stimulated the emergent fields of ethology, ethnology, craniology, phrenology, anthropology, and (nonfantastic) archaeology. Douglas Hunter links the search for pre-Columbian whites to epistemological and theoretical conversations about natural history and human history. In *The Place of Stone* (2017), Hunter tracks how debates about pre-Columbian whites transformed the social sciences by filtering these conversations through various readings of Dighton Rock, a mysterious artifact linked to a variety of proposed possible archaic white populations. While Hunter demonstrates how "colonization employed the language and methodology of science to turn the displaced into the original displacers, the victims of conquest into the original aggressors, and to justify their removal" (13), his primary concern is how these explorations contributed to the history of ideas. Hunter's term "White Tribism" bears further consideration. Focusing mostly on Mound Builders, Hunter notes that many of the groups proposed as pre-Columbian whites were thought to have built the mounds: "Through what I call White Tribism, theorists turned to Indigenous peoples in whom they detected intellectual and cultural capabilities into white, or at least into Indigenous peoples who must have been improved in the past by the superior cultures, technologies, and blood of Europeans. This was also a form of possession, with the bodies and cultures of ancestral Native Americans colonized by newcomers" (10). By identifying such foundational theories, Hunter's study foregrounds my own. As such, as Terry Barnhart suggests, "Antiquarian writings are considered narrow, nonanalytical, and lack a problem orientation" (*American Antiquities*, 30). The same might be said of many of the "scientific" texts developed to explain white tribism: their concern was scientific and historical accuracy. While Hunter's narrative focuses on how many theories based in or even against white tribism led to modern antiquarianism, anthropology, and archaeology, by contrast, *Colonizing the Past* concerns itself more with the public literary, cultural, and political uses to which these theories were put. Poets, historians, travelers, novelists, and even advertisers took theories such as white tribism and engaged larger and less esoteric national conversations about expansionism, industrialism, national identity, and imperialism.

By embracing a "problem orientation" that transcended scientific evidence or historical logic, the literature in question imagined pasts more suited to explore and explain the new nation's evolving sense of itself moving forward. These efforts ultimately reflect more anxiety than confidence, fears at the core of settler subjectivity and sovereignty. To distinguish the scientific and the sensational from the what I call here *primordial*, I have culled mostly literary texts that conjectured alternative pasts to reimagine and reframe the national present. In them, nineteenth-century white settlers and events are linked to binding mystical pasts of legend and tradition, often directly, often through figurative language. More concise, primordialism imaginatively reconstructed a continental past based around ancient North American whites whose success or failure rehearsed or foreshadowed that of the new nation as it transitioned from loose confederation to global empire. As such, primordialist texts both claim the glory of archaic inheritance *and* ponder the possibilities of racial and social degeneration and obscurity implied by the inability of primordial whites to survive into the modern era. Such contradictory simultaneities, I argue, characterize and perform the internalized paradoxes of settler identity and its quixotic quest to overcome its roots in violence and theft.

As such, primordialism was never about Indians but rather always and already about settler representations of their refracted and mythologized selves. In most primordialist texts, Indians are undifferentiated, secondary role players. By foregrounding an archaic white past, primordialism gave settlers a home in continental history in ways conventional historiography denied. Without such a link, the land itself was arguably still the Indians' and settlers themselves forever invaders, guests, or foreigners. Aileen Moreton-Robinson notes, "White colonial paranoia is inextricably tied to an anxiety about being dispossessed by racial others" (23), a fear central to the development of the primordial sensibility. This precluded the creation of the genuine and durable nation they hoped was their destiny. So motivated to erase Indian history or to absorb it into white history, they turned to the primordial. This often led to absurd historical paradoxes, historiographic mismatches also foreseen by Irving. Frustrated by the lack of a grandiose subject, Knickerbocker misreads a series of fleeting allusions in obscure texts to create in the history of New Netherlands an otherwise absent depth, continuity, and Old World legitimacy. In the end, Knickerbocker accedes to the "vulgar opinion that America was discovered on the 12th of October, 1492, by Christovallo Colon, a Genoese who has been clumsily nicknamed Columbus" (7:33). As would all primordialists, Knickerbocker rejects documented history as useless because it was "sufficiently known": unable to provide the legends and traditions needed by a romantic nation. Oddly enough, an older Irving established Columbus as the "Great Navigator."[6]

One of the pressing issues throughout the era in question had to do with the interaction and entanglement of races in the new nation. In the eighteenth century and well into the nineteenth, it was thought that environmental factors determined racial identity. Initially, culture trumped biology as a source of social membership: *translatio mundi* transported a civilization and a worldview based on classical and biblical traditions, and it was more important to be aligned with these than to have the whitest skin. Nonetheless, whites were primarily the legatees of these bodies of knowledge rather than just the offspring of the northern Europeans who came to these traditions a millennium later and brought them to the New World. As such, Irving was working with an inclusive definition of race based more on civility than biology. In this case, white Americans had to avoid the fate of primordial whites who allowed the new natural setting to cause them to abandon the civilized lifeways that set them apart from nonwhites: the legends that they had darkened to become Indians.[7] Many primordialist texts warn white Americans of the dangers of racial slippage as modeled by the ex-white Indian savages whose ancestors had been primordial whites. Aware of this fear, Irving catalogs the many theories that reimagined Indians as degenerated Norwegian, Egyptian, Gaulish, Celtic, Roman, Phoenician, English, and Irish populations (7:37)—all classically or biblically referenced and so eligible for whiteness—even if their skin was not pale. Exhausted, Knickerbocker gives up, admitting: "First, that this part of the world has actually been peopled (Q.E.D.), to support which we have living proofs in the numerous tribes of Indians that inhabit it. Secondly, that it has been peopled in five hundred different ways. . . . Thirdly, that the people of this country had a variety of fathers, which, as it may not be thought much to their credit by the common runs of readers, the less we say on the subject the better. The question, therefore, I trust, is forever at rest" (7:39–40). But Americans would not let it rest. "The less we say on it the better" performs the strategy of evasion at the core of the settler's need to "disavow" both Indian distinctiveness and their own moral failures. Their century-long inability to let it rest demonstrates an anxiety intrinsic to their condition as settlers, as colonial, as nonindigenes.

By imagining the adventures of transplanted Old World whites or ex-white Indians as foreshadowing their own, authors of primordialist texts could do what actual, documented history could not: make continental history habitable for the white Americans. If settlers could imagine that either whites like themselves had a long history on the land or that the Indians were just long-lost relatives (or both), the history of conquest and colonization can be retrofitted to enact continuity and completion, rather than invasion and rupture, even as settler colonialism itself continued (and still continues) the messy processes of empire building.

In *Colonizing the Past*, I address the public and literary manifestations of primordial whites as they reflect the ambitions and paradoxes of settler culture. The texts examined here provide a coherent method of literary response to the settler culture, identity, and nation, often by directly linking pre-Columbian whites to nineteenth-century conversations about interlinked and evolving issues based in the nation's origins as a set of colonies. These include racial stability and the interracial frontier, the new nation's colonialist and later imperial ambitions, and the shifting roles and accommodation of racial and ethnic minorities. By rephrasing these transformations though fantasy, allegory, prophecy, and other digestible literary formats, they reframe present circumstances in the deep past of legend—just as they were in the Old World nations they admired. Through primordialism, white Americans could imagine themselves not as merely invaders and latecomers but as the heirs of an archaic past that imbued their nation and its metamorphoses with an authenticating mystique.[8]

Positioning pre-Columbian whites before documented history, primordialists provided the required national prehistory by conceding at least three centuries, from the departure of Welsh Prince Madoc to the arrival of Columbus (1170–1492 CE), of isolation. During these centuries, Europe initiated its transition to modernity, assuring the cultural authenticity of pre-Columbian whites, so positioning them to inhabit primeval America in ways more indicative of aboriginality.[9] "Primordial" thus connotes a past that is deliberately vague and mystical, bordering on mythology. This obscurity created a romantic veil beneath which the controversial ambitions of settler colonialism could be "disavowed" by repositioning the white presence in North America from the modern to the prehistoric.

Colonizing the Past tracks five episodes of varying length and scope in which primordial whites attracted significant attention in the new nation's print culture: the Welsh Indians, the lost tribes of Israel, the Mound Builders, the ancient Irish, and the Norse Vikings. For each, public interest was stirred when the group in question was invoked to contextualize concurrent conversations about a particular aspect of the nation's evolving identity. They share one key component: each episode diminished Indians to mere distractions or degenerates—erasing, diluting, or diminishing their role in territorial history. These support Jodi Byrd's observation that white settler cultures "relegate American Indians to the site of the already-doneness that begins to linger as an unwelcome guest to the future" (20). Byrd defines the settlers' "Indian" as having already passed from historical relevance, "already-doneness." Pushing further, primordialism reduced Indians to "never-wasness" by presuming a priori that Indian history and erasure is not *enough*: a nation as important as the United States intended to become *must* have a grander backstory of racial continuity lost in the mists of time.

As each episode waxed in the public imagination, primordial whites enacted a variety of historical patterns and precedents, albeit within the ambit of settler colonialism: some championed a trajectory toward empire, others reminded the settler nation of the risks of the venture at hand. Primordialist texts range from encomia and valedictories to jeremiads and elegies. As each waned, the link between contemporary events and the pre-Columbian past was no longer needed, and the relevant primordial whites faded into obscurity. For example, as discussed in chapter 1, the Welsh Indians attracted attention from 1790 to 1815, when issues of land title and racial degeneration shaped intrasettler debates about the legitimacy of expansion and the possible loss of whiteness among frontiersmen, rendering them unfit for membership in the republic. After the War of 1812, with the frontier secured and disciplined, such anxieties diminished, and the Welsh faded as the land was seized, and thus their utility faded. The five episodes studied here demonstrate a persistent and coherent predilection to find the only kind of past that could inform the nation's conversations with itself about its past and future: a white past.

Yet despite their constant preoccupation with archaic whites, and despite hundreds of texts, these five episodes have not been studied as a unified phenomenon. Individual episodes have been addressed—as in studies such as Gwyn Williams's on the Welsh Indians or Annette Kolodny's on the Vikings.[10] Nonetheless, as this book demonstrates, primordialism was a recurring proclivity—an underlying and telling leitmotif—of the settler imagination throughout nineteenth-century American culture. Its study unearths the long-standing compulsion to invent an American prehistory to validate the nation, belying feelings of incompletion based in their status as settlers. While it was never a dominant cultural mode, and its epics never appeared, primordialism reveals how the anxious new nation worried about its shaky claims to authenticity, land, history, and destiny. Among prominent writers, William Gilmore Simms, Timothy Flint, William Cullen Bryant, Ralph Waldo Emerson, Sarah Josepha Hale, John Greenleaf Whittier, Lydia Sigourney, Joseph Smith, and Henry Wadsworth Longfellow established primordialism as a vehicle for the expression of fantasies of settler colonialism and nationalism, alongside dozens of lesser figures such as Solomon Spaulding, Amos Stoddard, Cornelius Mathews, Ottilie Liljencrantz, and Ada Thomas.[11] In these, pre-Columbian whites did the things—fighting and/or civilizing Indians, building cities, establishing trade, and spreading their faith—that nineteenth-century whites imagined themselves doing in a shared effort to validate an authentic, predetermined, and foreordained modern nation rooted in the gravitas of archaic tradition.

The need to construct and contrive a mythic and mystic past, time and again, reveals a sense of illegitimacy and inauthenticity. This pattern reveals the enduring "colonial cringe" typical of settler colonials, the embarrassing and self-conscious fear that ex-colonies were always imitative, derivative, belated, and backward.[12] Like Irving, dissenting writers perceived in primordialism a telling irony: for them, the quest for an Old World–based white ancestry reflected a deeply ingrained sense of inferiority, the second-hand subjectivity of the colonial: James Fenimore Cooper, William Apess, Jeremy Belknap, Mark Twain, James Weldon Johnson, John Howard Payne, Micah Flint, Nathaniel Hawthorne, and William Ellery Channing, among others, recognized its derivative underpinnings, moral speciousness, racist origins, and, in fact, counternational potentials, based as it was in Old World emigration rather than New World innovation. Yet that is what makes primordialism worth sustained scholarly attention: each episode provides, in epitome, a cross section of a specific moment in the nation's transformation from fragile coalition of ex-colonies along the Atlantic seaboard in 1780 to the imperial and modern nation it had become by 1915. Primordialism especially flourished between the end of the War of 1812 and the beginning of the Civil War, a period ending in internecine war and before, mostly, its engagement with overseas empire building. Tracking that process, primordialism reframed formative debates about race, nation, and empire to represent a persistent yet understudied relation of American development to global patterns of "the settler diaspora."[13] Debates about primordial whites reflected profound and enduring anxieties intrinsic to the paradox of settler identity: the simultaneity of being subordinated colonials and subordinating colonizers. As settler discourse, primordialism reveals the fragile nature of settler pretensions to authentic inhabitation at a moment when the country itself was yet a frail set of former colonies whose citizens wore outdated clothes and whose books no one read.[14]

As primordialists contrived validating prehistories, they tested the coherence of settler culture by insisting on race—both acquired and in-born as its definition shifted—as the primary means of sorting the colonizers from the colonized. In fact, race itself *became* a primordialist fantasy during the period in question. Starting in the late eighteenth century, "race" evolved from a somewhat fluid condition that blended biological and environmental factors whose ultimate expression was morality and civility rather than birthplace. As the century wore on, "scientific racism" provided newer definitions more concerned with how and why one's ancestors developed different skin colors and other defining characteristics far back in the distant, prehistoric past. This shifted racial origins into the realm of the primordial, demanding the contemplation of speculative narratives based in competing versions of the archaic past.[15] Furthermore, "race" and "nation" became nearly synonymous in the romantic imagination, and national and racial histories thus strove to become one and the same. To create that authenticity nationalist writers—both Old World and colonial—participated in what Eric Hobsbawm has called "inventing tradition."[16] In the nineteenth century, romanticism demanded "tradition" to authenticate any given society's claims to territorial occupancy and legal sovereignty: "Modern nations and all their impedimenta generally claim to be the opposite of novel, namely rooted in the deepest antiquity, and the opposite of constructed, namely human communities so 'natural' as to require no definition other than self-assertion" (14), writes Hobsbawm. To suit romantic nationalism, nation-making mythography had to stretch from the primordial to the modern to create a linear trajectory, a collective and binding telos.[17]

A singularized primordial population, one sharing genetics as well as culture, then became the basis for every legitimate modern nation. Anthony D. Smith defines the role of the romantic nationalist: "The [primordialist] readily accepts the modernity of nationalism as a political movement and ideology but regards nations . . . as updated versions of immemorial ethnic communities" (*Nationalism and Modernism*, 159). Because members of nations share both biology and history, they can modernize without vacating that essential identity. By this reckoning, the true nation is natural: for these people, in this place, to be anything other than sovereign would be unnatural. Nations, then, grow out of a mystic continuity and deep intimacy of a race and a place. To serve these ends, primordialism envisions a linear connection between a distant white past and the modern white present to legitimate the nation's claims to both territory and sovereignty. Primordialism in fact predates modern nationalism: Augustus employed Virgil to craft a binding national narrative based in an undocumented, primordial past with *The Aeneid*.[18] A more recent instructive parallel might be the controversies over the "Ossian manuscripts." Having shuttered its parliament in 1707 to join the United Kingdom, Scotland expressed particular anxieties about its prospects as a nation, given (before Sir Walter Scott) its lack of a national(-ist) legend.[19]

Such efforts were particularly visible and problematic in settler nations. However, the redefinition of race as a biological category enabled a reconstruction of history based not on how people adjusted to their environments but rather on how they maintained essential identity despite environmental changes: racial integrity could withstand migration to colonial settings. In fact, adaptation became associated with degeneration. Tracey Banivanua-Mar writes, "[Racialized] History helped to discipline the world's infinite and scattered pasts into sequential and teleological metanarratives—or prerehearsed historical templates that reduced disorder into comprehensible ordered narratives leading inexorably to the present" (26). Such templates became the "tradition" at the center of efforts to invent nations. Hence, primordialism as an effort to create a "history" created "prerehearsed" pasts unavailable to white settlers and their descendants that dramatized the elimination of the Indians, for example, as the inevitable outcome of racial ordering—a teleological metanarrative.

As a coalition of ex-colonies sharing only a rejection of British dominion, the United States was far from a "natural" *nation*, as it lacked both a common biological identity (race) and historical community (tradition), despite Crèvecoeur's deluded Farmer James's effort to define "a new race of men" in America.[20] From the Revolution on, as Irving parodied, authors sought to construct a shared history, a common language, and a vision of a nation rooted in the pre-Columbian past from the mundane facts of the contact, conquest, colonial, and revolutionary epochs.[21] Yet none achieved the allure of legend. It was not the fault of the Connecticut Wits: there was an irresolvable mismatch between the source materials and the nation-making imprimatur. In fact, in more than a few framing narratives for primordialist texts—including Longfellow's "The Skeleton in Armor" and Sarah Josepha Hale's *The Genius of Oblivion*—nineteenth-century American narrators comment on their detachment from the nation before unearthing the primordialist materials that become the main text. As Cooper noted in 1832 in his introduction to *Lionel Lincoln*: "Perhaps there is no other country, whose history is so little adapted to poetical illustration as that of the United States of America. . . . There is consequently neither a dark, nor even an obscure, period in the American annals: all is not only known, but so well and generally known, that nothing is left for the imagination to develop" (6). For Cooper, the colonial and early national pasts provided no transcendent tradition ripe for romanticization, forcing the settler nation to confront the uncomfortable truth: it was a set of transplanted, former rival colonies on stolen Indian lands, always on the verge of dissolution.

In 1841, in an essay celebrating the translation and publication of the Icelandic sagas that confirmed the long-held belief that tenth-century Norsemen had temporarily inhabited Newfoundland, William Gilmore Simms elaborated: "It is something, surely, to be able to boast that we have an American antiquity. . . . The more rude the annals, the more susceptible of an original polish—the more imperfect the history, the more encouraging to the genius which adventures boldly" (*Views*, 2:57). As a settler, Simms silently ignores that Indians could provide a salutary or sufficient "American antiquity"; yet the Norse need nothing more than to have been white in the Western Hemisphere, and for only a few seasons, to overwrite centuries of Indian history. In an essay in his collection *Views and Reviews in American Literature, History and Fiction*, "Americanism in Literature," Simms linked annal-polishing to nationalist ends: "It must be remembered that the national themes seem to be among the most enduring. . . . It is only a more noble egotism which prompts us to speak of our country,—to make its deeds our subjects, and its high places our scene. It is because it *is our* country" (1:38; emphasis in original).[22] Simms theorizes primordialism as the linkage of a (white) American antiquity to the moral obligations of the writer by positioning nation as a natural outcome of racial consolidation. His "is" and "our," respectively, affirm that the nation has been established by 1841 and that white people have established it, an assumption Simms himself, as a Confederate nationalist by the 1850s and as the son of an Irish immigrant, would subsequently question, basing his claim for difference in the legend of a primordial Irish in the Carolinas (see chapter 4).

Such convolutions represent the complexities and the paradoxes of settler nationalism, nation building in the wake of settler colonialism's establishment of sovereignty, a process based on the denial of any indigenous potential for autonomy or modernity. Walter Hixson's *American Settler Colonialism* (2013) repositions the European occupation of North America as "settler colonialism" before and above any of its other iterations: "This study flows from a premise that the United States should be perceived and analyzed fundamentally as a settler colonial society. The American 'imperial settler state' originated in the context of Indian removal and forged powerful continuities over space and time. American history is the most sweeping, most violent, and most significant example of settler colonialism in world history" (1). Hixson's work refers to the study of white colonizers, colonists, creoles, and their descendants in Australia, New Zealand, Canada, and South Africa, denying exceptionalism's separation of American "pilgrims" or "pioneers" from these other, more ordinary diasporic whites.[23] It should be noted that primordialism features in the literatures of no other settler nation. However, American nationalism evolved during the early nineteenth century, when romanticism compelled the invention of such traditions. By 1867, when Canada confederated, and 1901, when the others were granted "Colonial Nationhood," newer nationalisms had displaced romanticism's.[24]

Settler theory defines white soldiers, farmers, missionaries, and others as continuing and even intensifying the colonization of the lands and peoples begun by the departed Old World empire. To this end, settlers cultivate more than territory and sovereignty: they also nurture cultures of complicity with the colonialist ideology. Hixson continues: "Settler colonialism typically unfolds in association with nation building. . . . Historical distortion and denial are endemic to settler societies. In order for the settler colony to establish a collective, usable past, legitimizing stories must be created and persistently affirmed as a means of naturalizing a new historical narrative" (9–10). For Hixson, settler colonialism creates a vortex, absorbing seemingly all aspects of settler culture. With an end in the creation of a natural, the means—distortion and misrepresentation—are justified. Hixson then views settler colonialism as a form of authoritarian hegemony. A more nuanced reading of settler culture, especially its literary productions, reveals a far more complex cultural terrain in setter communities, ones borne of anxiety: settlers' nervous efforts to "naturalize" themselves—to gain as organic and as genuine relationship with their land as "natural" Old World nations do with theirs—demonstrated an essentially imitative and subordinated subjectivity. Settler culture colonized, but was also colonial.

That being the case, while settler colonialism's drive for sovereignty unifies its ideology, settler *nationalism* reveals far more complex intrasettlement contradictions. This begins in the long-standing denial that the United States is or has ever been either a colony or an empire, in the global sense of each term. The resistance of American cultural studies to accusations of imperial nationalism might be traced to exceptionalism.[25] Empires, in the European sense of the word, were supposedly banished by the Revolution and the establishment of the republic. Yet while Thomas Jefferson sought an oxymoronic "empire of liberty," critics have always seen through such facades. At the start of the Mexican-American War in 1837, William Ellery Channing insisted that its older meaning had always characterized the nation: "Some crimes by their magnitude, have a touch of the sublime; and to this dignity the seizure of Texas by our citizens is entitled. . . . It is nothing less than a robbery of a realm. The pirate seizes a ship. The colonists and their coadjutors can satisfy themselves with nothing short of an empire" (20). Nonetheless, "empire" was long disavowed in American culture and Americanist scholarship. While Amy Kaplan in 1993 famously unmasked the "absence of Empire" in American Studies, Robert Beisner had charted it in 1968:[26] "Blind faith in a unique national morality (and forgetfulness of the past) renders people unable to recognize the enormities of their own history, or, more generally, to face honestly the role of power in human affairs; the myth of innocence causes them to forget three centuries of slavery, the massacres of Native Americans, the suppression of the Filipino insurrectionists, the shooting of striking Anglo-Saxon workingmen; and it makes them blind to American imperialism even when it stares them in the face" (xiv). In the decades that followed, Andy Doolen, David Kazanjian, John Carlos Rowe, Robert Gunn, and Malini Johar Schueller, among others, have carefully linked American literature to cultures of colonialist complicity and imperial ambitions.[27] Positioning the United States as an empire, these scholars have opened the study of American culture to theories of settler culture more nuanced than Hixson's, such as those developed by historians James Belich and Lorenzo Veracini and anthropologists Patrick Wolfe or Kevin Bruyneel.[28] This has led to a new taxonomy of empire among historians of American culture.

To be precise, "settler" has challenged "pioneer" or "pilgrim" to describe the white colonial in the territorial United States.[29] Renaming "pioneers" as "settlers" humbles the nationalist project by demanding that it is ordinary: a simple transplantation of European cultures as was happening in other settler cultures, a white diaspora that spun off nations that largely simply localized European cultures and communities rather than founding manifestly destined cities upon hills whose establishment will begin the end of history.[30] Reframed then as invasion and occupation, the white inhabitation of North America and the founding of the United States become closer to ordinary events in human history, not markers of epochal transformation. As settler colonies, the new nations are plagued by their entanglement with the metropolitan culture that founded them as colonies, regardless of political autonomy. Nira Yuval-Davis and Daiva Stasiulis identify "the unevenness and the fragility of settler identities, which were often forged in defense against metropolitan contempt" (qtd. in Coombes, 4). Incompleteness and anxiety open "settler" to historical revision in ways "pioneer" and "pilgrim" foreclose.[31] Patrick Wolfe notes: "The process of replacement maintains the refractory imprint of the native counter-claim" (387). Hixson asserts: "History remains a neuralgic subject in settler colonial societies" (12). In Wolfe's "process of replacement" the tragic fate of the original populations thus become the source of a neuralgic fear of illegitimacy and inauthenticity: even as settlers claim to have transcended their origins elsewhere, the resulting nation will always and inevitability be a "replacement" rather than aboriginal; it will never be natural or native—its true birth story elsewhere.

On the level of individual membership in the settler nation, Alan Lawson defines the settler colony as "the site of a very peculiar dual inscription; a place that is both colonized at the same time it is colonizing" (155).[32] Settlers anxiously await approval from the imperial culture, while anxiously announcing themselves as the land's natural inhabitants. To that end, settler culture pursues what Philip Deloria calls "playing Indian": "Indians provided impetus and precondition for the creative assembling of an ultimately unassemblable American identity" (5). Mythologizing a white archaic past, on the figurative level, reveals the same aspirational revisionism. Deloria tracks how whites, beginning with the Boston Tea Party, put on headdresses, called each other Indian names, pretended to be Indians on stage and in film, and "trained" in woodcraft as Boy Scouts. Deloria continues: "If Indian play allowed colonists to take on dual, metaphoric identities useful in creating a sense of Americanness, it also carried the threat that they would lose themselves—and their identity—in the netherworld between Briton and Indian" (35). Disavowing their preoccupation with that "netherworld"— and its analog in Lawson's colonial/colonizer simultaneity—allows settlers to hide from the complexities of history through purposeful acts of misappropriation. To that end, playing Indian and primordialism both represent more than settler attempts to co-opt Indian identity: they also enact an unwillingness to confront or accept their own. This corroborates Matthew Crow's note that, "in the American context, settler colonialism has worked by allowing the predominant settler populations to not recognize itself as one" (107). Such sleight of hand both justified imperial violence and disavowed it through the providential logics of exceptionalism by recurring to foundational traditions such as the Puritan covenant.[33]

Worse yet, awareness of being a latecomer cripples settler claims to distinctiveness: "American literary nationalism didn't modernize the *mythomoteur* of an ethnie—there being no white ethnie to modernize in America," writes Ojibwe scholar Scott Richard Lyons; "it simply stole its cultural meaning from someone else" (150). Tracking the imprimatur of romantic nationalism, Lyons corroborates Irving's and Simms's (and later Hawthorne's and James's) recognition that the "rude annals" of white American history offered a bare cupboard for settler-writers. Yet the unending quest for a binding narrative, one that would establish the settler nation as a moral and political equal to the natural nations of the Old World, demonstrates how the settler is never settled. Foundational denial haunts settler identity: Alissa Macoun and Elizabeth Strakosch assert the scholarly imprimatur to expose "the settler colonial project [as] fundamentally incomplete—and unable to be completed" (432). There was reason for such anxiety. Alyosha Goldstein notes, "United States colonialism is a continuously failing—or at least a perpetually incomplete—project that labors to find a workable means of resolution to sustain its logic of possession and inevitability by disavowing the ongoing contestation" (3). Along the same lines, Ed Larkin notes, "Instead we ought to recognize the serious dissent, the unsettled state of affairs, and the general incoherence that characterized much of early US politics and culture. . . . The possibility of fissure, rupture, and breakdown was always in the foreground" (39). While Larkin refers to the early republic, the same argument might be extended through the antebellum decades more generally. The Monroe Doctrine proved ineffective when French forces intervened Mexico in 1837 and 1861. The continental ambit of "Manifest Destiny" failed north and south. In 1844, "54–40 or Fight," referred to United States' claims to territory beyond the current border with British Columbia, Manitoba, Saskatchewan, and Alberta. The Mexican War brought only the northern half of the sister republic to the south. Furthermore, internal fissures based in ethnicity, economics, and region—sectionalism, nativism, and expansionism—demonstrate how the new nation was never successful, stable, or even national.[34] Even before these fissures exploded in 1861, Americans were aware of the overbearing barriers to their genuine unification as an Old World–style singularized race or nation. Jason Phillips

comments, "Before the Civil War was fought or remembered, it was imagined by thousands of Americans who peered at the horizon through an
apocalyptic atmosphere" (4).

The trouble has long been the intransigent settlers' refusal either to recognize or to take responsibility for their inevitable incompleteness, or the derivative nature of the mission itself. Instead, they have obsessed on fantasies
of completeness such as Manifest Destiny. Kariann Yokota elaborates the
internal contradictions of settler identity suggested by Lawson and Deloria. "Both of and outside the dominant culture" (10), Yokota's settlers display contradictory responses to this irresolvable proposition: "Americans
feared being seen by the rest of the world, not least the British, as still mired
in colonial dependence. . . . The project of nation building and developing
national identity in the young United States was as much about its people's
struggles in 'unbecoming' what had made them British subjects before independence as it was about 'becoming' citizens of a new country" (9). Living in both an Old World backwater and a New World frontier, settlers
feared losing the racial preeminence that separated them from and perpetuated their dominion over the colonized—enslaved and indigenous nonwhite populations. Moreover, Yokota's idea of "unbecoming British" must be
understood literally as well as figuratively: if "British" was a race as well as an
empire, the new nation was also confronted with a twofold threat with regard to maintaining the racial singularity necessary for binding the "natural
nation" into a coherent whole.

Two factors threatened the stable preeminence of colonial whiteness: the
darkening environmental forces of the intercultural frontier *and* the influx
of immigrant populations whose whiteness was in doubt. Katy Chiles rhe-
torically asks, "If the white man displaces the Native man from his land,
and the land influences the human form, what will become of this white
man? Or the land? And the nation-state he so recently founded?" (130). On
a more global scale, Lorenzo Veracini notes, "Other neurosis-generating
settler anxieties include paranoid fears about degenerative manifestations
in the settler social body, apprehensions about the debilitating results of climate, remoteness, geopolitical position, racial contamination" (*Settler Colonialism*, 81).[35] These neuroses permeated all aspects of the new nation's
culture. Each threatened to dilute the northern European version of dominant whiteness left over from the colonial era. Each threatened to remove
the settler from the ranks of the colonizers and to demote, or perhaps replace, them among the colonized. As such, policing the borders of whiteness
has long haunted settler writing. What Toni Morrison said of the "Africanist" ghost haunting American writing might also be applied to Indians: "It

has occurred to me that the very manner by which American literature distinguishes itself as a coherent entity exists because of this unsettled and unsettling population" (5–6). By defining whiteness not as a thing in itself but as what it is not—black or, in this case, Indian—Morrison recognizes that a literature suited to and in service of a settled and sovereign nation is the aspiration of white American writers: settlement. The ghost of race—in terms of slippage, contamination, or even moral panic—binds the settler nation's writing around a textuality of paranoia and anxiety, one based in its origins as a loose conglomeration of settler colonies.

All these anxieties and more were accounted for in primordialist texts. In fact, each episode brought to light a specific set of contradictions rooted in the new country's status as a settler nation, based in the nexus of national and racial anxieties. In response to various issues that foreshadowed transformational shifts in the new nation—claiming western land, adjusting to industrialism, etc.—the primordialist impulse conjured up archaic continental metanarratives in which these complicated processes had been "prerehearsed": the ex-white Welsh could serve as a warning to frontiersmen not to lose their whiteness, serving to check undisciplined expansion; the Indians were lost Jews whose conversion would rewhiten them, thus revealing providential approbation of the settler nation. Even when primordialism becomes a form of critique, the nation's authenticity is still affirmed by its continuation of ancient patterns: when critique is repackaged as prophecy, it acquires a primordial authenticity. The resulting texts bear out these conflicts, reflecting the neuralgic and divergent nature of settler culture.

In every case, primordialist texts delegitimize Indian aboriginality and otherness, defining and celebrating the appropriation of indigenous lands as normal, natural, and even heroic. They displace and release the resulting tensions into an archaic past, shifting credit or blame for current conditions to long-established patterns that provided the legendary basis for national meaning.[36] In all cases, once white prehistory is established, Indian history becomes, at best, its ancillary, making the country, for white Americans, *theirs* in ways conquest and inhabitation alone could not, leapfrogging the "settler trauma" and ordinariness of migration and colonial history.[37] Almost immediately after the Revolution, as Irving demonstrated, flimsy legends were reimagined as grandiose triumphant or tragic allegories. For example, the "patriots" needed to define themselves as alienated from the Old World, and so a pretext that used victimization to justify migration, rebellion, and eventual sovereignty was found in the primordial past: "The settler . . . has suffered elsewhere and 'is seeking refuge in a new land'" (*Settler Colonialism*, 14), notes Veracini. This reframes invasion as escape:

Amos Stoddard's Welsh escape English expansion; William Warren's Jewish Ojibwa are chased into America by savage Asians who become Sioux; and Henry Wadsworth Longfellow's Norse lovers escape an angry Swedish father. Such escape-based narratives not only imagine rupture from the colonial parent but also reposition the New World as a welcoming refuge rather than an alien wilderness, justifying its appropriation.[38]

What ultimately binds all primordialist narratives, though, is the assumption that the only meaningful pre-Columbian prehistory is white. Even in its most sympathetic manifestations, primordialism eliminates Indians qua Indians, negates their otherness, and absorbs them, often in footnotes, in reimagined histories that deny the New World its newness. Each episode, as Simms noted, extrapolated "rude annals" into nation-building poems, novels, histories, and songs. Primordialism then enacts what Renato Rosaldo called "imperialist nostalgia": "an innocent yearning [used] both to capture people's imagination and to conceal its complicity with often brutal domination" (70). The resulting fantasies not only occluded both violent conquest and dull settlement but also mythologized the nation as a continuation of ancient traditions of white achievement and adventure in a land fated for their inhabitation.

The following chapters chart how conflicts within the nation's print culture over the pre-Columbian past reveal the unsettled nature of the settler nation. These conflicts were articulated in a broad range of literary and other narrative materials, across the belletristic spectrum. European materials on primordial Americans have mostly been omitted as immaterial to such intramural conversations. Old World conversations about primordial white Americans engaged different cultural contexts. In Wales, Ireland, and Norway, the same legends invoked local nationalisms.[39] But these were traditional nations, not settler societies, and they had the ancient legends, languages, and customs that linked the distant past to the modern present needed to satisfy the criteria of romantic nationalism. Overlaps occur, as when British poet Robert Southey's epic *Madoc* was published to fund a British settlement in America. Or when Irish poet Denis MacCarthy's epic of Saint Brendan was invoked in debates over Irish whiteness and immigration in America. Southey's poem will not be discussed below, as its failure left the planned settlement stillborn, but MacCarthy's poem will be for its participation in conversations concerning racial destiny and national membership.

As the century progressed, shifts in the shape and direction of primordialist fantasies reflected shifting ideas about race, nation, and empire in the nation. Early in the century, Welshmen, Jews, and the Irish become Indians, reflecting a fear that racial degeneration threatened the integrity of settler dominion. These metamorphoses imply that whiteness is unstable, the markers of civilization—literacy, technology, religion, etc.—transient. If they are, the raced mission of settler colonialism is inevitably destabilized and thus unreliable as a basis for national validation. Later, white Mound Builders, Irish monks, and Norse adventurers prefigure national engagements with industrialism, regional and ethnic diversity, and overseas imperialism. In each, crucial divergences reveal profound divisions among the several settler constituencies: are non-Anglo-Saxons genuinely white? Should Indians be integrated, removed, or annihilated? Should industrialism displace agrarianism? Should slavery be expanded into new states?

The fissures primordialism refracts to the archaic past had very real consequences. The internal conflicts in those texts reveal the heretofore fragmented and divergent models of settler colonialisms in post-Revolutionary, early republic, and antebellum cultures. While they shared a demand for settler dominion and sovereignty, the shape and trajectory by which those goals might be achieved in different regions varied widely; yet consistently, primordialism provided the archaic imaginative spaces onto which those tensions might be etched and thus displaced. As to the looming conflict that exposed settler nationalism's failure to achieve an authenticating cultural unity, Matthew Crow notes, "it is possible to understand the American Civil War as a war between two very different versions of expansion, or two very different settler colonialisms" (104). In the North and the South (and the West), competing settler colonialisms revealed contradictions that no amount of disavowal or denial could erase: the settler colony was based in a drive for dominion, including dominion over other whites whose ideas about the forms and uses of that dominion led to different and divergent forms of settler nationalism. In the final section—on the Norseman and the post–Civil War nation's overseas adventurism—the ultimate form of settler colonialism, its natural transformation toward global empire, is reconstructed as primordially foreordained.

In the opening chapter, the early republic's fascination with the twelfth century's Welsh Prince Madoc reveals contestation over western expansion. Madoc's supposed crossing and settlement and the possible survival of his descendants were thought to establish Anglo-Americans as the legal inheritors of western lands through the Doctrine of Discovery. However, all accounts also claimed the Welsh had become Indians. In response, the legend was reframed as a cautionary tale, policing the racial ideology of expansion and insisting on republican colonization of the anarchic frontier. Along with

Irving, Jeremy Belknap, Jedidiah Morse, and a host of others perceived in this fantasy the dubious morality of expansionist colonialism.

As described in chapter 2, it had long been conjectured that Indians were descended from the lost tribes of Israel, wandering since the fall of the Temple in the seventh century BCE. As they wandered, they lost their status as Hebrews—a "white" ethnicity in the early republic—and, like the Welsh, became savages, but on a much larger scale. During the Second Great Awakening (1810–40), this legend was disinterred to challenge Indian removal and other genocidal policies as violations of the nation's implied covenant with a Protestant God. Others simply argued that, as Old World refugees and lapsed whites, Indians deserved assimilation. Indigenous writers—including William Apess and William Warren—saw lost tribe theory as an aperture in white culture through which more humane racial policies might be brought in, and so endorsed it. Yet James Fenimore Cooper's refutation of it in *Oak Openings* (1848) best reveals its dangerous and covert colonialist suppositions.

In chapter 3, reimagining the Mound Builders as white entangled the growing economical with sectional crises of the antebellum decades. Primordialist texts, especially Cornelius Mathews's *Behemoth* (1839), depicted white Americans picking up where the Mound Builders left off, depicting Indians as latecomers. By contrast, in a number of texts, Indian savagery disrupts an otherwise continuous trajectory from the white Mound Builders to the white Americans, a fantasy that applied only to the industrial North, not the agrarian South. However, their vanishing, most notably in William Cullen Bryant's "The Prairies" and Joseph Smith's *Book of Mormon,* suggested a similar fate for the prideful settler nation. In the end, Indians were affirmed as the descendants of the Mound Builders, trumping the romantic fantasy of racial continuity, but not before skeptics, such as poet Charles Jones, inverted the corrupt motivations behind their whitening.

Chapter 4 addresses how two Irish primordialisms reflected the growing nation's need to incorporate diverse and divergent regions and populations. The first part of the chapter discusses how Simms saw his South as the victim of northern colonialism and conjured a southern primordialism to balance New England's nationalization of the Norse. Using the Norse sagas, Simms explores the stories of two tenth-century Norsemen who end up in even older Irish settlements in the South. However, the sagas' Irish savages threaten their Norse guests and so fail his intended model of a multiregional nation. In the second part of the chapter, the anxiety shifts from region to ethnicity. "Exogenous" whites were needed, threatening the ethnic singularity demanded by romantic nationalism. Denis MacCarthy's poem

"The Voyage of St. Brendan" whitens the Irish by showing sixth-century Celtic monks crossing the Atlantic, converting Indians, and exploring westward. Together, the two concurrent Irish miniepisodes contrived a multiregional and multiethnic nation—challenging the cultural singularity intrinsic to settler colonialism—but still base their narratives in white ascendance.

Finally, chapter 5 discusses how the Norse Vikings were split into two distinct traditions that shifted the locus of settler colonialism from place to blood. In the first part of the chapter, violent Norsemen became bucolic settlers in the poems of Whittier and Longfellow, leading to the founding of Norumbega, a settler colony, in tenth-century Massachusetts. Simultaneously, in the South, Norman traditions were appropriated to celebrate a feudal agrarianism. From this regional base, the Civil War became a proxy war of not just competing colonialisms, as per Crow, but also of competing primordialisms. The North's victory led to the subsequent embrace of the Vinland Vikings as globetrotting empire builders. In the latter part of the chapter, in the Vinland legend, primordial white inhabitation mattered less than the access it granted to racial inheritance and the traditions of overseas imperialism in administered rather than settler colonies. The Norse emerge as burden-bearing white men in the stories of Frank Norris and others. However, Jack London, James Weldon Johnson, and Mark Twain, among others, identify these claims as indicating the expiration of the romantic ideology primordialism was intended to supplement.

Yokota has noted the disturbing effect of the empty spaces on American maps in the early republic: "The preponderance of vast unclaimed tracts of cartographic emptiness and the lack of civility that this implied reflected poorly on the new nation. This was not desirable to those Americans who wished to propel America out of its 'savage' past and into a higher stage of development" (21). What Yokota says of its maps, primordialism says of its past: the vast unclaimed tracts of continental history before 1492 was unsettling, and primordialism was invented to fill them, assuaging the settler's neuralgia. Nineteenth-century Americans attempted to colonize that past by filling it with people who looked like themselves because, if its past was Indian, white settlers could never fully inhabit its future; it could never be home.

1

Welsh Indians in the Early Republic

From Cambria's shores, by civil discord driv'n,
By all forsaken, save a few and heaven
O'er the wide waves he seeks a friendly land,
And hails, America, thy fertile strand!

—W.P., "Madoc," 1806

In 1806, "W.P." published in the American magazine the *Port-Folio* a brief piece of "Original Poetry" called "Madoc."[1] It arrived in the midst of a widespread revivification of the old legend of a Welsh prince who purportedly fled to America in 1170 CE, returned to Wales, and finally settled in the New World with up to ten ships full of refugees from his nation's internecine wars. As to the wave of interest in Madoc, Gywn Williams reports: "By the 1780s a tidal wave of Welsh Indian stories was breaking on English-speaking America. . . . In the last years of the century, something of a Madoc fever broke in the USA and belief in Welsh Indians became universal" (*Madoc*, 37).[2] Reflecting the ideology of settler colonialism at the heart of Madoc mania, the poem's narrative allegorizes a peaceful acculturation and unilateral transformation of the "savages" into docile underlings, eager to assimilate to white lifeways.

Introduced as "A Poem sacred to the memory of Madoc, prince of North Wales, who, in the eleventh century, flying from his country, with a few followers, is supposed by many to have first discovered and settled in America," the poem rewrites contact as a peaceful parable of restraint and implicit Welsh noblesse oblige. W.P. deftly deploys the legend to reconceive a sanitized contact history, replacing Columbus with Madoc, who was not only three centuries in advance, but also embodied republican values six hundred years before their purported implementation.[3] This revision transforms white colonizers from invaders to benefactors by establishing parallels between seventeenth-century Anglo-American and twelfth-century Welsh New World settlement histories: for example, both left their homelands as refugees, a trope common to settler foundation narratives, such as both Pilgrim and Puritan exile narratives. American readers in 1806 were meant to see themselves in "Madoc's" allegory of peaceful settlement, benign acculturation, and progressive nation building.

Furthermore, W.P.'s assumption of providential guidance reimagines Madoc as an Old Testament patriarch, most directly Noah. His unnamed landing place becomes a Promised Land, and implies a predestined continental imprimatur:

> Heavens! What a scene of grandeur meets his eye!
> Around he gazes, lost in mute surprise:
> Here mountains lose their summits in the clouds,
> A boundless forest nature's bosom shrouds;
> Resembling Ocean each bold stream appears,
> As birds unknown salute his ravish'd ears:
> "Is this the paradise by the bards foretold?
> And may we expect here an age of gold?"

"Madoc's" prescient envisioning of Manifest Destiny embraces a nonsectarian protestant Christianity.[4] However, as would also hold for the primordial Norse when their turn came later in the century, the Welshmen's historical Catholicism was domesticated for a Protestant readership, sectarian differences erased in their race-based superiority to the savage paganism of the Indians: the Welsh "all their God adore; their God, who led them over untravell'd seas / And promised security and ease." These values are tested when the "Natives" greet the Welsh:

> Soon on the shore the native bands appear,
> And gaze with wonder, devoid of fear,
> To all his ready hand the chief extends,
> And uses them as brethren and friends.
> What tho no words were understood, their eyes
> Witness'd at once their kindness and surprise.

Exchanging gifts and bonding over a feast and "metheglin"—Welsh mead—the two peoples become friends, silently glossing over the long-documented, even in 1806, deployment of alcohol as a means of colonization.[5] However, only one group is transformed by contact:

> To industry were all his [Madoc's] vows addressed
> Thus heaven work'd pity in the savage heart,
> Who, taught the God of heaven to adore,

Made cultivation glad the willing shore;
And soon, instructed in each useful art
Gave to humanity the glowing heart.

Madoc is thus credited with succeeding where all later white efforts at peaceful conversion and acculturation going back to the 1620s had failed. Madoc's successful subordination, colonization, and transformation of the indigenous population reflects a fantasy of benevolent paternalism, a narrative that conceals the longer and far messier facts of contact and conquest.

The poem ends with a direct effort to replace Columbus and his linkages to Catholicism and the Black Legend of Spanish Conquest with Madoc and a more benign fantasy of conquest without confrontation:[6]

Madoc! Th' Iberian chief to thee must yield;—
He dy'd with human blood the ravag'd field
But thou shalt justly boast unceasing fame;
Intent the cruel savage to reclaim,
Thou Gavest him, emulous in virtue's course
Reason, religion, liberty, and laws. Columbus!
Then withdraw your haughty claim
And bow with deference to Madoc's name.

A year later, the *Port-Folio* would publish a scathing review of Joel Barlow's *Columbiad* (1807), condemning the poet, the poetry, and the subject.[7] By contrast, "Madoc" expresses a desire for a new, sanitized pre-Columbian American past for a nation that wanted so badly to define itself as humane and benevolent, based in a republican admixture of reason and virtue to which the poem added a primordial depth and authenticity. In just a few lines, "Madoc" compressed the settler nation's hopes for racial dominion, religious conversion, and moral righteousness by sanctifying their practice in a distant past, an alternative history of interracial contact to model the republic's purportedly humane colonialist ambitions: Madoc bears an early version of the white man's burden, and in turn, the lucky Indians pass from savagery to servitude. Implicitly, the Welsh, undiluted by the messy histories of contact and cohabitation, can now take sovereign responsibility for both the Indians and their lands. Silently, the Indian's pre-Madoc past fades into irrelevance, their present and future safely entrusted to the benevolent white man.

Yet "Madoc" was only a minor contribution to the widespread literary re-creation and contemplation of the Welsh legend in the early republic. Most of the dozens of other texts describing Madoc and the Welsh legacy in pre-Columbian America lacked its clear exposition of a fantasy of nonviolent settler ideals. In the decades following the Revolution, undocumented reports from the frontier kept reporting *surviving* Welsh Indians. In almost every other account, the racial dynamic of the poem was reversed: these Welsh had become Indian. They had lost their Christianity, their metallurgy, and their literacy, everything but their language, according to the many travelers who claimed to have met and conversed with Welsh-speaking Indians in various places west of the Appalachians.[8] W.P. instead ceases his tale before the Welsh could lose their whiteness, a viable potential in an age where it was widely held that the "race" of an individual or a group could shift from one to another even in the space of one lifetime.[9] Writers less sanguine than W.P. would deploy the racial reassignment of the Welsh to study how this transformability might redirect or undermine the expansionist goals of the early republic. In the process, the Welsh Indians became proxies in debates over expansion, race, and authenticity as this fragile set of ex-colonies that dreamed itself a nation debated whether or not to colonize the interior without sacrificing racial identity or republican values.

Madoc's linkage to colonialism dates from the first British dreams of seizing and settling North America. In the 1590s, the Spanish Armada defeated, Elizabethan courtiers plotted their late entry into the American land grab already undertaken by Spain, Portugal, and France. Yet for the Elizabethans, the "Black Legend" of Spanish savagery toward the Indians—perhaps on account of the semiwhiteness of the Iberians, or their degenerate Catholicism—complicated their plans.[10] Similar ambivalence characterized American thought in the 1790s. In the 1790s, the British defeated and their Proclamation Line of 1763 erased, new Americans staked out Ohio and imagined themselves legally, morally, and racially entitled to colonize these open lands.[11] Thus in both the 1590s and the 1790s, settler colonies were projected to fill the empty spaces on the left sides of maps. However, in both, doubts about both whether and how to undertake these conjectured colonialist endeavors catalyzed ethical, moral, and legal debates. Neither the British nor the Americans wanted to be accused of repeating what John Locke called the uncivilized application of "force without right" whose practice led to the demonization of Spanish conquests.[12] To avoid repeating Spanish barbarism, or at least of being tarred with the same brush, the Elizabethans and the republicans pondered by what right they could claim lands already occupied by indigenous inhabitants and how colonizers could be restrained from becoming conquerors. In Great Britain, decisions could be imposed, despite resistance, by the emergent imperial bureaucracy.[13] New

Americans faced a more vexing paradox: How could a nation born of the anticolonialist self-assertion based in the "consent of the governed" plant its own colonies without violating the rights of those they intended to colonize? Worse yet, the lands in question were populated by French, Indian, squatters, and others, many of them Christian, complicating their aspiration to justify unilateral land seizure in the name of proselytization, a central tenet of the Doctrine of Discovery.

In both Elizabethan England and early republic America, Madoc and his Welsh Indians were evoked both to establish and trouble the legal and moral right of English-speaking whites to invade, seize, and settle the land through an invocation of the Crusades-based Doctrine of Discovery. The Doctrine required that the land on which the prospective colony was to be planted was empty, terra nullius. Emptiness, of course, requires a prehistory wherein the markers of an occupied place as defined by invaders are imagined as absent—*space* undefiled by the human imagination's recreation of it as *place*. For both the Elizabethans and the early republicans, the absence of both Christianity and European-style inhabitation qualified any given place as empty, as void space. Once a land was deemed empty, the first Christian European discoverers could claim it to the exclusion of all other Christian Europeans and do with it as they pleased, so long as it followed the Christian values at the foundation of the Doctrine: mine, trade, proselytize, and, most important, colonize.

Carole Pateman links this thinking to settler colonialism:[14] "A settled colony simultaneously presupposes and extinguishes a terra nullius. Settlers plant themselves in order to create a civil society out of a state of nature, an empty, vacant land where there is no pre-existing title. All title is created by civil government" (67). Under this rubric, Indians were imagined as having never achieved civil legitimacy. By contrast, the Welsh—on account of their whiteness, civility, Christianity, and their Old World origins—were positioned in both the 1590s and the 1790s to have assumed legitimate legal title to the continent extending into perpetuity, extinguishing any and all indigenous claims, as well as any post-1170 European claims. This positioned Indian inhabitants as well as prior French and Spanish colonizers as trespassers, criminals whose claims to the land were void, no matter how civilized they might subsequently become. By forming a civil society—as opposed to Indian savagery, French anarchy, or Spanish monarchy—the Welsh were positioned as the only pre-Jamestown population in North America fit to establish first British and then American title.

Here's how the story was reconstructed to serve this end: in 1170, Madoc supposedly fled Wales; in 1289, Edward I conquered Wales and, implicitly,

all places settled by the Welsh.[15] Three centuries later, Elizabethans looked
west to colonize Virginia, so their version of Madoc landed there. Six hundred years after Madoc's purported landfall, early republic settlers imagined themselves as the rightful legatees of his accomplishment, and not just
in reference to wherever he had landed or settled but for nearly the whole
continent. This claim was taken seriously as a point of law: in the 1790s, the
British invoked Madoc's prior occupancy in their dispute with the Russians
over Nootka Sound.[16] However, in the 1790s, accounts emerged in American
print culture of Madoc landing at Mobile Bay and his travels across the
Mississippi valley before settling in various places from North Carolina to
Tennessee—all disputed places claimed by both settlers and Indians—before
finally heading up the Missouri River and settling in the Dakotas. The legend grew to suit the territories desired by the colonizers in question.

The legend's heyday between 1780 and 1815 featured dozens Welsh
"Indians" whose presence bolstered claims to the Doctrine, though it did
not begin with this intent. Prior to this era, the legend's growth reflected
English ambitions on French colonial holdings in the Mississippi valley. In
1740, London's *Gentleman's Magazine* published a series of reports that the
Tuscarora Indians were speaking Welsh; in 1768, Charles Beatty reported
accounts of a Welsh village near New Orleans; similar accounts in 1752 and
1791 claim the Conestogas of western Pennsylvania were Welsh. Like Jonathan Carver, George Croghan offered a similar narrative in 1753 and even
claimed to have been told that the Welsh Indians still had Bibles they could
not read. Croghan, however, reported the Bibles were in the Welsh language. Yet the Bible was translated into Welsh only in the fifteenth century,
making Madoc's ownership of a Bible in his native tongue an obvious fiction.[17] Similar wishful fabulations accompanied more specifically American
accounts. Gwyn Williams notes, "Literally scores of people reported direct
conversations in Welsh with Indians, several Indian chiefs swore that their
ancestors had been Welsh. . . . At least thirteen real tribes were identified as
Welsh, eight others invented to fit" (*Madoc*, 37).

After the Revolution, and working from a strictly ethnological (rather
than literary) perspective, Frederic Cozzens, George Ruxton, Henry Rowe
Schoolcraft, and George Catlin repeated stories of meetings with Welsh-
speaking Indians, overlooking the fact that the Welsh language, like English,
had evolved in the intervening centuries: a nineteenth-century Welshmen could no more converse with his twelfth-century countryman than
Catlin could have with Chaucer. Still, Welsh Indians were supposedly still
living up the Missouri valley, fishing in coracles (leather dinghies) and building villages. "Proof" was delivered in purportedly non-Indian fortifications

along the Tennessee River. In some accounts, Welsh remnants lingered in the language of the "lighter skinned" Tuscaroras, and copper and iron arrowheads indicative of lost metallurgic skills unknown to "red" Indians among the Mandans, and fragments of medieval books were found scattered among the relics of various tribes.

However, aside from these rather superficial remnants, almost all reports conceded that the Welsh had degenerated to savagery: they had "Indianized" physically and culturally.[18] The Welsh were said to have become the Mandans—or maybe the Padoucas, or the White Padoucas. Variants of the legend—and there are dozens—have them going up the Red River or further west to become the Pueblo or the Texians or south to become the Aztecs.[19] Katy Chiles has identified this potential for racial transformation as a central anxiety for white Americans in the decades following the Revolution: "If the New World influenced the appearance of indigenous peoples of America and if transported Africans became white, would it be possible that whites might become something else? And—most urgently—under what conditions could a person of one race transform into another?" (9). Six hundred years in North America had transformed the Welsh from white to Indian, behaviorally and, perhaps, biologically. This exposed central early republic fears as well: Would westward expansion degenerate more recent white settlers? Could frontiersmen be trusted with the responsibilities of citizenship?

While these were crucial and pragmatic questions, more culturally minded Welsh primordialist texts reframed these disturbing potentials in allegories that merged direful degeneration and diligent maintenance: cautious Federalists found in the purported Welsh transformation a model of degeneration to be avoided; expansionist Democrats found in their version of the legend a pretext for white legitimacy and inhabitation. In almost every case, the fate of the Welsh became entangled in early republic debates over what is recognized today as the ambitions and methods of settler nationalism as the new country debated expanding into the trans-Appalachian West and, eventually, beyond. The controversy over the Welsh Indians serves as a crucible, then, for working through the nation's anxieties concerning the West, and, in turn, how these debates reveal what type of nation it might become. Moreover, as the first pre-Columbian group to emerge in post-Revolutionary print culture, the Welsh also provoked debates over primordialism itself: What kind of country needs a legendary past? As such, it paved the way for later episodes by opening alternative American pasts in which complex disputes would be reframed within the allegorical framework of a distant, undocumented past.

The Doctrine of Discovery and Settler Nationalisms

> God, in Locke's voice, mandates that improving productive labor is
> key to the entitlement of property. So mandated, colonizers felt the
> entitlement, even the duty, to appropriate, enclose, develop and subdue
> the "vacant lands" of America that were regarded as lying to waste
> by the inhabitants, who were seen as "actively neglecting" the land. . . .
> These "settled" or "planted" justifications were a way to ideologically
> distance the British from the Spaniards, whose colonies they saw as
> being founded on violence and destruction, instead of on planting and
> "improving."
>
> —Eva Mackey, *Unsettled Expectations*, 2016

Eva Mackey's reading of John Locke's *Second Treatise of Government* (1688) discusses how European "fantasies of entitlement" such as the Doctrine of Discovery served the ends of settler colonialism (50–51).[20] The strategic deployment of the Madoc legend grounded this fantasy in a purportedly genuine white occupation of the territory that would become the American West through the application of the Doctrine to preempt French and Spanish claims as well as to erase Indian rights. Shawnee legal scholar Robert J. Miller has traced the concept back to the Crusades and its use to "claim" lands held by non-Christians.[21] When the "New World" became an issue a few centuries later, England, a latecomer to trans-Atlantic colonization, added the necessary element of inhabitation, better known as colonization: "England and France thus added to the Doctrine the element of actual occupation and possession as a requirement to establish European claims to title by Discovery" (19) in order to claim North America, even though the French, Spanish, and Portuguese had hit the beaches first.

In 1576, Elizabethan courtier Sir John Dee revived the Madoc legend to establish British legal title to North America.[22] In a privately circulated memo, noting that England had absorbed Wales in 1289 and thus all its rights and properties, Dee wrote: "The Lord Madoc, sonne of Owen Gwyndd prince of North Wales, leaving his brothers in contention, and warre for their inheritance south, by sea (westerly from Irland), for some forein, and— Region to plant himself in with soveranity: with Region he had found, he returned to Wales againe and hym selfe with Shipps, vituals, and men and women sufficient for the coliniy, . . . nowe named America" (qtd. in Barone). Dee's memo found its way to George Peckham, Thomas Powell, and Richard Hakluyt, whose texts influenced Samuel Purchas and Thomas Heriot. Peckham made the crucial link to the Doctrine of Discovery: Madoc's settlement "doth shew the lawful tytle, which the Queen's most excellent Majestie hath unto those countries" and that the English were entitled to "restore her [America] to her Highness's right and interest" (qtd. in Barone). Dee's claim that Madoc meant "to plant himself in with soveranity" distinguishes the civilized Welshmen from the nomadic Indians, as well as earlier traders or explorers, such as both the French and the Spanish: once they arrive, the land is no longer empty. The expanding role of the legend in British imperial rhetoric can be seen in Hakluyt's revisions to his earlier work: in his 1582 *Divers Voyages* Madoc merited a brief mention; in his 1589 *Principal Navigations*—published after the defeat of the Spanish Armada—his section is expanded to a full chapter, revealing Madoc's growing role in propaganda as the window for colonization opened.

Miller also identifies missionary work as validating the Doctrine.[23] The Pilgrims applied it so in 1626, as Robert Cushman claimed:

> And first, seeing we daily pray for the conversion of the heathens. . . . This then is a sufficient reason to prove our going thither and live lawful: their land is spacious and void and there are but few and do but run over the grass, as do also the foxes and wild beasts. They are not industrious, neither have art, science, skill or faculty to use either the land or the commodities of it. . . . As the ancient patriarchs, therefore removed from straiter places into more roomy, where the land lay idle and waste, and none used it though there dwelt inhabitants by them (as Gen. 13:6, 11, 12 and 34:21 and 41:20) so it is lawful now to take a land which none useth, and make use of it. (91–92)

Linking proselytization to colonization, framed within Old Testament typology, Cushman articulates the Doctrine's most important codicil: the discoverers' claim to replicate the social, ecclesiastical, and commercial institutions of the home culture in the terra nullius of colonial space is not only righteous but also, in fact, required.

Two centuries later, the "West" had moved from Massachusetts to the Ohio valley, and both the Welsh legend and the Doctrine were revived to justify colonization. However, two centuries of dubious behavior by "Christian" whites on the frontier troubled the applicability of the Doctrine as a vehicle for building God's empire: missionary work had been half-hearted, and many settlers, like the Indians, were hunters—"new-made Indians," not husbandmen. After the Revolution, the masses of largely undocumented squatters in the Ohio and Mississippi valleys could no longer be ignored or evicted, as the British had endeavored. As many of these were Revolutionary veterans, they claimed membership and therefore incorporation into the coalescing national narratives. Settlers were streaming west without preexisting social, cultural, economic, religious institutions, and, most important, ideas of white nationhood, given the multiracial nature of the frontier. Chaotic militia-based defeats at Chillicothe and Kekionga as well as the settlers' flagrant violations of the Treaties of Paris (1783) and Greenville (1795) and the Jay Treaty (1794) suggested that white frontiersmen were poor candidates for full republican membership. The Whiskey Rebellion (1791–94) in western Pennsylvania directly rejected eastern tax law with violence, and adventure stories that re-created the Indian-killing Paxton Riots of 1763 and white savages such as Tom Quick and Lewis Wetzel valorized irrational interracial violence that could not be disavowed by republican culture.[24] Gouverneur Morris worried that the West "would not be able to furnish men equally enlightened to share in the administration of our common interests" (qtd. in Rakove, 14). George Mason asserted that if western states were not equally represented, they "will either not unite or will speedily revolt from the Union" (ibid.). The early republic, then, faced some hard choices: whether or not to colonize the West, and, if it did, how to stop abandonment of republican order on the western frontier.

At the same time, other early republic thinkers feared another kind of slippage: the loss of the Revolution's sense of unified, intercolonial mission to more strongly connect this group of diverse ex-colonies into a unified nation. They feared that, without transcendent, binding narratives, such as those based in essential commonalities of language and tradition, their nation would be simply an administrative unit, its citizens void of any cohering sense of common or unique purpose. The resurgent embrace of a sanitized Columbus during these decades signifies the quest for a national mythology, for example. A primordialist text addressed the issue even more specifically: Sarah Josepha Hale set her primordialist narrative about Tyrian Mound Builders, *The Genius of Oblivion* (1823), in the 1790s, with her young hero disgusted with the lack of national enthusiasm, a void filled by his discovery of primordial whites in the West. For *both*, white Westerners posed distinct risks of the settler nation: living in the woods, eating wild game, and interacting with the "savages," they had become "new-made Indians," in the terms of Hector St. John de Crèvecoeur's farmer James.[25] The slippage moved from theory to history: during the ongoing Indian Wars (1714–1815), white children captured by Indians returned to the forest upon "liberation," as did Indian children held by whites, as noted by Cotton Mather, Hector St. John de Crèvecoeur, Benjamin Franklin, and Cadwallader Colden.[26] All of these substantiated German race theorist Fredrich Blumenbach's idea of racial degeneration, "since . . . it is very easy to degenerate into brown, but

Story of Marcoo: justification for settler colonialism?

very much more difficult for the dark to become white" (qtd. in Jacobson, *Whiteness*, 1).

In brief, on its western frontier, the new ex-colonial nation was failing to achieve the ideals of and justifications for settler colonialism: sovereignty based in a shared sense of historical necessity and providential imprimatur based in the expansion of a European civilization and Christian virtue. This final pairing threw into relief competing eighteenth-century theories of nationalism: civic and romantic. Civic nationalists depended on the creation of the nation through the rule of law, such as in a republic. Romantic nationalists depended on the creation of the nation through commonly held transcendent narratives, such as those based in race or religion. As to the difference, Lloyd Kramer comments: "The first form of nationalism, which is often called liberal [civic] nationalism, typically includes individual rights in its definition of the nation's fundamental ideals. The second form of nationalism, often called integral [romantic] nationalism, typically subsumes the individual into a national community and identifies the nation in terms of race, ethnicity or culture rather than politics or individual rights" (24). As a product of the Enlightenment, civic nationalism was forward-looking and rules-based. Given the chaos intrinsic to colonizing the West, civic-minded Federalists sought to delay further colonization and instead focused on developing republican ideals among the thirteen former colonies on the Eastern Seaboard. This distinction by no means absolves American civic nationalists of the crimes of settler colonialism; however, it provided a foundational counternarrative of ambivalence and sensibility, slowing and limiting expansion.

Nonetheless, by the 1790s, the settler nation—like most former colonies—was already behind the times in their "colonial cringe," as European nations had been seeking their archaic foundations since midcentury. Romantic nationalism, as identified by Kramer, rejected the future- and rules-based ideals of the civic nation to define the modern nation as organic and distinctive from its neighbors. Eric Hobsbawm views such efforts skeptically: "It is clear that plenty of political institutions, ideological movements and groups—not least in nationalism—were so unprecedented that even historic continuity had to be invented, for example by creating an ancient past beyond effective historical continuity" (7). In the new United States, to meet the standards of romantic nationalism, the lack of historical continuity compelled the invocation or fabrication of, ultimately, transcendent categories and narratives binding the primordial past to the post-Enlightenment present. Unlike Europeans nations, whose neighbors shared their whiteness, to police the

borders of the nation—both geographically and culturally—Americans
settlers sought transcendent identity in race, as they viewed their borders,
and thus their national integrity, as threatened by nonwhites and ex-whites:
from within by African Americans, from without by Indians, and from both
by frontiersmen.[27]

Binding, foundational narratives in settler nations turn to race to make
the crucial identificatory distinction: sorting the colonizers from the colonized. In the late eighteenth century, according to Nell Irvin Painter, Robert
Young, and Bruce Dain, "race" displaced "nation" as the center of collective identity within political bodies seeking binding and distinguishing
narratives. By this thinking, "race" defined the territorial boundaries that
created the borders for any political entity. This shifted the criteria for the
settler nation from political sovereignty to transcendent cultural integrity shared by the inhabitants of a place as the source of the authenticating "historical continuity" for the nation. This would provide a depth and
a legitimacy lacking in nations based in the artifice of political organiza-
tions, such as republics. For romantics, nations must be natural, as opposed
to older arrangements based on kingdoms or feudal dominions. Anthony
Smith comments: "[Romantic] nationalism holds that the world consists
of natural nations, and has always done so . . . ; that the members of nations may, and frequently have, lost their national self-consciousness along
with their independence; and that the duty of nationalists is to restore that
self-consciousness and independence to the 're-awakened' organic nation"
(*National Identity*, 146). Like all expressions of romantic nationalism, primordialism aims to reawaken the natural nation suppressed by modernity's
unnatural artifice by locating its true members as having been present since
a fictional, Edenic moment *before* politics, when more natural and genetically unified communities formed based in tradition and values, rather than
by princes and popes.[28]

While this model worked for the ancient nations of Europe, its application in settler nations was problematic. *Settled* nations housed the raw
materials for imagining a nation based on a transcendent linkage of people
to place: language, continuity, and legend. *Settler* nations do not. Debates
about the nature of American nationalism still reflect divisions between
civic and romantic ideologies. One effect has been a permanent uncertainty in settler/Indian relations. Kevin Bruyneel states the problem: "The
dilemma this creates for scholars of US-indigenous politics is that it leads
them . . . toward either a more internal or a more external location for indigenous people and tribes" (5). While a civic nation might include Indians
as individuals capable of participation in the republic's self-governance and

commons democracy, a romantic nation is more exclusive: Indians cannot join because they share neither culture, tradition, nor history with the other members of the nation. Federalist Indian policy recognized Indian land rights, and their treaties emphasized training in literacy and skilled labor; later, policies created by romantic expansionists led to exclusion, whose endgame was Jackson's Indian removal.[29]

Here's where the legend of the Welsh became a stand-in for debates about the future of the nation in the West. Civic-minded Federalists simply did not need the Welsh or primordialist authentication they supplied. However, because romantic expansionists kept dredging up increasingly expansive versions of Madoc and his descendants, the Federalists had to rebut repeatedly what they viewed as dangerous distractions in the civic nation, a pattern of exchange and finally compromise that structures this chapter. On the whole, the legend of the Welsh Indians rehearsed how intranational conflicts would be contained in the early republic, albeit temporarily, through a narrative of synthesis that served the ends of both groups. The early republic's hybridization of romantic and civic nationalisms, however, would be short-lived, with the former becoming dominant in the 1820s. Nonetheless, as played out through competing versions of the legend of Madoc, the new nation's settler colonialist ambitions were momentarily adjusted to accommodate disagreements as to its methods and practices. In the end, both nationalisms and their ultimate synthesis were played out in microcosm through the disputed mythology of the Welsh Indians.

Madoc and the Romantic Nation

By calling the attention of mankind once more to this subject, he may be the means of procuring a more accurate inquiry into its truth, which, if it should even refute the story of the Welsh, will at least perform the important service to the world, of promoting a more accurate discovery of this immense country.

—John Filson, *The Discovery, Settlement, and Present State of Kentucky*, 1784

In his *Discovery, Settlement, and Present State of Kentucky*, John Filson, despite this ambivalence, subsequently identifies the Welsh as the Mound Builders who were later "expelled by the Natives" (56), as would Noah Webster a few years later. Moreover, whether the Mound Builders were Welsh or not, Filson encourages the potential legal and historical significance of primordial whites in the American West. He includes a number of such testimonials in search for investors in his Kentucky Company. By recasting the "dark and bloody ground" of Kentucky as a long-standing abode for white people, he attracted speculators, hoping to turn a profit for his company through semideliberate historical distortion. In doing so, he joined with other expansionists in deploying the Welsh as the region's original occupants whose efforts the new American settlers would continue, evading the more arduous and morally complex task of beginning their own.[30] Even before the Louisiana Purchase in 1803, the Welsh legend provided a prefiguration of colonization based on the racial and religious hierarchies at the heart of the Doctrine of Discovery. To confirm the whiteness of the elusive descendants of Madoc, more recent Welsh immigrants were repeatedly taken West to identify their long-lost cousins. Meriwether Lewis was tasked by Thomas Jefferson to find his fellow Welshmen up the Missouri River, for example. For romantic nationalists, the Madoc myth offered a potential binding narrative for an otherwise improvised settler nation, a covert romantic epic of white survival and racial unity.

Transatlantic Madoc enthusiasts contributed to this discourse by saturating the legend in larger narratives of more general racial dominion. In 1804, Robert Southey, a British poet, published *Madoc*, an epic whose profits were to fund a white pantisocratic settlement in Ohio. The book failed, and Southey and his partner, Samuel Taylor Coleridge, abandoned the project.[31] *Madoc* itself describes the emergence of the Welsh *as* the Aztecs, based on shared leopard imagery in their regalia.[32] Others imagined the West as the destined Welsh homeland. After a lengthy publicity campaign to finance such a venture, Welsh Methodist minister Morgan John Rhys, conceding Federalist fears of frontiersmen, wrote, "'Tis to be lamented that the frontiers of America have been peopled in many places with people of bad morals" (qtd. in Gwyn Williams, *The Search*, 19). To correct this, with his partner, Benjamin Rush, Rhys proposed a Welsh colony, and they purchased land along the Ohio. With Morgan citing Madoc as his predecessor, he founded the short-lived village of Beulah in 1794.[33] Other Madoc-based texts embellished his legend to serve nation-making cultural imperatives. Like a deus ex machina, the Welsh had supposedly settled everywhere—landing in Alabama, east to North Carolina, north to Ohio, and finally west to the Dakotas. Bernard DeVoto commented that the Madoc story "became by far the most widespread legend of pre-Columbian discovery. In the United States, it became our most elaborate historical myth and exercised a direct influence on our history" (qtd. in Gwyn Williams, *Madoc*, 31).

This elaboration can be seen most completely and extensively in the work of General Amos Stoddard. Coming near the end of the Madoc moment.

Stoddard's *Sketches Historical and Descriptive of Louisiana* (1812) culminates the legend's meaning, dismisses the fear of deracination, and introduces other concepts that reveal both the settler colonialist ideology and the implicit anxiety—the fear of inauthenticity—concealed within the primordialist impulse. Stoddard, a decorated military veteran and territorial governor who officiated the ceremony marking St. Louis's transition from French to American occupation in 1804, anticipates American victory in the War of 1812 and presents his compendium of information concerning the space his countrymen would soon occupy.[34] The first four hundred pages present a fairly extensive catalog of the peoples and resources awaiting Americans as they colonized the lands and peoples of the Louisiana Purchase.

However, his final section, "A Welsh Nation in America," fundamentally establishes the story of the Welsh as the only regional—or even continental—history that matters. In these chapters, Stoddard indulges a lifelong fascination with primordial whites: for decades, he had gathered "information" concerning "evidences" of purported pre-Columbian populations from the Phoenicians to the Polynesians, just as Knickerbocker mocked and later "fantastic archaeologists," such as Josiah Priest, would continue. In the opening sections, he describes the continent as actively interconnected to all other ancient civilizations. He concedes its global populations had melded into a single race by 1170, implying that Indian culture was a recent development—provisional and hence disposable—and really just constructed from the leftover fragments of Old World traditions.

By contrast, Stoddard positions the Welsh as the first permanent settlers, as opposed to the other Old World populations whose presence was fleeting, never really inhabiting the land by establishing a civil society. In other words, North America had housed imperial outposts but never settler colonies, not until the Welsh. As such, for Madoc, the place was a tabula rasa and thus eligible to be claimed, colonized, converted, and cultivated by those worthy of such a mission. Following this pattern, Stoddard positions his narrative to foreshadow a republican, and thus paternalistic, version of Anglo-American history. By this reckoning, before 1170, North America was an empty continent: occupied but not inhabited, not yet on a path to historical meaning. Stationed in St. Louis, Stoddard had long interacted with Spanish and French who, likewise, had *not* imposed civil order on their imperial holdings and so had left the *terra* functionally *nullius,* and still a tabula rasa ripe for Anglo-American colonization. For Stoddard, the French and Spanish were unworthy of the Doctrine's privileges, as they had ignored its demand to convert and improve the land's denizens. By staying in place and not only retaining their culture but also imposing it upon the indigenous populations (as in W.P.'s poem), Stoddard's Welsh provide a counternarrative for American occupation and colonization, one based in the as-yet unstated ideology of the white man's burden. To do this, Stoddard addresses at length the influence of the Welsh on Indian culture during those three centuries (1170–1492) and finds that, in fact, "Indian" culture as a whole owed its most central defining characteristics to Welsh cultural influences.

To begin, Stoddard domesticates Madoc's settlement by drawing parallels between it and early Anglo colonial history, transplanting by 430 years the foundational settler narrative of European refugees seeking a haven for liberty and autonomy. Like Jefferson in *A Summary View of the Rights of British America* (1774), Stoddard begins in 1066 by establishing Wales as "the last refuge of British liberty" after the Norman invasion.[35] Next, he creates a narrative that mostly substitutes the Welsh for more familiar Pilgrim and Puritan colonial experiences: "Invaded from without and convulsed within, the Welsh had strong motives to abandon their country, and to hazard their lives in pursuit of another, especially at a time when they had nearly lost all hope of maintaining their liberties" (467). Like the seventeenth-century Anglo immigrants, the Welsh migrated for liberty when their rights in Europe had been denied. This positions settlers as refugees, not invaders, victims rather than victimizers.

Then Stoddard conducts a thorough review of the printed sources of Madoc mania. He begins with Hakluyt's contemporary David Powell (1584) but makes particular reference to eighteenth-century British traveler Charles Beaty, who claims to have seen "a Welsh Bible [that] they kept carefully wrapped up in a skin because they could not read it." Nonetheless, for Beaty, "both men and women observed the rites and ceremonies prescribed by Mosaic law" (477), suggesting an even older primordial link between the Welsh and the Old Testament.[36] To Stoddard, however, this is not proof of degeneration; instead, he reconfigured the standard narratives about how the Welsh interacted with Indians, breaking from the standard identification of one tribe or another as Welsh. Instead, for him, the Welsh had subdued the indigenous populations and spread themselves among them as cultural ambassadors, transforming Indian populations by installing themselves as each tribe's de facto patriarchal elite—Jefferson's "natural aristocracy"—tasked with bringing civilization to the savages. Stoddard also uses this notion to refute accusations that the Welsh purportedly appear in so many places proved their actual presence in none: "Against these authorities several plausible objections may be urged, calculated at first blush to weaken their validity. In the first place it may be said that, if they prove anything, they prove too much" (479). While Stoddard never claims *all* Indians are Welsh, he does imply that all meaningful Indian culture is Welsh-based. Their range envisions a saturation of the eastern half of the continent by Welshmen charged with cultural colonization.

To demonstrate the Welsh ubiquity in thirteenth- and fourteenth-century North America, Stoddard inserts a Malthusian study of population growth. From an original base of eleven hundred (in ten ships), he calculates a doubling every fifty years, so that by the time of the first "recorded" sighting of Welsh Indians in 1660, there would have been 1.26 million Welsh in North America. He also supposes a third Welsh fleet—no longer just ships, but fleets now—landed separately from the first two. Finally, he presumes universal military superiority for the Welsh in any conflicts with resisting Indians: "Hence we are led to believe, that population was rapid among them; and perhaps the more so as they had exchanged a foggy and barren country, for one of a serene atmosphere, and more prolific in the necessaries of life, both vegetable and animal. No doubt they preserved many of the useful arts a long time, particularly the art of war, which enabled them to reside in regions of their choice, and to multiply in security" (480–81). This is a palimpsest of seventeenth-century colonial history transferred six centuries into the past and a thousand miles west. Next, Stoddard builds upon Southey's narrative that the Welsh either conquered the Aztecs in Florida and then supplanted them in Mexico or that a fraction of the Welsh *became* the leaders of the Aztecs. To support this, he cites the similarity of Montezuma's seal and the Welsh coat of arms: "a griffin with expanded wings, holding a tiger in his talons" (481).[37] Conveniently for Stoddard, however, the Spaniards destroyed Aztec culture, erasing evidence of its Welsh origins.

Stoddard concludes with a portentous paragraph linking the Welsh to the practices of Freemasonry so prevalent among the Founders: "Travellers describe certain private societies among the Indians which apparently resemble our lodges of Freemasons. Their rules of government, and the admission of members, are said to be nearly the same. . . . The ceremonies of initiation, and the mode of passing from one degree to another, would create astonishment in the mind of an *enlightened* spectator. Is not this practice of European origin?" (488; emphasis in original). This passage serves two functions. First, it completes the Welshization of Indian culture: the few "civilized" aspects of pre-Columbian indigenous culture had Welsh roots. The ubiquity and dispersal of Welsh people and culture, coupled with their exogenous dominance (Aztec) and endogenous influence (secret societies), imagines a Welsh-descended elite informing and shaping indigenous culture. Of course, this resembles how republican culture intended to impose

order on the democratic chaos of post-Revolutionary America and its racially slippery western border. In the early republic, Freemasonry was at
its apex. Steven C. Bullock analyzes Masonic claims: "The new language
of Masonic science first placed the fraternity into the accepted genealogy of
learning and civilization, giving it a central role in the lineage of progress.
The scientific principles that underlay these changes, furthermore, had
continuing significance at a time when Americans had embarked on an
unprecedented experiment in liberty and equality" (143). Stoddard, likely
a Mason himself, parallels Madoc's moment and his own, at the moment
when the United States began to realize its continental ambitions through
its projected victory in the War of 1812. In both narratives, communities
founded on fair-minded principles of liberty and Freemasonry overcame
forces of tyranny and ignorance. Stoddard writes: "In the early periods of
English history, the knowledge of freemasonry was mostly confined to the
druids; and Wales was more fruitful of this description of men, than any
other part of Europe. They were almost the only men of learning in those
days. They executed the functions of priest, historians, and legislators. Those
in Wales in particular animated their countrymen to a noble defense of
their liberties, and afforded so much trouble to the first Edward that he
ordered them to be barbarously massacred" (488). On the eve of a second
war with England, Stoddard makes the cause of the Welsh the cause of the
new nation, as the war threatened recolonization. More precisely, however,
Freemasonry's staffing of the "priest, historians, and legislators" in every
tribe prefigures the establishment and empowerment of an elite class to preserve the archaic traditions intrinsic to romantic nationalism.

Yet as much as he intended to celebrate the "Welsh nation" uncritically,
Stoddard ultimately betrays the anxiety intrinsic to settler colonialism's
claim to historical transcendence: racial regression. He reproduces a letter
from Tennessee governor John Sevier that refers to a thirty-year-old conversation about the remains of a fort in Tennessee with a "Cherokee" chief:

> It is handed down by our forefathers, that the works were made by *white
> people*, who had formerly inhabited the country. . . . At length it was discov-
> ered that the *whites* were making a number of large boats which induced the
> Cherokees to suppose, that they intended to descend the Tennessee River
> [and attack the Cherokees]. At length, the whites proposed to the Indians
> that if they would exchange prisoners and cease hostilities, they would
> leave the country, and never more return; which was acceded to, and, after
> the exchange, parted in friendship. The whites then [went] up the Muddy
> River (Missouri) then up that river to a very great distance. They are now on
> some of its branches: But they are no longer a *white people*; they are now

become like all Indians; and look like the other red people of the country. (484; emphasis in original)

In their surrender to the Cherokee, the Welsh lost more than their land. By conceding to Indians, they seem to have lost their sense of difference and dominion, the first step toward becoming "like all Indians," and so vacating their whiteness and its attendant historical privileges. To Stoddard, whatever civilization pre-Columbian America had attained was based in the interventions of the Welsh. By conjecturing a legend of white people resisting tyranny and establishing republics in North America, Stoddard transfers a *racial* pride in the achievements of archaic whites to a *national* pride in the more recent reenactment of that legacy, demonstrating romantic nationalism's equation of race and nation. Yet despite himself, he betrays the settler's fear of racial instability. Civic nationalists would dwell more tellingly on the loss of Welsh whiteness and its troubling implications.

The Primordial Past and the Civic Nation

In respect to the Welsh Indians, I have only to inform you that I could not meet with such a people, and from intercourse I have had with Indians ... I think you may with safely inform our friends that they have no existence.

—John Evans, 1797

In 1797, even as Rush and Rhys planned their Madoc-modeled asylum, John Evans, a Welsh farmhand, was specially recruited to travel up the Missouri River to Mandan territory to test their Welshness.[38] Upon his return, he reported none. Meriwether Lewis would likewise come up empty (Gwyn Williams, *Madoc*, 148). While this did nothing to stifle enthusiasts such as Stoddard, the growing lack of evidence only fueled the fire of those who found little use for Madoc, primordialism, and romantic nationalism. In their efforts to quell what they viewed as a useless distraction, skeptics repositioned the Welsh Indians to challenge both romantic nationalists and land speculators (such as Filson) by denouncing expansion as driven more by profit seeking than by republican ideals or the implicit patriotism of racial mythmaking.

This also reflected the changing "science" of race. Chiles notes that, by the late 1790s, there had been "a shift in the understanding of race from a malleable feature of a person's exterior to a trait lodged within one's corporeal interior" (202). By this line of thinking, the Welsh Indians—fixed in their whiteness—had either vanished, never existed, or so interbred with the Indians to have vanished as a distinct population. In all three scenarios, claims on the Doctrine of Discovery via Madoc's inhabitation were voided by a loss of whiteness—as well as of Christianity, literacy, and other forms of "civil" society. More direct, though, even as fantasy, civic nationalists considered Welsh Indians dangerous distractions for a divided and divergent set of ex-colonies claiming to be a nation that still lacked a cohesive and durable political, economic, or cultural identity as it confronted more meaningful internal threats based on frontier policy, slavery and trade, multiregional cooperation, and staggering structural debts and deficits.

Most prominent was Jeremy Belknap in *American Biography* (1794–98). In an opening chapter that considers a gathering of proposed pre-Columbian explorers, Belknap not only refutes the Madoc legend for its implausibility but also links it to pro-expansionist propaganda going back to Dee, accusing Hakluyt and Purchas of being Dee's propagandizing pawns. Their accounts—claimed as legitimate history—become worse than mere legends as they perform the work of deceitful advertising for venture colonialists. Belknap's rejection of Hakluyt in the 1590s as a reliable historian, then, might also be read as a critique of the expansionists in the 1790s: "National prejudice might prevail, even with so honest a writer, to convert a Welsh fable into a political argument to support, against a powerful rival, the claim of his sovereign to the dominion of the continent" (137). Belknap refutes the Doctrine of Discovery's enabling of settler claims to western land as they are based in greed, not virtue. He identified the promulgation of the Welsh Indians as a front for unregulated land grabbing, not a basis for a foundational narrative for a civic republic. Had he lived so long, Belknap, like most New England Federalists, would have likely challenged the Louisiana Purchase and other westward ambitions, as he had anticipated in his political satire *The Foresters* (1787).[39] For such skeptics, national identity needed no basis in a preliterate past.

Jedidiah Morse denied Madoc twice. In his *Universal Geography* (1792), Morse commented, "The pretensions of the Welsh to the discovery of America have but a slight foundation. . . . He [Madoc] and his colony have not been heard from since [their departure from Wales]" (46). In his 1795 *History of America*, Morse concluded a long satire with "It may be added that the Welsh were never a naval people, that the age in which Madoc lived was particularly ignorant in navigation; and the most which they could have attempted was a mere coasting voyage" (2). In 1807, Pittsburgh writer Zadok Cramer would comment, "Before the cession of Louisiana to the United States, this was the region of fable. Fancy peopled it, and a thousand miraculous tales were related.—The mammoth, that wonder of creation, was thought might be there, and Welsh Indians" (271). In 1805, Charles Brockden Brown reprinted a scathing review in the *American Magazine* of Southey's *Madoc* that mocked not only the poem but also its theft of Spanish conquest history to invent an epic scale absent from the legend itself. Like Belknap, these writers demand more of historiography than biased speculation done in the name of forwarding unfounded and unjust claims on the land. By their reckoning, the Madoc legend illegitimately defined a nation as based in legend rather than law.

A secondhand tale about a medieval prince based in obscure sources and flimsy material proof compelled other writers to reconsider the primordial impulse more generally. Benjamin Franklin's "Edict by the King of Prussia" (1773) mocks British claims to the "Rights of Discovery of America" by having the German ruler invoke his own sovereignty over Great Britain eight hundred years after its Saxon "Discovery." Washington Irving's *A History of New York* (1809), aside from mocking the Madoc myth (as he had in *Salmagundi* as well), asks, "What right had the first discoverers of America to land, and take possession of a country, without asking the consent of its inhabitants, or yielding them an adequate compensation for their territory?" (7:412). Ultimately, Irving reduces the Doctrine to its true essence: "the Right of Extermination, or, in other words, the Right by Gunpowder" (7:419). Beneath primordialist claims to national validation, Irving identifies greed and violence as the primary drivers and methods of settler colonialist aggression. On the whole, it mattered little to these skeptics if there had been Welsh Indians or not: primordial events are irrelevant to a nation based on the forward-looking identity of a civic nation.

Finally, consider Henry Marie Brackenridge's rejection of Madoc and his practice of civic nationalism. The son of novelist Hugh Henry Brackenridge, Henry was raised in the West, becoming fluent in Spanish and French.[40] In *Views of Louisiana* (1814), he affirms: "That no Welsh nation exists at present on this continent is beyond a doubt. . . . We are often tempted by a fondness for the marvelous to seek out remote or improbable causes for that which may be explained by the most obvious" (169–70). Three years later, Henry was in the Maryland legislature when the Jew Bill was introduced, banning Jews from public office, legislation typical of the emergent racial unilateralism innate to romantic nationalism. Henry fought and lost, resigning in protest. Next, in the early 1820s, he insisted on maintaining the land rights of hispanophone Floridians when serving under territorial governor Andrew Jackson, who wanted to distribute those lands to his fellow plantation owners. This time, Henry was dismissed. Later, as John Quincy

Adams's emissary to South America, he insisted on recognizing the governments in Bolivia and Venezuela although Indigenes were in power, a decision that again cost him his job. To a civic nationalist like Brackenridge, ethnic identity—Jew, Catholic, Spaniard, or indigenous—had nothing to do with citizenship or legitimacy. Of course, he had no use for Madoc.

Still, as W.P. showed, the legend might still have some use. In response, Federalists explored another use for the Welsh Indians: as symbolic extrapolations of undisciplined white frontiersman. As noted, almost every account of the supposed Welsh Indians noted that, aside from their language, the Welsh Indians had become just that—Indians. One 1792 account reported that "the people subsist by the produce of the chase; that the instruments they use on the occasion are generally bows and arrows. . . . They had several books which were most religiously preserved in skins and were considered by them as mysteries" (Gwyn Williams, *Madoc*, 88–89). In brief, they seemed just a few steps ahead of white frontiersmen on the path toward losing their whiteness. Hence, an impasse based on differing conceptualizations of the prioritization of the criteria for national membership for both the nation among other nations and for genuine citizens among noncitizens: for romantic nationalists, race trumped republicanism; for civic nationalists, the republic trumped race. Yet the concept of racial transformability offered a means for the Federalists to accommodate expansion and for the expansionists to concede the benefits of republican order. To this end, the most popular version of the Welsh legend offered a binding narrative of racial and republican redemption.

Synthesis: The Story of Maurice Griffiths

American writers were particularly fascinated by the Welsh Indians' historical indeterminacy, or their liminal status as neither savage nor civilized, Indian nor European. Welsh Indians perhaps represented the at once frightening and exhilarating possibility that European settlers might adapt to the conditions of frontier life with going entirely native and without renouncing all the cherished ideas of civilization.

—Juliet Shields, *Nation and Migration*, 2016

Juliet Shields has recently commented on the mixed legacy of the Madoc legend as a whole as to how early republic American imagined the process of colonization. The story of Maurice Griffiths, as it traveled from a newspaper report to inclusion in Harry Toulmin's *Description of Kentucky*

(1793; the version used here) brings together elements of romantic and civic nationalisms to craft a narrative of synthetic rewhitening that serves not only both forms of nationalism but, more profoundly, settler colonialism at base. This version of the Madoc legend suggested frontiersmen could be both rewhitened and reintegrated into the republic. In this story, if frontiersmen had lost their whiteness, whiteness itself was unstable. If whiteness was unstable, it could be regained as easily as it was lost. And if frontiersmen could regain it, and again be trusted with the privileges and responsibilities granted white men in a settler republic, could the instability of "race" be repurposed both to discipline racial slippage and serve settler colonialism? The Welsh Indian narrative most often reprinted even long after the early republic, Griffiths's story demonstrates a defining hope to gloss over and disavow the paradoxes intrinsic to the colonization of the West.

While theories of race shifting had been largely debunked in "scientific" circles by 1800, they lingered in the popular imagination.[41] In fact, racial transition came to be viewed in very fluid terms, if the literary record reflects popular opinion. If a person or group had been transformed racially, could they also be switched back? Although no Indianized Welsh could provide a model for reversing degeneration or a model of archaic and heroic whiteness as none could be found, their narrative might still be applied to the rewhitening of those unstable frontiersmen, the "new-made Indians." Moreover, if new Indians could become white, what of older ones? Thomas Jefferson told a group of Indians in 1808, "Temperance, peace, and agriculture . . . will prepare you . . . to mix with us in Society, and your blood and ours united will spread again over this great island" (qtd. in Nichols, 193). Foreshadowing the Dawes-era motto of "Kill the Indian but not the man," such statements imagine a unified, coherent, and authentic settler nation gesturing toward *both* an inclusive civic nationhood that deemphasizes *race* and an exclusive romantic nationhood privileging the settlers' Old World origins.

This would turn on rescripting the frontiersman as redeemable—his lost whiteness found—through the imposition of republican discipline, a process subsequently to be imposed on Indians. As Juliet Shields suggests, a version of the Welsh Indians emerged that reimagined them as stuck between Indian and white, savage and civilized, and indigene and settler. Early republic frontier experience demonstrated a vast range of possibilities along this spectrum. The titles of recent books like David Andrew Nichols's *Red Gentlemen and White Savages* and Nancy Shoemaker's *A Strange Likeness* emphasize the racial multiplicity of the early American frontier. Shoemaker describes the function of race on the eighteenth-century frontier: "In practice, skin color was not a foolproof indicator of identity. No one could count on being able to tell people apart simply by looking at them. Whites adopted by Indians, either through captivity or by their own choice, looked like Indians to other whites. At the same time, the thorough intermixture of some communities and families confounded any attempt to categorize people by either physiology or culture" (137). In this context, the Welsh were reimagined as having integrated elements of both racial categories and so became a means of uniting the primordial past and the republican present. Chiles writes, "Late eighteenth-century environmentalism provided a counterintuitive way to account for that distinction: fundamentally similar to whites, North American Indians were different only because of the circumstances in which they had lived" (17). If the frontier had caused Indians to become "red," the process could be reversed; moreover, if environmental conditions had fairly recently reddened the Indian, had they ever *really* been Indian? Or just temporarily darkened whites? Was racial difference temporary and reversible, as Jefferson suggested? While this vision of racial plurality seems progressive, however, with its end goal of universal whiteness, its covert colonialism belies a benign facade. Denying the Indianness of the Indians reframes settler colonization as laudable correction rather than damnable conquest. In the carefully curated story of Maurice Griffiths, a fiction of absolution was first tested on a single white frontiersman. Later, it would help reimagine Indians as lost Jews, as addressed in the next chapter.

Although it uses the Welsh as foils in the story of a frontiersman's redemption, Griffiths's story offers an intriguing alternative that complicates any notion of racial otherness to embody, by contrast, the more complicated racial transformation observed by Shields and Chiles. This transmutes the Welsh from a foundational legend about colonizing Indians and their lands—as with W.P.'s poem—to a narrative of settler self-rewhitening that preserves the nation as both civic entity and romantic adventure by restoring the whiteness of the West. In Griffiths's tale, and in the story of how it worked its way through the early republic's print culture, a very different role is imagined for primordial whites, one that in fact incidentally reveals the moral and racial precariousness of the settler nation. In December 1792, the *Kentucky Palladium* in Frankfort published the extended account of a Welshman, Maurice Griffiths, as provided by Judge Harry Toulmin. After Hugh Henry Brackenridge, Toulmin was the most prominent western man of letters in the 1790s.[42] Toulmin reportedly heard Griffiths's account from a fellow Kentuckian farmer named John Childs and offered his personal endorsement of Childs's reliability. Small wonder Belknap accused the legend's believers of excessive credulity.

Nonetheless, Griffiths's hearsay-based account was reprinted at least a dozen times and on both sides of the Atlantic over the next sixty years. The Filson Society reprinted it in the late nineteenth and early twentieth centuries, including in a comprehensive 1908 edition that collected dozens of Welsh Indian testimonials. Josiah Priest and other fantastic archaeologists cataloged it as a reliable source as well. In its initial reprinting in his collection *A Description of Kentucky* (1793), Toulmin addressed the doubters: "Sir,—No circumstance relating to the history of the Western country probably has excited, at different times, more general attention and anxious curiosity than the opinion that a nation of white men speaking the Welsh language reside high up the Missouri. By some the idea is treated as nothing but the suggestion of a bold imposture and easy credulity; whilst others regard it as a fact fully authenticated by Indian testimony and the report of various travellers worthy of credit" (96). Subsequently, Toulmin frames the story within a settler colonialist narrative, referring to the Welsh as "white Americans" and offering proof that they were "an agricultural people," and their relics reveal the "genius who relied more on their military skill than their numbers" (97)—craftsmen and farmers, a republican yeomanry. In Griffiths's own account, however, something very different lurks: a radical Indianization, one closely resembling depictions of white frontiersman, such as the "back settlers" in letter 3 of Crèvecoeur's *Letters from an American Farmer* (1782), a text Toulmin reprinted adjacent to Griffiths's in *A Description of Kentucky*. As Griffiths experiences both the Shawnee and the Welsh, the text offers an informative contrast between the unredeemed, deracinated Welsh, and the recovered, rewhitened frontiersman, a narrative that sanitizes the rough westerner in preparation for his forthcoming reentry into the republic.

Toulmin records that Griffiths was sixteen when he migrated to Ohio from Wales. He was promptly captured by the Shawnee and subsequently spent a number of years as an adopted warrior. As already noted, the ease of white acculturation to Indian lifeways had long disturbed settlers, such as Crèvecoeur's farmer James: "By what power does it come to pass that children who have been adopted among these people can never be prevailed upon to readopt European manners?" (213). When the Shawnee undertook a three-man exploratory expedition up the Missouri River, Griffiths was included as a full member of the tribe—an Indian in all but birth. After traveling for a month, past the Sandhills of Nebraska, the tribesmen adopt a policy of rotating the role of intermediary with the other tribes they met. Like the fictional Alonso Decalves in John Trumbull's *New Travels to the Westward* (1786), they soon find an all-white tribe close to the headwaters

of the Missouri:[43] "After passing the mountains they entered a fine fertile
tract of land which having traveled through for several days they acciden-
tally met with three white men in the Indian dress." Griffiths immediately
understood their language as "pure Welsh" (101). Yet as it is not his turn as
intermediary, he says nothing.

Griffiths and the Shawnee are then taken to "the village of these white
men" where "the whole nation was of the same color, having all the European complexion." They are taken before "the king and chief men of the nation," and the Welsh Indians deliberate the fate of Griffiths and his Shawnee
companions. In the end, they rule that their "fire-arms, their knives, and
their tomahawks" indicate they are "a war-like people" who would likely
come back with "a powerful body of invaders" if they were allowed to escape
down river. When a death sentence is pronounced to protect the isolation of
the tribe, "Griffiths then thought it was time for him to speak. *He addressed
the council in the Welsh language*" (102; emphasis in original) and assures his
captors, "It was their wish to trace the Missouri to its sources; and that they
should return to their country satisfied with the discoveries they had made
without any wish to disturb the repose of their new acquaintances." Subsequently, "An instant astonishment glowed in the countenances, not only of
the council, but of his Shawnee companions" (102), and they are released.
At this point, the Shawnee functionally vanish from the account: once aboriginal whites are found, Indians become irrelevant to both the past and
the future of North America.

Now able to communicate with his long-lost cousins, Griffiths stays
among the Welsh for eight months. Yet consistently, Griffiths reports that
Madoc's descendants had lost the characteristics that set them apart from
Indians, aside from skin color and language. Toulmin records that Griffiths
noted their degenerated state: "They had no books, no records, no writings. They intermixed with no other people by marriage: there was not a
dark-skinned man in the nation. . . . Their clothing was skins well dressed.
Their houses were made of upright posts and barks of trees. The only implements they had to cut them were stone tomahawks; they had no iron.
Their arms were bows and arrows. . . . They had neither horses, cattle, sheep,
hogs, nor any domestic or tame animals. They lived by hunting" (104). The
particulars of the Welsh Indians' retrogression to subsistence lifeways—
the loss of metallurgy and architecture, the abandonment of literacy—had
all also been observed among "white" settlers of the frontier. Having passed
the winter, Griffiths and the Shawnee finally travel back east. The Welsh
Indians are decidedly not candidates to "readopt European ways" and so are

left in isolation, unfit for rewhitening. At this point, the narrative shifts to Griffiths himself.

Next, Toulmin reports that his Frankfort correspondent John Childs recounted Griffiths's escape from the Shawnee and his subsequent acquisition of a Kentucky farm. Griffiths's abandonment of his Shawnee captors and his own rewhitening, a fiction, given the observations of Crèvecoeur, Franklin, and Colden, demonstrates how a frontiersman, even one who lived as a Shawnee, could reenter civil society. As a Kentucky farmer, Griffiths likely became a slave owner and a full participant in the settler colonialist project, his moment of having been an Indian a fleeting memory. In brief, Toulmin champions a narrative wherein white frontiersmen such as Griffiths could readopt European ways and thereafter regain the privileges of white citizenship. In many ways, Griffiths's story is entangled with that of Crèvecoeur's narrator, or, more precisely, his father's. As noted, in 1793, Toulmin excerpted both Crèvecoeur's letter 3, the well-known "What Is an American?" essay, and Filson's biography of Daniel Boone in his collection *A Description of Kentucky* directly following his reprint of Griffiths. In letter 3, often cited as articulating the "American Dream" at the heart of settler identity, Crèvecoeur's narrator observes race-shifting frontiersmen, including, briefly, his own father:

> In all societies there are off-casts; this impure part serves as our precursors or pioneers; my father was one of this calling, but he came upon honest principles, and was therefore on of the few who held fast; by good conduct and temperance, he transmitted to me his fair inheritance when not above one in fourteen of his contemporaries had the same good fortune. . . . Thus our bad people are those who are half cultivators and half hunters; the worst of them are those who have degenerated altogether to the hunting state. As old ploughmen and new men of the woods, as Europeans and new-made Indians, they contract the vices of both. (72–73, 78)

As it was for Griffiths's Welshmen, a key moment in the process of deracination occurs when the switch is made from commercial farming to subsistence hunting. Civilized whites farm; savage ex-whites hunt. Such passages have been more recently cited to establish an ironic distance between the colonialist propaganda of the thoroughly upbeat farmer and Crèvecoeur's own darker vision.[44] The twinned redemptions of Griffiths and James's father suggests the process can be reversed by "good conduct and temperance."

Toulmin's placement of Griffiths's narrative adjacent to Crèvecoeur's in his anthology juxtaposes four "new-made Indians"—Welsh Indians,

James's father, Griffiths himself, and Daniel Boone. Unredeemed, the Welsh alone have irrevocably "Indianized" (213), while Boone, James's father, and Griffiths have engaged the stage-based process wherein republican self-control overwhelms the savage-making environment, thus making the West safe for settlement and frontier whites safe for republican self-government. The Welsh in that narrative provide a counternarrative signifying that, after so many generations, racial transition can become irreversible. By contrast, Griffiths's double transformation from Welshman to Shawnee warrior and then from Shawnee warrior to yeoman farmer provides a fantasy of whiteness regained, and his return to farming—and presumably slaveholding—a model for assuring the transplantation and perpetuation of settler colonialism in a hostile setting.

Crèvecoeur, of course, knew things were far more complex than Toulmin and other Anglo-Americans imagined, and his *Letters* ends with James foolishly attempting, or so he thinks, to become an Indian. In letter 12, when the violence of the Revolution arrives, James responds by endeavoring to forgo his whiteness to move west among the western Indians: "I will revert into a state approaching nearer that of nature . . . far removed from the accursed neighborhood of the Europeans" (211). Like Colden and Franklin, he ponders how white captives happily acculturated to Indian life before deciding, as Philip Deloria would recognize, to play Indian: "You may therefore, by means of anticipation, behold me under the wigwam" (219).[45] Yet Crèvecoeur presciently sees in this aspiration elements that mark James as a settler colonialist despite himself: as much as he wants to, he cannot simply decide to shift races and instead ironically simply starts the process of colonization over again at a safe distance from the Revolution, absolving himself of its violence but replicating its hierarchies nonetheless.

In his new western settlement, despite his rejection of "the Europeans," James means to transform Indian agriculture from subsistence to commercial: "In order to supply this great deficiency of industrious motives and to hold out to them to prevent the fatal consequences of this sort of apathy, I will keep an exact account of all that shall be gathered and give each of them a regular credit for the amount of it, to be paid them at the return of peace" (223). In the process, their diet and economy would shift from hunting and subsistence to agricultural and commercial. In other words, Crèvecoeur has his fictional narrator flee the violence of settler colonialism by settling a new colony and beginning the same patterns of transformation and dominion, a dark commentary on the prospects of the new nation doing anything other than replicating the violence it sought independence to disavow. In the end,

James envisions himself the same way W.P. envisioned Madoc: as a refugee from a corrupt and degenerate society whose inhabitation of the Indian-based terra nullius brings enlightenment and stability through unilateral intercultural dominion and benevolent paternalism.

Toulmin, like generations of subsequent editors and historians, had not read *Letters* through to letter 12. Or, if they had, they refused to incorporate its deep critique of settler colonialism. By fetishizing James's idyllic letter 3, they, settler colonialists themselves, disavow the violence and hypocrisy of noncanonized letters 9 and 12. The deliberate nonreading of those later letters in the next two centuries of anthologies—starting with Toulmin's—demonstrates the complicity of nationalist print culture in the promulgation of colonialism.

These debates continued to feature a primordial Welsh leitmotif, at least until the era of Andrew Jackson. In the famous Marshall Trilogy, the Doctrine of Discovery was repeatedly invoked to justify various gradations of settler land seizure and ethnic cleansing, all of which left Federalist ideas of restraint on history's dustbin. Leftover Federalist chief justice John Marshall ruled on the Doctrine's lasting relevance but shifted language between 1823 and 1833 in ways that reflect his increasing awareness of its moral and legal slipperiness.[46] When ruling on *Johnson and Graham's Lessee v. William M'Intosh* (1823), he embraced it: "This principle was, that discovery gave title to the government by whose subjects, or by whose authority, it was made, against all other European governments, which title might be consummated by possession. The exclusion of all other Europeans, necessarily gave to the nation making the discovery the sole right of acquiring the soil from the natives, and establishing settlements upon it."[47] Yet having affirmed it, Marshall wavers, echoing a fear of the masses when it came to the act of "acquiring the land," as conquest was now conducted by commoners, not kings. As such, Indian rights had been violated: "In the establishment of these relations, the rights of the original inhabitants were, in no instance, entirely disregarded; but were necessarily, to a considerable extent impaired."[48] Marshall's telling concession that Indians *had* rights, even if they were impaired, breaks from previous applications of the Doctrine. Marshall recurred to Federalist fears of racial degeneration by removing degenerated frontiersmen by shifting the Doctrine to the Federal government alone, disallowing its use by all whites. While the ruling is usually read with attention to indigenous rights, the exclusion of the frontiersmen must be noted: Marshall retained earlier Federalist fears about racial and, hence, moral degradation, a transformation that subverts the Doctrine's basis in stable conceptions of race and civility.[49] Thus the specter of race-shifting haunted Marshall's faith in the Doctrine as a narrative of justified colonialism.

Jackson and his fellow settler colonizers persisted, and the resulting lawsuits again found their way to Marshall. In 1832, with Indian removal under way, Marshall's ambivalence had grown into outright doubt.[50] By affirming the semisovereignty of Indian nations ("domestic dependent nations") Marshall undermined the Doctrine's basis in the concept of unused land: if prior to European colonization the Cherokee had had a "civil" society, the *terra* had not been *nullius*, and the doctrine becomes inapplicable. Andrew Jackson's defiance of John Marshall's leftover Federalism defined the age. Supposedly, Jackson responded to the majority opinion in *Cherokee Nation v. Georgia* by shouting, "John Marshall has made his ruling. Now let him enforce it!"[51] Marshall's rulings failed to revive the republican values of the 1790s, when the Madoc legend reflected meaningful debates about whether expansion was in the best interest of the republic, marking a step in the nation's transition from civic republic nation to romantic Jacksonian empire.[52]

In this new historical moment, Madoc's story faded, the problem to which it had been oriented solved by the triumph of Jackson's romantic nationalism and its legitimation of settler colonialism. The legacy of white primordial inhabitation he provided to buttress the settler nation's continental and racial ambitions via the Doctrine of Discovery were simply no longer needed. Nonetheless, as mere obscurantism, the legend of Madoc has lasted well into the modern era, spawning a new book "proving" its truth about every decade.[53] In 1953, the local chapter of the Daughters of the American Revolution erected a monument on the beaches of Mobile Bay attesting to the truth of legend. Its text claims it was erected "In memory of Prince Madoc, a Welsh explorer who landed on the shores of Mobile Bay in 1170 and left behind with the Indians, the Welsh language." Yet most of the inscription lists its sources—"Authority of Encyclopedia Americana copyright 1918—Webster's Encyclopedia—Richard Hakluyt 1552–1616, a Welsh Historian and Geographer—Ridpath's History of the New World, etc.," an excess of citation belying the DAR's unstated anxiety about their historical veracity. In fact, when the plaque was damaged by Hurricane Frederic in 1979, the park rangers, calling it a "pseudohistorical embarrassment" placed the plaque in storage. In 2012, however, a bill passed by the Alabama legislature restored it to its former setting, perhaps foreshadowing more recent nativist strains America culture.[54] The internet has also proven a fertile site for all manner of speculative history and combative argumentation, most of which simply rehashes the older disputes between modern-day Belknaps and Stoddards. Through all these convolutions, the function of the legend remains the same: to assuage settler neuralgia that their nation might be unassembleable.

The specter of the loss of whiteness, however, would outlast both Madoc and the eighteenth-century environmentalist "science" in which it was based. The notion that Indians had descended from a white, Old World refugee population that had found its way to the Western Hemisphere somewhere in the primordial past would be revived in nineteenth-century controversies that identified them as descending from the lost tribes of Israel. Again at stake were the borders of whiteness: how to distinguish the colonized from the colonizers. The possibility of an Indian Hebrew lineage also disinterred long-smoldering ideas about religion, the Reformation, and the function of prophecy among God's chosen, an elevation white Americans increasingly assumed for themselves as they imagined and embraced their Manifest Destiny. Lost tribe theory would then test the limits of race and national membership as the new nation continued to pursue its anxious and impossible goals of consolidation and completion.

2

The Lost Tribes and the Found Nation

When I look at their children, I imagine myself in the Jewish quarter
of London. . . . God declared that he would carry away the Jews into a
country undiscovered and uncultivated, and who proposed this was able
to execute his designs.

—William Penn, 1683

Beginning in 1492, and because they believed in biblical history, Europeans
were befuddled by Indians: if the Bible was a divinely inspired and comprehensive account of human history, who were all these people? Starting
almost immediately, in European intellectual and religious circles, supposedly with Amerigo Vespucci, it was proposed that Indians descended from
the ten lost tribes of Israel, scattered after the Babylonians sacked the Temple at Jerusalem in the eighth century BCE. Conveniently, this also solved
the mystery of their disappearance, bolstering the Bible's infallibility.[1] This
primordialist tradition crossed the Atlantic with Puritan John Eliot and was
shared by Roger Williams and William Penn, among others. Subsequently,
these few enlightened colonists treated Indians as fellow "people of the
Book" and sought to treat them justly, more humanely than did their fellow
settlers. Williams's negotiations with the Narragansett and Penn's with the
Lenapes represent gestures toward consensual cohabitation.[2]

Yet cohabitation was conditioned on acculturation. The motives behind the erasure of Indian identity—rewhitening them, converting them to
Christianity—differed greatly. In New England, Williams and Eliot believed
converting these apostate Jews would catalyze the millennium—Christ's
glorious return to earth to begin the Apocalypse. In Pennsylvania, while he
was less concerned with conversion, Penn, as William Pencak and Daniel
Richter observe, "had the choice of either submitting to European mores
and laws or leaving" (xii). Such gestures, while well intended in their insistence on the humanity of the Indians, were still based on a primordialist precondition: Old World roots whitened the Indians and thus qualified
them for cohabiting with other whites but only after their whiteness was

reestablished and millennia of supposed degeneration peeled back. Lost tribe theory then denied the distinctive otherness of the Indian by writing them into a white history that disregarded their own and offered at best the same marginality in the New World that subordinated Sephardic and Azkenazi Jews in the Old.

Their fellow colonial settlers castigated Eliot, Williams, and Penn—and their followers—for their resistance to the more overtly violent genocidal orientation of the colonizing project. Eliot's "Praying Indian" towns were under constant pressure to relocate, and Quakers were put in internment camps during the Revolution.[3] Lost tribe theory offered, if nothing else, a premise for halting outright slaughter to contemplate alternatives to how the settlers might colonize without (bodily) extermination. If slaughter was not an option, how might interracial relations be reimagined? In their own day, Eliot and Penn applied lost tribe theory in two distinct ways: Eliot favored millennial conversion and Penn paternal reform, respectively, each of which endured into the first half of the nineteenth century. Typical of settler anxiety, each enacted a nervous solipsism: lost tribe theory had more to do with validating the white nation than with a genuine gesture toward decolonization or racial equality. While both redirected the more popular urge for wanton destruction by making Indians Jewish, both, in the most basic sense, were ultimately about establishing the settlers themselves as God's new elect and establishing the providential imprimatur of colonialism by bringing the lost and apostate Jews into the fold, monopolizing biblical cosmology for themselves.

In other words, both reflected a colonialist desire to prove the righteousness of settler culture by policing a self-assigned covenant between the Protestant God and his New (World) elect. The stakes were high: in both New England and Pennsylvania, righteousness indicated God's mandate for the colonizers to colonize the Promised Land. By this logic, failure to convert the apostate Jewish Indians would invoke God's wrath, and the land would be forfeit. How colonists treated the lost tribes, once they were aware of their Hebrew and thus primordially white origins tested the righteousness and validity of the settler venture. Primordialist texts that featured lost tribe theory reveal profound ruptures in colonialist practice: business as usual—genocide and other violence—might forfeit the settlers' status as God's elect.

These complications recurred when lost tribe theory was revived in the nineteenth century, now in reference to the nation, not a colony or a sect. While eighteenth-century deism disregarded such suppositions as absurd, the Second Great Awakening returned it to public conversations about

Indian policy and national identity.[4] Once again, it was embraced mostly by radical religious minorities within settler culture who faced ridicule for their rejection of genocidal violence. Fundamentally, lost tribe theory clung to eighteenth-century theories of race as an externalized reflection of environmental origins that could be adjusted rather than placing people in fixed, scientifically designated subcategories of the human species. In the era immediately prior to the religious revival, racial identity "was socially symbolic rather than a biophysical category, and hence was absolutely distinct from the modern notion of race as an essential and immutable biological property" (qtd. in Chiles, 9), comments Ezra Tawil. Katy Chiles then notes, "Unlike Africans . . . Indians were generally expected to become more like whites specifically through their adoption of white social practices and social habits" (18). Moreover, if Indians were Lost Jews, their conversion and assimilation seemed to be even more viable and salutary.

Eran Shalev tracks how lost tribe theory resisted the age's romantic justifications of ethnic cleansing and polygenetic racism: "For at least three decades during the first half of the nineteenth century, the Israelite-Indian theory flourished, and was an important element in the United States' intellectual discourse, its national identity, and its imagined history" (151). More specifically, the Second Great Awakening reawakened the sense of covenant between settlers and the Protestant divinity whose blessing for continental appropriation they claimed. Covenants, while affirming exception, also invite critique in the form of Old Testament–style prophecy based in God's anger with and punishment of his elect. Temporary earthly setbacks, correctives, were more often found to indicate God's displeasure.[5] Moreover, prophets often raised the stakes for either earthly or national destruction should the offenses be so profound.

Lost tribe theory's kinder, gentler colonialist corollaries—Eliot-based millennialism and Penn-style reform—inspired prophetic critiques of not only the settler nation's occasional transgressions of the covenant they claimed, but also their claim to covenant itself. Shalom Goldman writes, "A biblical self-concept dominated much of early American thought. . . . The notion that the United States is a nation with biblical roots, a nation chosen by God to play a major role in world affairs, is very much with us" (God's Sacred Tongue, 2). Inclusion in the nation depended on any given subpopulation's place in that biblical narrative. Lost tribe theory offered Indians a chance to join that narrative, but only on terms set by the colonizers. As to the colonizing nature of those terms, David Spurr writes, "The ultimate aim of colonial discourse is not to establish a radical opposition between colonizer and colonized. It seeks to dominate by inclusion and domestication rather than by a confrontation which recognizes the independent ideology of the Other" (32). By assigning a primordial Jewishness to Indians, Anglos who believed in lost tribe theory—in the 1600s and the 1800s—conquered by "inclusion and domestication."

This fantasy impinges on the "whiteness" of nineteenth-century Jews, a premise that may seem incongruous, given the anti-Semitism that informs so much Jewish experience in America. "Prior to the early nineteenth century, all Europeans in the United States were more or less equally white," writes Karen Brodkin in *How Jews Became White Folks* (1998). Early republic Jews—mostly Sephardic but also some Ashkenazi—were simply another colonial population: "Prior to the early nineteenth century, all Europeans in the United States were more or less equally white" (53). However, the Second Great Awakening's evangelism reinscribed covenantal ideologies that demanded the nation's otherwise diverse populations identify with far more unified collectivities, a process resulting in the accelerated exclusion and racial unwhitening of Jews. Robert Michael in fact dates theories of anti-Semitism to the Second Great Awakening by contrasting them to the tolerance of Jews by the Founders and during the early republic. As the new century began, "Jews feared, with good reason, that the state and federal governments could deny them equal treatment under the law if those political entities were officially to recognize the Christian religion in their constitutions. Most American Christians had already begun a strong movement in this direction; they believed America to be a Christian nation, and they argued that this condition should be recognized in the state and federal constitutions. Those who denied Christianity as the true faith were at best wrong and at worst evil" (75). Maryland's Jew Bill of 1817 excluded unconverted Jews from holding public office, for example; later, more stringent forms of anti-Semitism led to more stringent forms of marginalization. As such, the viability of lost tribe theory as a vehicle for offering nongenocidal models of interracial cohabitation enjoyed only a brief window to contribute to an improved status for Indians. Until or unless they converted, however, in the national imagination, Jews switched from endogenous whites in the early republic to exogenous others in Andrew Jackson's America, and Indians reverted to, as ever, people without history.[6]

Nonetheless, during this window, as potential converts, Indians, reimagined as Jews, offered a special opportunity for newly "awakened" Protestants to demonstrate and police their claim on God's favor on behalf of the nation for both Eliotian millennialists and Penn-style reformers. According to the Revelation to John, conversion of the Jews was required to evoke the Apocalypse. As such, the proselytization of Jews—Indian, Ashkenazi, or, *justification for colonization?*

later, Sephardic—became the evangelized settler's main mission under the New World covenant.[7] As such, progress toward, or regression from, converting the lost tribes became a crucible for covenantal score keeping, thus entangling lost tribe theory with the longer tradition of prophecy expressed through literary exposition. Lost tribers embraced the outsider tradition of the biblical prophetic traditions: the Old Testament jeremiad. Calling it "an adversarial celebration of America," Sacvan Bercovitch clarified his placement of the prophetic jeremiad near the center of American self-expression: "Following the logic of the jeremiad, [prophetic writing] castigates the defects of the present so as to give voice to an abiding national identity" (*American Jeremiad*, xvii). Jeremiads threatened divine punishment for the covenanted community not in the afterlife but in the here and now, and so prophetic enunciation often led to the castigation of the prophet.

Because lost tribe theory provided the scriptural basis for a prophetic condemnation of the violence of conquest, its advocates became pariahs in Andrew Jackson's America. In particular, "the defects of the present" they identified were colonialist policies and practices of violence and other antagonistic behaviors that alienated rather than welcomed the Jewish Indians and prevented and precluded their conversion and redemption. For both millennialists and reformers, conversion began with convincing Indians of their Jewish heritage, compelling them to view their Indianness as recent and hence disposable, defining racial difference as evidence of apostasy and sinfulness. By this logic, as "strayed" Israelites, the Indians were always already white. Their redemptive rewhitening, their conversion, simply brought them back into history. God's agents of this change, of moving history forward, then, are the proselytizing, Protestant whites and their covenantal nation. Jews and Jewish Indians depended upon the benevolence of the elect to bring them back into meaning. The elect move providential history forward; the converted are moved by it. Prophecy's primary subject, then, is the elect and their covenant: lost tribe theory is about white settlers far more than it is about Jewish Indians.

Even the most condemnatory prophetic utterances still affirmed national destiny and chosenness: just as when God's first chosen strayed, they atoned and were redeemed by the Lord, so it was imagined that his new chosen—white and Protestant Americans—might undergo a similar process of purgation, atonement, and reaffirmation in preparation for the millennium. This process was to begin with the white nation's admission and confession of its sins, the most glaring of which (after slavery) was its treatment of Indians. To call attention to these national sins, lost tribers condemned historical racism and genocidal violence and demanded whites prove their worthiness as God's chosen by prioritizing the nation's divine mission over its territorial and material ambitions. This tested the limits of settler discourse: the Second Great Awakening *also* spawned movements toward egalitarianism, feminism, abolitionism, etc.[8] However, at its core, its liberal humanism concealed deep and implicit colonialist motivations.

Therefore, the older Eliot/Penn schism recurred in nineteenth-century lost tribe theory. Millennialists and reformers differed as to the terms of their atonement. For the former, the Apocalypse was the goal, and so they advocated conversion and repatriation of converted Indians to their biblical home—Palestine—to bring about Christ's return. The work and redemptive sacrifice of the settler elect in bringing this about, in turn, affirmed their chosenness based in a covenant of grace. By contrast, reformers acted upon a more practical covenant of works: the elect found redemption through virtuous behavior and Christian charity. For them, inhumane white behavior—now reconfigured as violence against fellow whites and biblical forebears—signified a national sin. To atone, reformers gladly bear an early version of the white man's burden by uplifting the Jewish Indians, even at the cost of wealth and power. Until white Protestants did so, divine wrath would imperil the nation; events such as the Panic of 1837 or the looming Civil War itself were said to be signs of the coming dies irae.

A comparatively secular book revived lost tribe theory: James Adair's 1775 *The History of the American Indians,* based on his forty years as a trader in the South, is free of religious invective.[9] Reflecting a critical reading of the Bible and an Enlightenment-style epistemology, Adair outlines his methodology: "You know the uprightness of my intentions as to the information here given, and that truth hath been my great standard. I may have erred in the application of the rites and customs of the Indians to their origins and descent—and may have drawn some conclusions exceeding the given evidence—but candor will excuse the language of integrity" (dedication). Early on, however, Adair draws a conclusion that, for an eighteenth-century intellectual, seemed harmless, but that nineteenth-century Christian nationalists would dangerously redirect: "From the most exact observations I could make in the long time I traded among the Indian Americans, I was forced to believe them lineally descended from the Israelites. . . . This descent, I shall endeavor to prove from their religious rites, civil and marital customs, their marriage, funeral ceremonies, manners, language, traditions, and variety of particulars" (14). When Adair does cite the Old Testament, it is as a historical source, not a religious text. Nonetheless, Adair was rephrased at great length, and not for such disinterested ends, but to reduce Indian culture to merely an outcropping of Hebraism.

rationalizing 2,

Reflecting the eighteenth-century notions of racial transformation, Adair domesticates the Cherokee and explains their traditions as degeneration rather than difference or divergence.

When the new nation's military had contained Indians as a meaningful threat to the nation's survival by 1815, settlers were in a position to do with the indigenes as they pleased. For those who sought solutions other than eradication—given their newly awakened Christianity—lost tribe theory opened both millennialist and reformist narratives of white redemption through their assumption of responsibility for the still-degenerate Indians. These were expressed in polemics, poems, fictions, testaments, and historiographies featuring Indians as lost Jews. Millennialism struck first, in Elias Boudinot's *A Star in the West* (1816). Ethan Smith and Mormons Joseph Smith and Sidney Rigdon carried on Boudinot's Eliotian tradition to prepare for Christ's return through conversion. Reformers, such as Lydia Sigourney and John Howard Payne, advocated the lost tribe theory to confirm the covenant by making the white nation worthy of becoming New World Canaan by behaving more humanely. At the same time, Indian intellectuals William Apess and William Warren used the reformist platform to find sympathetic audiences. Perceiving not only its historical impossibility and its veiling of a more insidious paternalism, Samuel Drake, C. S. Rafinesque, and, most important, James Fenimore Cooper and Nathaniel Hawthorne critiqued both the concept of the lost tribes and its colonialist applications.

Millennialism: Covenant and Colonization

> But when the Protestant millennialist theory was formed, logically, there
> came with it a need to find a new chosen nation, or nations. If history
> is theodicy, if redemption is historical as well as individual, if evil is to
> be finally and decisively bound through these great conflicts, God must
> operate through cohesive bodies of men.
>
> —Ernest Tuveson, *Redeemer Nation*, 1968

Ernest Tuveson's observations about millennialism's origins in the Reformation reverse engineer Manifest Destiny (139): Calvinism needed to transcend the New Testament's emphasis on the individual's relationship with Christ and coalesce larger collectivities to move its apocalyptic agenda forward. It called for a millennial nation, and so one appeared, as Nathan Hatch observes: "Americans of all ranks sensed that events of truly apocalyptic significance were unfolding before their eyes. Judging by the number of sermons, books, and pamphlets that addressed prophetic themes, the first generation of United States citizens may have lived in the shadow of Christ's second coming more intensely than any generation since" (184). The Second Coming would complete history, and completing history required a Christian nation to assemble all the necessary pieces and assure their seamless unity.[10]

As the last empty space on the map, the unmapped West became the crucible for apocalyptic preparation.[11] In dozens of texts, millennialists deployed a covenantal perspective to chide the settler nation's long history of violence and abuse because it prevented and delayed the divinely intended transformation of the Hebrew Indians, thus hindering and delaying the Apocalypse. By millennialist logic, along with conversion, all the disbursed People of the Book must be returned to their biblical homelands, or destined homelands, prior to Christ's return. North America, then, must be wholly white and Protestant, as it was so destined. "Ethiopeans"—the nineteenth-century term used for all biblical Africans as established in the translation of the Bible used throughout the Second Great Awakening—must be returned to Africa; hence the same millennialists supported efforts to "colonize" Africa by "repatriating" former slaves to Liberia. In addition, all Jews—Indian, Sephardic, or Ashkenazim—needed to be returned to *their* Promised Land: Palestine. Indianness, then, becomes merely a temporary condition of degeneration, reversible through conversion and repatriation. In the end, repatriation affirms that the New World was never really the Indians': it was always predestined for God's newly chosen, the white Protestant nation.[12]

This complex process began with conversion. Potential missionaries to the Indians must be taught that their work will be among once and future Old World whites rather than New World savages. To this end, Boudinot, Ethan Smith, and the Mormons all rehash Adair, update his research, mix in Calvinist orthodoxy, and transplant the narrative further west to keep pace with the shifting contact zone of the frontier. Each relates how ancient Jews came from the Old World, imagining both transatlantic and Bering Strait crossings. Each also considers possible interbreeding with Asiatic tribes, or that perhaps only *some* Indians are Hebrews. Despite these variations, millennialists considered pre-1492 Indians Jewish *enough* to be both functionally white and the missing Israelites. Therefore, missionaries needed to bring the outcasts back into the fold. Describing the zeal of the era, Goldman observes: "Many wealthy and publicly minded Americans . . . felt that encouraging the 'conversion of the Jews' in the United States would hasten the Second Coming and highlight America's destined role in the events of the End Time" (*God's Sacred Tongue*, 90). This mission impinged on the survival of the nonconverted People of the Book: if the Indians were degenerated Jews, killing them violated the covenant, a controversial stand in Jackson's America.[13] After establishing their versions of lost tribe theory, Boudinot, Smith, and the Mormons admonish white readers for their un-Christian treatment of Indians and their disregard for their assigned mission.

When Boudinot published *A Star*, he was already such a well-known Federalist politician, minister, and Indian advocate that a young Cherokee—Buck Watie—would later borrow his name.[14] The Boudinot who authored *A Star in the West* wedded the evidence of Adair to the Calvinism of his French Huguenot ancestry—closely linked to New England Puritanism—to produce an extended argument for and commentary on the Jewishness of the Indians. Born to wealth, he dedicated his life to public service. As a congressman from New Jersey (1777–95), signer of the Treaty of Paris while serving as president of Congress (1783), and then as the director of the mint (1796–1805), Boudinot had extensive experience with Indian issues.[15] Throughout his career, Calvinist orthodoxy and well-intended republican paternalism informed his political and public works. His first book, *The Age of Revelation, or the Age of Reason Shewn to Be an Age of Infidelity* (1790), critiqued Thomas Paine's *The Age of Reason*. As founder of the American Bible Society in 1816, Boudinot funded extensive distribution of Bibles and missionaries in the West.

In *A Star*, Boudinot sees the white nation failing in its covenanted assignment. Especially in its preface and conclusion, Boudinot excoriates settler behavior but then predicts that, once they understand the Indians' Israelite origins, whites can redeem themselves by embracing their nation's millennial responsibilities, rehearsing the jeremiad's pattern of castigation followed by affirmation. In the preface, Boudinot first traps casual Christians with a discourse on the patriotism of the War of 1812 and then chastises their un-Christian behavior toward Indians: "The compiler of the following sheets, animated by this blessed eastern prospect, can no longer withhold the small discovery that has been made of a rising Star in the West, from the knowledge of those who are zealous and anxious to behold the returning Messiah coming 'in his own glory and the glory of the Father,' attended by all the saints; which star may in the issue, turn out to be the star of Jacob, and become a guide to the long suffering and despised descendants of that eminent patriarch, to find the once humble babe of Bethlehem" (ii). The knowledge of the star in the west—the soon-to-be converted Jewish Indians—creates an opportunity to catalyze the Second Coming, aligning the destinies of the chosen of both Testaments. Having affirmed the need to proselytize the Indians, Boudinot shifts to admonition: "For more than two centuries the Aborigines of America engaged the avarice and contempt of those who are commonly called the enlightened nations of the old world. These natives of the wilderness have always been considered by them as savages and barbarians and therefore have given them little concern, farther than to defraud them of their lands, drive them from the fertile countries on the sea shores, engage them in their wars, and indeed destroy them by thousands with ardent spirits and fatal disorders unknown to them" (ii). Seeking a more secular indictment of settler atrocities, Boudinot simply reprints Washington Irving's "Traits of Indian Character" (1814) in its entirety, as would Apess.[16] Irving delineated the long-standing moral bankruptcy of settler colonialism, made worse by white claims to providential righteousness. By contrast, Boudinot offers whites a narrative for atoning for these crimes that still functions within the metanarrative of settler colonialism: before Boudinot's announcement, frontiersmen thought Indians were outside of biblical history, and so white abuse might be excused as a case of mistaken identity. However, Boudinot insists that knowledge of their biblical origins makes the continuation of such behavior a far greater transgression: "There is a possibility, that these unhappy children of misfortune may yet be proved to be the descendants of Jacob and the long lost tribes of Israel. And if so, that though cast off for their heinous transgressions, they have not been altogether forsaken; and will hereafter appear to have been, in all their dispersions and wanderings, the subject of God's divine protection and gracious care" (iii). The banishment of the lost tribes to America was God's punishment of his first chosen, for sins detailed in the Old Testament. As such, the chosenness of these Jews—at least those who convert—remains in force: unlike Old World Jews, they had nothing to do with Christ's crucifixion. The covenant protects converted Indians because their attendance, as biological Jews, at Christ's return is required. Subsequently, for 280 pages, Boudinot biblicizes Adair's observations. In his final chapter, biblically reshaping Adair's "evidence," Boudinot returns to his jeremiad in fuller and more direct terms:

> What could possibly bring greater declarative glory to God, . . . that these wandering nations of Indians are the long lost tribes of Israel; but kept under the special protection of Almighty God, though despised by all mankind, for more than two thousand years, separated and unknown to the civilized world? Thus wonderfully brought to the knowledge of their fellow men, they may be miraculously prepared for instruction, and stand ready, at the appointed time, when God shall raise the signal to the nations of Europe, to be

restored to the land and country of their fathers, and to Mount Zion the city of David. (280)

The point of conversion is to prepare Indians to return to Palestine. Implicitly, of course, this leaves North America to white Protestants, having performed their role in the restoring the Indians and re-placing them in the land promised to their ancestors. Jewish Indians are not, therefore, indigenous to North America, and their future—and humanity's—requires not their involuntary removal westward but their voluntary return eastward.

Boudinot's whites still need to redeem themselves, to atone for the violence done to Indians when they were unaware of their shared biblical kinship. A few pages later, after restating that "the house of Israel shall be discovered, and brought from the land of their captivity a far off, to the city of God," he notes that "all those who have oppressed and despised them, wherever they are, will become subjects of the anger and fury of God" (296). So, he asks: "Will it not be wise then to consider our ways betimes, and sincerely to repent all improper conduct of oppression and destruction to any, who may turn out to have been the continual objects of God's regard, though suffering under his just displeasure? . . . Let not our unbelief, or other irreligious conduct, with a want of an active more lively faith in our almighty Redeemer, become a stumbling block to these outcasts of Israel" (297). If whites, armed with the revelation provided by Boudinot, mend their ways, two centuries of sin might be forgiven, and their New World covenant reaffirmed. Boudinot reminds them: "Who knows but that God has raised up these United States in these latter days, for the very purpose of accomplishing his will in bringing his beloved people to their own land?" (299). Reflecting a settler anxiety that American whites have yet to earn their election, Boudinot concludes with a list of "European" sins to be undone by Americans, an inverted schedule for redemption; moreover, he warns against anti-Semitism as creating a premise for further exploitation, earning divine retribution not unlike that suffered by the Indian Jews themselves: "We go on under the similar threatening of the same Almighty Being. We shew much the same hardness of heart, under the like denunciations of vengeance, that he will afflict and destroy, without mercy, those nations who join in oppressing his people" (301). Settlers can thus become a nation destroyed by God to protect his Jewish chosen, or they can be "raised up" to their own covenant. This prophecy began forty years of lost tribe–based exchanges about the Jewish Indians, Jews, and white settlers' election.

The next major millennialist was Ethan Smith, whose first book, *A Dissertation on the Prophecies Relative to the Anti-Christ and the Last Times* (1811), does not mention the lost tribes but still obsesses over the Apocalypse. As befits a small-town Vermont Calvinist minister, he writes in a more direct and less cosmopolitan style than Boudinot, though he cites and quotes from *A Star* at length in *View of the Hebrews; or the Tribes of Israel in America* (1823).[17] However, Smith parses the issue more carefully. While Boudinot's invective to convert the Jews—Indian and non-Indian—is relatively direct, Smith makes a crucial distinction: "I shall here . . . note some passages which distinguish between the *dispersed* state of the Jews, and the *outcast* state of the Ten Tribes" (70; emphasis in original). Dividing Jewish populations between Christ-killing Old World Jews as "Judah," and the lost tribes as "Israel," Smith distinguishes Israel's loss of whiteness as a punishment for more recent New World sins.

To establish the separate punishments God would impose on each, reflecting their ancestors' sins against the Abrahamic covenant, Israel (the Indians) has been "cast out from the nations; from society; from the social world; from the knowledge of men, as being Hebrews" (70). The white missionary compels atonement by instructing them of the stakes of those crimes, given their potential as covenanted people: "The present outcast tribes shall be convinced from their own internal traditions, and by the bid of those commissioned to bring them in, that they are the ancient Israel of God. . . . Here is a branch of the tribes, till now, and for a long time unknown. But themselves finding out who they are, they plead with God for the entail of the covenant, and their covenant right to Palestine; and that the Turkish possessors of it were never called by God's name; nor were they under his laws" (71–72). Identifying white American Christians as "commissioned by God," Smith would have them ship converted Jewish Indians back to their Promised Land. This plan also reflects a global effort at preparation: for Smith, the elect would remove Muslim "Turks" from Palestine because the Turks were "never called by God's name" (72), implying that each nation has its place: the Turks do not belong in Palestine; ipso facto, the Israelites no longer belong in America.

America is the Jewish Indians' exile—punishment—thus they have not been merely wandering but deliberately suffering in savagery. However, some Israelite Indians have sinned more than others: he divides "Israel" as having split into two races, one that remained whiter than the other, which led to an internecine war won by the darker, and hence more sinful, Israelites who then became Indians. The mounds of the Ohio valley, he argues, were constructed by whiter, more civilized Israelites prior to their eradication by the "red" savages: "These partially civilized people became extinct. What account can be given of this, but that the savages extirpated them, after long and dismal wars? And nothing appears more probable than that they were the better part of the Israelites who came to this continent, who for a long time retained their knowledge of the mechanic and civil arts; while the greater part of their brethren became savage and wild" (173).[18] Isolation in the New World itself alone did not rob the Jews of their whiteness, as it had for Boudinot. Reduced to savagery, the ancestors of the surviving Indians compounded their sins by slaughtering their fellow New World Jews. The redemption of nineteenth-century Jewish Indians, then, impinges upon not just conversion but also atonement: they must understand Indianness in and of itself as the indication of sin.

Smith ends, like Boudinot, with an explicit jeremiad to the settler nation that begins with the whites' neglected covenantal duty to proselytize the Indians but describes it as a more complicated process on account of the more complicated history of their deracination and subsequent violence against the settlers themselves: "The duty of sending them the gospel, and of being at any expense to teach them Christianity and the blessings of civilized life, is great and urgent on every principle of humanity and general benevolence. And this duty peculiarly attaches itself to the people, who are now in possession of the former inheritance of those natives; and from too many of whom that people have received insufferable injuries" (227). The occupation of the vacated—morally if not materially—"former" lands by violent white frontiersmen is divinely mandated if and only if they forgive Indian violence and turn to reconciliation and proselytization: "We are the people especially addressed, and are called upon to restore them; or bring them the knowledge of the Gospel, and to do with them whatever the God of Abraham designs shall be done. The great and generous Christian people who occupy much of the land . . . must of course be the people to whom this work is assigned" (230). Paraphrasing Isaiah 40:31, Smith urges: "Let not those tribes of my ancient people whom I have borne as on eagles' wings for so many ages; let them not become extinct before your eyes; let them no longer roam in savage barbarism and death! . . . Send them the word, the bread of life. You received the book from the seed of Abraham. . . . Remember then your debt of gratitude to God's ancient people for the word of life. Restore it to them, and thus double your own rich inheritance in blessings" (249). Smith positions whites as more than just the last in a series of God's intermediaries for the restoration or punishment of the Jews. Instead, they become God's partners in the work of restoration, so long as "your seed of salvation" takes root. Moreover, "your land" implies the righteousness of the white occupation of America and the divine nature of the duty to reabsorb Indians into Hebraic, not American, history. Smith is ultimately admonitory: by neglecting and abusing the Indians, Americans risk becoming "heathens" themselves and so risk becoming "eternally undone" (250). In fact, continued genocide, as it had for the Israelites, would signal not just conquest but racial regression—to destroy Indians is to become Indian.

The Mormon prophet Joseph Smith, like the unrelated Ethan, believed that Indians were descended from the Jews of the Old Testament and that their darkened skin indicated their descent from those who had regressed into savagery and annihilated the more civilized outcast Jews. Hence accusations of plagiarism have motivated Joseph Smith's followers even into the twenty-first century to keep Ethan Smith's *View* (as well as Solomon Spalding's *Manuscript Found*) in print so as not to appear to conceal the intrinsic and extrinsic differences of *The Book of Mormon* from these prior texts, forestalling accusations of plagiarism.[19] However, strictly as a primordialist narrative, *The Book of Mormon* reflects the ongoing pattern of literary primordialization of continental history in white print culture, proof of the constant yearning for an archaic racial legacy in American culture between the War of 1812 and the Civil War.

While Joseph Smith likely read other lost tribe primordialist texts, his far more layered story embodies a more complicated narrative and, hence, eschatology, starting with the notion of multiple primordial white populations occupying ancient America. As perhaps the most accomplished and extended primordialist text, *The Book of Mormon* can be read from the perspectives of literature and culture rather than more narrowly as testament.[20] First, the Jaredites were the initial Old World immigrants to an empty New World—non-Jewish Semites (descended from Noah's son Sem) who crossed the Atlantic after God's destruction of the Tower of Babel. However, the Jaredites had nearly destroyed themselves through civil war, rendering them vulnerable to annihilation once the displaced Jews appeared. Initially, Smith's Israelites are a small fugitive group who fled southeast after the fall of the Temple, the family of Lehi. They sail across the Pacific, leaving, on their way, the Pacific populations who will ultimately arise as members of the dispersed chosen to be collected prior to the Apocalypse.[21] Once in North America, the Lehites mop up the Jaredites and soon divide, like Ethan Smith's, between more and less civilized groups, the Nephilites and the Lamanites. Around the same time the Lehites arrived from the West, another group of nontribal Jews, the Mulekites, escape Babylon and cross the Atlantic, merging with the Nephilites. With no unifying event, such as the fall of the Temple, Smith's Jews are a far less unified group, united more by race and shared exile or punishment. As such, the white responsibility toward them has less to do with Old World history than New World prospects and preparation.

When the Nephilites and the Lamanites begin a war of extermination, Christ arrives in America after his crucifixion and resurrection in Palestine, converting both before ascending to heaven, and they live in peace for a few centuries. This complicates the standard narrative in that the Indians in 1492 were no longer unconverted Jews but apostate Christians. Eventually both the darker, savage Lamanites and the lighter, mound-building Nephilites forget the union forged by Christ, the long-postponed war re-ignites, and the Lamanites wipe out the Nephilites. The surviving Lamanites become the Indians—Jewish by birth but ex-Christians in fact—now cursed with unending internecine war as God's punishment for their apostasy. No return to Palestine was needed because, as lapsed Christians, they have detached from their Jewish origins and must be relocated to a new Zion in the New World. The last surviving Nephilites—Mormon and his son Moroni—create the gold plates that become *The Book of Mormon.*

In the *Book,* Joseph Smith—like Ethan Smith—adds a moral component to the old environment-based theories of race shifting: darkness indicates savagery. This redirects Boudinot's millennialist reiteration of Calvinist eschatology in important ways. First, he does not demand the repatriation of the surviving Lamanites to the Holy Land. Second, *The Book of Mormon* rarely breaks into jeremaic prophecy, limited as it is by the framing narrative of Moroni's Golden Plates; there is little direct condemnation of the white treatment of Indians. Instead, Smith allows the stories of corrupt, transplanted Old World civilizations—first the Jaredites and then the Nephilites—to stand as models of American empires that failed through collective hubris revealed by the abandonment of their foundational ideals. As such, the *Book* still invokes covenantal critique and prophecy. Near the end of the concluding "Book of Moroni," Moroni, the last Christian Nephilite, after pages of adventure and divine wrath, writes: "And now my beloved brethren, if this be the case that these things are true which I have spoken unto you, and God will shew unto you with power and great glory at the last day, that they are true, has the day of miracles ceased? Or will he, so long as time shall last, or the earth shall stand, or there shall be on man upon the face of the earth to be saved?" (594). From this, then, Moroni extrapolates a message of proselytization for his readers who, in their obedience, in their acceptance God's gifts, *become* Latter Day Saints, each of whom is gifted with specific divine powers and responsibilities: "And again I exhort you, my brethren, that ye deny not the gifts of God, for they are many; and they come from the same God. . . . For behold, to one is given by the spirit of God, that he may teach the word of wisdom; and to another, that he may teach the word of knowledge by the same spirit; and to another exceeding great faith; and to another the gifts of healing by the same spirit" (597). As in all millennialist texts, then, the Apocalypse depends upon gathering those blessed by God—the saints. As the Israelites had once been chosen and Christian, their (re-)conversion is then demanded, as is the conversion of Polynesians, the leftovers of the Lehites. Subsequently, Mormon missions to the South Pacific began in the 1840s, just as more secular American imperial efforts in the same region were also initiated.[22]

Closer to home, Smith left explication to his followers. Sidney Rigdon, known as "Aaron to Smith's Moses," published a series of essays laying out the new revelation:[23] "The only thing which God promised to the world after the great Apostasy, which was to corrupt all nations, and defile all the kings of the earth, and terminate in the overthrow of the gentiles . . . was the return of the scattered remnants of Jacob, and gathering of the house of Joseph, bringing them as he did at first, and building them as he did at the beginning" (qtd. in Grant Underwood, 29). Rigdon demanded more than other millennialists: for him, modern whites exist in a corrupt state, the gentiles threatened by "overthrow" and "termination" until they found a New Jerusalem (or Zion) by following the teachings revealed to Joseph Smith. Only then could white Americans become elect. Unless such a gathering is endeavored, the end days will never come, and Christ will allow Americans, like the Jaredites, to die off, unredeemed: "Unless the scattered remnants of Joseph should be gathered from all the countries whither they have been driven, that no such thing as a millennium could ever exist; or that God never promised such an era to mankind on any ground than that of the gathering of the house of Jacob to the Lord of their fathers and that predicated on the fact of the gentiles having forfeited all claim to divine favor by reason of their great Apostasy" (qtd. in Grant Underwood, 29). The salvation of the new elect, then, depends on their conversion of the old elect, a humbling shrinking from white presumptions of divine primacy to a subordinate relegation to serving God's first chosen. For Rigdon, all the descendants of Abraham through Jacob and Joseph, the Jews, the Polynesians, and the lingering Laminites must be gathered. The sons of Noah's son Japeth, gentiles—white Americans—must gather them, but are not themselves, by birth, saints. There are no predestined saints among the whites, signaling a break from Calvinist orthodoxy. Nathan Hatch notes that

Smith identifies "the rich, the proud, the learned who find themselves in the hands of an angry God. Throughout the book [*of Mormon*], evil is most often depicted as the result of the pride and worldliness that comes from economic success and results in oppression of the poor" (117). Yet gentiles can be redeemed and achieve sainthood for themselves and their country by doing God's Work, though the Sons of Ham (Africans) and Yam (Arabs and Asians) need not apply, as the darkness of their skin reveals the corruption of their souls. Mormon historian Grant Underwood explains: "Even Europeans like Smith, Rigdon, and the bulk of antebellum Mormons could be 'adopted' into the House of Israel through conversion to Gods' latter-day work and thus become equal participants in the promises of the 'new covenant.' In this sense all white Americans could with perfect propriety describe themselves as gentiles" (31). The ignorance of the Lamanites—the Indians—of their identity and history and their unreconverted apostasy meant that God's servants must gather them. As such, unlike other millennialists, Mormons endorsed Indian removal as it concentrated the Indians and moved them toward Utah and the end times.[24] Smith's ideas, even as translated by Rigdon—which included Old Testament–style polygamy—of course offended both mainstream American Christians and the Calvinist orthodoxy. The Mormons were chased from the United States yet allowed to settle, like the remaining Lamanites, on de facto reservations, in empty and supposedly unprofitable western places unwanted for colonization by the settler nation.[25]

Other non-Mormon millennialists wrote the story of the Israelite Indians and their righteous white rescuers in more popular forms yet met with similar excoriation. Harriet Livermore's 1835 hymnal, *The Harp of Israel,* was written while she was a missionary among the Cherokee before being forced back to Philadelphia under orders of the US Army, preceding the Trail of Tears.[26] She witnessed the same "similarities" as Adair and dedicated her work to Boudinot. Her hymns are to be taught to Indians, giving them words to thank God and his missionaries and to express their joy at returning to Palestine. Quoting Psalms 33:7, she begins:

> "Rest in the Lord:" O sweet command;
> And patient till he shall come,
> To summon us to Canaan's land,
> And welcome outcast Israel home.

Later verses describe their retention of Mosaic law and tradition, though ignorant of their origins. Her intended ventriloquism silences the Indians, as do all primordialist texts. Livermore concludes with a jeremiad affirming whites' role in the restoration of the outcast Jews: "I declare to the rulers of the people of this land, that the declaration of God to Abraham, more than three thousand years ago, is received at this eventful period, and by the spirit of truth is addressed to every Indian that prays to the Great and Mighty One! Yea—the Indians are Israel!!!" (178). Similar materials rarely ventured beyond the evangelical press or crossed over to a general readership. In the end, millennialism was too insubstantial and eschatological and therefore too easily marginalized in an impatient and pragmatic print culture. As an intrinsically Orthodox construct, millennialism recurred to the mysticism of a covenant of grace. The Second Great Awakening, however, mostly transcended the mysticism of the Puritans' covenant of grace in favor of the immediacy of a covenant of works, stressing the simultaneous interplay of sin, punishment, and redemption, individually and collectively. By shedding eschatological trappings, reformers identified settler violence as a national sin that threatened a collective covenant of works. For them, the stakes were not the end of the world, but the end of the nation.

White Reformers and the End of Tribes

Revivals of the 1740s drew upon millennial themes to challenge believers to a greater commitment to traditional values. Democratic ferment in the early republic, however, convinced many that they should erase the memory of the past and learn all they could about the gospel of equality.

—Nathan Hatch, *The Democratization of American Christianity*, 1989

As Nathan Hatch suggests, reformist texts spent far less time interrogating the Jewish legend and more on how knowledge of the Jewish Indians' Old World origin created moral and racial obligations for whites, following more closely the colonial models of Roger Williams and William Penn than that of John Eliot (186). However, the reform version of lost tribe theory demanded only that: the improvement of white behavior toward other races and other peripheral populations.[27] A reformed settler community, among other things, would be defined by its ability to cohabit with yet still command exogenous populations, based around a model of Christian progressivism that required adherence to a single model of national identity and "civilized" behavior. Reformist prophecies—jeremiads—punish and correct settler colonialism but rarely ponder whether Indians, even Jewish ones, could be fully members of the nation. This reflected both traditional anti-Indian racism and the creeping anti-Semitism that was increasingly unwhitening Jews. Nonetheless, these newly awakened Christians took a more "egalitarian" approach to non-Protestants and other exogenous communities in their midst than did most white Americans and sought ways to redress the mistreatment of these groups—slaves, debtors, women, and others victimized or marginalized by the sins of the settler nation—to redeem themselves and their nation, restoring the covenant, now relabeled as Manifest Destiny. In the end, however, this demarcation of the saved and the salvageable ironically removed Jews from the borders of white privilege, switching them from endogenous to exogenous, from white to somehow less than white.

In fact, by seeking and enunciating prophetic insights, reformers sought for themselves the semioutsider status from which to offer prophetic critique. After the Revolution, Robert Abzug notes, "The religious virtuosos . . . revived the covenant tradition of their ancestors, transferring a sense of chosenness from New England to the United States. . . . Reformers positioned themselves both within the culture and just outside, taking as their mission a kind of alienated engagement with the discourse of society" (7–8). Abzug links the Awakening to temperance, abolition, labor organization, women's rights, and, most important for lost tribe theory, Indian policy. In this rubric, Indians achieve meaning only through their Jewish semiwhiteness. The new covenant depends on the elect "sacralizing" their behavior toward their former victims. This paternal liberalism foreshadows the globalization of impulses later used to justify both the Dawes Act at home and "altruistic" overseas imperialism abroad, the white man's burden. This section features texts by two popular writers from the 1820s and 1830s. Both link Jewish Indians to Christian reform but with no reference to conversion, Apocalypse, or deportation. Lydia Sigourney's extended verse narrative *Traits of the Aborigines of America* (1822) and John Howard Payne's story "The Uses of Adversity" (1837) both critique millennialism and seek more immediate uses for lost tribe theory to catalyze liberalized Indian policy and white betterment. Their call for such introspection reveals a telling ambivalence, a possibility of doubting the settler nation. Yet their prophetic insistence on liberal acculturation made the fate of the Indians, even Jewish ones, secondary to the settlers' own biblical mission.

For a poem entitled *Traits of the Aborigines of America*, Sigourney's near epic spends very little time on Indians or their traits.[28] Most of it rephrases Western history running from ancient Israel through Napoleon. Consistently, she reveals the savagery, futility, and hubris of "civilized" white nations, reminding her white readers that the actions for which they condemn

Indians closely resemble those of their ancestors. First, citing Boudinot, Sigourney establishes the Indians—"Free and unconquered," "Majestic and alone"—as Israelites, conceding that some tribes had completely shed their Hebrew habits and culture:

> Some with mystic rites,
> The ark, the orison, the paschal feast,
> Through glimmering tradition seem'd to bear,
> As in some broken vase, the smother'd coals,
> Scatter'd from Jewish altars. . . .

> The christal tube
> Of calm inquiry, to the patient eye,
> Meek Boudinot! Reveal'd an unknown star
> Upon this western cloud. (8)

While she concedes the millennial impetus to "bring again / His banish'd" home to Palestine, more important to Sigourney is that America "hast left / Mourning on earth, 'mid those who feel the ills / Of Penury" (9). Yet here and throughout, the poet must remind herself to return to the Indians, to pay them more poetic attention: "But whither art thou fled, / Adventurous strain" (9). By confessing her own tendency to ignore the Indians, Sigourney both exposes and practices colonialist practices of erasure and disregard.

Next, her panoply of European sins reaches America, and she blames colonial whites for not behaving as Christians during conquest, yet typically disavows the violence of settlement:

> Long had the natives drawn,
> From the storehouse of the Christians' sins,
> Weapons against his faith. Long had they heard
> A language from his lips which by his life
> Was contradicted. Long, too long inquir'd,
> Of a perfidious race, ye, who command
> Us, the Indians, to observe the righteous rule
> Which ye transgress, by breaking that just law. (8)

"Beloved Michon," William Penn, alone models Christian generosity. Sigourney's Penn, in the legend of his fair-trading and gentle accultura-tion of the Delaware, stands as a model for nineteenth-century reformers. Given their active role in the abolitionist movement, the Quaker model—if not the faith—drew converts of the Second Great Awakening as fellow travelers along the road to liberal progressivism. As to charges of Indian savagery, as a moral relativist, she holds out Alexander the Great:

> How will they differ in the Forest Chief,
> And him of Macedon? . . .

>   Those forest sons
> Taught from their youth, to twine the vengeful creed
> With soul's honour, shrink not to demand
> Sternly, like ancient Israel, eye for eye,
> And life for life. Their rash, misguided hands
> Rais'd for retaliation, in blind wrath
> And ignorance, with no controuling force
> Of heaven-taught precept, oft are deeply stain'd
> With cruelty. But how shall we excuse
> The deeds of the favour'd Christians? (123–24)

Sigourney contrasts Old and New Testament versions of race and violence, expiating the Israelite Indians for vengeful habits that were normal when they departed for the Old World. Christianity, for her, makes such violence by settlers inexcusable. For her, the settler nation is Christian in name but not practice:

>   And thou,
> My country! What has thy example been?
> Thou, who hast sometimes sent thy men of peace,
> To warn the savage of His holy will,
> Who hath no pleasure in the ways of wrath,
> Revenge or cruelty? (126–27)

A catalog of war crimes follows, leading to removal: "Thus the sad race / Of subjugated Judah, bent the glance / Of speechless, hopeless, agonizing woe" (140). Like Boudinot and Ethan Smith, Sigourney concludes with a jeremiad aimed at the settler nation. Unlike theirs, however, her goal is not eschatological but a more direct evocation of the covenant of works to demand the white nation establish their election through simple kindness and generosity:

>   Oh! Then impart
> To your blind brother, in his heathen woe,
> The surplus of your luxury; . . .

Christians! Who listening, love the word divine . . .
Think of your brother, (for our God hath made
All one blood who dwell upon the earth)
Think of your brother, in your very gates,
Wand'ring, unsatisfied, benighted, sad,
Down to his grave. (171–72)

Ultimately, her concern is "your salvation"—that of the white reader and nation. After discussing Kateri Tekakwitha—the seventeenth-century Mohawk saint—Sigourney appeals directly to her women readers to find among Indian women a gender-based unity: "Think of these sisters! Think of that blest word, / That pure religion, which has raised your lot" (173).[29] Understanding the sentimental nature of her appeal, Sigourney directs her female readership to their role in these transformations, as the Second Great Awakening emplaced middle-class white women as the arbiters and enforcers to the nation's claim to moral righteousness.[30]

Finally, Sigourney's universalism invokes social equality but with an eye toward the salvation of the settler as well as assimilating Indians to the norms of liberal capitalist democracy. From white frontiersmen, she demands,

Think once more:
The Indians are their neighbors, deeply stung
With sense of wrong, and terrible in wrath,
What shall restrain their hatchets. . . .

Oh! Make these foes
Your friends, your brethren, give them the mild arts
Social and civiliz'd, send them that Book. (177)

Ultimately, her jeremiad becomes national: "My Country! Rouse / From thy deep trance!" (178). By asking whites to teach Indians "The mild arts, Social and civilized," she projects their acculturation in terms of their conversion to white religion and lifeways, if not their assimilability. As former Jews, by this reckoning, Indians are redeemable, but the security of the nation impinges on whites doing better than they have done simply because this is what Christians should and must do. Sigourney appeals to sympathy and female solidarity to mobilize the culture of sentiment to oppose the culture of violence. Those "mild arts," the same ones later taught in the Dawes Act's boarding schools, perform a subtler, covert cultural violence, thus serving the ends of the colonialist dominion she intends to critique.

John Howard Payne, writing later in the removal era, represented a more direct linkage of institutionalized racism to God's actual punishment of the nation, not just the prophecy of it. By trade, Payne was an actor and playwright, trained in London, where Mary Shelley rejected his marriage proposal. However, royalties from his song "Home Sweet Home" (1821)—one of the most popular of the era—provided a steady, though often squandered, income.[31] Traveling in the South during the early 1830s, he became involved with the Cherokee resistance to removal, even, at one point, spending time in prison for obstructing the army. Many scholars, in fact, believe Payne co-wrote the Cherokee Memorials (1836) with John Ross.[32] Moreover, Payne collaborated with missionary and historian Daniel Sabin Butrick, creating a vital and extensive collection of tribal history and lore. Although it went unpublished until the early twenty-first century, it has since emerged as crucial documentation of preremoval Cherokee life.[33] In it, Butrick and Payne reiterate Adair's lost tribe theory, especially as to linguistic similarities. Like Adair as well, they ignore eschatology. The failure of Payne and Butrick's book to find a publisher forced him to a more direct strategy: a jeremiad announcing God's implementation of the punishment phase of the covenant of works hidden in a story in one of the nation's most successful monthly journals.

Published in *The Ladies Companion: A Monthly Magazine* in the summer of 1837, "The Uses of Adversity" reflects Payne's work as a playwright.[34] Mostly a series of conversations set in the comfortable drawing rooms of Washington Square, its actions link the Panic of 1837 directly to the violence of Indian removal by way of lost tribe theory. Mrs. Huntley, the young married stand-in for the reader, looks forward to an upcoming gala so she can show off her diamonds. As more guests arrive, the conversation soon turns to the recent findings at Petra and the contemplation of how a civilization can be so soon lost to oblivion, a foreshadowing of the new nation if its ways go unmended. They next discuss the theory that every classical and biblical population had visited North America as espoused by Josiah Priest and Amos Stoddard, among others, demonstrating the widespread familiarity of Americans with primordial white fantasies during the antebellum decades.

Payne, however, next puts his own twist on the lost tribes tradition, one not unlike Joseph Smith's multimigration narrative. His Jeremiah in waiting, Mr. Westbrook, tells the story of Petra, focusing on the Edomites, the descendants of Esau, called the "Red Men" of the Old Testament, whose later members included Job and the family of Herod. As such, they are biblical Jews, but of a peripheral tribe. Eventually, the Edomites are punished for their sins after the fall of the Temple but, because of alliances with the

Phoenicians, and later the Romans, end up sailing west to America along the trade routes long established by Old World populations who traded, but never settled, in the New: "Surely there can be nothing outrageous in supposing that the remnants of a doomed race at a crisis of its extremist peril might avail themselves of their long-existing maritime facilities by escaping at least as far as the merchants of Solomon had ventured in pursuit of Gold." Westbrook then relates the story of the Edomites to the American empire: "If our own country should ever invite this fate, it is not be averted by mere shouts among ourselves for our superior blessings as a people, our liberty as citizens and our enlightened happiness as men! We must not hope to see the blow averted till we lay aside our vindictive contemptuousness whence ruin springs, and which is assured to fall upon America if she deserve it, as it ever was in the days of yore upon the now extinguished Edomites, the Red Men of the East" (171).[35] Westbrook's condemnation of jingoism redirects the conversation to how the nation's treatment of its "Red Men" reflects its covenantal standing. Several non-American lost tribe theorists are mentioned—Mordecai Noah and Frederick Turner, for example.[36] This exposes how pretensions to millennial significance are absurd for a brand-new settler nation. Soon, another character introduces the multiple Jewish migrations theory. Considering the mounds as evidence, Westbrook responds in the interrogative: "May not the result prove that the Red Men of the East were the builders of the Wonders of the West? May not the Red Men of the East after a residence for ages have been exterminated in some contest in the land where they had taken shelter?" A layman cuts in: "'Yes,' cried Mr. Burton, 'and by the objects of their ancient antipathy to the sons of Judah, the lost tribes of Israel who had entered from another direction and have since overspread both Americas and becomes known as the same as what we call Indians,'" reflecting familiarity with the Smith's ideas (172).

Mrs. Heywood initiates the crucial transition to atonement: "What impressive reflections . . . are awakened by the imagination that even in this New World, the race of Esau should have struggled with the race of Jacob and have here experienced the final fulfillment of the prediction of Isaac to his son Israel 'cursed be he who curseth thee'" (172). Having established the Indians as an Old World People of the Book, and thus as sufficiently white, Payne shifts the conversation to how white Americans are now obligated to them in different ways. Mr. Burton expounds:

> If this be so . . . and if our own Indians be indeed the lost tribes who are yet to be restored by miracle, how awful the responsibility of our republic in becoming their curse . . . we ourselves must then tremble at the sentence,

"cursed be he that curseth thee!" . . . if we did as Edom did . . . to their brethren, we have not only pursued them, but pursued them *after their iniquities
had an end,* do we not stand toward them in precisely the same relation held
by the Edomites towards their ancestors, and may we not infer what must be
the penalty of our present persecutions from the awful monitions from the
past? (173; emphasis in original)

This extended syllogism invokes Isaac's curse on the nation for its abuse of
the Indians. However, simultaneously, like all prophecy, it operates under
an exceptionalist assumption of a covenant for American Protestants, one
that compels God both to reward virtue and punish sin, thus affirming election while ignoring the sins of the un-Chosen. Westbrook gets to the root
sin: "Our conduct to the Indians arises from our covetousness; and that
this is so, our frontier people who are its prompters candidly and unabash-
edly vow, 'All we desire of the Indians,' say they openly, 'is their lands. We
care not where they came from, nor whither they are to go. But their lands
we want, and their lands we shall have.' Thus it is that we make ourselves li-
able to the denunciations against idolatry" (173). For Payne's spokesman, the
republic's behavior has violated two cardinal sins: covetousness and idolatry.
Coupled with the possibility of Isaac's curse, God's wrath awaits the nation.

In the story, divine retribution comes in the form of financial collapse,
one largely based in the deflation of western land prices. First, one character learns of the murder of her uncle by Indians. When some characters call
for revenge, it is revealed that he had been defrauding the Indians: shooting
him was "Mosaic" retribution. Next, Mr. Huntley enters, blanched. Financial
houses are falling, causing bankruptcies, suicides, and homelessness—the
collapse caused by Jackson's defunding of the National Bank: the Panic.[37]
In the weeks to follow, Mrs. Huntley perceives the immorality of her grandeur and sells her diamonds to pay debts. The Huntleys avoid poverty when
a long-lost client appears, for whom Huntley had forgiven a debt, now
wealthy. He provides a home in the West, meaningful labor for Mr. Huntley,
and a school for Mrs. Huntley full of Indian children, allowing the Huntleys
to escape New York and seek atonement by farming and educating and assimilating Indians. Impervious to the irony that their new land was recently
Indian land, the Huntleys, and implicitly Payne himself, view the transition from idolatrous Manhattanites to humble westerners as doubly bene-
ficial: redemptive for whites and salutary for Indians, a moral leap based in
"true religion."

Acknowledgment and atonement restore the covenant in Payne's
narrative but fail to either reverse or even impede the progress of settler

colonialism. By redirecting conquest from violence to acculturation, even the most humane versions of lost tribe–based reform ideology recur to paternalism. Moreover, anti-Semitism's creeping insinuation threatened the utility of lost tribe theory as a vehicle for sympathy or inspiring reform. As he transcribed it in his and Butrick's collection, Payne recorded a conversation with Major James Lowery, administrator of the Trail of Tears, who states that if the Cherokees were proven to be Jews, it "would militate against their continuance in this country" (*Payne-Butrick Papers*, 1:87) as much as their identity as Indians.[38] Moreover, given the shrinking interest in both Jews and Indians among American whites, in a letter to John James Audubon, Payne writes in frustration of his appeals to the government: "But why should I continue to prolong this communication? Sheet after sheet, sheet after sheet might be written and still leave the subject yet unfinished; and as I fear the whole of what I can say will not be so defective as to be unworthy of notice, I forbear, adding only a few words relative to Indian customs relative to a few of many Indian customs resembling those of the Jews—." (*Payne-Butrick Papers*, 2:132). Payne had hoped that demonstrating the Jewishness of the Cherokee would forestall their removal in the name of a simple Christian sympathy for another People of the Book, as had Sigourney. Yet settler colonialism in the form of racially restrictive nativism carried the day, and Indians were lost to the reform movement's investment in larger and noisier causes.[39] Nonetheless, two Indians who converted, and survived schools like Mrs. Huntley's, testified to their desertion by white liberals.

Making the Book Talk Back: Apess and Warren as Lost Jews

One can see at least three reasons for Equiano's underscoring of the correspondences between biblical Jews and contemporary Africans. One was to assert the idea of mutual creation. . . . A second was pedagogy. . . . A third reason was to remind his white readers that their own cultural practices were found wanting and did not measure up to the required biblical standard. . . . After his conversion to Christianity, . . . Equiano was able to make the white man's book talk back in a black man's voice.

—R. S. Sugirtharajah, *The Bible and the Third World*, 2001

R. S. Sugirtharajah's analysis of eighteenth-century African-British autobiographer Olaudah Equiano's use of Nigerian lost tribe theory to frame an Africanist critique of slavery anticipates the use of its American version by "native intellectuals" William Apess and William Warren (Sugirthara-jah, 84, 86).[40] Shorn from both the covenantal trappings of millennialism and the sanctimoniousness of liberal reform—although each acknowledged both as fellow travelers—both of these Indian writers appropriated lost tribe theory to resist settler colonization by claiming a biblical basis for indigenous cultural sovereignty. In particular, lost tribe theory features in the appendix of Pequod William Apess's *A Son of the Forest* (1831) and in his sermons "Increase of the Kingdom of Christ" and "The Indians: the Ten Lost Tribes" (1831), as well as in Metis Ojibwa William Warren's *History of the Ojibway People* (1885; composed 1852) to help each author localize lost tribe theory and make his book talk back in the red man's voice. Each appropriates and abrogates lost tribe theory to discredit the settler nation's claim to righteousness on account of its anti-Christian acts of conquest. In the process, each seeks access to a tribal cultural autonomy modeled on the political and economic semiautonomy of Jewish survival in western Europe.[41] Each seeks to replicate the Jewish tradition of negotiated cohabitation—of being in but not of the Christian nations that "hosted" them—and of insisting on the preservation of language, religion, and customs. The survival, both material and cultural, of Jews catalyzed their acquiescence in lost tribe theory.

One such strategy employed by both Apess and Warren (as well as by Jews) is pretended compliance. About such distracting dissimulation, Frantz Fanon writes: "In answer to the lie of the colonial situation, the colonized subject responds with a lie. Behavior toward fellow nationalists is open and honest, but strained and indecipherable toward the colonizers. Truth is what hastens the dislocation of the colonial regime. Truth is what protects the 'natives' and undoes the foreigners" (14).[42] Donning a mask of conciliation and cooperation, Apess and Warren concede a possible Jewish heritage to lay claim to the historical success of the Jews' historical embrace on the margin. While neither necessarily "lies," each plays trickster to enact a prioritization of survival through misdirection. They echo the reformers' critique of white abuse but without echoing their paternalistic resort to liberal universalism. In her article "Nations of Israelites," Sandra Gustafson has attached this strategy to Apess and his endeavor to transfer the Old World Jewish covenant to the New through lost tribe theory: "In taking up this figure, mixing Native meanings with it, and transforming it into a vessel for American Indian autonomy, Apess ultimately sought to force his Boston audiences, and Americans more generally, to acknowledge the suppressed history of King Philip and America's native peoples" ("Nations of Israelites," 34). Native versions of lost tribe theory create—more so for Warren—a space within "neuralgic" settler discourse, particularly from within the evangelism of the Second Great Awakening, from which to critique white violence. By offering their critiques as intraracial, or at least intrasectarian, they implicitly compel whites to look inward to understand the disqualification of their claim to benevolent colonization because of their long history of savagery.

Some recognized the trickster strategy: Joseph Snelling denied Apess was a "real" Indian. Minnesota congressman Henry Sibley observed: "Warren is a *blatherskite* with just enough education to make him mischievously disposed, and no confidence can be placed in his statements" (qtd. in Schenck, 87). That each mask was occasionally penetrated only affirms that both dabbled in double-talk. In their publications, the mask of the Jew allowed the articulation of counterhistories, ones created from within the Christian community but based on older and more authentic claims to the divine covenant than that of Protestant nationalists.

Apess was exposed to millennialist theodicy early on.[43] Adopted as a child by a Massachusetts Calvinist minister, he rebelled by attending revivals, before becoming a Methodist preacher. Hilary Wyss speculates that lost tribe theory allowed him to suggest that the Indian covenant is not only older than the whites' but that it had weathered their outcast condition: "In advocating this theory, Apess further buttresses his argument for the superiority of Native Americans. As descendants of the Israelites, Natives are the chosen people of God. By inverting a theory originating in the dominant culture, Apess has appropriated the language and the logic of dominance, arguing for his own superiority in terms that have their roots in the culture that least wants to hear such arguments" (163). Apess's provocative stance demands recognition of the Indians' older and first bond with God, an intimacy conceded by Boudinot, whom Apess quotes at length. For Apess, the Indians' covenant was reaffirmed by their conversion to Christianity, doubling rather than supplanting their older covenant. Yet Apess has no intention of removing to Palestine or hastening the Apocalypse. Rochelle Raineri Zuck has observed, "The rhetoric of the lost tribes operates as more than just an expression of Christian orthodoxy, a reaction to white narratives of American exceptionalism: it provides a means to challenge 'Vanishing Indian' narratives with stories of sovereignty and continuing presence" (2–3). Zuck identifies Apess as abrogating colonial discourse—a stance of initial acquiescence that masks subversive acts of appropriation—to create an ironized strategy of resistance—a mask, for all intents and purposes. Apess leverages the biblical primacy of Jewish Indians to demand a special place in, but not of, the settler nation.

This occurs mostly in the extended appendix to his autobiography *A Son of the Forest* (1831). Apess begins by reviewing how Europeans morally debased Indians to reduce them from pre-1492 civility to a state of deliberate savagery, erasing their otherwise intact precontact Mosaic customs. Apess then shows how postconquest Indians were abject, reduced to subalternity by colonialist brutality, literal and figurative: "When I reflect upon the complicated ills to which my brethren have been subject, ever since history has recorded their existence—their wanderings, their privations, their many sorrows, and the fierceness of the persecution which marked their dwellings and their persons for destruction—when I take into account the many ancient usages and customs observed religiously by them, and which have so near and close resemblance to the manner, etc., of the ancient Israelites, I am led to believe they are none other than the descendants of Jacob and the long lost tribes of Israel." Citing Boudinot, Apess claims that, as Israelites, they "have not been altogether forsaken and will hereafter appear to have been in all their dispersions and wanderings, the subjects of God's divine protection and gracious care" (53). The bulk of the appendix, then, collects material from Adair, Boudinot, and others to establish the Hebrew origins of the Indians. Anticipating objections to the legend's viability, and reflecting the popular idea that many Old World cultures had visited ancient America (see Priest and Stoddard), Apess concedes possible complications and dilutions: "It is not presumed that the ten tribes of Israel alone did this. Many of the inhabitants might have gone with them from Tartary or Scythia . . . but the great body of the people settling in North and South America must have originated from the same source. Hence it would not be surprising to find among their descendants a mixture of Asiatic languages, manners, customs, and peculiarities" (86). Despite this complication, Apess still affirms, despite the impure blood and culture of the Indian Jews, their access to the covenant of Abraham. In fact, Apess challenges the purity of all races and cultures, as history reflects infinite collisions, exchanges, and overlaps. Gareth Griffiths has suggested that colonialist discourse assumes geographic primordial "zones of cultural purity" (238) in which prehistorical races emerged in isolation from one another.[44] By asking his audience to dismiss the notion of a pure Indian Judaism and with it any claim to undiluted racial or ethnic identity, Apess implies the absurdity of the very idea of primordial or originary "cultural purity," the basis for romantic definitions of race, including whiteness itself, to "dislocate the colonial regime" of the settler nation.

Apess's sermon "The Indians: The Ten Lost Tribes" further parses the Jewish identity of the Indians by distinguishing Old and New World Jewish histories. In brief, Old World Jews suffered and destroyed their covenant with God because they "nailed the Lord of the universe to the cross" (114). However, the ancestors of the New World Jews had already left Palestine when this happened. Thus the Indians' Jewish forefathers are guilty only of older sins punished by the destruction of the Temple, for which all other Jews had been forgiven and their covenant restored. The ten tribes' exile to the New World and subsequent punishment by white invaders had certainly sufficed as covenantal atonement for whatever sins they had committed since. The Indians' punishment complete and their conversion under way, Apess asks for equality in the new nation, having debunked the biological, ecclesiastical, and cultural arguments that buttressed Indian removal, enacted the same year he was writing: "That the Indians are indeed no other than the descendants of the ten lost tribes, the subscriber has no doubt. He is one of the few remaining descendants of a once powerful tribe of Indians, and he looks forward with a degree of confidence to the day as being not far distant when ample justice shall be done to the red man by his white brother—when he shall be allowed that station in the scale of being and intelligence which unerring wisdom designed them to be" (114). The success of his efforts impinged upon *awakened* white Christians' willingness to subordinate themselves to the "unerring wisdom" of God's design, demanding they link their new faith to a new way to think about and act toward the Indians, now their long-lost biblical *elder* brothers.

In "The Increase of the Kingdom of Christ" (1833), Apess contemplates the punishment coming to white Americans should their behavior toward Indians not improve: "Woe, woe to the nations who tread upon the jewels of Israel. . . . The shield of the great Jehovah, veiled from human eyes by a thick cloud of judgment, still blazes like an orb of fire for their defense. Earth and hell are not able to accomplish their extermination, or to amalgamate these dispersed people with strange nations" (106). Despite often being "in ruins," Jews have survived diaspora, sojourning, and threats of absorption through the centuries. As Jews, heirs of long centuries of embracing the margin to assure cultural and material survival, Indians maintain their chosenness, a narrative that positions settlers as Jehovah's objects—like the Babylonians or the Medes, minor characters in the unfolding of biblical history—rather than God's subjects. When the settlers overstep their bounds, their real sin is hubris, an overreaching pride in claiming anything other than a supporting role in divine history. Like their biblical forebears, once their function has passed, Jehovah has no more use for them: "Have not the great American nation reason to fear the swift judgments of heaven on them for nameless cruelties, extortions, and exterminations inflicted upon the poor natives of the forest? We fear the account of national sin, which lies at the door of the American people, will be a terrible one to balance in the chancery of heaven. . . . Has not one reason been that it was not the purpose of God that it should be done—for lo, the blood of Israel flowed in the veins of those unshackled freeborn men?" (106–7). Apess resists assimilation, then, on the premise that Jews had survived by *not* amalgamating with their various hosts during their long diaspora, by not interbreeding with their oppressors. Finally, Apess affirms the covenantal notion that America is the Promised Land but not for the settlers. Instead of aligning himself with the Americans, then, he aspires to fellowship with the global community of outcast Jewish populations: "When shall the proud, strong, fleet warriors of the western wilds, the remnants of the powerful tribes, come up to the help of the Lord against the man of sin, as strong and bold for Christ as they are in council, and in deeds of arms! Let us pray for Zion—and let us remember her scattered and peeled people in their sorrowful season of desertion. The lamp of Israel shall burn again, and the star of Judah shall rise again, never to go down, for it will shine over Bethlehem" (107). Ultimately, Apess prophetically turns the tables: the "man of sin" is the settler, not the Indian. The invocation of Zion as a place in the New World—America cleared of settlers by the converted "warriors of the western wilds"—completes his appropriation and abrogation of biblical textuality to articulate a counternarrative to Manifest Destiny.

Likewise, Warren would mingle a rigorous critique of colonialism through the lens of lost tribe theory to express a pragmatic and more immediate need for survival. Despite multiple disingenuous claims of being isolated and ignorant on the Minnesota frontier, Warren is in many ways more entangled than Apess in midcentury print culture and invested in the ongoing processes of colonialism and conquest.[45] For example, he astutely shows how lost tribe theory could be misread to challenge the polygenism of Samuel Morton and other forms of scientific racism: "Assume the ground that the human species does not come of one common head, and the existence of the red man is a problem no longer; but believe the work of the Holy Bible, and it will remain a mystery till God wills otherwise" (60).[46] This syllogism suggests a more sophisticated approach that leads back to biblical monogenism. Writing after the zealotry of the Second Great Awakening, Warren reflects a more sober detachment of religious dogma from continental history. His emphasis appears more historiographic than ideological and his appeal more rational than spiritual.

Perhaps this reflects the complexity of his heritage and the time and place in which he wrote. Warren's father descended from Mayflower passenger

Richard Warren, making early republic historian and playwright Mercy Otis Warren a distant cousin. His mother was Marie Cadotte, a daughter of the prominent Metis Ojibwa family on the Great Lakes frontier.[47] Warren wrote the essays that became *History of the Ojibway People* between 1850 and 1852 for a St. Paul newspaper when he was twenty-five and already the elected representative of the northern—mostly Metis—district in the territorial legislature. Yet despite his time in a New York boarding school, he at times dons the mask of the unlettered Indian, suggesting a Fanonian strategy of evasion, of opportunistic exploitation of the fissures and weaknesses in settler discourse. In the *History,* his constant smudging of his own identity and authority mark him as a "native intellectual": his loyalties, pronouns, and perspectives shift throughout. Sometimes he identifies as Ojibwa, others times as a generic (implicitly white) narrator. Spatially removed from the locus of nineteenth-century print culture, Warren discards convention and complicates a variety of assumptions about race, place, and faith in antebellum culture:

> I have never had the coveted opportunity and advantage of reading the opinions of the various eminent authors who have written on this subject, to compare them with the crude impressions which have gradually, and I may say naturally, obtained possession in my own mind, during my whole life, which I have passed in a close connection of residence and blood with different sections of the Ojibway tribe. Clashing with the received opinions of more learned writers, whose words are taken as the standard authority, they may be totally rejected, in which case the satisfaction will still be left me, that before the great problem had been solved, I, a person in language, thoughts, beliefs, and blood, partly an Indian, had made known my crude and humble opinion. (55)

Both tribal insider and cosmopolitan outsider, Warren claims a peculiar authenticity and authority. More than a few times, he identifies specific errors made by Henry Rowe Schoolcraft—the most noted "ethnologist" of the day.[48] Warren undermines Schoolcraft's reliability as an observer, finding his claim to membership in the secretive Medewewin Lodge purposefully deceptive and thus particularly offensive. Correcting Schoolcraft and earlier Jesuit accounts of the Ojibwa, "connecting them with their own crude and mythological ideas" (57), he confesses a tradition of deliberate misdirection performed to inoculate indigenous culture from white appropriation: "Their innate courtesy and politeness often carry them so far that they seldom, if ever, refuse to tell a story when asked by a white man, respecting their ideas of the creation and origin of mankind. These tales, though made up for the occasion by the Indian sage, are taken by his white hearers as their bona fide belief and, as such, many have been made public, and accepted in the civilized world" (57–58). Trickster informants have long misled white investigators such as Schoolcraft, drawing down a mask to protect their true culture by inverting the assumed power dynamics of colonial exchange. At the same time, Warren complicates lost tribe theory by claiming Hebraic descent for his tribe but not his race. His lost Jews had extensive contact with Asiatic tribes in their trek to the Bering Strait, and, instead of intermingling, "it is natural to surmise that they were driven into America by hostile tribes of Asia, and that they have been thus driven and followed till checked by the waves of the broad Atlantic" (72). Warren identifies the Sioux—inveterate enemies of the Ojibwa—as non-Israelite Asiatics: "Taking the grounds, the writer is disposed to entertain the belief that, while the original ancestors of the Dakota race might have formed a tribe or portion of a tribe of the roving sons of Tartary, whom they resemble in many essential respects, the Algics, on the other hand, may be descended from a portion of the ten lost tribes of Israel" (62). Warren concedes that Algics—Algonquians—may be linked to some of the absent Israelites, and that other Asian populations may also have legitimate claim to Hebrew identity. Nonetheless, he collects enough evidence to announce confidently a biblical lineage. He references Boudinot and others, but his familiarity came only after his independent conception of the Algics as Jews: "The belief which I now have expressed has grown on me imperceptibly from my youth, ever since I could first read the Bible, and compare it with the lodge stories and legends of my Indian grandfathers, around whose lodge fires I have passed many a winter evening" (62). Unlike Apess, Warren found his evidence not in Adair or *A Star*: instead, Warren relies upon direct evidence from the same native informants who lied to Schoolcraft while telling him, their fellow Indian, the truth.

Warren fleshes out his identification of the Ojibwa as semi-lost semi-Jews to claim the sympathy generated by the Christian reform aspects of the Second Great Awakening. First, he identifies the Ojibwa as victims of both Old and New World aggressors, mimicking settler narratives of white victimhood and refugee identity. This reflects that, as he wrote in 1850, Sioux aggressions still threatened Ojibwa settlements in western Minnesota; however, the Ojibwa themselves had been forced west from the eastern Great Lakes by white colonization: "This would account for the antagonistical position in which they and the Dakotas were first discovered, and which, as the Algics are now being pressed back by the white race, on the track of their old emigration, has again been renewed more deadly than ever. Truly are they a wandering and accursed race! They now occupy a position wedged in as it were, between the resistless tide of European emigration, and the still powerful [Sioux], their inveterate and hereditary enemies. As a distinct people their final extinction seems inevitable" (72). Like Apess, he recalls that these Jews were never Christ killers, and so they were absolved of God's punishment for the crucifixion. Instead, he asks for retributive justice from the awakened whites. When these moments occur, he switches to his Anglo mask to appeal to his implied white reader as an endogenous equal. In the preface, Warren demands "we" act with Christian mercy:

> The few tribes and remnants of tribes who still exist on our western frontiers, truly deserve the sympathy and attention of the American people. . . . Are not the bones of their ancestors sprinkled through the soil on which are now erected our happy homesteads? The red man has no powerful friends (such as the enslaved Negro can boast), to rightly represent his miserable, sorrowing condition, his many wrongs, his wants and wishes. In fact so feebly is the voice of philanthropy raised in his favor, that his existence appears to be hardly known to a large portion of the American people, or his condition has been so misrepresented that it has failed to secure the sympathy and help which he really deserves. (23–24)

The Second Great Awakening had, among other things, catalyzed abolitionism, as Hatch and Abzug have documented.[49] By 1852, the evangelical energy of the awakening had subsided, but many of the movements it had begun only accelerated. Whites were contributing resources and would soon go to war over issues originating in the "Negro's" presence while Indians were increasingly marginal in the nation's print culture. Writing as a white Christian male, Warren evades accusations of self-interest to voice a universal appeal for charity, mercy, and atonement.

However, when he writes as an Ojibwa, Warren, like Apess, reminds settler readers that Indians have a long and complicated history in both the Bible and in North America that the settlers cannot and will never have. Warren asserts the actual and ineradicable primordial intimacy of the land and the Indian, Jewish or not, and, by contrast, the recentness of the settlers, to delegitimize any such claim emanating from settler culture. As it was for Apess, lost tribe theory for Warren represented a last-ditch effort to continue and extend the Second Great Awakening's premise of interracial sympathy and reform to make larger claims about identity and sovereignty. In the end, Warren simply asks that Indians in general and Algics specifically—on account of their Israelite origins—be reconsidered by white Americans not as New World enemies but as Old World neighbors whose presence in America prior to white arrival should humble settler pretenses to eminence.

James Fenimore Cooper and the Demise of Lost Tribe Theory

This opinion based on some religious prejudices and slight acquaintance with philology and antiquity has been entertained by Penn, Adair, Boudinot, and several other superficial writers. . . . It is astonishing to me how in our enlightened age, any such unfounded belief can be sustained; if greater absurdities still not prevail as yet among a few.

—C. S. Rafinesque, "The American Nations and Tribes Are Not Jews," 1833

In 1833 C. S. Rafinesque, in a review of Ethan Smith's *View*, offered a broad rejection of lost tribe theory in particular and primordialism more generally. Echoing Jeremy Belknap's criticism of the Welsh Indian enthusiasm, he attacked "Mormonitism" (Mormonism) as proof of how "false beliefs can be spread and made subservient to crafty purposes" (99). Similarly, Samuel Gardner Drake in *Biography and History of the Indians of North America* (1834) writes: "It can add nothing to our stock of knowledge respecting our antiquities, to talk and write forever about Nebuchadnezzar and the Lost Tribes of the Jews; but if the time which has been spent in this manner had been devoted to some useful pursuit, some useful object would have been attained. As the matter now stands, one object, nevertheless, is clearly attained, namely, that of misleading and confounding the understandings of many uninformed people" (48). Like Rafinesque, Drake accuses lost tribers, and all primordialists, of bad science, beginning with a theory—a fantasy—and adjusting facts to suit it to serve the selfish and violent ends of settler colonialism. Promulgating these falsehoods, they argue, renders their readers, the American public, misled, confounded, and uninformed, besotted by the self-congratulatory clamor of having achieved one of the authenticating criteria of romantic nationalism. At this same moment, the settler nation's most famous novelist subverted these pretensions to identify lost tribe theory's unintended abetting of both anti-Indian racism and anti-Semitic prejudice.

Always a skeptic of the practices, if not the end goal, of settler colonialism, James Fenimore Cooper provided the most comprehensive dismissal of lost tribe theory and all that it represented in *Oak Openings* (1848). This largely forgotten novel was written well after the hopeful yet corrective tone of his earlier, better-known novels had been replaced by a far darker perspective catalyzed by his rejection of Jacksonian materialism.[50] The plot of *Oak Openings*, set in Michigan at the beginning of the War of 1812, is twice interrupted for extensive set-piece debates over lost tribe theory. With his usual disregard for historical chronology, Cooper sends one of Boudinot's missionaries, Pastor Amen, to Michigan to convince hostile tribesmen of their Israelite origins. Amen preaches to a group of Indians representing a variety of Algic tribes, all under treaty alliance with the British and thus ready to kill the encroaching American settlers. Indian voices in these conversations are largely counterdiscursive, critiquing settler history rather than asserting an indigenous alternative. At one point, an Indian disingenuously summarizes lost tribe theory, exposing its many absurdities: "The Great Spirit divided mankind into nations and tribes. When this was done, he picked out one to be his chosen people. The pale-faces call that favorite, and for a long time much-favored people, the Jews. The Manitou led them through a wilderness, and even through a salt-lake, until they reached a promised land, where he permitted them to live for many hundred winters" (273). This could be, of course, Mosaic Jews and their encounter with the Red Sea, or lost Jews encountering Salt Lake in Utah, implying, like Apess, the primacy of the Indian occupation of North America. However, it is most likely an affirmation of the accurate narrative of the Bering Straits crossing by Asiatic tribes, linking Indian veracity to truth and white conjecture to fantasy, inverting the usual dynamic. Thus the Indian voices Cooper creates are more counterdiscursive than indigenous, reactionary rather than original. Yet through this perspective, as articulated by the Potowatomi Crowsfeather, positioned as a Socratic skeptic, Cooper's own doubts emerge. Pastor Amen counters: "It is no matter which path the lost tribes travelled to get here. The main question is whether they came at all. I see in the Red Man, in their customs, in their history, their looks, and even in their traditions, proof that they are these Jews, once the favored people of the Great Spirit!" (276). Crowsfeather responds, "If the Manitou so well loves the Indians, why has he permitted the pale-faces to take away our hunting grounds? Why has he made the Red Man poor and the White Man rich?" (277). Following that, the "tribeless" Peter summarizes: "My brothers have heard what the Medicine Man has had to say. . . . He has told them that which was new to them. He has told them that an Indian is not an Indian, that the red man is a pale-face, and that we are not what we thought we were. It is good to learn" (278). Amen's naivete reflects his misconception of the

Indians' ignorance. Yet Cooper's Indians are well aware of history's power, more cognizant than the settlers themselves of the broader by-products of settler colonialism as its victims than its practitioners could ever be.

Crowsfeather soon brings up white anti-Semitism, as described—though not practiced—by the novel's hero: "There is a bee hunter in these openings. He has told me who these Jews are. He says they are people who do not go with the pale-faces but live apart from them like men with the small-pox. It is not right for my brother to come among the red men, and tell them their fathers were not good enough to live, and eat and go on the same paths as his father" (282). Confused by the Indians' perceptive understanding of racial and material asymmetries based in the settlers' racial hierarchies, Amen concedes a degree of anti-Semitism in settler culture but promises conversion would end it: the trouble for white Protestants is not the Jews themselves but rather their faith. Next, they debate recolonizing Palestine. Crowsfeather responds: "If this be so why do not the pale-faces let us keep our hunting grounds to ourselves? We are content. We do not wish to be Jews. Our canoes are too small to cross the great salt lake. . . . My brother says there is rich land under the rising sun, which the Great Spirit gave to the red man? Is this so?" (283). Amen answers, praising a Palestine he has never seen: "Beyond all doubt! It was given to the children of Israel as a possession forever; and though you have been carried away from it for a time, there the land is still open to receive you and awaiting the return of its ancient masters. . . . Jews alone can make Judea what it was and will be again. If my people owned that land, they could not use it. There are too many of us to go away in canoes" (283). Cooper has Amen inadvertently and presciently ventriloquize three settler colonialist concepts here. First, he foresees the settler colonization of Palestine to establish a Jewish state. Second, reiterating settler colonialism's grounding in land acquisition and white sovereignty, Amen imagines both Palestine and precontact North America as intrinsically empty and therefore available for legal inhabitation. Third, the missionary assumes settler intimacy with and hence indigenous alienation from the land of North America: as the Indians/Jews *belong* in Palestine, they have never really inhabited America.

The Indians have an answer for each. For example, Peter queries, "Did not the fathers of the pale faces come in canoes?" implying their exit could be by the same means. Amen's response reveals the flimsiness of lost tribe theory's implicit colonialist agenda and the illogic that undergirds settler claims on the land: "No, the Great Spirit, for his own wise ends, has brought my people hither, and here they must remain to the end of time. It is not easy to make the pigeons fly south in the spring" (284). The Indians are wise enough to know that millennialist proselytization simply cannot be argued against from any rational perspective due to its basis in romantic mysticism. This ends the discussion of lost tribe theory, though the theme recurs occasionally through the next hundred pages, as war approaches. Worse yet, throughout, Amen's promotion of lost tribe theory heightens tensions and invites violence, engendering animosity rather than conciliation. In the end, these tensions force Amen to back off his millennial obsession and resort to reform-based "pure Christianity."

While the Indians cannot accept Amen's revisions to continental history or his apologies for white violence, they come to admire his resilience. Near the end, an Indian, Bear's Paw, undermines the pastor's arguments when they address the crucifixion and resurrection, the basis of the Protestant covenant: "My brother wishes us to think that red men are Jews. No; red men never harmed the Son of the Great Spirit. They would receive him as a friend and treat him as a chief. . . . This tradition is a wise tradition. It tells us many things. It tells us that Injuns are not Jews. They never hurt the son of the Great Spirit. It tells us that the red men have always lived on these hunting grounds, and did not come from towards the rising sun" (421). Bear Paw's identification of the many paradoxes of settler Christianity mirrors that of deist and agnostic skeptics such as Thomas Paine, whose *Age of Reason* had been challenged by Boudinot's *Age of Revelation*. Yet, through Bear Paw, Cooper establishes the ultimate incompatibility of orthodox Christianity and settler colonialism. In sum, Cooper identifies a flawed ideology in which the operatives of colonialism remain oblivious to the cruelty of their actions, blinded by the rhetoric of romantic nationalism as it was hidden within supplementary narratives such as lost tribe theory and other primordialist fantasies. In turn settler-readers have been granted permission to absolve themselves from genuinely engaging the larger paradoxes and cruelties intrinsic to the violence of settlement.

Still, as Amen is American, the Indians are treaty-bound to kill him along with all the other Americans. However, instead of torturing him with the gauntlet, they take him into the woods, allow him to pray, and grant him a quick death. Yet Amen's pleas and sincerity convert the tribeless Indian, Peter, who subsequently helps most of the other Americans escape downriver. Cooper, that is, still views settler colonialism as inevitable and settlers as heroes but only if they act in accordance with the Christian values they claim rather than the colonialist violence they perform. In a coda set thirty years later in the 1840s, the narrator returns in search of Peter. He finds Michigan transformed by settler colonialism and soon meets a wholly Christianized Peter. Yet when queried about "Indian traditions," "a cloud passed before his countenance" and "he seemed anxious to atone for this involuntary expression of regrets for the past" (433). This language of loss links *Oak Openings* to Cooper's long-standing critique of the environmental damage of colonialism, the "wasty ways" first condemned in *The Pioneers* (1823).[51] After a description of Elias McCormick's thresher, the naive narrator reflects: "Altogether it is a gigantic invention, well adapted to meet the needs of a gigantic country. Old Peter went afield with us that day. There he stood, like a striking monument of a past that was still so recent and so wonderful on the very prairie, which was now teeming with the appliances of civilization" (451). Although the narrator remains oblivious, Cooper's ambivalence is clear. The country is gigantic and productive, yet nothing here in the old "prairie" is as "wonderful" as the naïve narrator would hope. Lost from both Peter and the land itself is anything interesting or adventurous. The narrator makes the standard encomiums about the glories of American civilization, but, for Cooper, something has been lost.

By 1848, lost tribe primordialism had become pointless: Why make Indians Jewish or write them into white history when Jews were themselves no longer white? As Brodkin notes, Jews were losing their whiteness: as the century progressed, "'inferior' religious cultures became inferior races. In the nineteenth century, anti-Catholicism and anti-Semitism overlapped and fused with racial stigmatization of southern and eastern Europeans" (55). The unwhitening of the Jews—Indian and otherwise—served romantic nationalism's strengthening efforts to singularize a white identity more rigidly than it had for the first half century after independence. In response, lost tribe theory morphed to serve new ideas about race and empire. Reflecting the ongoing need to find a primordial justification of white dominion, a wave of books announced that the lost tribes had traveled west from Palestine to become the British and other Gothic peoples rather than east to become Indians. Henry Poole's *Anglo-Israel; Or The British Nation as the Lost Tribes of Israel* (1879) and *Fifty Reasons Why the Anglo-Saxons Are the Lost Tribes of Israel* (1882) and Edward Hine's *Forty-Seven Identifications of the Anglo-Saxons with the Lost Ten Tribes of Israel* (1878) gave northern European whiteness a primordial and biblical depth of its own at the moment of its most imperial, globe-dominating aspirations.

In 1841, Nathaniel Hawthorne identified a far more powerful force that distracted Americans from the moral and religious complications raised by lost tribe theory. In *The Whole History of Grandfather's Chair*, Hawthorne wrote an anecdotal history of Puritan New England for young readers. In its framing narrative, a grandfather tells his grandchildren about the Puritan past. One of his heroes is John Eliot, whose translation of the Bible into Algonquin qualifies him as an American "Apostle." The grandfather positions Eliot's missionary work against more obvious elements of settler colonialism. One night, Eliot meets with Puritan leaders: "They inquired, it may be, how they could obtain possession of such and such a tract of [the Indians'] rich land. Or they talked of making the Indians their servants; as if God had destined them for perpetual bondage to the more powerful white man. Perhaps, too, some warlike Captain . . . laying his hand upon his sword hilt, he would declare that the only method of dealing with the red man was to meet them with the sword drawn and the musket presented" (473). Through these allegories of his own moment's solution to "the Indian problem"—removal, assimilation, or genocide—Hawthorne juxtaposes over two centuries selfish, racist, and brutal settler colonialism. The oldest grandson, Laurence, thoughtfully doubts the effectiveness of Eliot's efforts and is directed to a biography. Seeing this as an opening, the grandfather expands, using lost tribe theory to consider Christian alternatives: "Treat these sons of the forest as men and brethren . . . and let us endeavor to make them Christians. Their forefathers were the chosen race when God delivered them from Egyptian bondage. Perhaps he has destined us to deliver his children from the more carnal bondage of ignorance and idolatry. Chiefly for this end, it may be, we were directed across the Ocean" (475). Then he recounts many of various corollaries of lost tribe theory but ends, as does Cooper, by stripping away eschatology and pretense to argue for a simple Christianization of Indian relations. While the paternalism of the colonialist covenant remains, Hawthorne uses lost tribe theory to excoriate white Christians.

More telling, the other grandson, Charley, has already been lost to print culture's celebration of interracial violence. When the conversation turns to the role of Eliot's Christian Indians in King Philip's War, he gets excited: "'I do wish, Grandfather,' cried Charley, 'that you would tell us about the battles of King Philip's War!' 'Oh no!' exclaimed Clara, 'Who wants to hear about tomahawks and scalping knives?'" (476). The grandfather resists: "I have no time to talk about battles"; yet Charley persists: "Who was the Captain of the English?" To which the grandfather responds: "The most noted captain was Benjamin Church, a very famous warrior. . . . But I assure you, Charley, that neither Captain Church nor any of the officers or soldiers . . . did anything a thousandth part as glorious as Mr. Eliot when he translated The Bible for the Indians." To which Charley mutters under his breath, "Let Laurence be the Apostle . . . and I will be the Captain" (477). Charley's fascination with the adventure of violent racial extermination reflected the genocidal print

culture of Jacksonian America. Laurence's intellectualism and Clara's senti-
mentalism, by contrast, seem flaccid and subordinate, lost in the noise and
glamor of battle. Hawthorne's vision is thus very dark: Eliot's story cannot
compete with the more pervasive narratives wherein white men find glory
and affirmation by slaughtering Indians. More telling, none seem to care
about the Indians' Jewish origins, implying lost tribe theory's demise as a
challenge to the settler narrative.

Responding to the new racial climate, later episodes in primordialism
in American culture would reflect a different set of anxieties. Like the legends of the Welsh Indian, lost tribe primordialism was rooted in eighteenth-
century beliefs in the instability and malleability of racial categories: like
Madoc's Welshmen, the lost tribes had regressed, and so might white
settlers if they did not attend to covenantal directives. These reflect, as Lorenzo Veracini theorizes, "paranoid fears about degenerative manifestations
in the settler social body, apprehensions about the debilitating effects of climate, remoteness, geopolitical position, racial contamination, inappropriate
demographic imbalances, and concerns about the possibility that the land
will ultimately turn against the settler project" (*Settler Colonialism*, 81). As
regressed ex-whites, it was hoped by their advocates that stories about the
Welsh and the Israelite Indians would force the new nation to reflect on
these fears and perhaps gain a degree of sympathy for the race they had supplanted, given the instability of their own racial identity and its potentially
fleeting ascendance.

As racial categories hardened by mid-nineteenth century, their central metamorphic premise—once and future whiteness—became a useless
anachronism. Reflecting these transitions, later episodes of pre-Columbian
whiteness reflected a new paradigm, shifting from anxieties about the savage past to anxieties about the encroaching future. This had already begun
in primordialization of the Mound Builders as ancient whites who had
maintained their racial identity, as already seen in the number of texts that
identified both the Welsh and the Lost Jews as potential Mound Builders.
However, the vanishing of the Mound Builders (whatever their origin),
along with the inability of both the ancient Irish and the Medieval Vikings
to survive in North America, suggested new forward-looking anxieties:
Why had these whites failed? And how could Anglo-Americans at once
claim their legacies as justifying their occupation of the land *and* stay and
prosper while they had failed at both endeavors? If the Welsh and the Jews
had become Indians, what might be learned from the mysterious vanishing
of the Mound Builders, the Irish, and the Vikings?

3

White Mound Builders and
the Lessons of Prehistory

All of these vestiges invariably occupy the most eligible situations for towns or settlements; and on the Ohio and Mississippi, they are most numerous and considerable—There is not a rising town or a farm of an eligible situation, in whose vicinity some of them may not be found. I have heard a surveyor of the public lands observe, that wherever any of these remains were met with, he was sure to find an extensive body of fertile land.

—Henry Marie Brackenridge, *Views of Louisiana*, 1814

In 1794, at age eight, Henry Marie Brackenridge traveled down the Ohio River by flatboat, when his father—novelist and politician Hugh Henry Brackenridge—sent him to learn French from the habitants of Ste. Genevieve, Missouri.[1] The elder Brackenridge also wanted his son safely away from Pittsburgh, as George Washington was sending an army west to quash the Whiskey Rebellion. Hugh knew he, along with "that surveyor of public lands," his friend Albert Gallatin, would soon be arrested for their minor yet public roles in the insurrection. Like the younger Brackenridge, Gallatin would travel the Ohio many times and had always been perplexed by two things:[2] first, the many complex mounds and other intricate man-made earthworks that dominated its banks and, second, the long portages and inconsistent ground transportation that impeded the river's navigability and thus the West's profitability, impeding its settlement.

Both must have crossed Gallatin's mind that summer, as access to the markets downriver was among the rebels' main complaints. Making the river navigable—along with pursuing dozens of other internal improvements—would require large-scale geophysical and political interventions.[3] As the younger Brackenridge later observed in his 1814 book *Views of Louisiana*, the mounds informed settlement patterns: they always "occupy the most eligible situations for towns or settlements," as the Mound

Builders seemed more able to accommodate the geophysical difficulties of the region than were the Anglo-Americans. These locales had supported the type of highly organized communities and concentrated populations that were the dream of Americas gazing west.[4] Settlers had only to plot their villages among the ruins. Much later, in 1876, John Patterson MacLean commented, "Attention was called years ago to the fact that nearly every town of importance in the valleys of the Ohio and the Mississippi and their tributaries is founded on the ruins of these ancient people" (17). Having served this function, however, the mounds themselves had diminished in the public imagination, reduced to mere curiosities for tourists or looters, as Gordon Sayre has noted.[5] William Stone's 1834 story "The Grave of the Indian King" explicitly links such vandalism to the cultural politics of imperialism. He describes a greedy "English *savant*" violating a mound: "The gentleman had travelled much and had been a great collector of curiosities. . . . He had rescued an urn from the ruins of Herculaneum and dug an Ibis and a thigh-bone from the pyramids of Grand Cairo. And he was resolved to penetrate the secrets of the grave of the Indian King and if possible to obtain the pipe, the tomahawk, and the hunting apparatus, if not the canoe, for the use of the British Museum" (220). Although such ravages continued (and still do), they represent carrion gathering as the final stage of colonization's—literal—removal of colonized cultures, the literal theft of its history. Mounds were ploughed over, vandalized, or otherwise ignored, especially in the South.[6] Moreover, after 1870 or so, scientific confirmation of their Indian origins relinquished the mounds to the realm of only archaeologists and antiquarians: their "problem orientation" diminished as whites lost interest, as they had in all things Indian at that time, just as William Warren had attested.[7]

Between the War of 1812 and the Civil War, American print culture produced a near unanimous narrative that the Mound Builders had been white. In this way, primordialization repurposed the mounds, not by celebrating them as the achievements of pre-Columbian Indians but rather through imagining Old World whites constructing (and later abandoning) them before vanishing themselves. For a generation, the mounds were represented as the remains of archaic whites whose work of civilizing North America had been disrupted and whose transformation of the land could now be taken up by the settler nation to complete the continent's ascending but momentarily disrupted yet destined trajectory toward industrial modernity. Steven Conn comments on their cumulative achievements, "The desire to use the Mounds as a way of filling up the continent's pre-Columbian history linked archaeology to the process of nation building" (128). The mounds and their white builders were re-created in planning documents, natural histories, novels, poems, polemics, and other belletristic texts. However, these contemplate how the mounds foreshadowed *both* positive and negative outcomes for the new nation. In doing so, they allowed authors to use the vanishing of the Mound Builders to track the settler nation as it endeavored to realize either a progressive narrative of transformation and wealth or a darker path to self-destruction and obscurity. As the Civil War approached, the latter seemed more likely, and such potentials were reflected in the literary representation of the Mound Builders. In sum, this episode enacted the growing divide between the nation's future and past, between an agrarian southern culture that disregarded the mounds and an industrializing northern culture that reimagined the Mound Builders as figurative ancestors.

Intersectional and interregional controversies had revealed themselves in the Whiskey Rebellion itself. In 1794, farmers of western Pennsylvania could not ship their grain down the Ohio because of problems of navigability and the Spanish control of the Mississippi River, nor could they pay the taxes on their distilled grain imposed by Alexander Hamilton to fund the annual military campaigns against the western Indians. Tax relief alleviated Washington's aggressive response, and the immediate crisis passed. Moreover, even with the removal of the Spanish and the French after 1803, and the Indians mostly defeated after 1795, the rivers were still a morass of rapids, falls, and sandbars, all of which both impeded getting the crops to markets and radically expanded the price of doing so.[8] Canals, locks, and safe portages were all needed. Debates about these improvements, their costs, and their nation-building utility would be cast back upon the white Mound Builders. An undercurrent of fear regarding national fragmentation defines literary Mound Builder narratives, as they imagine primordial nations more united than their own yet still fated for oblivion. When unity is lost, present and primordial, the nations end. The white Mound Builders could then be repurposed both to model a trajectory toward modernity and to forewarn of trajectories toward dissolution.

Fear of such failure haunted early republic culture. George Washington hoped internal improvements would foster a durable union among the diverse former colonies. In a letter to Henry Dearborn, he wrote: "Extend the inland navigation to the eastern waters—connect them, as near as possible, with those which run westward—open these to the Ohio towards Lake Erie, and we shall not only draw the produce of the western settlers and the fur trade of the lakes to our ports—thus adding an immense increase to our exports, and binding these people to us a by a chain never to be broken"

(Dearborn, 32). Internal improvements might then serve national union as well as economics. By this reasoning, they prevent regional, sectional, or secessionist impulses, reflecting distinctly settler fears that their improvised nation was not viable and, by implication, that they themselves were incapable of genuine nation making. In addition, the growing West compelled the imagining of a continental nation. The terraforming of such a massive space would require infrastructure interventions on an almost unimaginable scale. Furthermore, the coming of steamboats accelerated the conversation after 1798: during the flatboat era, the rivers' lack of navigability could be minimized.[9] To this point, settlement had been only as fast or as slow as the rivers. In the end, man-made navigability was key to the mechanics of colonization.

In 1806, Jefferson asked his secretary of the Treasury—the same Albert Gallatin—to plan internal improvements on a national scale: a system of projects to open western waters and to build durable roads designed to enable the transformation and capitalization—the colonization—of the land. In short, Gallatin was tasked with building the infrastructure of empire, the last act of conquest: terraformation perpetuated colonialism's effects through irreversible topographical transformation, overwriting nature. At the same time, what Washington, Jefferson, and Gallatin sought was a nation built on communication, exchange, and cooperation, all core republican values. Even at the level of form, Gallatin's proposal embodies collaboration: his *Report on Roads* (1807) is more compiled than composed, a collection of coordinated projects designed not only to maximize resources but also to foster connections between distant communities. In the follow-up, *A Treatise on Internal Navigation* (1808), Gallatin extols improvements as building more than roads and canals: "Good roads and canals will shorten distances; facilitate commercial and personal intercourse; and unite, by a still more intimate community of interests, the remote quarters of the United States. No other single operation within the power of government can more effectually tend to strengthen and perpetuate that union, which secures external independence, domestic peace, and internal liberty" (8). While the plan explicitly forwarded commerce, Gallatin's hope was a durable multiregional nation, the end goal of the settler nation, a transformation that would perpetuate its sovereignty by synthesizing and combining the goals of communitarian cooperation and personal gain. These plans would take time and multiregional, multistate buy-in—taxes, tolls, tariffs—all investments Jefferson and Gallatin assumed their countrymen would pay, deferring more immediate gains for long-term improvements. Moreover, they asked individual states to subordinate themselves to federal authority, as the federal government would select and design the projects to be undertaken. They assumed Americans' loyalty to the collective national mission when making their plans.

This assumption, however, was already on shaky ground, as its weaknesses were exposed during that fateful summer of 1794. Republicanism depended on a model of civic nationalism defined by subordination and the common good. Just as romanticism had deployed, among other things, the legend of the Welsh Indians to enable unrestrained expansion, so again did the romantic trump the republic. Whereas before the question had been whether to colonize, now the issue was how. Again, this began in reaffirmations of the Federalist fear of the undisciplined frontier. First, Anthony Wayne banned local and state militia in his battle against the Shawnee Confederacy at Fallen Timbers, noting that their incompetence had contributed to the losses of Generals Harmar and St. Clair in 1791 and 1792. Instead, Wayne deployed only the larger collectivity of the national army.[10] At the subsequent Treaty of Greenville in 1795, although more aggressive colonizers sought to remove all Indians west of the Mississippi, Wayne drew the line at the Wabash River, enraging eastern land speculators who wished to profit from the further theft of Indian lands.[11] Second, that same summer Washington sent another army west to quash the Whiskey Rebellion, but, recognizing the legitimacy of its causes, only briefly jailed Hugh Henry Brackenridge, Gallatin, and Congressman Timothy Findley. Charges were never brought. Instead, Washington sought ways to use the federal government to open the western rivers and so discourage regional identification, a goal further pursued by Jefferson and the older Gallatin.[12]

Toward these ends, Gallatin's internal improvements were intended to unite the diverse multiregional nation by inculcating a sense of loyalty to nation as more important than loyalty to state, region, or self. Aware of creeping interregional tensions, Gallatin used Jefferson's assignment to craft a counternarrative of national coherence based in sacrifice and cooperation. To convince his fellow settlers to subordinate short-term profits for the long-term investment, he appends a letter from Robert Fulton, famous for inventing the steamship: "When the United States shall be bound together by canals, cheap and easy access to market in all directions, by a sense of mutual interests arising from mutual intercourse and mingled commerce, it will be no more possible to split them into independent and separate governments, each lining its own frontiers with fortifications and troops . . . than it is it now possible for the government of England to divide and form again the seven kingdoms" (qtd. in Gallatin, *Treatise*, 114). Like Washington, Gallatin and Fulton understood the precariousness of the settler nation and hoped these projects would craft crucial transregional economic and cultural interdependencies. However, they all underestimated how many Americans distrusted the federal government and preferred more local decision making and uses of their tax dollars. Widespread resistance to the plan was based on a common fear of cooperation for fear of sacrificing local self-determination. As these projects required multistate and multiregional buy-in, they were viewed as impinging on states' rights, so revealing the weakness of any sense of national membership or coherence. The former colonies, as Washington feared, still viewed each other as rivals more than as siblings, and the paradigm of federalist collaboration would soon be abandoned in favor of models of a less unified nationalism. This led to the social, cultural, and economic differences that, among other things, cleared the path to the Civil War. Restrained republican thinking would not survive the nation's transitions after the opening of the West.

As to internal improvements, in early 1817, Gallatin's reformulated plan, now known as the "Bonus Bill," was vetoed by lame duck James Madison because he feared its trumping of the emergent doctrine of states' rights.[13] After the veto, state-based projects in the North continued, while southern projects were largely abandoned. When promises of national improvements were not kept, western land values plummeted, and the depressions of 1818 and 1819 ensued. Subsequently, individual states undertook their own projects, such as New York's Erie Canal in 1824.[14] Reginald Horsman has linked the pattern of localization and individuation to larger transitions: after 1815, "a new Romanticism was present—an emphasis on personal, individual traits rather than on abstract institutional excellence" (38). The centralized, institutional early republic, as an intellectual premise (rather than a political scaffolding), ended after 1815, for all intents and purposes. Yet its mythology lived on, as republican iconography served the ends of the romantic empire. For example, the mythologized lone American farmer, the Jeffersonian republican yeoman, the vaunted *settler* of settler colonialism, was in fact highly dependent upon the cooperative and collective efforts of a communitarian republic.[15] However, he had instead come down as thoroughly individual and independent.

To lend primordial depth to the contest for settler self-definition, the Mound Builders were whitened. Even as Jacksonian romanticism and individualism ascended, those retaining republican values turned to stories of Mound Builders to model the large-scale communitarian achievements they hoped would still be engaged. Hoping to accommodate the romantic nationalists and their obsession with racial destiny, the Mound Builders would need to be white. Gallatin and many others believed ancestors of living Indians had built the mounds, rendering their ability to provide the necessary archaic heft in the racially obsessed romantic nation void. Roger Kennedy claims Gallatin was "the first American statesman to employ the evidence of ancient Indian architecture to justify exertions to redeem the Republic" (24). This paradox serves to demonstrate the many forms of settler colonialism competing with each other in antebellum America: while Gallatin imagined completing the colonization of the continent by using terraforming projects both to stabilize the nation and maximize profits drawn from its natural resources, he also imagined colonization as a collective and nonraced activity, openly and respectfully borrowing from ancient Indian cultures not just a model of terraformation but also a communitarian sensibility.[16]

Gallatin's later study of the linkages between Indian languages demonstrated that Mound Building Indian culture was a continental endeavor, coalesced through unifying efforts to build massive earthworks.[17] And he assumed this would be enough to impress his countrymen to reconsider their resistance to subordination. Kennedy comments that Gallatin "hoped that America would drop such notions and embrace all races as equal partners. Then 'there will be no trace left of the pretended superiority of one of those races above the other . . . the claim is but a pretext for covering and justifying unjust usurpation and unbound ambition'" (31). To Gallatin, it did not matter if the Mound Builders were Indians; it did matter that they were good engineers. For others as well, it did not matter if the nation's archaic role models were Indians. Henry Marie Brackenridge had more directly linked the mounds to a more generally advanced culture: "It is not every country, however, which can of itself attain the full extent of the population of which it may be rendered susceptible. In unfriendly soils and climates, nature must be forced by the arts and labors of agriculture, to afford sustenance for a numerous population" (*Views*, 192). For Brackenridge, the Indian Mound Builders had only gotten started: "America may have been less fortunate than Europe in those happy inventions which serve in some measure to perpetuate improvements, and yet, in some of the arts [the Indians] may have attained greater excellence" (*Views*, 194). Their trajectory toward modernity, he implies, if taken up by settlers willing to accept Indian forebears, could surpass Europe's.

Gallatin and Brackenridge were not alone in their identification and celebration of the Mound Builders as both role models and Indians or in displaying the same anxieties. Before 1815, nearly unanimously, republican scholars perceived the mounds as the productions of the ancestors of "living" Indians.[18] Benjamin Smith Barton dedicated his *New Views of the*

Origin of the Tribes and Nations of America (1797) to Jefferson with an extended and startlingly forward-thinking commentary on the role of history in the formation of policy:

> Natural History, which opens the door to so much precious knowledge concerning mankind, teaches us, that the physical differences between nations are but inconsiderable, and history informs us, that civilization has been constantly preceded by barbarism and rudeness. It teaches us a mortifying truth, that nations may relapse into rudeness again, all their proud monuments crumbled into dust, and themselves, now savages, subjects of contemplation among civilized nations and philosophers. In the immense scheme of nature, it may be our lot to fall into rudeness once more. There are good reasons for conjecturing, that the ancestors of many of the savage tribes of America are the descendants of nations that had attained a much higher degree of polish than ourselves. My inquiries at least seem to render it certain, that the [Indians] are not, as some writers have supposed, specifically different from the Persians, and other improved nations of Asia. The inference from this discovery is interesting and important. We learn that the [Indians] are capable of improvement. (v–vi)

Barton's claim that the ancestors of the Indians built the mounds guarantees their humanity and thus their potential for eventual national inclusion. Moreover, his recognition of the fragility of the coming American empire enacts a measured humility. Gallatin, Fulton, Brackenridge, Barton, and Washington all implicitly accede the instability of the new nation—a collection, like all settler nations, of disparate former colonies—whose best chance at survival was based in accommodation and inclusion.

However, as noted in chapter 1, after 1815, the concept of racial difference was reconfigured as more oppositional. After this, for any parable or allegory to be useful, the Mound Builders needed to be white. Barbara Mann comments, "By 1830, any authors openly championing the Natives as Mound Builders were simply silenced" (67). The Mound Builders had to be white, or else their legacy could not be claimed. The Mound Builders became either a "lost race" of whites, or, more often, the descendants of an Old World population who journeyed to the New: Phoenicians, Tyrians, Vikings, Welsh, Romans, or Aryan "Hindoos." Some suggested that whitened Indians, such as the lost Jews, built the mounds. Noah Webster identified Mound-Building Welsh Indians.[19] The popularity of white Mound Builders also emerged: writing as a young widow Sarah Josepha Hale deliberately began an epic of Tyrian Mound Builders in her 1823 poem *The Genius of Oblivion*. At the same time, the study of mounds became regionalized: while thousands of mounds were in the South, only those north of the Ohio

River received serious scrutiny; most in the South were desecrated or ignored.[20] This was reflected in both scientific and literary descriptions of the mounds. In the Mound Builders' rise and fall, American writers imagined their own, and they were not wrong: as much as the Mound Builders provided a model for growth and cooperation, they modelled self-destruction. In those texts, on the level of allegory, the writers positioned themselves as prophets, holding up abandoned republican values as a forsaken covenant. This evoked traditions of prophecy and retribution in which extreme forms of settler colonialism became the subject of critique: the Americans could vanish as easily as the Mound Builders, as Barton had implied. Their vanishing generated a series of speculative scenarios in texts by authors ranging from William Cullen Bryant to Timothy Flint and dozens of others. Like the jeremiads based in lost tribe theory, these were intended to humble Americans—obsessed as they were with dark romantic fantasies—that all human endeavors crumble in time, and that the nation, in fact, would very soon.

To do this, literary writers drew from a vast body of "natural history" texts. Politically and racially complicit amateur scientific "information" allowed white readers and writers to leapfrog the Indians to claim the Mound Builders as earlier versions of themselves. Yet as the century progressed, better trained and more professional archaeologists affirmed Gallatin's earlier theory that the mounds were built by Indians, a shift that, while historically accurate, greatly diminished their meaning in the race-obsessed nation by erasing their whiteness, the only racial designation that bring them into ongoing conversations about its past, present, and future. However, before the Civil War, primordial fantasies of white Mound Builders haunted both scientific and literary texts. Early texts, such as Caleb Atwater's *Description of the Antiquities Discovered in the Western Country* (1818), defined the mounds as defensive structures, protecting embattled populations from the surrounding savages, much as frontier Americans imagined themselves before 1815. Later, in Ephraim Squier and Edwin Davis's *Ancient Monuments of the Mississippi Valley* (1848), the Mound Builders became accomplished craftsmen and protoindustrialists, reflecting northern transformations toward modernity. Atwater's and Squier and Davis's texts, in fact, bookend the transition between the early republic and antebellum appropriations of Mound Builder "science" in ways that reflect their changing role in the national imagination, changes simultaneously reflected in primordialist literary production.

The White Mound Builders: The Textuality of Archaeology

[This] is a work which will prove an undecaying monument to those bold spirits who at that period adorned our legislative halls; and the great advantages and blessings of whose exertions will be more surely handed down to a later posterity, and prove to them a more enduring honor than the mounds of a former race of our own country, or the marble monuments of others could be for us or for them.

—Unattributed, New York Legislature, 1838

The mounds were never too far from debates over internal improvements in the North, as seen in the foregoing statement from the 1838 debates in the New York Legislature concerning widening the Erie Canal. The Mound Builders—a "former race"—here seamlessly enter into a trajectory running from Greece and Rome through the Founders. During the antebellum decades, interest in the mounds peaked in the North, as did the entanglement of white Mound Builders and terraforming colonialism in antebellum America. The three decades between Atwater's 1818 *Description*, the first publication of the American Antiquarian Society, and Squier and Davis's massive 1848 *Ancient Monuments*, the first of the Smithsonian, reflect the shift from fragile postcolony to emergent empire, a shift replicated by the modernization of their methodologies. This becomes clearer in the authors' textual and cultural commentaries than in their presentation of their evidence. While Atwater relies upon the amateur investigations by friends in the spirit of republican collaboration to place the white Mound Builders as embodying an early epic in civilization's stage-based ascent, Squier and Davis deploy more scientific and systemic methods to describe preindustrial Mound Builders, reflecting their moment's more utilitarian and materialist milieu. Squier and Davis, publishing in the same year as the founding of the American Medical Association, demonstrate the same transitions toward professional and industrial modernity.

Atwater was a professional writer who spent his career in the Cincinnati literary circles that included Daniel and Benjamin Drake, James Hall, Julia DuMont, Timothy and Micah Flint, Alice and Phoebe Cary, William T. Coggeshall, and William Davis Gallagher, all of whom (and many others) would use Atwater's text for literary source materials.[21] Most of these writers had ties to Philadelphia, the most republican American city, and its spirit lived on there long after it had diminished elsewhere. The Cincinnati writers imagined themselves as "western"—regional but not sectional—and tasked themselves with bridging the gap between North and South, as was the intent of Gallatin's network of improvements. In fact, Atwater's book mostly assembles contributions from interested leaders from throughout the region. Amateur "observations" were sent to Atwater from both sides of the Ohio, making him as much editor as author, à la Gallatin and his plan. In fact, Henry Marie Brackenridge, Daniel Drake, Tench Coxe, Dewitt Clinton, Moses Fiske, and Samuel Hildreth, contributed to both Gallatin's and Atwater's volumes.

As to Atwater's mounds themselves, trans-Bering immigrants built them, but not Indians, who migrated separately.[22] At a time when distinction among Asian populations was unknown, Atwater speculates the Mound Builders had been "Hindoos," though little suggests he knew any more of Hindus than that their supposed Aryan descent made them functionally white. At the same time, Atwater imagined the Mound Builders living under threat from more savage, and eventually victorious, Indian neighbors to the North. The mounds themselves were imagined as defensive constructions to repel invasion. Beyond this, Atwater and friends observed an organized civilization that combined classical structure and internal improvement requiring cooperation and coordination: roads, levees, drainage canals, etc. As such, his Mound Builders resemble the settlers of Cincinnati only a generation before. By 1818, settlement north of the Ohio River had finally progressed to the point where the Mound Builders had been broken off: "Should the inhabitants of the Western States, together with every written memorial of their existence, be swept from the face of the earth, though the difficulties of future antiquaries, would be increased, yet they would be of the same kind with those which now beset and overwhelm the superficial observer" (10). Atwater accedes that the American West in 1818 for settlers was still more a promise than a reality, defined more by what it might become than what it was. And nothing was secure: were the whites to vanish or move on, they, like the Mound Builders, would have left mostly defensive ruins after fifty years of constant conflict. Before finishing his introduction, Atwater distinguishes two sets of "antiquities" he will not address: "Antiquities of Indians of the Present Race" and "Antiquities Belonging to People of European Origin." So when Atwater delineates his true subject— "Antiquities of the People who formerly inhabited the Western Parts of the United States"—he refers to the Aryans who had been displaced by other, more savage fellow ex-Asians: "It is time to consider the third, last, and most highly interesting class of antiquities, which comprehends those belonging to that people who erected our ancient forts and tumuli; those military works, whose walls and ditches cost so much labor in their structure; those numerous and sometimes lofty mounds, which owe their origin to a people

far more civilized than our Indians but far less so than Europeans." The obsession with defense reflected the Cincinnatians' experiences: Atwater and
his friends had mostly been brought to the West as children before 1812,
when conflict was nearly constant. Atwater was secondarily concerned with
how they lived, and notes that other remains were "cemeteries, temples, al-
tars, camps, towns, villages, race grounds and other places of amusement,
habitations of chiefs, videttes, watch towers, monuments, etc." (18). As an
amateur, however, he had neither the methods nor the skills to decipher the
significance of these aspects of the ruins.

Yet here's where the *Description* takes on primordialist aspects: he conjectures that they lived more like Europeans than did "our" Indians. In a
speculative concluding section, Atwater looks further beyond the defensive
earthworks to position the Mound Builders in the early republican framework for the settlement of the West: "The ancestors of our North American
Indians were mere hunters, while the authors of our tumuli [Mounds] were
shepherds and husbandmen" (119). To imagine the Mound Builders as
settled, domesticated and domesticating, is to imagine a primordial precedent for economic and social organization aligned with republican ideals,
maintaining the dichotomy Crèvecoeur established between durable settlers
who farm, and "new-made Indians," who hunt. Next, indulging in ethnological theorizing beyond his training, Atwater narrates a transition from
husbandry to specialization: "[The Mound Builder] improves the breeds of
his animals already domesticated; renders the implements of his industry
more perfect and extends the field of cultivation. At length the mechanic
arts become so necessary that some persons devote their whole time to
them, whilst others exchange their own articles of trade for those belonging to the people of neighboring nations. . . . The arts and sciences are cultivated; man puts off his rough, savage manners, and lays aside by degrees,
the ignorances and prejudices attendant on such a state of society" (125).
While not every mound evidenced such progress, "they evidently improved
their condition while residing here," rehearsing the progressive, stage-
based narrative intrinsic to settler colonialism, separating the dynamic and
the civilized from the static and the savage. In fact, Atwater here links his
Mound Builders to his American readers, as each had engaged a longer
process of colonization: expanding their holdings and customizing the land
to achieve an intimacy otherwise unavailable to the nonindigenous. In the
end, Atwater offers an even more speculative primordialist historiography
that opens the link to industrialism more thoroughly pursued by Squier and
Davis. First, Atwater reprints Moses Fiske's report of fragments of woven
fabrics that had sealed a child's mummy from disintegration in a Tennessee

mound: "Clothes of a singular texture, some of linen. . . . I am not apprized that the modern Indians or any indeed moderns of any description, could manufacture such cloths" (136–37). Next, Atwater notes the Mound Builders had found magnetic north and employed geometric symmetry: "Nearly all the lines of the ancient work found in the whole country, where the form of the ground admits it, are right ones, pointing to the four cardinal points. . . . Had their authors no knowledge of astronomy? These things never could have happened, with such invariable exactitude in almost all cases, without some design" (139). The observation of natural laws and the transference of those laws to human society epitomized the goals of the same American Enlightenment that produced the republican values of the new nation.[23] For Atwater, white Mound Builder accomplishments at logistics, weaving, and other protoindustrial skills brought American prehistory up to the point where settlers could imagine themselves continuing this trajectory toward modernity.

Thirty years later, Squier and Davis expanded the study of the mounds far beyond Atwater and the dozens of other, lesser white Mound Builder texts published in the interim. Squier and Davis describe the mounds on a national scale, well beyond Atwater's limits in the Ohio valley, and with far greater professional proficiency.[24] Moreover, they were compelled to respond to the vogue of Samuel Morton's *Crania Americana* and the rise of scientific racism, wherein racial markers switched from environmental and mutable to biological and immutable. Championing polygeneticism, Morton claimed each race was created separately, unrelated to each other, and so they were easily hierarchized and subordinated.[25] Under this rubric, for the Mound Builders to have historical meaning in a settler nation, Squier and Davis needed to identify them as more firmly white than had Atwater, as misplaced members of an Old World civilization, or else their historical meaning would be reduced to antiquarianism or mere curiosity.

Instead, Squier and Davis mobilize their findings to establish an affinity based primarily on achievement and only secondarily on biology. To reframe the Mound Builders as protoindustrialists, Squier and Davis spend far less time on the mounds themselves and more on nondefensive relics that mark them as doing what white people have always done. For example, while Atwater acknowledges a tendency toward manufacturing, Squire and Davis, working with new and more professionally gathered evidence, identify the Mound Builders as road builders, toolmakers, and mathematicians more directly: "There is a class of earthworks, occurring at various points of the west, which seems better to come up to the utilitarian standard of our day than any other, and the purposes of the popular mind, if not that of the antiquarian, seem very clear. These are the graded ways, ascending sometimes from one terrace to another, and sometimes descending towards the banks of rivers or water-courses" (*Ancient Monuments*, 88). Squier and Davis, in passages such as these, draw their reader's attention to the "utilitarian"—the byword for progress in the age of John Stuart Mill and Jeremy Bentham, figures excoriated in the South.[26] Aside from scope, the most significant difference between their work and Atwater's is their attention to how progress in the material sciences and manufacturing symbolizes protomodern achievements in technology and logistics rather defense and feeding "concentrated" populations. These Mound Builders represent a postfrontier community moving forward by investing in preindustrial infrastructure and craftwork. After noting the sophistication of their pottery and earthenware, Squier and Davis address more commonplace articles and objects: "Among the articles that exhibit the greatest degree of skill in their manufacture, may be mentioned a sort of boss or button. . . . These present a convex and plane surface and are identical in form with some of the old fashioned buttons which still linger on the small clothes of our grandfathers" (*Ancient Monuments*, 208). These items as well reveal systems of mass production, with similar or identical implements and statuary: "So far as fidelity is concerned, many of them deserve to rank by the side of the best efforts of the artist-naturalists of our own day" (*Ancient Monuments*, 272). As to mathematical and geometric precision, "Nothing can surpass the symmetry of the small work. . . . It will be remarked that we have here the square, the circle, and ellipse, separate and in combination—all of them constructed with geometric accuracy" (*Ancient Monuments*, 66). Just as Atwater noticed the earthworks had been aligned perfectly with the four points of the compass, revealing an awareness of astronomy, Squier and Davis extend the same attention to detail to their manufacturing skills. Squier and Davis sum up Mound Builder civilization as "numerous," "homogeneous," and a "single grand system" composed of "dense commercial and manufacturing communities . . . the offspring of a large agricultural population" (*Ancient Monuments*, 301, 302) whose materials—just as language had for Gallatin—reflect a cultural network stretching from the Sierra Nevada to Lake Superior, to eastern watersheds, and to the Gulf of Mexico, the borders of Manifest Destiny.

The "progress" the Mound Builders evince aligns them with the northern half of the settler nation rather than the purported stasis of the Indian or, implicitly, the South.[27] At the same time, Squier and Davis note the incompleteness of the evidence at their disposal. While they include a chapter on southern mounds, they concede that their information is as old as Atwater's or even William Bartram's: "We are in possession of very little authentic information respecting the Monuments of the Southern United States. All accounts concur in representing them as very numerous and extensive, and as characterized by a regularity unknown, or known but to a limited degree, amongst those which occur further north. . . . This extraordinary regularity, as well as their usually great dimensions, have induced many to regard them as the work not only of a different era, but of a different people" (*Ancient Monuments*, 104). Their chapter about southern mounds is a collage of descriptions, some reprinted from Atwater, some by northern writers who traveled in the South: Dewitt Clinton, Amos Stoddard, Henry Marie Brackenridge, and Walter Pigeon. Moreover, in their preface, they list dozens of scholars whose work preceded or complemented their own; yet only one, the Reverend W. B. Stevens of Athens, Georgia, is from a southern state. The effect is slightly tragic: the South, as indicated by its mounds, remains unexplored and underdeveloped. The South seems alien and other—"a different era, a different people" (*Ancient Monuments*, 104). The chapter ends abruptly, and the southern mounds never factor into Squier and Davis's general findings. As archaeology professionalized after the Civil War, the remaining southern mounds were explored, but by then the Mound Builders had become Indians and so useless as primordial forebears. Yet at the center of the Mound Builders' moment, the most extensive literary treatment of the primordial Mound Builders had already pondered all of these aspects: the rise of industrialism, the potential for national dissolution, and the role of internal improvements in its prevention.

Indigenized but Not Indianized: Cornelius Mathews's *Behemoth*

As our own history assumes a prouder and loftier crest in the noonday concourse and throng of nations, she will more fondly and reverently cast back her regards toward the first fountains of her origin. Is it too much a pastime of the fancy to believe that, as Americans, in the progress of time, attain the stature of a generous manhood, they will more affectionately grasp the shadowy hand extended to them by that dead old nation that built the mounds?

—Cornelius Mathews, *Behemoth*, 1839

The following sections examine both the tragic and triumphalist literatures of the Mound Builders, starting with Cornelius Mathews's 1839 novel *Behemoth: A Legend of the Mound Builders*, which, as much as any text addressed in this book, explicitly linked white Mound Builders to manufacturing, internal improvements, and settler nationalism and so set the standard for primordialist fantasy.[28] The one full-length antebellum novel about the Mound Builders fictionalizes their ultimate embrace of republican, Gallatin-style ideas about internal improvements and national union. Moreover, its absence of Indians—even as savages—represents a strong colonialist subtext. Together, they signal a paradigmatic shift in how settler literature imagined the nation's continuing need to colonize: with Indians out of the way, next was the land itself. While Gallatin's sympathy with and modeling of his projects after Indian achievements at least included them in the American past, his wholesale remaking of western lands through his plans for canals, roads, levees, and the like also assumed that the living Indians no longer had claims on the land and that, as such, the settler nation, as Fulton implied, could remake its interior along British lines through large, cooperative interventions in the topography of the continent itself. While Mathews would champion that process, others would recognize the nervous hubris it concealed.

In the meantime, in *Behemoth*, Indians are simply not there to challenge, share, or usurp the deeper indigeneity of the white Mound Builders as they respond to a nearly genocidal crisis by becoming a centralized nation defined by technology and cooperation. Mathews imagines the Mound Builders' near annihilation by an enormous mammoth, and, more important, their transformative response to it. Paul Giles claims, "The novel is predicated on an imagined affinity with the Mound Builders" that features "many analogies with European civilizations" (95). Nonetheless, Giles still identifies Mathews's Mound Builders as "Indians" (94). However, a plethora of references to the whiteness of the Mound Builders litters the novel. More direct, in the modernizing metamorphoses they undergo to defeat the behemoth, Mathews creates an explicit link between engineering Mound Builders and engineering Anglo-Americans. Necessary to this process is the end of violence as a vehicle for conquest, reflecting a settler hope to complete their naturalization as the continent's authentic inhabitants. Calling it an "epic" of national origins, Eric J. Sundquist links *Behemoth* to removalist politics of the 1830s: "The ideology of Removal was required to perform a double function. On the one hand, it had to provide a philosophy to justify purging the continent of 'alien' and potentially deadly people. On the other hand, it had to create a political and cultural medium in which conquest could be naturalized or set within a panoramic elaboration of predestined history, as in Cornelius Mathews's novel" (73). Recounting how Perry Miller linked Mathews to Herman Melville through their common use of an obsessive, individualist protagonist, Allen Debus forwards a similar removal-based allegorical reading: "While . . . Mathews extolled the sublime majesty of America's restless frontier, *Behemoth* also reflects fears contemporary men may have harbored concerning savage nature and frightening primitives to be encountered in the old, wild West, where hideous monsters from prehistory—metaphorical for what was then considered anthropologically primitive—dwell" (82). While Debus's argument concerning the "savage nature" of the West is born out, his equation of the mammoth and the Indians is not. By 1838, interracial war as a crucial aspect of conquest had outlived its colonialist function, and Indian removal was nearly complete. Instead, the Mound Builders' containment of the continent itself—as embodied in the behemoth—represents an important redirection of the paradigms of colonization more generally: the transition from fighting Indians to conquering nature. If intimacy with place, and thus indigeneity, eludes the settler through dominance of the Indian, why not seek it through dominance of the land?

As such, Mathews resurrected Gallatin's values concerning the role of infrastructure in the creation of a republican union, in the staving off of local, regional, and sectional distractions from the national, though not Gallatin's admiration for Indians. As Mathews discusses in his appendices, only by relearning the cooperative values of the Founding and mixing them with emergent industrial technology could settlers change their continent to suit themselves. Mathews's novel of primordial Mound Builders endeavors to establish not only a unifying history but a history of unification. To allegorize the concept of a population left alone with its continent, Mathews imagines the Mound Builders, as the novel opens, inhabiting a *postconquest* West in which all other human threats to peace had long been removed. To survive the next step in the development of their civilization's progress, when the behemoth appears, they must learn not to respond with violence but rather embrace other means of making the continent safe for their continued growth, and to do so as one. Mathews's Mound Builders' ultimate turn to technology and cooperation to defeat the mammoth represents the nation's projected maturation. The behemoth is defeated through extensive cooperation in creating a large-scale engineering project, performing the next step in colonialist nation-making: *building* the nation followed *removing* the Indian.

As the novel opens, the Mound Builders are agrarian settlers: following Atwater's developmental narrative, they have cultivated an organized and broad civilization in prehistoric America. They live in self-sufficient villages and practice a monotheistic faith. In a preface, Mathews writes:

"Simultaneous and co-eval with this [mammoth], the great race that preceded the red man as the possessors of our continent, have been called into
being. . . . In describing the Mound Builders, no effort has been made to
paint their costume, their modes of life, or their system of government. . . .
It matters not to us whether they dwelt under a monarchical or popular
form of polity; whether king or council ruled their realms; nor in fine, what
was their exact outward condition" (v). Yet the text clearly illustrates them
as whites: "The Mound Builders accomplished a career in the West, cor-
responding though less magnificent and imposing, with that which the
Greeks and Romans accomplished" (2); and after noting the discovery of
some crosses in Mound Builder graves, Mathews asks, "Can it be possible
that these antique warriors were Christian men?" (16). Skin is repeatedly described as "white" or "pale," and a "shock-haired lad" (67) makes an appearance. More telling, the forges, fields, and villages clearly depict the Mound
Builders as preindustrial whites whose way of life American settlers would
recognize as an earlier version of their own.

To complete the alignment, Bokulla, their leader, emerges to lead only
when needed, in the Washingtonian model of the Roman Cincinnatus.
However, Bokulla's eventual moral and intellectual progression from war
chief to civil engineer is the novel's most important transition. As leader,
Bokulla learns the hard lesson that violence was a remnant of a savage
past. In its place, terraforming and technological ideas become the next
step in the development of national unity and security. For Mathews, war
had served its purpose. Such a transition marks settler colonialist ideology:
as Lorenzo Veracini notes, "Ultimately, the disavowal of both a founding
violence and of indigenous presences systematically informs settler per-
ception. Accordingly, the only encounter that is registered is between man
and land" (*Settler Colonialism*, 84). Bokulla's final conquest of the mammoth, and the land he symbolized, completes the white appropriation of
North America.

The Mound Builders must learn this lesson by suffering massive loss.
As the novel opens, the civilization seems bored, stranded at a certain level
of progress and comfort, and so in danger of losing touch with the values
that had made it great. When the threat comes, they respond as they always
had to human threats: with organized violence. After the mammoth ravages thousands of villages, Bokulla urges a counterattack, and the war machine begins: "Hardened by custom, and familiar in a measure with the
object of their dread, they now ventured to lift their pale white countenances and gaze with some steadiness of vision upon the foe. Naturally of a
noble character and constitution, the Mound Builders needed only that the

original elements of their temper be stirred by some powerful conviction to excite them to action" (23). Bokulla's eloquence and careful planning reminds the Mound Builders of their glorious past, and "the national pulse beat true again" (31). Subsequently, Mathews describes technological advances far in advance of those documented by Atwater, his constantly cited source. He describes higher levels of metallurgy, including brass, steel, silver, and copper; medieval and classical implements of war such as boiling oil, siege towers, catapults; and "some internal machinery . . . so contrived that these solid weights of metal could be swung to and fro with fearful swiftness and violence, by the application of a small and apparently inadequate power" (35). This civilization is on the verge of industrial technology, armed with social and cultural scaffolding for large-scale organization, but only for purposes of war.

The older, wiser Mound Builders, however, know that, despite Bokulla's charisma and leadership, the mammoth cannot be defeated in this way: "'This army, five score thousand in numbers,' reiterated the old man, 'will be but as snow in the whirlwind before the breath of the Behemoth. They have forgotten, senseless men! the story of our fathers'" (35–36). Subsequently, the army trails the behemoth west, and, when they attack, all their military technology and organization is destroyed in minutes. They find the Behemoth swimming in the Pacific; he kills the Mound Builders by the thousands and chases Bokulla and a few stragglers hundreds of miles inland, yet the mammoth stops before reattacking the villages. The novel could easily have ended here, letting the mammoth destroy the Mound Builders and letting the ancestors of the Indians mop up the rest, suggesting a meditation on the futility and hubris of war. The Mound Builders could still serve as primordial role models: they were white and had advanced technology, noble leadership, and a concentrated population, and the new nation would have been warned of its growing hubris.

But the behemoth stops: Mathews has a more complicated story to tell. A few survivors trickle back to the villages, and the Mound Builder civilization seems ready to disband, to split into separate nations, all steps that might have turned them to Indians. Just as the problem of sharing the West threatened to split the United States into northern and southern nations, the question of defeating the mammoth threatens the Mound Builders: implicitly, the West *itself* is the behemoth whose monstrous vastness could either destroy or complete the nation. One day, Bokulla leaves his village to "discover in the broad wilderness toward the sea, whatever means of triumph he might, over a power that had hitherto proved itself more than a match for human strength and cunning" (78). He understands the stakes:

"He saw his people not only in the present time, but through a long futurity, scourged and suffering," and from the foothills of the Rockies, understands the scope: "From his lofty stand, the self-exiled chieftain looked down upon a country as broad as Europe. . . . Over those vast, verdant deeps, the prairies, were scattered like islands, countless cities in whose suburbs tall towers of granite and marble sprang to the sky" (81). To achieve the intimacy with the land necessary to be shown this vision, as would Henry David Thoreau, Ernest Hemingway's Nick Adams, William Faulkner's Ike McCaslin, Eugene O'Neil's Emperor Jones, or Toni Morrison's Milkman Dead in later American writing, the nonindigenous Bokulla must cleanse himself of the accouterments of civilization to find the settler's path to indigeneity, his true acceptance by the land: "He vowed to cast himself upon Nature and to be received and sustained by her as her worthy child, or to perish as an alien and outcast on her bosom" (83).[29] Like all settlers, Bokulla had been an outsider, whose emergent indigeneity empowers his further and final transition from colonial to colonizer, a transition sanctified by the land's opening itself to him. After long nights of visions, Bokulla tracks the behemoth to a "spacious amphitheatre of meadow, completely shut in by rocks and mountains, save at a single narrow cut or opening" (92), the mastodon's secluded lair.

That night, Bokulla, indigenized but not Indianized, finally dreams of the continent's secret history: he dreams of a battle between "beings of an inconceivable and super-human stature," creating mountains, the land telling him the story of its formation. In the novel's allegory, Bokulla's discovery of that valley represents providence, a transformation possible only after a painful purging and cleansing. On his return, Bokulla nearly starves, only to be delivered by a hawk, which brings him a partridge to eat and shows him where to find water and a horse to lead him home (95–98), another of the novel's glaring anachronisms incorporated to make the Mound Builders more like settlers and less like horseless pre-Columbian Indians. Upon his return, Bokulla inspires the Mound Builders to undertake a massive earthworks project to trap the behemoth in his valley. They begin planning to plug the five-hundred-foot opening in the distant valley with a massive wall strong enough to withstand the mammoth's charge.

Five days after Bokulla and the other leaders finalize the plan and travel to the canyon to wait for the mammoth, Mathews describes the Mound Builder nation's reunification and repurposing: "The Mound Builders arrived in considerable numbers, in a wood near the amphitheatre, bringing with them in wagons the tools and implements required in the proposed labor" (119). Thousands of twelve-foot square blocks are cut, each with a six-inch hole in its center for steel reinforcing rods to be inserted. Musicians keep the mammoth mesmerized, merging art and technology. Mathews also describes how individual Mound Builders subordinated themselves to the collective goal: "And yet there was no lack of spirit; every one labored as if for his own individual redemption" (121). The link to the nation-making power of cooperation is unmistakable. For the Mound Builders, the achievement is twofold: the conquest of the Behemoth *becomes* the reestablishment of internal collectivity, an Andersonian "imagined community."[30] Only after they change from destructive violence to constructive cooperation can modernity begin for these violence-trapped Americans, primordial and recent, in the premodern past.

Stymied by a wall 500 feet wide and 250 feet high, the mammoth rages for weeks, almost escaping once up a streambed. In the end, the walls of the Mound Builders are stronger than the mountains. As the behemoth declines, the nation gathers: "Hundreds and thousands of the Mound-Builders gathered from almost every corner of the Empire to look upon the last hour of the mighty Creature which lay extended, in his whole vast length, in the plain. A catastrophe and show like that was not to be foregone, for it might never (and so they prayed) come again. . . . Nations looked down from the wall and the mountains on the strange and terrible spectacle" (126–27). In this image, Mathews imagines an "Empire"—a multinational unification—without an emperor, as Bokulla is only a local chieftain who rises to the occasion. Like Washington's, his leadership is reluctant but firm and temporary. As Washington proposed in his letter to Dearborn, Bokulla had learned that peaceful projects built better nations than endless wars, never mind the environmental damage done to the land itself or the symbolic cost of the death of the great beast that embodied nature. These become collateral damage in the story of the industrial settler nation.

Moreover, Mathews expounds more directly than any other writer about his literary use of primordial whiteness. At the end of the story, in an introductory note to forty pages of endnotes and documentation (mostly Atwater's), Mathews betrays a virulent racial nationalism. Here he implores further archaeology of American antiquities, sure that other primordial whites will be unearthed. As it is, he views white prehistory as securing the nation's identity, establishing its place among the world's other immemorial civilizations: "The swifter the present time yields its concerns and its labors to the simple agency of steam and iron the more earnestly, it seems to me, will it look back to that great embodiment of natural and unmechanical strength, the Mastodon of the western prairie. As men and day-laborers we dwell in the present—as gods and diviner beings, we reside in the past and the future!" (132). In the novel, the ramparts' construction marks a transition from the "unmechanical" age to that of "steam and iron." Mathews positions his white reader as both figurative descendent of primordial Mound Builders and implied ancestor of future Americans defined by "generous manhood." Mathews concludes by suggesting that the primordialist imagination helps not only to create the nation but to realize its providential destiny. In perhaps the most succinct definition of primordialism as a whole, he betrays its inevitable colonialist machinations: "History nor chronicle presents to the mind a more august or imposing subject of speculation than the unrecorded race that has departed like a shadow from the glorious and magnificent west. Here we can enjoy a spectacle of which the imagination is the chief architect, where no vulgar circumstance intrudes, and where the actors are heroic and all the decorations in the highest style the fancy chooses to furnish. . . . A decaying bone, an old helmet, a mouldering fragment of wall or hearthstone, may call us back into centuries that are gone, and make us feel our kindred with generations buried long ago" (133). Indians used neither helmets nor hearthstones, and, despite Andrew Jackson's efforts, their bones were not yet decaying. Mathews's vision is only indirectly genocidal, although he shares the general public assumption of a glorious white future by fabulating a triumphant white past. Yet while Mathews concedes that the "red man" will temporarily displace his white Mound Builders before the coming of the modern whites, he never encourages fantasies of revenge: the empire unified by Bokulla seemed invulnerable to savage threats, a gesture that silently concedes a parallel invulnerability for his own settler nation. More likely would be a repetition of hubris and lassitude from the novel's opening, a course leading toward annihilation had not Bokulla humbled himself. Other writers contemplated the vanishing of the white Mound Builders as foreshadowing far darker outcomes for the proud nation.

The Decline and Fall of the Mound Builders

The unknown race, to which these bones belonged, had, I doubt not, as many projects of ambitions and hoped as sanguinely to have their names survive as the great of the present day. . . . Their hair seemed to have been sandy, or inclining to yellow. . . . We have seen mounds which would require the labor of a thousand men employed upon our canals, with all their mechanical aids, and the improved implements of their labor, for months.

—Timothy Flint, *Recollections*, 1826

Descriptions of American internal improvements often made proud and affiliative reference to white Mound Builders, as in this passage from Timothy Flint, internalizing the triumphant linkage of the archaic past and the modernizing present in the American imagination. Between 1820 and 1860, many literary writers in the North found in the Mound Builder legend the raw materials for crafting fables and cautionary tales for their nervous fellow settlers. Unlike the archaeologists and Mathews, other writers concentrated more on their vanishing than their triumphs. Moreover, these complex texts refuse to blame Indians for their demise, and so never call out for vengeance. Far more often than blaming genocidal savage violence, they craft stories of internal hubris and degeneration that prophesize how the decline of the white Mound Builders foreshadowed a potential American self-destruction. A few writers did exploit the possibility of archaic Indian attacks to inspire a modern genocidal response. The market was ripe for exploitative narratives of the Indian massacre of the innocent white Mound Builders, bloodbaths avenged by removal: William L. Stone, Samuel L. Mitchell, William Henry Harrison, and Walter Pigeon, among others, dwelt on the Indians' slaughter of the Mound Builders.[31] Even when Indians do attack, moreover, like Old Testament Egyptians or Babylonians, Indians become providential agents who punish the elect but are never the elect themselves: they appear only after the Mound Builders abandoned the founding values that had enabled them to build the mounds in the first place.

Far more often, and most often in the most accomplished literary texts, the Mound Builders are punished for imagining their nation to be indestructible: a warning to American readers that their own complacency and confidence invited self-destruction. Indians, then, are again an afterthought at best, written out of the history of their own continent.[32] By exploring both the vanishing of all civilizations and mixing in elements peculiar to antebellum America, these writers hold up the vanishing of the white Mound Builders as a precursor to a white nation haunted by the specter of disunion and internecine violence. In each, primordial whites live and then die in the shadows of the mounds, and their stories tell how they had long abandoned their large-scale, community-based, and nation-making origins. Solomon Spaulding's *Manuscript Found* (1812), Samuel Bellamy Beach's *Escalala: An American Tale* (1824), William Cullen Bryant's "The Prairies" (1833), and Daniel Thompson's novella *Centeola* (1864) share an implicit message: only white America can destroy white America.

The first presciently locates the coming conflict across the banks of the Ohio River. Spaulding's *Manuscript Found* has long been a source of contention in the Mormon community. Yet whether or not Joseph Smith read it in its manuscript form, it is a fascinating text in its own right and un-fairly overlooked in the annals of early American literature.[33] Its history re-flects the presumed marketability of Mound Builder novels, even before Atwater's publication, as the author wrote it specifically to pay off debts—as was the case with Hale's unfinished Tyrian Mound Builder epic *The Genius of Oblivion* (1823).[34] When his ill health forced him to abandon the manu-script, Spaulding gave it to a friend before he died in 1816. By the early 1830s the manuscript had circulated in the upper Hudson valley (Smith's home region) before it vanished, only be rediscovered in a Hawaiian attic in the 1880s, finally finding a permanent home in the Oberlin College Library. Ever since, Mormon scholars have used it to rebut charges that Joseph Smith had plagiarized it in *The Book of Mormon*. Like Ethan Smith's *View of the Hebrews*, the Mormons explained the text's similarities to Joseph Smith's as mere coincidences and, as such, counterevidence, keeping each in print to demonstrate their fair-mindedness.

Instead, Curtis Dahl suggests, "the critic can more profitably study [*Manuscript Found*] as an outgrowth of a common tradition of writings about the Mound Builders" (186) than as a proto-Mormon text, an observa-tion that reflects the persistence of primordialism in the antebellum decades. More recently, Adam Jortner, in the *Journal of Mormon History*, resuscitated the text as "a fictional frontier narrative of Native Americans from the Age of Jefferson. . . . [that] complicates historiographical conceptions of popular white understandings of race, history, and democracy" (229). Jortner reads the narrative as a parable of recent events on the frontier. However, *Manu-script Found*'s pre-Columbian Americans are not Indians: they instead re-semble a nonspecific Old World population. Physiologically, the Mound Builders are "white," as described by Spaulding's fictional Roman narrator: "As to their persons, they were taller on an average than I had seen in any nation. . . . As to their complexion, it was bordering on an olive tho of a lighter shade—Their eyes were generally dark brown or black. Their hair was of the same coular, tho I have sometimes seen persons whose hair was of a reddish hue" (27). While Spaulding could be referring to a Mediterra-nean origin, in 1744 Thomas Clarkson speculated that the original, mono-genetic human was "dark olive, . . . a just medium between white and black" (qtd. in Chiles, 156–57). Katy Chiles tracks how Clarkson circulated widely in late eighteenth-century transatlantic culture and was cited by figures ranging from Olaudah Equiano to Benjamin Smith Barton.

However, the circumstances of their decline in Spaulding's protonovel align them closely with the narrator's own Rome in the novel's framing narrative, and, allegorically, with Spaulding's own after Jefferson's 1807 embargo revealed the deep fissures soon to haunt the settler nation. To this end, *Manuscript Found* transposes Roman prehistory on the New World along the lines of Edward Gibbon's *The Decline and Fall of the Roman Empire* (1776–88), a very well-circulated book in the early republic. Gibbon's theme of imperial self-destruction often served as a warning to eighteenth-century Great Britain as it fashioned itself the new Rome in its embrace of the Augustan Age, a model of neoclassicism adopted by the ever-imitative settler nation.[35] In that sense, *Manuscript Found* shares ground with William Jenks's embargo-inspired *Memoir of the Northern Kingdom* (1808). Jefferson's embargo exposed how the North/South rivalry leftover from the colonial and constitutional periods remained extant.[36] Both Jenks and Spaulding conjecture alternative American histories to reframe the regional threat to national unity, with Spaulding looking backward and Jenks forward. Jenks's *Memoir* imagines a distant future in which the North and the South had become separate nations facing a war of extinction.

Casting the same sources of disunion on a distant past, and likewise deploying a series of framing narratives, *Manuscript Found*'s Mound Builders—the Ohians and the Kentucks—actually exterminate each other in such a war. Both Jenks's and Spaulding's texts end abruptly, withholding resolution, thrusting the task of finishing the story, of resolving these fissures, onto the reader. *Manuscript Found* accomplishes this through a complex frame that does in fact resemble that of Joseph Smith's *Book of Mormon.* The first frame has the modern "author" finding some ancient Roman manuscripts in a cave in southern Ohio. After noting that he has made some abridgements, he publishes them and addresses the reader: "Gentle Reader tread lightly on the ashes of the venerable dead—Thou must know that this country was once inhabited by great a powerful nation. Considerably civilized & skilled in the arts of war & & that on [the] ground where thou treadest many . . . a Battle hath been fought and heroes by [the] thousand have been made to bite the dust" (2). As the "translation" begins, the manuscript turns out to be the memoir of Fabius, a Roman shipwrecked in North America in the fourth century CE who mostly describes the decline and fall of the Mound Builders. Fabius had left Rome for personal reasons soon after Constantine converted the Roman Empire to Christianity and, more directly, about the time Rome split itself into two separately administered empires, Roman and Byzantine, a schism Gibbon viewed as suicidal. Fabius initially settles among the "savages" of the seaboard. Bored with his uncivilized neighbors and fearful of their children growing like them, the Romans head west to find the more civilized Mound Builders, whose "complexion, the form & construction of their bodies, their customs, manners,

Laws, government and religion all demonstrate that they must have originated from some other nation & have but a very distant affinity with their
savage neighbors" (2). More important, Mound Builder civilization—from
its monotheism to its complex system of roads and canals—is marked as
"white." After this, Fabius vanishes, until, fleeing from the concluding conflagration, he hides his scrolls where the modern "author" finds them.

The first section of Fabius's manuscript describes a near Utopia, with
matching empires on the north and south banks of the Ohio: the Siotans
and the Kentucks. Settled among the Siotans, or Ohians, Fabius learns that,
nearly five hundred years before, a wise man from the West—Lobaska—had
brought broad reforms, almost all reflecting republic values.[37] Lobaska
thwarted a Kentuckian attack with a disguised canal—needing a "thousand men with shovels"—that safely traps the Kentuckians, whose lives
are spared in the name of interregional brotherhood. Lobaska's subsequent
reforms—veiled republican ideals—spread to both sides of the Ohio as his
sons become the first emperors of each. Under Lobaska's regime, Gallatin-
like plans are put in place, education and literacy become universal, utilitarian architecture comes into vogue, and, while there is hereditary title,
leaders are subject to legislation: "Tho learning, civilization, and refinement
had not yet arrived to that state of perfection in which they exist in a great
part of the Roman empire—yet the two empires of Siota and Kentuck during their long period of peace and prosperity were not less happy. As luxury
and extravagance were scarcely known, to exist, especially among the common people, hence there was a great similarity in their manner of living,
their dress, their habbits and manners.—Pride was not bloated & puffed
up with enormous wealth—Nor had envy fewel to influme her hatred and
malice" (65). While these sections call to mind Thomas More's *Utopia,* they
also call to mind Gibbon's description of the early Roman republic. Yet the
reader's foreknowledge of the empires' ultimate self-destruction haunts
the text. Following Lobaska's death, nearly five centuries of peace ensue.

While Lobaska's republican reforms modernize the Mound Builders,
eventually, human impulsiveness, greed, and irrationality cannot simply
be eradicated. The seeds of self-destruction had been planted in Lobaska's
flawed plans, representing Spaulding's critique of Jefferson's republican ide-
alism. For example, Lobaska had insisted that every community build defensive earthworks, maintain an arsenal, and train its young men as warriors,
just in case the surrounding savages attacked. Given this militarized context, then, when the chance came, local Mound Builder chieftains needed
very little cause to slaughter their neighbors. Soon after Fabius's arrival, in
the fourteenth generation after Lobaska, a young Kentuckian prince carries

off his distant cousin, a Siotan princess who had been placed in an arranged marriage with Sambal, an older Siotan king, a plotline borrowed from *The Iliad*, another classical text about how civilizations end. Their elopement violates the constitution of each empire forbidding trans-Ohio marriages among the nobility. Irrational and overblown rhetoric inform the run-up to war, just as they had the prelude to the War of 1812.[38] Sambal, like Homer's Menelaus, responds selfishly: "How have I been insulted, abused, dishonoured & outraged. How have my prospects for glory been instantaneously blasted and my character become the ridicule of a laughing world" (83). Soon, he hires soothsayers to stir up public anger (89), and Lobaska's rationalist values are abandoned. In the Siotan parliament, literally, the loudest voices win. A lower noble, Boakim, articulates the rationale for war: "The injury, the insult and outrage has not been committed against us alone—if this was the case perhaps we might accept of reparation—but it is committed against the throne of Omnipotence and in defiance of his authority. . . . The mighty achievements of your warriors shall immortalize their names—& their heads shall be crowned with never fading laurels—& as for those who die, gloriously fighting in the cause of their country and their God, they shall immediately receive their ethereal bodies—& and shall arise quickly to the abodes of increasing delight & glory" (93). God and glory thus become the weapons of bullies, not thoughtful men. Soon, leaders of far-flung communities arrive with armies set on destroying everything on the other side of the river: "Ulipoon King of Michegan received the orders of the Emperor with great joy—War suited his niggardly and avaricious soul—As he was in hopes to obtain great riches from the spoils of the enemy—Little did he regard the miseries & destruction of others if by this means he could obtain wealth and aggrandize himself" (95). Sure enough, Ulipoon betrays the Siotan cause by trying to escape with his plunder, only to be slain by aggrieved Kentukians. In brief, everything Lobaska had built on reason and restraint vanishes. Spaulding, like Jenks, presciently foresaw the end of the republic, divided by the Ohio, and the coming of the Civil War. His Mound Builders thus destroy themselves and abandon republicanism. Writing before Atwater, Spaulding mistakes the mounds themselves as just earth piled atop the war's casualties. Soon, savages migrate into the depopulated Ohio valley peacefully and inhabit the abandoned constructions. In the end, Spaulding chides his countrymen for mistaking their momentary achievements for signs of an exceptional and perpetual destiny and warns them of their drift into hubris.

By contrast, Beach's verse narrative *Escalala* imagines the Mound Builders as wayward Vikings, but not ones linked to Leif Ericson and Vinland.

Writing prior to 1837, when the Norse revival was set off by the publication of Carl Rafn's *Antiquitates Americanae* (see chapter 5), Beach worked from a general idea of the tenth-century Norse in North America but repositions them as shipwrecked vagabonds.[39] His Vikings have found their way to the Ohio and Mississippi Rivers' confluence and have built the mounds over nine generations as their population grew to the hundreds of thousands. In the "Advertisement," Beach concedes the fantastic nature of this idea and deliberately satirizes the Mound Builder vogue in the wake of Atwater's publication:

> Who, or whence, were the authors of these ruins? And what has become of them? Are questions which curiosity has asked and which philosophers, theorists, and historians have attempted to answer, in vain. They have been ascribed to the Lost Jewish Tribes; to a Welch colony; and I know not what other strange origin; and grave and learned dissertations have been penned by learned and grave men in support of each of the theories. In this conflict of absurd opinions and unsupported conjectures, I have thought it allowable to embellish a poetic tale with a theory of my own: and one which, if it needs that merit, is at least as plausible and as well supported by authentic history and doubtful tradition, as either of those to which I have alluded. (v)

Beach's assumption of readerly familiarity with primordiality in general and Mound Builders in particular demonstrates their ubiquity by the 1820s. Along the same lines, while Beach observes primordial whites as a rich vein for fiction, he concedes that mistaking it for history is delusional. Yet while he claims to aspire to escapism, his disavowal is disingenuous. *Escalala,* like all primordialist texts, does the cultural work of settler colonialism in that it reduces Indians to mere foils in the story of a white North America. At the same time, like Spaulding, Beach critiques the dangerous complacency and self-congratulation of the Era of Good Feelings. As he begins, Beach recognizes the linkage of primordial whites to specific prefigurations of the nation's shifting identity. For him, the mounds evince the technological progress of a white population but without matching advances in morality or culture. In a poetic "Introduction," and in ennobling iambic pentameter, he comments on American prowess in the sciences:

> If Art, if science, of invention ask
> A helping hand, to aid their god-like task;
> Thy Franklin, Rittenhouse, and Bushnell stand,
> The chosen votaries of her high command;
> In Ocean's depths, secure, their journies ply,

Unfold the heavens, or pluck the lightnings from the sky
And Fulton, Whitney Godfrey, Evans share
Her gifts, with Clymer, Wilkinson, and Hare. (viii)

In an extended endnote, Beach adds: "No nation, embracing a similar extent of population, can boast a greater number of citizens who have become
the ornaments, or the benefactors of the human race through the medium
of ingenious or useful inventions, than the United States" (85). Admiring
the technical achievements of individual Americans, Beach sets the stage
for critiquing the materialist nature of settler identity. Although his Vikings
began as pirates, the American bottom transforms them to builders, marking Atwater's trajectory, yet they merit only iambic tetrameter, traditionally
a less noble form:

And there the wand'rers stayed their feet
And wept, like infancy, to meet
Unlooked, unhoped for, term so fair
To all their toil and their care.
And there a rustic vill they reared,
Gathered wild maize, the forest cleared;
. . . In peace they dwelt; the Indian, wild,
Bland nature's free but simple child,
Beheld, with terror and surprise,
Their race increase, their cities rise,
And hid him in some wildwood glen;
Deeming the gods had left the skies
To tabernacle there, like men. (18)

Indians, "Bland nature's free but simple child," can only watch in awe from
ahistorical stasis, as the dynamic and the godlike whites take ownership of
and terraform the region. Eventually, the Norse nation, Scania, grows to six
hundred thousand.

Soon, the crown prince, Ruric, corrupt and bored, kidnaps Escalala—the
beautiful Indian princess, despite a forewarning dream in which he had stolen a doe, leading to a vision where "The city seemed to melt." Worse yet,
Ruric proclaims, "For fate has cast her happy lot, / At Scania's royal court to
shine / My slave—perchance my concubine" (45). Her father, Warredondo,
and Teondatha, her "Chippeway" fiancé, set out to recapture her. As the war
begins, and in noble iambic pentameter, Warredondo ventriloquizes Red
Jacket's well-known 1805 speech "Religion for the Red Man and the White":[40]

> When first the Spirit, whose pervading power
> Chills in the blast, refreshes in the shower, . . .
> Then formed the Red Man from the finest clay
> And gave him free, his native woods to roam. . . .
> Since first, to soothe their cares and aid their wants,
> The Spirit gave our race these peaceful haunts.
>   At length—heaved upward by the yawning sea,
> Moved with the breath of some bad deity—
> The White Man came, a small and feeble band,
> And sought a dwelling in our peaceful land.
> Our sires received them, in their wild abodes
> And, blind to reason, deemed them like the gods. (65)

Beach would have no doubt been familiar with Red Jacket's well-circulated speech, and his oblique reference to it suggests a more serious purpose than he had stated in the front matter. In blunter tetrameters, Ruric echoes the colonialist narrative:

>   Spare thy vaunts
> For those who hear them: Scania's lords
> Contend not in a war of words.
> Spare too the fabled tale, for you
> And your uncultured line
> To lord it o'er these wide domains
> Exclusively by right divine.
>   Our valiant sires,
> Sought and secured this savage waste;
> Known only then to beasts of prey
> Or men as unreclaimed as they. (67)

Each line here rephrases debates of the 1820s surrounding removal, with settler pretensions humbled in the lower verse form Beach imposed on their shallow platitudes. His satire of the triumphalist narrative and the inarticulateness of its defense extend his critique to the long history of the hypocrisy of conquest.

However, soon thereafter, the Indians take a captive. The graphic nature of the torturous gauntlet run, borrowed fairly directly from the well-circulated accounts of Colonel William Crawford's torture and execution by the Shawnee in 1782, reveals their savage side as well.[41] Beach thus reverts to the dehumanizing images of the noble and ignoble savagery central to settler colonialist rhetoric. Despite this contradictory imagery, Beach has at the very least tricked his reader into a more critical perspective: promising escapism, he delivers ambiguity. When negotiations break down, full battle is engaged, and both races resort to savagery. Eventually, Escalala breaks free, fetches her pet mammoth (smaller than Mathews's), and tramples Ruric and his compatriots. Thereafter, she decimates the Norsemen:

> The battle is ended: the merciless slaughter
> The carnage, which knows or exemption nor quarter; . . .
> And each successive morning, far
> Down Time's dark tide, beheld the war;
> And other fields were fought and won,
> By that peerless Amazon . . .
> Swept all her [Scanian] children from the earth. (90)

Even as the Indians win by dint of sheer numbers, Beach both satirizes and participates in white-based primordialist fantasies. From a moral standpoint, what matters most is the moment of racial cohabitation at the opening of the poem. Writing in 1823, and in frontier Michigan, Beach references centuries of multiracial French and Anishnabeeg cohabitation only recently disrupted by more aggressive forms of settler colonialism as, after 1815, in the words of Richard White, "the Americans arrived and dictated" (413) and imposed the more rigid Anglo-American ideologies of settler colonialism to displace the less demanding form practiced by the French.[42] Beach's ending—extermination based in corruption and hubris—blames whites for their own extinction, a warning that their mistreatment of the Indians, more than the Indians themselves, imperils their achievements. A similar narrative arc characterizes the most famous primordialist Mound Builder narrative of the era.

In 1830, William Cullen Bryant visited his brother, an Illinois farmer. His route was peppered with mounds and, so inspired, he wrote "The Prairies," the most famous Mound Builder text.[43] Reflecting the poem's prophetic simultaneities of affirmation and critique, James Hurt linked the poem to primordial whiteness and settler colonialism:

> Interpreted as relics of a race that preceded contemporary Indians, the mounds also are incorporated into an ideology of settlement. If the Indians displaced a previous race, then their title to the land is no more legitimate than that of the white settlers, and white settlement can be seen as merely part of a natural cycle of rise and decline. If the "mound builders" were thought to be a white race . . . then the rationalization also contains disturbing racial overtones. . . . In Bryant's fantasy-history, the non-existent mound builders

are linked with white civilization, so thoroughly that the white settlers seem
their natural heirs and the Indian control of the land only a temporary
aberration. (15)

Hurt here points to a number of the uses of primordialism as a way of re-
framing public issues that transcended merely the quest to understand the
continent's history before 1492. In the poem itself, Bryant's use of primordial
whiteness was fairly typical but is in some ways more aggressively colonialist
in his accusing the Indians of unprovoked genocide. Wandering the West,
Bryant's narrator crests a mound and contemplates its meaning:

> A race, that long has passed away,
> Built them: a disciplined and populous race
> Heaped with long toil, the earth, while yet the Greek
> Was hewing the Pentelicus to forms
> Of symmetry, and rearing on its rock
> The glittering Parthenon. These ample fields
> Nourished their harvests, here their herd was fed
> When haply by their stalls the bison owed,
> And bowed his maned shoulder to the yoke. (300)

There was, of course, no evidence of the domestication of bison, but, aside
from this, Bryant strays little from Atwater. While Atwater and friends
imagined "a concentrated agrarian" population, Bryant depicts the Mound
Builders as herdsmen, the opening stage of Atwater's stage-based teleology.
The "toil" of mound building evokes public works, establishing republican
and classical themes of cooperative accomplishment.

Unlike Spaulding and Beach, Bryant depicts Mound Builders as not directly guilty of provoking their inevitable vanishing, reflecting shifts in the
culture linked to simultaneous efforts at Indian removal. The summer Bryant travelled west, the initial skirmishes of the Black Hawk War had com-
menced, as the army removed the Sauk from western Illinois. The Black
Hawk War was an overture to the Indian wars of the 1830s, culminating in
the Trail of Tears.[44] In the poem, Bryant's narrator collapses removal into a
longer Ozymandias-like vision of the transience of all human artifice. Settler
efforts at Removal, then, only accelerate an inevitable and natural passing of
the Indians' ascendance on the continent, as Hurt noted, absolving them
of direct culpability. Silently, then, completing an otherwise natural historical process, the whites' time has begun, making the settlers just as indigenous
in their moment as the Indians to the West had been in theirs. Yet Bryant's
concern is also humbling: man is diminished in deep time's unfolding, and

his attempts to find meaning enact an absurd and self-deceiving hubris. While, on one level, this absolves Indians of agency for their role in the destruction of the Mound Builders, on another, it justifies removal, as removal conveniently enables the transition to history's next stage, from Indian to settler. Disavowing the Black Hawk War and the series of wars set off by removal, Bryant envisions that this transition might have otherwise required violence, as it had during the last transition from Mound Builder to Indian:

> The red man came—
> The roaming hunter tribes, warlike and fierce,
> And the Mound Builders vanished from the earth.
> . . . The gopher mines the ground
> Where stood their swarming cities. All is gone;
> All—save for the piles of earth that hold their bones,
> The platforms where they worshipped their unknown gods,
> The barriers which they builded from the soil
> To keep the foe at bay—till o'er the walls
> The wild beleaguers broke, and, one by one,
> The strongholds of the plain were forced, and heaped
> With corpses. (300)

Bryant provides no backstory of hubris or provocation: the Indians attack because they are "wild beleaguers," whose turn to occupy the region has come. Bryant then imagines a sole survivor integrated into the Indian community: "Man's better nature triumphed then. Kind words / Welcomed and soothed him; the rude conquerors / Seated the captive with their chiefs" (301). By citing "*Man's* better nature" (my emphasis), Bryant implies a leveling monogeneticism. Yet despite such claims to transcendence, he recurs to primordialism's doctrine that white prehistory was the only meaningful American prehistory, as the Mound Builders had inhabited the region peacefully, whereas the Indians are just "wild beleaguers," as would be his own generation of white settlers, at least according to settler mythography.

On a more material plane, while each race takes its turn, the Mound Builders and the incoming Americans share affinities for organizing and construction, skipping the Indian's time in a progressive master narrative. Both Mound Builders and settlers mark the land that endures beyond their epoch, while the Indians have left no more than had the animals. Bryant reverts to same seeming fatalism: "Thus change the forms of being. Thus arise / Races of living things, glorious in strength, / And perish . . . The Red Man, too, / Has left the blooming fields he ranged so long, / And nearer to the Rocky Mountains, sought / A wilder hunting ground" (301). His use of "left" betrays either a profound misrepresentation, a naive misapprehension implicit to settler colonialism, or, most likely, a deliberate assumption of removal's completion: the verb's passive connotation conceals the active violence of removal. For Bryant, genocide and ethnic cleansing are veiled as details of a larger historical inevitability, of violence disavowed, absolving settlers for the sins of their replacement of the Indians. To communicate this, the poet imagines time-traveling to the moment between the departure of the Indians and the arrival of the Americans, as if these were not simultaneous and violently deliberate:

> I hear
> The sound of that advancing multitude
> Which soon shall fill the deserts. From the ground
> Comes up the laugh of children, the soft voice
> Of maidens, and the sweet and solemn hymn
> Of Sabbath worshippers.

The end looks even further: "All at once / A fresher wind sweeps by, and breaks my dream, / And I am in the wilderness alone." The Sabbath worshippers, like the Mound Builders, will pass: white colonization will not end history, and becomes only a momentary efflorescence. The end of American civilization in time's obscurity chastens his white readers. To think they or their nation can either escape death or, conversely, *complete* history represents a dangerous egotism.

Last, Daniel P. Thompson's extended short story "Centeola, or The Maid of the Mounds" (1864) most explicitly links primordial Mound Builders to antebellum fears of national self-immolation.[45] Writing in the midst of the war, Thompson synthesizes four decades of Mound Builder materials to show how the nation had not heeded the warnings about interregional divergence and national fragility. Curtis Dahl has speculated that "*Centeola* could not have been written early in the century" ("Mound Builders," 190), as the bellicose prophecies of the earlier texts had now been actualized. Even more directly, like Mathews's, Thompson's preface links the mounds to actual internal improvements: "The most remarkable specimens of this kind were brought to light . . . in excavating the earth for the Louisville canal" (ix–x). Thompson imagines the Mound Builders as descended from archaic Tyrians who crossed the Atlantic to avoid invading Babylonians, a backstory similar to Hale's unfinished *Genius of Oblivion*, in which her ancient whites never even get across the ocean to build the mounds. The refugee trope resembles that of both the Welsh Indians and the lost Jews, as all express the settlers' disguising of invasion as escape.

Recalling the prophetic paradigms of Spaulding and Beach, Thompson focuses more on the corruption that made both vulnerable to and deserving of Indian attack. Early on, a sage foresees the fall of the Mound Builders in terms obviously referring to America on the eve of the Civil War: "Our nation is here now, but is it destined long to remain so? The history of the past bids me to say no; and finally the portents of time all echo back the answer no!" (24). Those portents are matched by a falling away from republican values. The eponymous princess in hiding, Centeola, observes the many "flagrant violations" of their religious principles in the "Imperial City," "the fountain head of every corruption and wrong." She cannot but prophesize: "And hence she began, as if acting under some involuntary impulse, to predict, unless timely repentance and reformation might avert it, the approaching doom of the nation" (32). The story's seven tribes share the Imperial City as a capital but neglect to foster unity or any sense of shared purpose. The Imperial City soon sends out rapists to silence Centeola. At the same time, reports come in that savages in the North had seized the surpluses of metal axes, spears, and swords awaiting shipment from the copper fields of the Upper Peninsula of Michigan that the emperor had ordered for use on his own people. Thompson's Mound Builders would be killed with their own weapons.

As the heroes—Centeola, her stepfather Alcoan ("The Sage"), and Tulozin, her worthy beloved—head south on well-built roads to the capital, they find refugees who describe the coming savages as "rough savage monsters. They are much larger and taller men than our nation" (71). Moreover, the savages have domesticated mammoths, as had Beach's Escalala, as war machines. When Centeola and her friends reach the Imperial City, they find the king has ordered virgin sacrifices; Centeola objects and, of course, becomes the next virgin in line. Alcoan reveals her actual identity as the princess, and Tulozin saves her. The savages attack, and the city burns. Centeola and Tulozin lead the surviving Mound Builders into battle, and then into exile in the South, where the Tyrians become the Aztecs, displacing the Toltecs. Thompson's brief fiction, like the others, ends with the destruction of the Mound Builders. However, the Tyrians' eventual colonization of Mexico suggests an even deeper appropriation: most of the students of the mounds held out the Aztecs and the Incas as Indian groups whose achievements outstripped those of "our" Indians. By whitening the Aztecs, Thompson simply shifts the fantasy southward, exporting rather than erasing the primordialist mantra that the only important American prehistory must be white.

As creators of primordialist narratives about the displacement, replacement, or effacement of the Mound Builders, Spaulding, Beach, Bryant, and Thompson create alternative historiographies, in which they use the Mound Builders, to varying degrees, to inform prophecies about the fragility and corruption of the settler nation. Unlike lost tribe advocates, however, the covenant violated by the settler nation is not with a Christian God. Instead, the settlers had broken from the founding values of the republic, the nation's covenant with itself. In these texts, a shadow United States—the Mound Builders—is always already fated to oblivion on account of its inability to acknowledge the lessons of history and the violence at the core of its identity, so inviting civil war. While these stories redirected antebellum stresses through primordial speculation, a group of poets from Atwater's Cincinnati contemplated the mounds even more darkly.

The Mound Builders in the Poetry of Cincinnati

Fortifications would then frown from the magnificent cliffs on which the eye of the voyager now dwells with delight. The smoke of artillery would poison our evening mists, and contaminate our morning fogs, which rising from our plains, curl around the summits of the green hills. A sulphurous odour would blend itself with aroma from our flowers.

—Daniel Drake, "Remarks," 1833

Although many figures raised alarms about interregional divergence—including George Washington, Charles Brockden Brown, John Quincy Adams, William Jenks, and Solomon Spaulding—few lived near the border commonly acknowledged as the fault line for future conflagration. From 1820 forward, whites living west of the Appalachians, especially along the Ohio River, were particularly aware of their tenuous position as conflict approached. In 1833, following the Nullification Crisis, Daniel Drake, who contributed to both Gallatin's and Atwater's volumes, and whose 1815 *Picture of Cincinnati* celebrated the city's mounds and internal improvements, published "Remarks on the Importance of Promoting Literary and Social Concert in the Mississippi Valley." While Drake's fame rested mostly on his activities as a medical doctor, he also fostered the West's culture more generally, hoping to create it as a third regional culture, as a unifying bulwark against sectionalism and secessionism.[46] Like Washington and Gallatin, Drake advocated improvements to foster national identity, and he found in the mounds a model of cooperative achievement. In 1818, with Atwater, he had imagined the mounds as defensive fortifications built to save civilization from barbarity; by 1833, he presciently imagined Cincinnati's future fortifications as defenses against the South. Not surprisingly, then, Drake resists sectionalism by advocating a reasserted national collectivity, painting a foreboding vision of the coming conflict.

Like Drake, the city's poets felt imperiled in Cincinnati and turned to the mounds to enable their foreboding literary utterances. Starting in the 1820s, Ohio valley poets, as collected in William T. Coggeshall's massive 1860 anthology *The Poets and Poetry of the West*, deployed the mounds to draw parallels between the at-risk settler nation and the ruins upon which it was built.[47] Thematic transitions over time in these poems establish a trajectory wherein the Mound Builders shift from Bryant-like reminders of the passing of all human endeavors to more direct Spaulding- or Thompson-like prophecies of self-immolation. In the 1820s and 1830s, for Micah Flint, Moses Brooks, and Luella Rose, the mounds rebuked all human pride. As intersectional tensions grew in the 1830s and 1840s, among many others, Thomas Shreve, Julia DuMont, and Charles Jones depicted the mounds as foreshadowing conflict more directly. Finally, Hattie Tyng offered a darker critique in the late 1850s. Their common critique delves beneath the topical operations of frontier life to identify the deeper issue of colonialism's inevitable entanglement with violence and greed. Like Brackenridge and Gallatin, they reject the whitening of the Mound Builders, repositioning whites as usurpers rather than heirs. Instead, they focus on the settlers' disregard for and literal destruction of the Mounds in their blind rush to remake the land in their own image, a path leading toward self-immolation. For each, the mounds represent the settler nation's sins in its removal of a noble past, a profound disordering that foreordains the coming chaos. Especially for Jones and Tyng, a community built on undisavowed violence intrinsically sets the terms of its own violent end. This line of thinking, however, began as soon as the 1820s.

Micah Flint, son of Timothy, published *The Hunter and Other Poems* (1826), before dying from tuberculosis that same year.[48] More sensitive than his father to the ambiguities of expansion, Micah's poem "The Mounds of Cahokia" was also included in Coggeshall's collection and contemplates how the mounds remind settlers of the constancy of death and the tenuous nature of the white settlements. The narrator walks to the peak of the enormous Cahokia Mound at sunset and contemplates the view:

From the dark summit of an Indian Mound . . .
I saw the lesser mounds which round me rose,
Each was a giant mass of slumbering clay,
There slept the warriors, women, fiends, and foes.
There, side by side, the rival chieftains lay;
And mighty tribes, swept from the face of day,
Forgot their wars, and found a long repose. (Coggeshall, 57)

Basing his idea of the mounds on Atwater's prioritization of their defensive and funerary functions, Flint invests the continent with a rich Indian pre-Columbian history and grandeur. However, next, "Your names have perished; / Not a trace remains" of their actual stories. After wondering if their ghosts still linger around the mounds, Flint offers an apology:

If so, forgive the rude, unhallowed feet,
Which trode so thoughtless o'er your mighty dead.
I would not thus profane their low retreat,
Nor trample where the sleeping warrior's head
Lay pillowed on its everlasting bed. (57)

In refusing responsibility for the removal of the Mound Builders' descendants, and by ignoring the violence of their displacement, like Bryant, Flint writes as a settler, mournfully, but still self-righteously. At the same time, he portrays white settlement as built atop a haunted graveyard rather than the usual tabula rasa of the colonialist imagination, an image foreboding impermanence but one in which the Indians killed each other and settler violence is omitted. Nonetheless, his apology demonstrates, if not atonement, a position of "rude, unhallowed" humility. Flint's paradoxical combination of colonialism and contrition enact an emergent awareness of the settler's conflicted subjectivity.

A decade later, Charles Jones offers a more pointed critique of white misbehavior as refracted through both the mounds' history and their ongoing neglect and abuse. Perhaps the best western poet prior to Alice Cary, Jones often addressed historical themes from a contrary perspective. For example, his poem to Tecumseh calls out raced nationalism and the erasure of genocidal violence from the national record.[49] Before his poem "The Old Mound," Jones places a note explaining the condition of the mound in question: "In the western part of Cincinnati (demolished years ago by a Vandal curiosity), near what is now the junction of Fifth and Mound Streets" (Coggeshall, 205). The term "Vandal" in a town with a Roman name, and in a nation claiming a classical legacy, suggests the whites pillaging the mounds were not the heirs of Rome but rather the descendants of the barbarians who sacked it. In the poem itself, his opening stanza maintains this attack: "Lonely and sad it stands: / The trace of ruthless hands / Is on its sides and summit, and around / The dwellings of the white man pile the ground" (Coggeshall, 205). Next, from "Upon its top," he critiques the pervading materialism of the new city: "And see around me spread / Temples and mansions, and the hoary hills, / Bleak with the labor that the coffer fills, / But mars their bloom for the while, / And steals from nature's face its joyous smile" (Coggeshall, 205). "Labor" could refer to either exploited labor in Cincinnati's mills or slavery across the river in Kentucky. Either way, greed mars the landscape. Turning back to the Mound, Jones writes:

> It too must pass away:
>   Barbaric hands will lay
> Its holy ruins level with the plain,
> And rear upon its sight some goodly fane.
>   It seemeth to upbraid
> The white man for the ruin he has made.
>   And soon the spade and mattock must
>   Invade the sleepers' buried dust
> And bare their bones to sacrilegious eyes,
> And send them forth some joke collector's prize. (Coggeshall, 205–6)

The "white man" here sacrilegiously desecrates antiquities in the name of profit and self-gratification, thus mocking white claims to the moral righteousness at the base of all claims to providential or civil dominion. Jones links the mounds, removal, grave robbing, and the violence of conquest as the driving forces of white conquest, invalidating the nation's claims to Christian, republican, and moral righteousness. Destroying the mounds inverts Cincinnatian values and glorifies materialism, but without any evidence of covenantal atonement or reaffirmation. Settlers' greed is not a momentary flaw but rather a defining characteristic. There is no sense of one great nation succeeding and building upon the ruins of another to achieve its and mankind's destiny before returning to dust. There is only vandalism.

When Coggeshall published "Ruins," Hattie Tyng was eighteen years old, at the start of a long career as a teacher, biographer, novelist, and poet under her married name, Hattie Tyng Griswold.[50] Written in 1859 on the eve of the war, "Ruins" calls attention to Americans' fascination with the Old World and their devaluation of the New, indicting the imitative cringe of the cultural

colonial. She begins with wondering why Americans value Old World antiquities more than their own:

> O'er all ancient lands they wander,
> Ever with a new delight,
> Seeking ruins which are sacred
> To their wonder-loving sight.
> But they know not that around them,
> Close at home, are ruins spread,
> Strange as those that glimpses give them
> Of the ages that are dead.
> Crumbling fane or fallen turret,
> Ruined mosque or minaret,
> Teaches not the solemn lesson,
> Which we learn but to forget. (Coggeshall, 686)

As settlers, Americans have assumed that their New World, in its newness,
has no antiquity, a position from which the violence of colonization can be
disavowed. Then Tyng turns to the mounds, working from Atwater's assumption of their defensive and funerary functions:

> Everywhere around are scattered
> Ruined lives and broken hearts,
> Wrecks of manhood far more shattered
> Than these fragments of lost arts.
> And we need not go seek them
> Far from our native land
> For unnoted and forsaken
> Near us many ruins stand. (Coggeshall, 686)

Tyng's ambivalence is on direct display as the poem ends. Like Gallatin
and Brackenridge, she recognizes not only that the Mound Builders have
become Indians but, more than the mounds, she recognizes that Indians
themselves are now forced to live with "Ruined lives and broken hearts," embodying the damage done by settler invasion. Her later work extended this
sympathetic portrayal of Indians. In this early poem, however, like Jones,
she is more concerned with how the settler's disregard for the mounds represented a more general reluctance to engage a continental history that was
not only not theirs but that they themselves had damaged rather than improved. As Jones mourned the wreckage of the mounds, Tyng addressed
the wreckage of Indian lives, thus making the New World as damaged as

the Old. For both, greed and self-centeredness doomed settler culture to self-destruction.

In the end, the interregional cause of the war seems incidental; instead, the violent rejection of republican values and the unchecked avariciousness and violence of the antebellum decades assured that American ruins would soon litter the New World. Jason Phillips has recently described how Americans—all well aware of the inevitability of the coming conflict—imagined a variety of sources: "When individual imaginations of looming civil wars coalesced, they depicted different conflicts depending on the visionaries' perspectives. . . . Somehow the real war combined all of these antebellum prophecies without fulfilling any of them in detail" (4). For these visionary poets, the violence and, subsequently, the vanishing of the ancient nation had begun to recur in the present. The coming war thus became a symptom of a larger and longer disorder: the settler nation's nervous desperation to unify and justify itself by any means necessary, to assemble the unassembleable, to recall Deloria.

The end of the early republic unleashed divisive local and sectional impulses, suppressed but never extinguished since the Revolution. After the Missouri Compromise and then during the Nullification Crisis, crucial fissures continued to appear. Paul Quigley quotes Thomas Cooper of South Carolina's 1827 plea before appending his own finding: "Is it worth our while to continue in this union of states, where the North demand to be our masters and we are required to be their tributaries?" to which Quigley adds, "To nullifiers and secessionists, the Union of affection, sympathy, and brotherhood that had been envisioned by Madison and Jefferson's generation of Republicans had disappeared, if it had ever existed at all" (57). Consequently, each region imagined its own models of settler colonialism.[51] For decades, the Mound Builders had been refashioned as primordial whites to invoke and raise the alarm about interregional divergences, as the emphasis shifted from hopeful stories of unification to despairing ones of division.

Looking even further, one other text linked the mounds to industrialism even more directly, and doing so, foresees postbellum conflicts. The Philadelphia-born James Hall settled in Cincinnati in 1833, moving east from Illinois, where he had witnessed and strenuously objected to the colonialist violence of the Black Hawk War, a war Hall's friend Benjamin Drake (Daniel's brother) condemned in his biography of Black Hawk.[52] While still in Illinois, Hall had edited the *Illinois Monthly Magazine* and published, thereby endorsing its sentiment, a story called "Three Hundred Years Hence," attributed to an anonymous "Bluffton." This story foresees a violent

future for the nation based in settler greed and selfishness, though along
the fissures of class rather than region.[53] At the opening, "Bluffton's" narrator is hiking through Cahokia, across from St. Louis, stops, and takes in
the view: "In the edge of the landscape was an Indian Mound of the largest
dimensions. . . . As I gazed upon the Mound, a fit of dreamy musing came
over me. I thought of the people who reposed in that sepulchre of other
years. 'The flood of ages' had rolled over them, and in its unceasing wave
was still sweeping on" (497). The narrator is then sent three centuries into
the future by "the Genius of the Valley." The mounds, true embodiments
of the region's history, are the only remaining familiar landscape features,
calling to mind the depths of precontact time, the long nonwhite continental history primordialism was designed to erase. When the narrator awakens, he first thinks he is in paradise: he sees fields and people, ships from all
over the world in St. Louis, and a burgeoning manufacturing sector. After
walking on good roads and an "iron bridge"—internal improvements—the
narrator becomes ambivalent. "An antiquary" informs him that the "very
names" of "our present great men were unknown," evoking reflection: "Man,
brief in his mortal existence, is yet more brief in the remembrance of others.
The shouts of the mob at the success of a political partizan is not the voice
after ages" (498). While this sentiment critiques the clamor surrounding the
Black Hawk War, it also suggests a lack of historical curiosity or introspection in this purported utopia, the ascension of bland materialism. Likewise,
the factories seem dangerous to the narrator, who increasingly cannot account for the complexity of the situation, causing him to miss telling flaws:

> A thick cloud of smoke hung over that portion of the city, caused by the thou-
> sand fires of the steam engines. . . . Here was the theater of the most exten-
> sive manufactories of the west. . . . The artizans were retiring to their houses
> in the high buildings of the dirty and narrow streets. I rejoiced, as I saw this
> multitude of all ages and sexes, that employment and sustenance was afforded
> to so numerous a population, and I remembered with exultation, that I had
> warmly advocated every plan that was suggested, to induce emigration to
> the west. . . . Now was the good policy of these measures apparent wherever I
> went, in the overflowing population of country and town. (4)

The narrator—a thoroughgoing advocate of western settlement—sees what
he wants to see and congratulates himself, blinded by his self-congratulatory
pride to encroaching signs of trouble. These superficial images of prosperity
"obscures the means of its production," to recall Veracini's comments on
settler colonialism more generally (*Settler Colonialism*, 14). In fact, the

colonizer also conceals it from himself through a determined and willful ignorance that the story soon deconstructs.

Next, a riot breaks out, with the mob screaming for "Bread! Bread! Bread!" as they burn down the homes of the wealthy—full-blown class warfare, complete with a militarized police force violently imposing martial law. When the narrator is "declared one of the insurgents," "An officer ordered me to be instantly put to death" (502) upon which he awakens back in the nineteenth century, the mound still dominating the landscape. "Bluffton" correctly perceived war as the result of the "success" of settler colonization: in the story, the narrator's advocacy of "emigration to the west" precipitates self-destruction in the distant future. When the narrator awakens, he admits that his calls for colonization and settlement are at an end. Instead of time-traveling to the past to celebrate the settler nation, as primordialism normally does, this story time-travels to the future to condemn it. "Bluffton" implies that patterns and tendencies toward violence and dominion that started even before the removal of the Indians continue into the future and find new victims in the white working classes of the West, many of whom would be Irish, a group whose precarious membership in the nation would likewise be cast upon the archaic past in primordialist literary texts.

Yet "Bluffton" was writing before mass Irish immigration later in the 1830s. In this dystopian future, the emphasis is class more than race or ethnicity. Disavowing or ignoring these transient conflicts resulting from greed and materialism, the mounds' endurance symbolizes permanence in the midst of an American society defined by transience and impetuousness, silently rebuking the self-important settler nation that, unless it learns from the past, will destroy itself, even as the mounds persist.

4

Dwarf Epics and the Ancient Irish

That picture is a picture of freedom; the home of free men, the homes
of Christian families; the dignity of labor; the freedom of knowledge;
the inviolable sanctity of worship; the peace and smile of God. . . .
That vision of yours was not the mere dream of the prophet; it was a
prophecy inspired of God, and my children shall yet read your prophecy
fulfilled upon these teeming prairies.

—The Reverend Joseph Thompson, "Oration," 1856

At an 1856 abolitionist rally, the Reverend Joseph Thompson recited the final
stanzas of William Cullen Bryant's primordialist ode to the white Mound
Builders, "The Prairies," while Bryant himself awaited his turn on the dais,
before omitting the poem's fatalist ending.[1] Thompson's point is that Bryant's vision of an American paradise on the prairies stands in stark opposition to a southern vision of a national future featuring violence, chains, and
misery. As noted in chapter 3, images of the white Mound Builders were
increasingly contrived to model northern industrial images of the nation
moving forward. For Thompson and other abolitionists, only the northern
version of the nation, authenticated in the primordial past, could move the
nation into a civilized future. Yet that vision was covertly based on careful
processes of exclusion; Thompson's language referenced the nativism that
often shadowed abolition. Other sources were more explicit about how this
vision might be achieved, and how it might be threatened. In his 1835 sermon "A Plea for the West," Protestant minister Lyman Beecher had put a
finer point on it: "Catholic Europe is throwing swarm upon swarm upon
our shores. They come, also not undirected. There is evidently a supervision
abroad—and one here—by which they come, and set down together, in city
or country, as a Catholic body, are led or followed by a Catholic priesthood
who maintain over them in the land of strangers and unknown tongues an
ascendency as absolute as they are able to exert on Germany itself" (100).
Throughout the essay, Beecher elaborated on the fundamental incompatibility of democratic values and Catholic discipline.[2] While he does not

reference an explicitly primordialist fantasy such as Bryant's, his point is the same: only democratic values based in Protestant individualism, commercial capitalism, and republican values (based implicitly in primordial Gothic traditions) would allow the exceptional nation could fulfill its destiny. Implicitly, non-Protestant, non-Anglo-Saxon whites could only dilute and corrupt the trajectory established by Bryant's Mound Builders.

The trouble was that the antebellum WASP-based nation still needed both the participation of the slaveholding South and the demographic bulk provided by Catholic immigration from Ireland and from south and central Europe. Without them, it would have been impossible to fulfill the settler nationalist fantasy of a coherent nation that inhabited and controlled the continent as a whole, by the presumption of right of the Doctrine of Discovery. The Doctrine's moral codicil (that colonizers must better the colonized), for preachers like Thompson or Beecher, had been violated by both the material violence of slavery and the spiritual violence of Catholicism. In brief, how could they accommodate Southerners and Catholics in a protestant and industrialized nation? To that end, the northern elite advocated forms of cultural conformity intended to discipline otherwise white places (the South) and peoples (semiwhite Catholic immigrants), shifting them from the ranks of the colonizers to those of the colonized. Only after a process of subordination, "Americanization"—one not unlike that of Hector St. John de Crèvecoeur's Andrew the Hebridean (for whom the term was first used)—would the southern states and the Catholic immigrants be considered worthy members in the imperial nation governed by the North.[3] Obviously, each generated resistance.

To resist such subordination, the Irish and the "Southrons" turned to narratives of primordial Irish inhabition. Irish southerners and their sympathizers countered nativists like Beecher by defending difference, by insisting that the primordial Irish had performed the ideals of the settler nation. As aspirant settler colonialists, however, they still assumed that primordial presence justifies modern inhabition and Indian erasure. In doing so, they ask WASP nation to "expand"—as defined by Nell Irvin Painter—the peoples and places that counted as "white." They imagined a more diverse nation by insisting that intraracial difference with regard to ethnic, sectional, and regional difference could be accommodated. The first section of this chapter discusses how second-generation Irish immigrant William Gilmore Simms, to resist what he perceived as the colonization of the South, mined the Icelandic sagas to find tenth-century Irishmen in the Carolinas. The second section discusses how the Irish themselves, to defend their potential as republican citizens while retaining ethnic and religious identity, turned to Saint Brendan, a sixth-century ocean-crossing monk. In the end, the legends only expose and reaffirm the same colonialist anxieties they were designed to resist: Simms's Irishmen resemble the ex-white Welsh, and Brendan's monks foreshadow the transient imperial Vikings of the simultaneous Norse revival. Yet as antebellum thought experiments that contemplated diversity and difference, the two Irish primordialisms anticipate emergent conflicts over ethnicity, divergence, and immigration in the decades that followed.

Hvitramannaland eda Irland ed Mykla: Great Ireland, or Whiteman's Land

> The Southern States now stand exactly in the same position toward the Northern States that our ancestors did in the colonies towards Great Britain.
>
> —South Carolina's Secession Convention, 1860

Going back to the Articles of Confederation (1781–89), the problem of multiregional nationalism plagued American politics, as it has virtually every settler nation.[4] In the process of nation formation, ex–settler colonies either joined with or departed from the prospective confederation. Their decisions were based on the varying histories, populations, and expectations among their proposed partners in nationhood. Even after confederation, conflicts arose as one region or former colony often sought to model the nation after itself and relegate its neighbors to positions of subordination or marginality. In some cases, divergence related to differing imperial parents: Quebec was French, the Orange Free State adamantly Boer. Or it may be geographical: New Zealand opted out of the proposed nation of Australasia. Settler nations, in every case, were forced to confront intrinsic geographical and demographic divergences that, in turn, both threatened their own coherence and impeded their own ongoing colonization of both contiguous and overseas territories.[5]

To aid in the process of national stabilization, settler colonialist texts performed two kinds of cultural work: externally, they identify and celebrate a stable and knowable national authenticity: demographic union, cultural distinctiveness, and shared history so that outsiders know they are a nation and no longer a colony; internally, they work to erase or ignore markers of disunion: section, gender, class, ethnicity, or religion, so as to convince themselves. Such persistent obsessions call to mind Philip Deloria's notion of the "unassembleable" settler.[6] Transcending the more balanced concept of regionalism, and predating even political self-determination, the most immediate threat was sectionalism, the privileging of local over national loyalties and the identification of irreconcilable intersectional differences as to culture, economics, and politics. In the United States, from the Founders' compromise on the three-fifths clause, the incompatibility of North and South constantly shadowed prospects for stable and sustained nationhood. This affected the nation's colonization of the West as it redefined how new states would enter the Union: Which form of settler colonialism would be reproduced and so come to define the new states? The Missouri Compromise in 1820 resulted from internal conflicts over which version of itself to export into its colonies west of the Mississippi River: the industrial North or the agrarian South.[7]

Intersectional alienation reflects dueling modes and methods of creating and perpetuating the settler nation. While the South sought to expand its race-based model, the North favored more economic forms of self-replication. Susan-Mary Grant remarks, "From the start, it seemed clear that if the Union were to come apart, it would do so because of the essential differences between the industrial North and the plantation South" (25). Grant also notes that northern efforts to nationalize the South exacerbated interregional tensions: "Ultimately, the northern view of the American nation sought to be inclusive, but at a price. That price was the acceptance of a specifically northern outlook and ideology, and it was one the South proved reluctant to pay. . . . By identifying the North as a separate society that was not only different from but actively hostile to the South, southerners were able to create and sustain a coherent sense of their own uniquely southern identity" (20–21). The alienated southern identity evolved from regional to sectional to separatist between 1789 and 1860. Sectionalism, as a subset of nationalism, has a peculiar relationship with settler colonialism. Sectionalism might best be understood as a proto- or even counternationalism that endeavors to advance its own local colonialist adventures—such as the South's filibustering and annexation of Texas—even when they vary from national policy. At the same time, sectionalism impedes the nation's ability to colonize, as colonization requires a stable and singular metropolitan culture to be imposed on the lands and peoples over whom it would establish dominion.[8] Grant continues, "That the South came to be seen in this way derives directly from the process of American national construction in the antebellum period, a process that involved the construction of a distinct northern nationalism that became national but certainly did not start out that way" (35). Sectionalism, that is, represents a reaction against the attempted consolidation of a national culture that transforms regionalism—the hope for a horizontal arrangement of communities within the larger nation—into a vertical nationalism that, in turn, demands subordination, a form of imperialism that transcends the accident of geographical contiguity. For the antebellum southern sectionalist, the only outcomes were either southern nationalism—hobbling the colonization of the West as well as the nation's other nascent global endeavors—or colonial subordination, thus joining the colonized and abdicating the dignity of the colonizer.[9]

As was often the case, this fissure in the national culture was cast back upon the primordial past. As I explore in chapter 5, the South eventually settled on a Norman version of Norse culture as its defining primordial fantasy.[10] Before this, William Gilmore Simms contemplated an Irish model. Before southern regionalism transmuted to Confederate nationalism, Simms imagined a multisectional nation composed of equivalent regions that accommodated different traditions, economies, laws, and politics.[11] For him, the North's efforts at monopolizing the nation's culture—both domestically and through print culture—eroded the unity of the nation. This is reflected in his literary production. In his many novels before 1850, Simms sought to balance the northern appropriation of American history and imagery with an equivalent southern contribution to the nation and its settlement. Initially, the young Simms was fiercely nationalist. Jeffrey J. Rogers has charted Simms's transition from regionalist to sectionalist to Confederate Nationalist as beginning in South Carolina's Nullification Crisis in 1830. As a regionalist, "Speaking against this hostile sectionalism, Simms argued that, as in the past, both sections, each in its own distinctive way, contributed to the greatness of the Union" (31). As a newspaper editor, he rejected Nullification (and faced an angry mob for doing so) as overly sectional yet defended states' rights, a functional regionalism. Yet his transition to sectionalism began soon thereafter. In 1842, Simms responded to James Fenimore Cooper's attempted northernization of the nation as a "slander upon the country at large": "Mr. Cooper committed the precise error which is so much the error of British travellers among us, that of confounding the commercial metropolis the country. We protest, again and again, against this false assumption the city of New York is to be taken as a fair example of the character of the United States. . . . He is apt to generalize too much from small beginnings. . . . That was published as 'Notions of the Americans.' It is very evident that the work should have been called 'Notions of the New Yorkers and New Englanders'" (Views, 1:232, 234).[12] This imbalance is supported in current scholarship. Writing of the need to "nationalize" the South, Jennifer Rae Greeson comments: "Taking the new political borders of the United States as a given, a new national culture had to explain not only how that which was within those borders was different from the rest of the world, but also how that which was within the borders was a homogeneous whole, a unit, a union" (109). Along the same lines, Simms questioned westward expansion for its threat to republican values, and he resisted funding the internal improvements needed for such efforts, as expansion upset the inter-regional balance of the nation and served northern interests at the expense of the South.[13]

For the loyal "Southron" (Simms's term), the choices would become the Scylla of northern nationalism, or the Charybdis of southern sectionalism.[14] While the South in general and Simms in particular would choose the latter by 1860, in the 1840s he sought a pragmatic middle ground. However, settler colonialism requires a singular national culture for its ideology of self-replication and sovereignty. Ultimately, Simms's fantasy was untenable: sectionalism intensified, and war violently reunified the nation. These contradictory presences are reflected in Simms's attempts to excavate a white primordial South. Yet in the early 1840s, when Simms became aware of the possibility of a southern primordialist heritage, he hoped to check the North's attempted usurpation of national identity in the same source they used to claim a dominant Norse inheritance: the Icelandic sagas. To begin, his source text's publication history ironically mirrors the inter-regional asymmetry he meant to resist: the legend of Irish settlement in the archaic South is an adjunct to the larger and longer Norse primordialism claimed by New England for the North. As is discussed in chapter 5 below, the Norse primordial episode began with Carl Christian Rafn's popular translation of the Icelandic sagas in 1837 and Irish historian Ludlow North Beamish's translation of Rafn in 1838. The sagas' affirmation of the Norse exploration of the coast of New England inspired northern writers to claim the Norse and their primordial presence as a national inheritance. Almost immediately, Henry Wadsworth Longfellow and John Greenleaf Whittier, in particular, used the sagas to concretize a Teutonic legacy for white Americans, one based in New England and expanding from that base. This intensified, for Simms, the North's overt efforts to monopolize the nation. Part of this account reveals the anxiety lurking beneath settler primordialist fantasies: the American sections of the sagas themselves are relatively minor, the story of a failed colony. Yet northern antiquarians and other literati celebrated those sections as foundational and affirming, demonstrating their own colonial cringe.

In a long review essay first published in the southern literary magazine *Magnolia* in 1841, Simms focused on the sagas' references to an *older* southern, pre-Norse claim on primordial whiteness. Simms dwells on two relatively minor episodes—as had Beamish—that featured an already established Irish colony in the South that bespoke an Irish crossing perhaps centuries prior to those of Leif Ericson and his Vikings in 1000 CE.[15] The sagas of Ari Marson and Bjorn Asbrandson, tenth-century Norsemen blown off course during voyages to Vinland who ended up among Irishmen in, as Simms lifts the phrase from Beamish's translation, "Hvitramannaland eda Irland ed Mykla; Great Ireland, or Whiteman's Land," a place identified as coastal Carolina, attracted Simms's interest. Simms claimed those Irishmen and their settlements for the South, asserting for the South a less rigid, less Teutonic, legacy that, he hoped, could coexist alongside Norse-based New England.

However, despite Simms's best intentions, the sagas show the southern Irishmen as degenerated to semisavagery, though decidedly not one identified with becoming Indian. Unlike the Welsh Indians and the lost tribes, the Irish retain value in raced nineteenth-century print culture strictly because, as whites, they crossed the ocean and maintained, for at least a while, a settlement comparable to the Norse in the North. Despite Simms's calls for fellow Southrons to use the adventures of these forebears to authenticate the region as a subnational yet still sovereign cultural entity, the source material was too ephemeral, and his call became a dead letter. Nonetheless, Simms's effort to imagine an Irish South reflects the entanglement of the settler nation in the global politics of imperial self-creation. Annette Kolodny studies how other Irish historians likewise cherry-picked the sagas in the name Irish cultural nationalism: "Beamish also had a political message for those same readers. Thus his goal was to rehabilitate 'a neglected of portion of Irish history' and, with that, the reputation of Ireland itself" (*In Search of First Contact*, 125). As he was primarily concerned with creating a primordialist legacy for Irish nationalism in the face of British colonialism, Beamish edited Rafn to emphasize a specifically Irish distinctiveness.

Along the same lines, Simms mined some fairly obscure materials to authenticate southern difference. Cognizant of the iconography of Columbus's legacy as a nationally binding narrative, Simms adds that the southern sagas never "lessen the merits of Columbus, nor do we refer to it for this purpose, but simply to show a frequent concurrence of tradition, in a matter the clues to which must depend in a great degree upon the sincerity and boldness with which the investigation is pursued" (*Views*, 2:84). Yet like most primordialists Simms frequently diminished Columbus's achievement, even referring repeatedly to his purported visit to Iceland in 1477, where he supposedly learned of Vinland.[16] Simms in 1841 is a thoroughgoing settler nationalist, more regionalist than sectionalist; he just wants his region and his ancestors to be among the colonizers, not the colonized. In fact, Simms concludes his review of Rafn by betraying an ultimate loyalty to race rather than region to mark himself as ultimately more settler colonialist than sectionalist. In a rather lengthy commentary on pre-Columbian whites and the failure of Indians to create a meaningful history, Simms identifies the unlikeliness of "our" Indians creating the mounds, rephrasing the finding of mound historian Caleb Atwater.[17] Contrasting the response of the Irish to British conquest with that of the Indians by the whites more generally, Simms writes:

> The genius of an oppressed people who had once been civilized and distin-
> guished is apt to become more pure, vivid, and even energetic in the midst of
> bonds than it ever proved itself in the day of its conscious freedom.... As the
> genius of the individual man becomes refined by trial, and grows at length
> into a noble and religious gravity, so that of a people, subdued to humiliation
> by a sense of inferiority, chastened by its overthrow and the restraints of its
> new condition, acquires strength for future greatness in the very necessity of
> endurance, to which it yields passively and without a struggle. (2:128)

This passage defends his fellow Irishmen as simply "subdued" and their culture dormant, as opposed to the Indian, who had never developed, even during its age of "conscious freedom" prior to contact. Thus the Irish and Southrons deserve the full privileges of whiteness because they had once been free and civilized. For Simms, the Indians had been neither: "They exhibited no proofs of emerging, remote or recent, from a state of bondage; but were a wild, untamed, and seemingly, untameable race, to whom the arts of civilization were wholly unfamiliar" (2:129–30). By this logic, then, only "whites" could have built the mounds and founded Mesoamerican civilizations.[18] While his readings of the sagas appeal to a specifically southern primordial distinction, in the end, Simms was mostly concerned with race and nation, especially as they provided cover for the behavior of the archaic southern Irish in the sagas.

Building from Rafn's translation, Simms's version of Marson's saga begins in Vinland when the Norseman Bjarni Karlsefne captures two Skraeling (Indian) boys who describe a region Simms recognized as the Chesapeake and Albemarle areas. The boys describe their neighbors: "Beyond them, on the other side of a great strait, just opposite their country, they described the people as being white, as wearing white garments carrying flags upon poles and shouting loudly. This description recalls to the Northmen a tradition of their own people; and they came to the conclusion that the country just described must be one of which they had frequently heard before which they called Hvitramannaland eta Irland ed Mykla, that is, 'White Man's Land'"

(*Views*, 2:63). Starting in the eighth century CE, Vikings had been raiding and, at times, ruling Ireland, constructing Dublin under the reign of Ivar the Boneless in the ninth century.[19] As such, their familiarity with Ireland is not unreasonable, nor would be Irish suspicion of Norse invaders. Venturing south to investigate, Karlsefne finds Marson, and Simms localizes the story: "The earliest tradition in regard to White Man's Land is found in the Landnamabok, AD 982. It appears that Ari Marson, one of the fearless adventurers of the North Seas, was driven by a tempest to a country lying west of Vinland the Good and vi (or xi or xvi) days sailing west from Ireland. This region, according to Professor Rafn, must be the tract of country which is now occupied by the states of Carolina and Georgia." Here, Marson had found the people described by Skraeling boys: "habited in white, carrying banners and speaking a dialect resembling the Irish and such as he could understand. Once in custody, the people of this region would not suffer Ari Marson to leave. They kept him, christened him, wived him, and made a chief of him" (2:63–64). Karlsefne is eventually allowed to return Marson to Iceland, and some of his descendants became the sagas' poets themselves. As to the origins of these primordial Irishmen, the sagas and Simms refuse to speculate in any specific way. More to the point, they had survived Indian hostilities, retained their Christianity, and still spoke Irish. Moreover, these Irishmen assimilate Marson, rather than being assimilated by him, demonstrating the cultural steadfastness intrinsic to colonizers, not the colonized. In Simms's allegory, a northerner is welcomed, treated well, and allowed to leave, implying a model of neighborliness based in Christian values. The Marson saga allows Simms to conjecture multiregional and multiethnic white inclusiveness but without extending to multiracialism, as the same courtesy had not been extended to Indians.

In Asbrandson's more extended saga, however, this model fails. Asbrandson is described as having arrived in Greater Ireland soon after Karlsefne took Marson home. Simms begins Bjorn's story with romantic and courtly misadventures in Norway that result, around 1006 CE, in exile. Before leaving, Bjorn was a legendary warrior and poet, and his disappearance the subject of wonder and legend: "He was a bard and a warrior, a great sea-captain, a man of warm passions and vigorous frame. These qualities rendered him rash and venturous, and, while yet very young, he had also provoked numerous enemies. . . . His blood sometimes triumphed over his morality" (2:65). This model of romantic chivalry would find fuller expression in the Norman legacy a decade later. Living in an antebellum Charleston, South Carolina, where duels often resolved affairs of honor among the creole elite, Simms recognized Bjorn as different from the otherwise stern

Norsemen embraced elsewhere in the sagas.[20] Escaping a jealous husband, Bjorn leaves Denmark in a ship sailing west and is lost. Thirty years later, blown off course, the Norse merchant Gudleif Gudlaugson and his crew land in a strange place. Simms thus rephrases and italicizes Rafn: "They found there a good harbor, and when they had been a short time on the shore, came people to them. They knew none of the people, *but it rather appeared to them they spoke Irish*. Soon came to them so great a number that it made up many hundreds. These men fell upon them and bound them and drove them up into the country" (2:70). Unlike Marson and Asbrandson, these Norsemen arrive in a group and, as such, represent a more organized threat. Soon they are brought before a large council and learn the danger of their situation. Perhaps given the recent desertion of Marson, the Irish are unrelentingly hostile:

> The Icelanders *understood enough of the language in which their captors discussed their fate to discover that some were for putting them to death, others for distributing them and subjecting them to slavery*. But whilst this matter was yet pending, they beheld where rode a large and dignified man who was much in years and whose hair was white. To this old man a very marked deference is paid by the people of the country. He is received with many outward shows of homage, and the question, touching the fate of the captives is, in some degree, submitted to his decision. This old man spoke to the Icelanders in the Northern tongue. (2:75; emphasis in original)

Bjorn, like Marson, has become a chief among the American Irish. He tells his countrymen who he is, and they remember his tale. Moreover, while he has become a chief among the Irish, he is a minor one, and he tells his fellow Norsemen to trust their fate to him, before his violent and xenophobic superiors arrive. The limits of his authority are soon manifested: "The people of the country become impatient, and suspicious of a conference between the strangers conducted in an unknown dialect. They demand an instant decision upon their fate; and the venerable chief finds it his policy to comply with their demands" (2:75). Bjorn quickly empanels a twelve-man jury. This causes Simms to recognize, in a footnote, the Nordic origins of this democratic institution usually claimed by Anglo-Saxonists.[21] Bjorn returns the verdict: "I have talked with the people of the country about your business and they have left the matter to me; and I give ye leave to depart whither ye will. Yet remove you must immediately from hence; let not the lateness of the summer discourage ye. The people here are not to be trusted—are hard to manage; and they think, moreover, that their laws have been broken to their injury by your coming. . . . They would show little mercy to a stranger"

(2:76). Bjorn sends mementoes to his lover and son but stays in White Man's Land, warning the others not to disclose his location. Yet this ending reflects a telling ambiguity. On one level, cognizant of the growing sectionalism in his city and in the more antagonistic work of colleagues such as Nathaniel Beverly Tucker, Simms may have paraphrased Bjorn's saga to warn off overly aggressive northern nationalists.[22] Staying true to his source material, Simms seems to have run up against an uncomfortable truth: these Irish, like Griffiths's Welsh, seem to be reverting to savagery. Many of his white frontiersmen, in *Richard Hurdis* (1838) or *Border Beagles* (1840), likewise demonstrate the racially metamorphic effect of frontier life in their savage tendencies.

The inchoate nature of this story, ironically, was reflected in Simms's own somewhat confusing comments on it. After his review, Simms calls for a literature based in Greater Ireland:

> In the adventures of Bjorn Asbrandson, the hero of Breidavik, the national poet may one day find the substance of a dwarf epic, quite as happy as the border tales of Scott. . . . From the very volume before us [Beamish]—a bald abridgment—fifty spirited ballads might be manufactured with ease; and a judicious artist might make a most romantic tale of the colony of Green Erin upon the shores of Carolina and Georgia; showing how . . . the wandering Irishmen pitched their tents for good; how they built cities; . . . how suddenly, the fierce red men of the Southwest came down upon them in howling thousands, captured their women, slaughtered their men, and drove them to their fortresses; how they fought to the last and perished to a man. (2:100)

Although the sagas bear no evidence of any "fierce red men," Simms deploys a settler colonialist trope to establish a more conventional sympathetic narrative of race-based settler victimhood. In another essay, Simms justifies such extrapolation: "Considered with reference to its intrinsic uses, the bald history of a nation, by itself, would be of very little importance to mankind. . . . Hence it is the artist only who is the true historian. It is he who gives shape to the unknown fact,—who yields relation to the scattered fragments—who writes the parts in coherent dependency, and endows, with life and action, the otherwise motionless automata of history" (*Views*, 1:25).[23] In those unwritten "dwarf epic[s]" and ballads, Simms foresees that intraracial and interregional hostilities could have most likely vanished by offsetting each other, balancing and equalizing North and South in their common mission to colonize the continent. Yet these books were never written, even by Simms himself. Throughout his long and prolific career, he never returned to the primordial Irish. When he did turn to non-Anglo historical fiction set in the South, he disinterred the Spanish settlements along the Carolina coast in *The Cassique of Kiaweh* (1859). Nonetheless, in 1841, he still held that southern writers should do for their Irish as Longfellow and Whittier would for their Norsemen: "The Irish settlers, like the merchant Northmen, might have been driven by stress of weather from their course, and might have felt compensated in the loss of ships by finding a new and fertile country. If we have proofs of Irish adventure and civilization in the bells, hooks, and crosiers in Iceland in the tenth century, why should not the Carolinas and Georgia have been vouchsafed the symbol of the cross from the hands of the wandering [savages] at the same period the Norsemen were driven by a northeast storm across the vacant waste of the Atlantic?" (*Views*, 2:87). By equating northern and southern primordialisms, Simms hoped to establish a balanced yet diverse multiregional primordial paradigm for national unity, a leveling directly at odds with the uniformity demanded by the hierarchies of romantic and settler nationalisms.

As the antebellum era progressed, Simms increasingly resisted northern efforts to subordinate—or, as Greeson affirms, to "colonize"—the South. He addressed this theme explicitly in *Southward Ho!*[24] There, an "Alabamian" offers an extended diatribe on "Yankee" violence, beginning with the Pequot War and extending through violence against the Quakers and other exogenous whites, including the Irish. Clearly, the South is next on this trajectory of dominion: "Our Yankee brethren are not the people to suffer their neighbors to be long at peace, or to be themselves at peace. . . . What was to be done with the devouring appetite of these rabid wretches, who so well discriminated always as to seek their victims to peril their own skins" (*Views*, 2:250–51). "Yankee" dominion, to Simms, was a quest for national homogenization, or interregional nationalization, based in violence, representational or, soon, actual. Southrons seem to be next on the list to be colonized. Simms's Greater Ireland has never been as well known as other primordial traditions, perhaps because, like Simms himself, much of southern culture was suppressed after the Civil War.[25] After the war, as a settler nation supplementing continental conquest with global imperialism, the North continued to eradicate internal distractions on its path to overseas dominion.[26] To ground that unity in primordialist precedent, the nervous settler nation still aspired to romantic nationalism's vision of a uniform and unified national identity, and so the Norse emerged as the final and most enduring primordialist fantasy in American culture. Reflecting this, Greater Ireland slipped into obscurity, as is demonstrated in its literary re-creation: in *The Vinland Champions* (1904), Ottilie Liljencrantz depicts young Norse heroes building a boat to trade with the Irish to the south. However, the

boat is destroyed, the Irish remain offstage, and the only region worthy of
a primordial past is the North, the basis for the imperial nation. Having no
primordial past to claim as a modern place in the New World, then, the Irish
would also employ a less regional strategy to prove their whiteness in the
Anglo-Saxonized settler nation by refuting Beecher's accusations of their
feminizing obedience.

This Pleasant Land Again Shall Reappear: Saint Brendan's Manifest Destiny

Every hour sees us elbowed out of some employment to make room for
some newly-arrived emigrant from the Emerald Isle, whose hunger and
color entitle him to special favor. These white men are becoming house-
servants, cooks, stewards, waiters and flunkies.... If they cannot rise to
the dignity of white men, they show they can fall to the degradation of
black men.

—Frederick Douglass, 1853

Writing in 1853, Frederick Douglass observed that the thousands of Irish who
arrived in the wake of the potato blight of the 1840s had unfair advantage
over the free African American population in the market for unskilled labor
in the industrial north. To him, the Irish willingly forgo the racial dignity
for which he and his fellows were fighting so hard and accept lives of spiritual, political, and economic subordination. The paradoxes of Douglass's
statement (qtd. in Ignatiev, 111) reveal the peculiar place of the Irish in the
settler nation's racial hierarchy. At once, they are "white" but simultaneously
"cannot rise to the dignity of white men." Their white "Color" gives the Irish
their first advantage, but one they willingly forgo by continuing habits of sub-
mission learned under both British and papal authorities. For doing so, the
Irish are not promising potential republican citizens, just as Beecher feared.

Douglass's statement, moreover, is typical in its pairing of African
Americans and Irish as outsiders looking in on the privileges of fully white
national membership. As I have argued elsewhere, the Irish occupied a peripheral place in the racial calculus of settler colonies, one acknowledged
by indigenous writers.[27] However, not all immigrants from Ireland counted
as "Irish": those from Northern Ireland and the adjacent counties had been
arriving en masse since 1750 but had been designated as "Scots-Irish" and
therefore fully white.[28] However, Irish from the southern counties enjoyed
no such privileging and were designated as, at best, semi- or subwhite, to

be marginalized with more visibly nonwhite races. As early as 1829, Ralph Waldo Emerson chimed in, "I think it cannot be maintained by any candid person that the African race have ever occupied or do promise to occupy any very high place in the human family. . . . The Irish cannot; the American Indian cannot; the Chinese cannot. Before the energy of the Caucasian race all the other races have quailed and done obeisance" (qtd. in Painter, 111). At the other end of the antebellum era, in 1861, an unsigned editorial in the *Atlantic* observed, "All the qualities which go to make a republican, in the true sense of the term, are wanting in the Irish nature" (qtd. in Jacobson, *Whiteness*, 48). Clearly, in the mid-nineteenth century, white skin did not guarantee the privileges of whiteness.

Yet the nation needed the Irish, and it needed them to be white, or nearly so, for their labor, demographic heft, and potential for mediating their relations with the more exotic and alien darker races. Industrialism and imperialism needed able bodies, unskilled labor, and men able to do the labor increasingly "beneath" the elite race's status. Compromises were sought. In 1835, James Kirke Paulding addressed immigration: "I would receive them with hospitality—most especially the children of Brave Old Ireland, who become good republicans the moment they set foot on our soil—and admit them, if not a political, at least to a social equality. . . . For a time they should be content with the protection of a just and beneficent government without attempting to usurp a share in its administration" (150, 152). Despite his claim that they might someday become "republican," Paulding views citizenship as earned rather than innate or inalienable. His idea of semicitizenship reflects the semiwhiteness of non-Gothic "white" populations. His pronouns—"our" and "them"—establish that essential distancing. This had been reflected in literary representations of the Irish in early republic writing. Hugh Henry Brackenridge's comic Teague O'Riordan in *Modern Chivalry* (1792–1815) or Charles Brockden Brown's dangerously unstable Clithero Edny in *Edgar Huntly* (1799) reflect the same ambivalence concerning the potential for the Irish to become Americans.[29]

Yet despite their centuries under the British colonial yoke, as Noel Ignatiev has argued, the Irish proved unsympathetic to the causes of their new home's enslavement of African Americans and dispossession of Indians. In fact, by self-identifying as white—as opposed to the nonwhiteness of blacks and Indians—they aspired to be counted among the colonizers rather than the colonized, especially through their participation in the Mexican-American War, an overtly settler colonialist aggression.[30] While these efforts made them something other than red or black, they did not necessarily make them white. In 1852, Emerson revisited the subject: "The worst of charity is, that the lives you are asked to preserve are not worth preserving. The calamity is the masses. I do not wish any mass at all, but honest men only, lovely & sweet & accomplished women only; and no shovel-backed Irish, & no Five-Points, Saint Gileses, or drunken crew" (qtd. in Painter, 139–40). Emerson's reiteration of the nativist tropes of Celtic savagery and Catholic ignorance and drunkenness, echoing his friend Beecher, suggests that the moral and military sacrifices made by the Irish in the Mexican War had gone for naught. They were still exogenous others based on their primordial racial identity; as Nell Irvin Painter notes, "As Celts, however, the poor Irish would also be judged racially different enough to be oppressed, ugly enough to be compared to apes, and poor enough to be paired with black people" (133). This also problematized the racial politics of settler colonialism as settlers sought to bring other brown and black peoples under their imperial sway both at home and abroad.

The partial inclusion of the Irish destabilizes settler culture through its introduction of intraracial multiethnicity, destabilizing the binary identification of whites as colonizers and nonwhites as colonized. Lorenzo Veracini notes, "All settler projects are foundationally premised on fantasies of ultimately 'cleansing' the settler body politic of its (indigenous and exogenous) Others" (*Settler Colonialism*, 33). As primordial Celts, as well as Catholics, the Irish were exogenous others. The failure to cleanse them from the Anglo settler nation, demographically or ethnically, foreshadows the ultimate inability of the settler nation to complete the project of demographic homogenization, a troubling sign of its unassembleability, to recall Deloria. Jenny Franchot suggests that Beecher's and Emerson's nativism belies an even deeper insecurity: "An unintended irony of this reductive process was its eventual disintegrative impact, for the attack on Roman Catholicism, in its enumeration of Rome's suspicious charms, often led to an uncomfortable recognition of the spiritual deficiencies and psychological pressures of Protestant culture" (137). Settler nativism is born not from an extrinsic fear of Irishness or Catholicism but rather from the settler culture's intrinsic awareness of its own colonial inadequacy, the disavowed but still internalized recognition of the illegitimacy of the secondhand settler nation.

Yet nation making still required Irish bodies to do the work that commodified black bodies could not be put at risk to do and that Anglos would not. In response, racial nationalists imagined a vertical ranking of acceptable exogenous ethnicities with the Anglo-Saxon ascendant. To claim at least a place above African Americans on this scale, Irish Catholics had to prove they possessed the "republican" qualities they had been accused of lacking. This section addresses how a primordial Celtic legend based in ethnicity (as opposed to Simms's based on region) was mobilized to sanitize the redefinition and empowering of the diasporic Irish as "white." While such efforts seem to challenge colonialist ideology, in fact this primordialist mythmaking only affirmed it by joining the Irish to the settler nation without disrupting its racial strata. Ironically, subordinating themselves to characteristically American traits enacted the obedience Beecher viewed as antirepublican: Irish efforts at national membership accede to the dominance and righteousness of the colonialist Anglo-Protestant hierarchy. Simultaneously, however, intraracial diversity is pondered in ways that will ultimately force the settler nation to contemplate expanded versions of whiteness. This began with an old legend repurposed to make Celts seem more Anglo-Saxon, but without forgoing Celtic pride or Catholic faith. During the 1840s, the primordial fantasy of Saint Brendan and his sixth-century sojourn in America both asserted Irish republican manhood intended to compel the settler nation to enlarge its concept of whiteness to include and embrace the Irish, a venture that met with mixed results.[31]

In the 1840s, in the midst of the mass migration catalyzed by the famine, Irish poet Denis MacCarthy published "The Voyage of St. Brendan" in the *Dublin Review*, a revisioning of the old, nearly lost legend.[32] MacCarthy republished the poem in his collection *Ballads, Poems, and Lyrics, Original and Translated* in Dublin in 1850, copies of which found their way across the Atlantic to be scurrilously republished. In the poem, MacCarthy affirms both the full whiteness and the independence of mind required for republican citizenship for the Irish by rejecting the essentialist stereotypes of drunkenness, obedience, violence, and intellectual subordination to Catholic orthodoxy and papal infallibility, the usual disqualifiers.[33] Breaking from older versions of the story, MacCarthy's poem revises the narrative to make the ancient Irish more like contemporary Americans, domesticating their otherness for an American readership. MacCarthy's invention mostly occurs when Brendan and his Monks land in America and travel as far as the headwaters of the Ohio River only to be turned back by an angel urging patience, enacting a fantasy of primordial whiteness to establish the destined presence for the Irish in the manifestly destined nation.

Since the sixteenth century, Brendan and his voyage had been mostly considered a Catholic odyssey, an allegory of a saint's faith and fortitude, with little speculation that the wondrous lands he visited may have been in North America. As the Counter-Reformation downplayed miracles and wonders, stories such as Brendan's were deemed superstitious

embarrassments, and the legend was repurposed as a transatlantic crossing. As romanticism reintroduced and reauthorized more speculative
narratives, beginning with a brief reference in Pierre Mallet's *Northern
Antiquities* (1770), Brendan's momentum began to grow. As it did, so did
skepticism of its veracity and meaning. In 1828, Washington Irving, having examined Brendan manuscripts in Spain and France chimed in: "As the
populace, however, reluctantly give up anything that partakes of the marvelous and the mysterious, as the same atmospherical phenomena which
first gave birth to the illusion may still continue, it is not improbable that
a belief in the island of St. Brendan may still exist among the ignorant and
the credulous . . . and that they at times behold its fairy mountains rising
above the distant horizon of the Atlantic" (12:305–6). As such, prior to the
famine, the legend of Saint Brendan was mostly derided as just one more
antiquarian legend with no "problem orientation," and thus a mere curiosity with no power to impact more recent conversations. However, the primordialist impulse in a settler nation, as well as in early nationalist Ireland
beginning in the late eighteenth century, shared a need to "invent a tradition" to validate claims to modern nationhood rooted in a distinctly unified
and unifying primordial past. Brendan was repositioned to reclaim, retro-
actively, the lost place of the Irish as both worthy inhabitants of their own
nation, and, as expatriate Americans, worthy members of the settler nation.
Interest in Brendan culminated in the publication of Denis O'Donoghue's
Brendaniana (1890), a comprehensive history, retelling, and bibliography
that went through a number of Irish and American editions.[34]

MacCarthy, a popular Irish poet, engaged the Brendan legend, setting
off a series of retellings and reformulations that moved the ancient priest
from a picturesque bit of trivia, as he had been for Irving, to a meaningful
hero and leader. His adventures legitimize the Irish role in the nation's present and future on account of its reimagining of a primordial past that shared
and complemented the dreams of the Anglo-Saxon nation. The primordial
Brendan was needed, primarily, to establish Irish whiteness, for both the
Irish themselves and for the growing settler nation. To do so, he was reinvented not as ethnically Irish or slavishly Catholic but rather as a hero
more aligned with classical than medieval or Celtic standards—white by
skin color, rational in thought, and masculine in deed. As described in blank
verse iambic pentameter—the form selected by neoclassicists to translate
epics in the nineteenth century—MacCarthy's literate, sober, and rational
Brendan matched ideals of republican leadership and manhood by embodying models of classical rather than Celtic leadership.[35] This retelling was not

wholly unfounded: prior to the Viking invasion in the ninth century, Ireland was the last resort of post-Roman culture. Thomas Cahill observes in *How the Irish Saved Civilization* (1995): "Ireland, a little island at the edge of Europe that has known neither Renaissance nor Enlightenment—in some ways, a Third World country . . . had one moment of unblemished glory. For, as the Roman Empire fell, as all through Europe matted, unwashed barbarians descended on the Roman cities, looting artifacts and burning books, the Irish, who were just learning to read and write, took up the great labor of copying all Western literature—everything they could lay their hands on" (3). Cahill's equation of Ireland with sites of global imperialism—the "Third World"—establishes the historic place of the Irish among the colonized, despite the whiteness of their skin. However, the monks were doing more than scrivening: they were building schools for boys and girls and actively engaging and incorporating leftover Celtic and Druidic traditions. Had their representation not been hijacked by centuries of British dominion and the accompanying misrepresentations, they might have been remembered as enacting the protorepublican values esteemed by white Americans and, as such, may have been fodder for narratives of inclusion in the settler nation.

Written at the height of Irish emigration, MacCarthy's poem becomes a distinctively American primordial fantasy, or at least the poet carefully reconstructed the legend to make it so. Like much of the poetry of primordiality, MacCarthy's was designed for public performance, and so it included extensive notes that fill out the narrative and guide untrained readers toward prefabricated interpretations. He begins with a headnote establishing the story's significance and the legitimacy of his sixteenth-century sources: "[That] the legend is overlaid, almost buried, beneath the weight of fable must be admitted; but that its two principal incidents—namely the voyage and the discovery—are facts, will scarcely now be denied by anyone who is aware of the strongly corroborative evidence on the subject" (91). MacCarthy then summarizes the narrative, freeing the poem itself to recreate his literary re-creation of a limited first-person voice through which Brendan himself narrates the story. In MacCarthy's hands, the story runs thus: growing up in sixth-century Ireland, Brendan heard legends of a western land, undertook the voyage, landed in Virginia, and traveled west to the Ohio River, where he was told by a "noble figure" to return to the coast, that valley having been destined for later explorers. He returns to Virginia, spends seven years building and proselytizing among the Indians, and returns to Ireland to tell his story and then retire. MacCarthy's mention of the possibility of pre-Brendan Irish crossings further burnishes claims on a deep Gaelic claim on North America.[36] Like Simms and the Irish interpreter of the sagas, North Ludlow Beamish, MacCarthy cherry-picks the legend to make it seem less like a fable and more like, as he notes, a historical romance in the mode of Sir Walter Scott. Once the readers know the plot, its real subject becomes Brendan's reconstructed character and virtues. The narrative voice MacCarthy establishes for Brendan belongs to a masculine republican leader who personifies the autonomy and reasonableness key to the legitimization of Irish character and Catholic individuality. The frame describes Brendan recalling his adventures to Saint Ita, his foster mother, after his return. She represents a model of feminine domesticity in opposition to the masculine world of monks sailing the Atlantic, establishing a sympathetic likeness familiar to MacCarthy's proto-Victorian transatlantic readership. Her presence establishes a normalizing link to the republican familial social model, ones Catholic monks were thought to have rejected.[37] Through her, he becomes a good son and a moral patriarch, if not a father. Brendan next recounts the Edenic myth of America, more familiar to readers of Rousseau and the other philosophers of settler colonialism:[38]

> Who but to thee my mother should be told
> Of all the wonders I have seen afar
> Islands so green, and suns of brighter gold,
> Than this dear land, or yonder blazing star—
> Of hills that bear fruit trees on their tops,
> And seas that dimple with eternal smiles,
> Of airs from heaven that fan the golden crops. (873–74)

Such passages, in more allegorical versions of the legend, compelled earlier scholars to consider Brendan's tale mere religious allegory, as had Irving. However, MacCarthy's version avoids all such allusions. For example, while traditional sources include two Easters celebrated on the back of a whale, MacCarthy's excision of such incredulities, and his grounding of the tale in simple conversation, reflects his effort to make the story do the cultural work of making the Irish more, not less, other to the practically minded Americans, skeptical as they were of Catholic mysticism. MacCarthy then affirms the manhood of the monks, at a time when anti-Catholic activists often depicted monks and priests as effeminate and homosexual, or as the rapists of children and nuns, softened and corrupted by ecclesiastical privilege. MacCarthy's response:

I grew to manhood on the western wave,
Among the mighty mountains on the shore;
My bed the rock within some natural cave,
My food, whatever the seas or seasons bore. (74)

Brendan becomes a pioneer, an explorer, enduring the privations of adventure and becoming hardened by them, unlike the soft, bookish priests of nativist fearmongering. Gazing west, then, Brendan dreamed of "Some clime where man unknowing and unknown / For God's refreshing word still grasps and faints . . . / Where Nature's love the sweat of labour spares / Nor turns to usury the wealth it lends" (76). Typical of primordialist imagery, the Western Hemisphere awaits in prehistory, and history arrives with the whites: the American tabula rasa represents a chance for primordial whites, often refugees from Old World oppression, just as Americans considered themselves and their ancestors, to begin their history again. MacCarthy then equates the Irish with the Americans through their mutual escape from British subordination—erasing centuries-long "usury." As Brendan contemplates sailing west, he is visited in a dream:

But angels came and whispered as I dreamt
"This is no phantom of a frenzied brain—
God shows this land from time to time to tempt
Some daring mariner across the main
By thee the mighty venture must be made." (77)

Brendan is a man, not just a monk, and his mission becomes exploration and liberation, mirroring American imperial aspirations, a new empire in which the immigrant Irish would be among the colonizers, not the colonized. As perhaps the ur-settler, Brendan paradoxically both disavows the British model of imperial behavior *and* mimics it in his visionary occupation of America. This cognitive dissonance—the refusal to equate the displacement of the Indians with the historical subordination of the Irish—demonstrates how efforts to Americanize the Irish were designed to transform them from refugees to settlers without changing the essential racial calculus of colonialism.

As they set sail, they see in the clear water the ruins of an ancient, sunken city. One monk tells a story, whose plot resembles Henry Wadsworth Longfellow's "The Skeleton in Armor," of a doomed Old World couple escaping to the New World. For Longfellow, it was Norsemen to New England; for MacCarthy, the Irish to Hy-Brassail, a western land of Irish myth.[39] Next,

American birds come to greet the monks: "I left the brothers wondering and amazed / Thinking that the choir of heaven was near" (101). When they land, they find paradise:

> There may not be rage of frost, nor sleet nor rain,
> Injure the smallest and most delicate flower
> Nor fall of hail would the fair, healthful plain
> Nor the warm weather, nor dark mountain caves
> Nothing deformed upon its bosom lies— (104)

Yet the monks, like American colonists themselves more than a millennium later, still gaze west and soon depart in that direction:

> Such was the land for man's enjoyment made
> When from this troubled life his soul doth wend;
> Such was the land through which entranced we strayed
> For fifteen days, nor reached its bound nor end. (106)

Brendan then describes a journey of privation and endurance familiar to readers in the 1840s as typical of the narratives of western exploration from Lewis and Clark and Zebulon Pike up through more recent sources such as Francis Parkman or Nathaniel Wyeth.[40] Brendan's monks, that is, are masculine and strong, undertaking and overcoming the same physical challenges offered by the frontier to Anglo-Americans at the time of MacCarthy's writing.

However, MacCarthy, building from an obscure reference in only one of the many medieval Brendan manuscripts, brings the story to a climax when the monks are stopped at the Ohio River, "whose bright waves flowed from east to west." Here, an angel appears, promising the West to the future white nation the Irish mean to join:

> We went to cross the placid tide
> When Lo! An angel on our vision broke
> Clothed in white upon the further side,
> He stood majestic, and thus sweetly spoke—
> "Father return, thy mission here is over;
> God who did call thee here now bids thee go,
> Return in peace to thy native shore
> And tell the mighty secrets thou dost know.
> In after years in God's own fitting time
> This pleasant land again shall reappear

And other men shall preach the truths sublime
To the benighted people dwelling there
But ere that hour this land shall all be made
For mortal man, a fitting natural home." (106)

Twelve hundred years later, the first whites to preach in the Ohio Valley were, like Brendan, Catholic priests: the Jesuit French. Moreover, Indians, "benighted people," occupy their "natural home" as they wait in stasis for history to begin when the white Christians return, when God decides the time is right for the bearers of meaningful history to enter the valley. As Brendan returns eastward, the valley remains pristine, "natural." The erasure of Indians from this colonialist fantasy reflects primordialism's core narrative: nonwhite history is prehistory.

Before sending them eastward, however, the angel foresees and sanctifies a binding commonality between Ireland and the United States as fellow victims of British dominion:

But in the end, upon that land [Ireland] shall fall
A bitter scourge, a lasting flood of tears
When ruthless tyranny shall level all,
The pious trophies of its early years;
Then shall this land prove thy country's friend,
And shine as a second Eden to the West
Then shall this shore its friendly arms extend
And clasp the exiled outcast to its breast. (107)

MacCarthy binds the Irish of the sixth century to Americans of the nineteenth through their shared victimization by and subordination in the British Empire, creating a primordial sympathy. Moreover, the loss of "the pious trophies of its earlier years" engenders a narrative of British (or similar Norse) invasion as the root cause of the broken state of modern Irish culture: the "Third World" conditions have resulted from intrinsic flaws based not in their racial whiteness or in their Catholicism but rather in their victimhood by the forces of various empires.

Other transatlantic Irish writers forwarded MacCarthy's version of Brendan. In his *History of the Irish Hierarchy*—published in Dublin and New York in 1854—Thom Walsh describes one of his fellow travelers: "This saint is mentioned in the voyages of St. Brendan, and his travels in a western country are alluded to in the Acts of the Saints: *Terra repromissionis sanctorum quam Dominus daturus est successoribus in 'tempore novissimo.'* The land of the repromise of the Saints, which the Lord is about to give to our successors in distant ages. Let the reader pronounce on the coincidence between this passage and the great emigration from Ireland to America in these late years" (503). Walsh's inclusion of the Irish in a narrative of Manifest Destiny suggests that Brendan and his seagoing monks provided a transformative primordial whitening and masculinization of Celtic and Catholic cultures. In turn this would place the Irish in America's past, present, and future. Small wonder, then, that Irish American journalist John L. O'Sullivan coined the phrase that crystallized the prophecy MacCarthy's angel foretold.[41]

Ignatiev has studied efforts like MacCarthy's to whiten and thereby Americanize the Irish: "The Catholic Irish, an oppressed race in Ireland became part of the oppressing class in America. . . . To enter the white race was a strategy to secure advantage in a competitive society" (1–2). In sum, MacCarthy's version of Brendan's legend expands whiteness, to recall Painter's term, but only in terms of sheer numbers; it never supplants whiteness as the ground zero of settler nationalism. At the same time, by loosening Anglo-Protestantism's monopolization of whiteness, the primordial Irish were positioned to provide a template for further expanding whiteness to meet the growing nation's need for the doers of the dirty work of imperialism who expected a minimum of its profits. Despite Ignatiev's claim to colonialist complicity, this lingering marginality—their semiwhiteness—exposes Irish migration as diasporic rather than assimilative. For the creole settler, *home* must be or become the colony, despite a nostalgia for his Old World origins. As such, "settler" becomes a poor descriptor for the Irish in the sense that home remained Ireland, making them exiles whose inclusion, though sought for the sake of survival, could never be complete. In the end, they seek a place in but not of America. Anglo-Saxon efforts to perpetuate Irish cultural, racial, political, and economic subordination, in fact, peaked in the 1890s, hardening the Irish sense of exile rather than inhabitation.

Sensing the intractability of the Anglo-Saxon refusal to grant them more than the trappings of citizenship, the Irish nurtured their rebellious reputation in draft riots during the Civil War and "agitation" in the emergent labor movement.[42] In 1884, Alexander Sullivan observed: "Those fastidious people who complain of Irish agitation in the United States, would show more reasonableness if they attached their censure to the causes of the agitation. . . . The Irish race will never cease agitation, in whatever part of the world its people may be found, until Ireland shall have achieved its national independence" (36). Even as the century passed, Sullivan observes that the Irish still look to Ireland as home, and that its reasons for agitation, wherever they are, become theirs. Small wonder, then, that the Irish played a prominent role in the Anti-imperialist movement of the early twentieth century. Kristen Hoganson notes that "Irish Americans equated US policies with British imperialism" (248); Benjamin Beede recounts how "Irish Americans . . . identified US imperialism with Prussian militarism and British rule in Ireland" (26); and Alexander Saxton remarks, "The roots of American anti-Imperialism were thus both internal . . . and external (from the arrival of European revolutionary exiles, . . . most of all, Irish migrants)" (64–65). In other words, the Irish recognized American expansionism for what it was: European-style imperialism. This distinction indicates that the Irish Americans' own semiassimilation—the settler nation's cultural colonization of semiwhite outsiders—has always been incomplete, and the Irish reaction has drawn them back to Ireland as their true *home*. Even this was grounded in MacCarthy's primordial prognostication. The angel sends Brendan back eastward, not to the American coast but to Ireland: "Seek thine own isle—Christ's newly-bought domain, / Which nature with an emerald pencil paints; / Such as it is, long, long, shall it remain / The School of Truth, the College of the Saints / The student's bower, the hermit's calm retreat" (107). Referencing the linkage of early medieval Ireland to the retention of classical and Christian learning, MacCarthy ends by praising Ireland and reminding his readers that the nineteenth-century Irish fled Ireland by force, not choice.

In sum, the two "dwarf epics" of Irish primordialism trouble settler nationalism by exposing critical intraracial fissures based in region and ethnicity. The incomplete absorption of both the ethnic Irish and the sectional South displays fractures in the myth of the unified Anglo-Protestant nation upon which settler identity depends. While settler colonialism established dominion over indigenous Americans and their lands, even as aided by exogenous semiwhites, the Irish, and semi-Americans, the Southrons, these episodes reveal that settler ambitions for cultural unity were highly fraught and deeply contested by intraracial and interregional rivalries and exclusions. Without the articulation and perpetuation of a singular national culture, its transplantation to overseas imperial holdings would always be unstable and easily challenged. The uncolonized Irishness of the Irish, and the unregenerate southernness of the Southron, problematized that model by enacting the unassembleability of American whiteness, a complication far more explicitly on display in the long and complex traditions of Norse primordialism that ran throughout the long nineteenth century in America.

5

The Norse Forefathers
of the American Empire

The Louisiana Purchase was pure Imperialism though it did not
require any fighting. . . . So long as American Imperialism was confined
to the North American continent . . . we did not call it Imperialism.
Now however that the American merchant people find it possible and
profitable to reach out after the opening market of Asia, they begin to
show some of the more familiar traits of Imperialism; and some who
have grown old under the delusion that this spirit was something quite
different so long as it was cooped up between the Canadian border, the
Mexican Gulf, and the oceans, are now mightily alarmed at the "new
manifestation." It is about as new as primordial slime.

—Albert Richardson Carman, *The Ethics of Imperialism*, 1905

Between the Revolution and the de facto settler inhabitation of the continental nation after 1848, primordial fantasies contemplated strictly the space
occupied, or to be occupied in the near future, by white Americans. Only
when the nation indulged in the Spanish- and Philippine-American Wars
(1898–1902) to acquire the leftovers of the erstwhile Spanish Empire was
"imperial" used to describe its acquisition and domination of geographically noncontiguous places and peoples. Yet Albert Richardson Carman's
insistence on the constancy of "imperialism" from the origins of national
history identifies a far longer implicit, but disavowed, empire-building aspiration in the politics, poetics, and economics of "expansion" (102–3).[1] Moreover, Carman's use of "delusion" presages Lorenzo Veracini's "disavowal"
in the twenty-first century: both characterize the settler project as denying its replication of the violence and dominance at the core of every empire. Each reflects on how acquiescing in the nation's "imperial" identity
signals a deep-seated anxiety, an unwillingness to concede the settler's imitative reproduction of Europe's nonrepublican forms of imposed hegemony.

Carman conflates internal and external forms of colonialism as distinct modes of imperialism, each equally rooted in "primordial slime."

This chapter tracks that slime to the nation's embrace of two interlinked Norse primordialisms that reflect Carman's linkage of contiguous and non-contiguous forms of imperialism. This division also characterizes settler colonial theory. Veracini makes the key distinction between "settler" and "administered or exploitative" colonies: "Whereas settler colonialism constitutes a circumstance where the colonizing effort is exercised from within the bounds of a settler colonizing entity, colonialism is driven by an expanding metropole that remains permanently distinct from it. . . . Settlers, by definition, *stay*, in specific contradistinction, colonial sojourners—administrators, missionaries, military personnel, entrepreneurs, and adventurers—*return*" (*Settler Colonialism*, 6; my emphasis). By this reckoning, before 1898, the United States had practiced only settler-based colonialism; after 1898, overseas colonialism was added to its repertoire. However, Carman would respond that each was just an opposing side of the same coin: dominion is dominion. Both contradict the settler narrative of victimhood, stage-based progress, and republican values that characterize settler self-representation: both disregard the settler nation's claimed bases in "the consent of the governed," and other nods to Lockean rule of law. The undisavowable "imperialism" of the Spanish- and Philippine-American Wars finally revealed earlier denials of empire as naive: the move into noncontiguous territories represented continuity with rather than breakage from long-established practices of empire-building: imitation rather than innovation.

This is not to say that settler colonialism ended when those wars began or when Frederick Jackson Turner announced the frontier closed: on the contrary, the Dawes Act of 1887 simply supplemented land-based material forms of colonization with one based in cultural genocide.[2] After 1898, Anglo-American imperialism thus took on *both* forms of "imperialism"— each of which was supplemented by Norse primordialist fantasies. For the overseas ventures, however, primordialist mythologies would be needed to ascertain and assure a nonterritorial link to an empowering archaic inheritance that justified or even required these violent interventions in global politics and economics, since intimacy with place was no longer necessary: Americans in the Philippines, for example, would *return* rather than settle. Deploying new biological understandings of race, nineteenth-century white Americans instead sought that link not in land but in blood, claiming a genetic, blood-based inheritance from a primordial population whose achievements they meant both to claim and to reproduce.[3]

As such, the tenth- and eleventh-century history of the Vikings—as ex-
emplars of *both* settler and exploitative forms of colonialism—spawned two
entangled fantasies: even as they planted settler colonies in England, Ireland, and North America, they also raided and traded from North Africa
to the Russian steppes. Textual reimaginings of the Norse, based on only
flimsy historical and archaeological evidence, provided both the geographic
and genetic premises for both nation building and empire making for white
Americans. This chapter tracks the simultaneity of settler colonialism
and the emergence of "exploitative" colonialism as expressed, celebrated, and
even undermined in representations of the primordial Norse in American
print culture from the time of the Mexican War to the aftermath of the
Spanish War. The appropriation of the Norse was split between the settler
colonization of the continent and the imperialist exploitation of noncontiguous sites of dominion.

In this chapter, first, literary re-creations of the mythical Norse city of
Norumbega in southern New England will represent the Norse as primordial settlers; second, the ephemeral Vinland encampments were used to
characterize the Norse as imperial "exploiters." This dual purposing not only
demonstrates the supple nature of Norse primordialism but also solves the
problem of the Norse abandonment of North America: the Vikings shifted
from American to global spaces, just as modern Americans looked overseas when the "closing" of the frontier announced the purported (but disavowed) end of the geographical colonization of American territory. Central
to the elaboration of both Norumbega and Vinland was the iconography of
the "discoverer" of Viking North America: Leif Ericson.[4] During this period, Ericson was reinvented several times to serve the shifting needs of the
settler nation for alternative foundational narratives. This would bring Ericson and the primordialist authentication he represented into conflict with
the similarly emerging (and equally conjectural) legacy of 1492.

Immediately after the Revolution, "Christopher Columbus" had been
reinvented as a Founding Father.[5] Only after the Revolution, "Americans
began to look for a new unifying symbol and Christopher Columbus
emerged as their choice," according to Inga Bjornsdottir (220). Books and
epics followed, cementing his heroic reputation. Cities, colleges, and other
institutions eagerly linked themselves by name to his legacy of reputed virtue, boldness, and leadership. To those ends, Kirkpatrick Sale has traced
the gradual invention of "Columbus"—as opposed to the more exotic and
unassimilable "Cristobal Colon"—in eighteenth-century print culture as
an unqualified hero, the embodiment of the Doctrine of Discovery's linkage of primacy and righteous mission. Yet Sale comments: "What was not

included . . . was the Black Legend of Spanish misdeeds, beginning with Colon's government in Espanola; missing as well, here as in every other account, was a good sense of Colon's land, Colon as governor, Colon as the increasingly demented malcontent in his last years in Spain" (332). "Columbus" might be said to represent a series of constructs, sanitized and de-exoticized versions of the actual Colon. For Italy and Spain, he was the Great Navigator, enabling exploration and empire; in America, the Discoverer, the first and foremost settler colonialist. Susanna Rowson's *Reuben and Rachel* (1799), for example, acknowledges the Black Legend, but exculpates Columbus as the victim of Castilians, who committed the Black Legend's atrocities in his absence.[6] Likewise, Washington Irving's definitive biography followed up Joel Barlow's *Vision of Columbus* by redefining Columbus as a de facto Protestant victimized by Catholicism's doctrinal and intellectual limitations, a rescripting that American readers found far more digestible.

Yet from the start, Colon's crimes and actual Catholicism were hard to conceal, and Ericson and other Norsemen—equally fabricated—were repeatedly revived as alternatives throughout the long nineteenth century. For example, the 1794 edition of Jeremy Belknap's *American Biography* accords the Viking settlement a mere ten pages and focuses not on Ericson but on Bjarni Herjólfsson: "But if it be allowed that he is entitled to the honour of having discovered America before Columbus, yet this discovery cannot in the least detract from the merit of the celebrated navigator" (86). Belknap then moves to his scathing rejection of Madoc. Bjornsdottir concludes, "These and other attempts, honest and otherwise, to deploy [Ericson] in order to oust Christopher Columbus failed. [Ericson] never caught the American public imagination in the way Columbus did. Columbus's voyage across the ocean had, after all, pointed the way for millions of European immigrants to escape poverty, persecution, war, and starvation, and to start a new life in America" (223). Nonetheless, in the decades around the Mexican-American War and those surrounding the Spanish- and Philippine-American Wars, the Norse enjoyed moments of, if not ascendance, widespread attention, especially as each came at a moment when issues of race, religion, and empire were defining national debates. The "Norse revival" began in 1837 with the translation of Carl Christian Rafn's *Antiquitates Americanae*, which inspired the recurating of the earlier sources as well. For example, when Belknap's literary executors reprinted *American Biography* in 1847, they added forty pages lifted from Rafn. In this excerpt, Ericson is a bold adventurer at the forefront of Christian civilization, a rendering at odds with Belknap's disregard for the romantic indulgences of primordialism.

Although materials on the Norse presence were initially in Pierre Mallett's *Northern Antiquities*, widespread interest began with Rafn.[7] Translated to English and published on both sides of the Atlantic, Rafn's book, the interpretive translation of the Icelandic sagas originally transcribed by Snorri Sturluson and other Skaldic poets in the fourteenth century, catalyzed a transatlantic fascination with all things Viking.[8] This would encompass more than the expected primordial land-based fantasy of a Norse origin. It also catalyzed a more durable blood-based fabrication that pushed the American appropriation of Gothic Anglo-Saxon identity deeper into the legendary past to its fictional roots in Scandinavian Teutonism by designating Anglo-Saxonism as a subculture of Norse Teutonism. After Rafn's book appeared, dozens of well-known writers celebrated and extended a new and improved foundation myth that promised greater imaginative potential than both the ephemeral fantasies addressed earlier in this book, the tarnished legacy of Columbus, and the dull and documented history of Anglo colonization and colonialism. Ralph Waldo Emerson, James Russell Lowell, Lydia Sigourney, Henry Wadsworth Longfellow, John Greenleaf Whittier, William Cullen Bryant, Washington Irving, William Gilmore Simms, and Bayard Taylor contributed to or commented upon the purported Norse origins of American culture, as did historians and translators George Perkins Marsh, Joshua Toulmin Smith, Thomas Wentworth Higginson, and Edward Everett. Later, during a resurgent Norse revival later in the century, reflecting the nation's leap into imperial adventures in non–North American territories, writers and historians who contributed to these debates range from Justin Winsor, Jack London, and Frank Norris to Mark Twain and even James Weldon Johnson, along with dozens of lesser figures working in a variety of genres.

The addition of a transcendent, blood-based inheritance allowed more foundational commentaries and critiques of the orthodoxies of nation, masculinity, whiteness, and the ongoing struggle for identity and legitimacy in the aging settler nation. Aside from bolstering romantic nationalism, the popularity of the Vikings reflected their ability to fit any number of national and global aspirations. On both sides of the Atlantic, Norsemen would be retrofitted to embody the demands of colonialist adventure, at home and abroad. Annette Kolodny's concept of the "plastic Viking" best articulates the malleability of the reconstructed primordial Norseman: "Depending on the purpose at hand and the sources cited, the Norse could be depicted variously as heroic warriors and empire builders, barbarous berserker invaders, fighters for freedom, courageous explorers, would-be colonists, seamen and merchants, poets and saga men, glorious ancestors, bloodthirsty pagan pirates, and civilized Christian converts" (*In Search of First Contact*, 204). Kolodny transmutes a Hydra-headed fantasy of a morphing white male identity into a source of heroism and endurance regardless of geographical or chronological setting, a utilitarian primordiality fit for establishing and practicing dominance in any given situation. Speaking of the same British claims on and usages of Norse genetics, Andrew Wawn writes: "The old northmen are variously buccaneering, triumphalist, defiant, confused, disillusioned, unbiddable, disciplined, elaborately pagan, austerely pious, relentlessly jolly, or self-destructively sybaritics. They are merchant adventurers, mercenary soldiers, pioneering colonists, pitiless raiders, self-sufficient farmers, cutting-edge naval technologists, primitive democrats, psychopathic berserks, ardent lovers and complicated poets" (4). Kolodny's and Wawn's lists define the multiple capabilities both Great Britain and the United States expected from the white men they sent out to settle, build, administer, and rule their empires. The imperial Anglophone man synthesized these Norse-based elements and shifted shapes as the demands of the colonial enterprise varied in each site and moment of colonial dominion.

Writing at the advent of the first Norse revival, Emerson described this man and his Scandinavian roots in "Self-Reliance" (1841):

> If we cannot at once rise to the sanctities of obedience and faith, let us at least resist our temptations; let us enter into the state of war and wake Thor and Woden, courage and constancy in our Saxon breasts. . . . A sturdy lad from New Hampshire or Vermont, who in turn tries all the professions, who teams it, farms, it, peddles, keeps a school, preaches, edits a paper, goes to Congress, buys a township, and so forth, in successive years, and always like a cat falls on his feet, is worth a hundred of these city dolls. (154, 156)

Emerson draws a transcendent biological link between the primordial Norsemen and the modern Anglo-Americans as the pinnacles of human development. In *English Traits* (1856), Emerson lingers on transatlantic Teutonism as the primordial source of the institutions of their common civilization: "The Heimskringla, or Sagas of the kings of Norway, collected by Snorro Sturleson, is the Iliad and the Odyssey of English history. . . . The Sagas describe a monarchical republic like Sparta. The government disappears before the importance of citizens. . . . The heroes of the Sagas . . . are substantial farmers whom the rough times have forced to defend their properties" (414). Emerson concedes the "sanguinary and piratical" qualities of the Vikings, with their "singular turn for homicide" (413): when forced to violence, they are the best at it. Implicitly, Emerson justifies white savagery, as those savages will eventually be redeemed by their intrinsic Teutonic dynamism when the moment that called forth their rage had passed: "Twenty thousand thieves landed at Hastings. These founders of the House of Lords were greedy and ferocious dragoons, sons of greedy and ferocious pirates. . . . It took many generations to trim and comb and perfume the first boat-load of Norse pirates into royal highnesses and most noble Knights of the Garter; but every sparkle of ornament dates back to the Norse boat" (416). By the latter half of the century, the cultural utility of the Norse had long undergirded the sanguinary and piratical qualities needed by Anglo-American men on the imperial frontiers of their empires. As the frontiers were tamed, these qualities became latent, dormant but never wholly disappearing. In sum, when needed, white men had access not only to the superior virtues of an advanced culture but to the atavistic superiority of their savage origins.[9]

Yet Emerson, in a Turnerian move, distinguished Norse-descended Americans from the equally Norse-descended English by expanding on how white Americans had surpassed their British cousins after having been molded by conquest, colonization, and settlement. Because they had more recently exercised these transitional and metamorphic potentials, Americans were the most authentic inheritors of the Norse legacy of intellectual superiority and physical dominance: "The American is only the continuation of the English genius into new conditions, more or less propitious" (419). More directly, contemplating the potential English financial collapse in the recessions of the 1850s, Emerson concludes: "If the courage of England goes with the chances of a commercial crisis, I will go back to the capes of Massachusetts, and my own Indian Stream, and say to my countrymen, the old race are all gone, and the elasticity and hope of mankind must henceforth remain on the Allegheny ranges, or nowhere" (442). The "Indian Stream" Emerson considered "his own" reflects his primordialist sensibility: he claims *both* the Norse legacy and the conquered Indians' acquired place, supplanting both the erstwhile colonial parent and the vanishing indigene.

Still, genetics troubled the American claim on the Norse: the most direct Gothic forebear of both the imperial English and their American mimics had long been designated as the Anglo-Saxon.[10] However, Anglo-Saxons made for poor literary subjects: farmers and craftsmen, their stories hardly fired the romantic imaginations needed to inspire either to realize its potential as a global empire. To meet this need, "Teutonism" was repositioned as the purest and most primordial form of the Gothic culture, as it was better suited to literary extrapolation. Despite objections from historians on both sides of the Atlantic, this romantic merging of all non-Celtic Northern Europeans was solidified throughout the 1840s and 1850s, with many writers explicitly identifying the Teutons as the genetic, cultural, moral root of Anglo-Saxon culture.[11] Within this, the Norseman was fabricated as both ur- and uber-Goth. Reginald Horsman's main focus in *Race and Manifest Destiny* is Anglo-Saxonism, but he affirms Teutonism as its purest expression: "The English were attracted to the idea of their race as a regenerating force for the whole world, for in Great Britain, throughout her colonies, and in the United States the Anglo-Saxons were apparently completing the march begun in the dawn of history by Aryan tribesmen. It was this aspect of the new Teutonism that also found the most fertile ground on the other side of the Atlantic, in the United States" (77). Teutonism, for the British, was genetic; for Americans, a more complete access to Teutonism was conjectured through both Vinland and their "blood" as English creoles, the same blood, as Emerson noted, whose latent power had been more recently activated by the settler colonial adventure. In the end, what mattered most was that the romance of Norse primordiality could be claimed, mostly through Ericson, without disconnecting from the Anglo-Saxon base. More recently, Barbara Bush has linked these imaginative leaps to settler identity: "Aryanism merged with new theories of social Darwinism, scientific racism, and older classifications to justify white superiority. All these fused into the powerful discourses of Anglo-Saxonism that emphasized the greatness of Teutonic peoples, Germans, Norsemen, and Anglo-Saxons, including the English, who had colonized the world and were superior to other races, including the Celts and 'inferior' southern and eastern European peoples" (30). On the literary scale, the stolid Anglo-Saxon, made bold by his Teuton roots, becomes *the* American. Horsman notes that this linkage generated a "fresh literary dimension . . . to the existing emphasis on government and law among primitive Germanic and Norse peoples" (26). The resulting Norse primordialist literary canon, featuring Emerson, Whittier, and Norris, demonstrated how their plasticity helped Americans reflect and confirm the settler postcolony as it annexed a global empire in the name of expanding an Anglo-Saxon-based civilization.

William Gilmore Simms likewise projected the Teutonic literary base for American Anglo-Saxonist literature in his 1841 review essay of Rafn and his many interpreters: "The Saxon, in all probability, obtained his first lessons, as well of war as of civilization, from the invasions of the northern sea-kings, as, in after periods, he rose into the highest rank of humanity, by the scourge and the bondage to which he was held in the grasp of the superior genius of another portion of the same conquering stock" (*Views*, 2:223). Simms knew most white Americans were not descended from Vikings, so he claimed the legacy for the "nation, but not the race," creating space for cultural Teutonism both to survive dilutions of the blood and to be assumed even by non-Teuton whites. His immediate purpose is the instigation of a literature suited to the primordial prerequisites of romantic nationalism, as noted above in the introduction: "It is something, surely, to be able to boast that we have an American antiquity. . . . It is so much raw material to our artists in fiction—a quarry to which the poet and novelist may repair with confidence, without much fear of exhausting their resources. The more rude the annals, the more susceptible of an original polish" (*Views*, 2:23–24). Simms recognizes that the scant and flimsy material proofs of Norse presence alone cannot give the United States access to primordial intimacy on a European scale needed to construct a "natural nation."[12] However, it allows American writers a source for a more legitimizing mythmaking: "It is because we shall, from these shapeless masses erect new fabrics, as from the ruins of ancient Rome, a new and scarcely less magnificent Rome is made to rise" (*Views*, 2:225). The American empire can be thus "made to rise" on the Roman model through the power of literary mythmaking by constructing national identity from the "rude annals" of a primordial myth.

These were given literary expression in distinct and overlapping land- and blood-based fantasies most explicitly during the Mexican- and the Spanish- and Philippine-American Wars. As to land, the fictional Norumbega, supposedly just outside Boston, writers explored founding narratives that both enabled the disavowal of the violence of conquest and decentered Columbus's primacy. As to blood, Ericson's temporary settlement at Vinland modeled blood-based imperialist narratives able to move beyond the geography of North America. During the Civil War, both North and South claimed the Viking legacy, as the North claimed the Norse and the South the Norman. These shifts minimized the role of place in the logic of the primordialism and enabled the shift in emphasis from land to race as the American colonization, as well as the primordial imagination, shifted from settlement to imperialism.

Norumbega

Not on Penobscot's wooded bank the spires
Of the sought City rose, nor yet beside
The winding Charles, nor where the daily tide
Of Naumkeag's haven rises and retires,
The vision tarried; but somewhere we knew
The beautiful gates must open to our quest,
Somewhere that marvellous City of the West

Would lift its towers and palace domes in view,
And, lo! at last its mystery is made known— ...
It lends its beauty to the lake's green shore,
And Norumbega is a myth no more.

—John Greenleaf Whittier, "Norumbega Hall," 1869

Although Mallett's *Antiquities* had been in circulation for some time, the first sustained public attention to the Norse began in 1837 with Rafn's *Antiquitates* and its many English-language translations, summaries, and explanations. Yet Rafn and his translators distinguish savage *Viking* conquest from peaceful and trade-based *Norse* settlement. Noting this transition, American writers immediately began extrapolating the latter to create a distinct place-based antebellum Norse primordialism, the poetic deaths of Whittier's and Longfellow's Vikings clearing the path for the Norse settler. In this process, the settlement would need a city, and, based on erroneous readings of old French maps, Norumbega was conceived and a more direct narrative of the Emersonian progression from warrior to settler begun.[13] At the same time, both poets articulate a subtle ambivalence: less confident than Emerson, both poets see in Norse culture both the heroic strengths and the tragic flaws of settler identity.

Henry Wadsworth Longfellow's "The Skeleton in Armor" (1842) has been commemorated as the foundational narrative of the Norse revival. Longfellow's Vikings, and his American narrator, both represent the embrace of authenticating white antiquity and initiate the settler-based pattern of disavowing its darker edges. In her reading, for example, Kolodny argues for a nuanced ambivalence. The protagonist hero kills his countrymen as he escapes Sweden with his bride, serving only a selfish need for sanctuary, doing nothing to forward the cause of his race or community: "If this is a love story, it is a decidedly disturbing one. Longfellow reifies the unromanticized image of the Vikings as piratical marauders rather than employing the newly emergent rehabilitated image of romantic explorers and freedom-loving warriors" (*In Search of First Contact*, 159). From this base, Kolodny argues, Longfellow constructs a broader critique of Andrew Jackson's abandonment of republican restraint and accompanying ideologies of public interest: "The illustrious history that began with the Goths and morphed into Vikings was not simply a glorious pageant of freedom-seeking heroics that led inexorably to the Reformation and then to Plymouth Rock. It was also a pageant of individuals seeking only the satisfaction of individual desires, whether for conquest, gold, land, love or salvation" (162–63). For Kolodny, the Norse revival both celebrated and disciplined the settler by tracing the sources of each to the more authentic primordial past. Yet Longfellow's corrective also exists within settler discourse as self-critique, letting stand the primordialist assumption that the only genuine American prehistory is white.

The absence of Indians from the poem, for example, enacts a common trope of settler literature: the disavowal of founding violence in settler historiography more generally. Veracini notes: "Settler colonialism also needs to disavow any founding violence. . . . Settler collectives are also escaping from violence. . . . A settler society is commonly articulated . . . [as] a fantasy of communities devoid of disturbances or dislocations" (*Settler Colonialism*, 75–77). Settlers needed to identify violence as left over from Old World corruption, thus validating settlement as escape rather than as invasion. "The Skeleton" does this by depicting violence as an unfortunate necessity to escape from the Old World's antidemocratic restraints. While there is violence when Longfellow's Viking departs Sweden, it resembles Revolutionary rupture, not attacks on or by Indians. As with Madoc's escape from civil wars, or the Lost Israelites fleeing Asian aggressors, Longfellow's Norse lovers become refugees rather than invaders. As such, they model the foundation of the settler community as cathartic and desperate rather than deliberate and avaricious. Read from this perspective, "The Skeleton" serves precisely that function. Longfellow wrote his poem upon the purported discovery of a buried Viking warrior in Fall River, Massachusetts.[14] The poem found unequivocal and broad popularity in the moment of the Mexican-American War's aggressive colonialist expansionism, a war framed as self-defense, protecting the white Texans from Mexican incursions.[15] The poem's popularity was such that sixty years later, Chicago novelist Ottilie Liljencrantz based *Randvar the Songsmith* around the descendants of its characters, as I discuss below. In the poem itself, Longfellow describes a young white Scandinavian couple and begins with a democratic premise: they defy aristocratic rules against marriage between a commoner and a princess, kill her father's crew, and venture to the American wilderness to found a farm and a family. Longfellow's narrator begins by contemplating the skull, and, as the aurorae borealis lights the skeleton's eyes ("Pale flashes seem to rise; / As When the Northern skies Gleam in December"), the skeleton chants:

I was a Viking old!
My deeds, though manifold,
No skald in song has told,

No saga taught thee
Take heed that in thy verse,
Thou dost tell a tale rehearse. (90–91)

The ghost has sought the poet, not unlike Coleridge's Ancient Mariner sought the "one in three" who could understand and retell his story.
Like Simms's unrealized "runic" poet, Longfellow assumes this special
mission to tell how a savage becomes a settler. Recalling his Old World
life, the skeleton first became a hunter: "Oft through the forest dark /
Followed the were-wolf's bark." As he ages, he joins the Vikings, and "Many
the souls that sped, / Many hearts that bled, / By our stern orders," demonstrating the requisite savagery. Yet when he and the chief's daughter fall in
love, he is rebuffed by the chief: "So the loud laugh of scorn / Out of those lips
unshorn," evoking the social mobility central to the democratic values Teutons were said to have founded. The skeleton continues: "She was a Prince's
child, / I but a Viking wild" (92). After killing his former shipmates in his
escape, the Viking and his princess sail westward and arrive in New England
three weeks later. Having landed, the skeleton transforms from berserker
to farmer:

There lived we many years;
Time dried the maiden's tears
She had forgot her fears,
She was a mother. (94)

When the Viking, heartbroken at his wife's death, kills himself, his "soul ascended": having repented and transformed, the Viking can be repositioned
as a Christian, even without formal conversion, by being a good husband,
farmer, and father. As a younger man, the Viking had fought as a berserker,
a "roving" marauder. In America, however, he becomes a farmer, killing no
Indians as he does so. Longfellow weds the Teutonic ideal to settler culture
in three ways. First, its hero wins freedom by defeating oppressive European
superiors; the skeleton, that is, had to be the *best* Viking—better than those
who stayed behind and never came to America—to escape from effeminizing feudalism. Second, the poem concedes that intraracial violence may
be required to establish freedom and independence, to separate the settler
from the colonizing Old World culture. Third, the poem sanitizes contact and colonialism by omitting the Skraelings altogether and imagining
the New World as an empty romantic idyll for the white couple alone. Yet
Kolodny's critique lingers: in his exposure of the selfish core of Jacksonian

individualism, Longfellow casts a shadow on the image of the Viking as the forefather of a settler nation. Longfellow identifies the self, rather than the nation or even the race, at the heart of the primordial white experience in the New World: the self-based nature of his story, while romantic, does nothing, as Kolodny suggested, for the republic, and his slaughter of his shipmates is committed merely for self-gratification. Nonetheless, "The Skeleton" established the Norse cottage in New England that others would expand into Norumbega.

These more sustained and sustaining narratives validated the settlers as the heirs of the strengths of a "race" they believed to represent the best of the Old World. Yet the Norse abandonment of North America within a single generation posed a problem for long-established primordialist conventions. Unlike other primordial whites discussed here, there was no premise for tracing degeneration toward nonwhiteness or extinction at the hands of savage hoards. In fact, the Vikings in many ways were the worst candidates for primordialization on account of their hasty retreat to the Old World, and thus the most difficult to link to ideologies of settler colonialism. Nonetheless, based on a few very sketchy references to sixteenth-century French maps and records, nineteenth-century Anglo-American writers conjectured the city of Norumbega, and Norumbega soon expanded from virtually nothing to the archaic locus of the permanent domestic inhabitation the historical record could not provide.[16]

John Greenleaf Whittier most directly developed the poetic reconstruction of Norumbega, although he arrived at Longfellow's ambivalence more gradually.[17] In three poems, including the sonnet quoted as this section's epigraph, Whittier describes a chimeric city up the Penobscot River, now lost in the forest, save for a fragment of a stone cross, an explicit marker of Viking Christianity. Yet in all Whittier's poems, Norumbega is never quite realized. At one level, this represents the colonialist method of repositioning invasion as adventure: the quest itself becomes the goal as the territory is appropriated. However, as Whittier revisited the subject over the course of four decades, that quest grew from illusion to delusion, representing his own darkening perspective on American prospects. The earliest, "The Norseman" (1841), ends, like William Cullen Bryant's Mound Builder fantasy "The Prairies," rehearsing the inevitable settler community to come:

> I hear the common tread of men,
> And hum of work-day life again;
> The mystic relic seems alone
> A broken mass of common stone;

And if it be the chiselled limb
Of berserker of idol grim, . . .
I know not. . . .
Quicken the past to life again,
The Present lost in what hath been. (12–13)

The New England workday Whittier imagines, the prototypical nonviolent
settler fantasy, exists literally atop the Viking ruins, granting it a primordial
foundation. The second poem, written after the Civil War and Whittier's
tireless abolitionism, "Norembega" (1871), reflects a more jaded perspective. In it, Whittier reimagines the city as always just beyond reality, perhaps
one reflected by the different spelling of the poem's subject. In it, an old and
dying "Christian Knight," apparently returning from questing through New
England, perceives "the domes and spires of Norembega town." His "hench-
men," however, understand it as a mirage, a correction the knight refuses
to recognize: "Your spire is but a branchless pine" (92). As the knight re-
alizes his error, he also knows that he will die before finding Norumbega
and that he does so as a colonial exile: "My life is sped; I shall not see / My
home-set sails again; / The sweetest eyes of Normandie / Shall watch for me
in vain." He sends the henchman to look over a nearby hill—"Perchance
the valley even now / Is starred with city lights"—only to find nothing:
"He saw nor tower nor town, / But through the drear wood, lone and
still, / The river rolling down." Before the knight expires, he asks, "Is Norembega yet a dream / Whose waking is in heaven?" Finally, the poet concludes,
"He needs the earthly city not / Who hath the heavenly found" (93). Indeed,
this ambiguous evocation ponders whether Norumbega, and hence the primordial Norse more generally, were always an illusion, a distraction from
nobler goals.

The final poem, "Norumbega Hall" (1887), was composed for the com-
memoration of a monument to Norumbega whose location had been
supposedly verified by Harvard engineering professor Eben Horsford, as
discussed below. Here, the poet imagines the city as a fantastic place full of
beautiful women and noble knights, re-creating Sir Walter Scott's medieval
Europe. While Horsford may have found a place on a map, for Whittier, it
remains chimeric: "at last its mystery is made known— / Its only dwellers
maidens fair and young, / Its Princess such as England's Laureate sung / And
safe from capture, save by love alone" (239). In filling the city with passive
Victorian virgins rather than Norse shield maidens, the sonnet becomes
wholly fantasy, articulating both the fantasy of Norse inhabitation and its
impossibility. In sum, Longfellow's and Whittier's Norse microsagas identify

the desire for such grand and race-based national narratives as delusional. In response, they position them as romantic distractions from the real work of building a nation truly aligned with Christian and republican values: each still affirms the colonialist mission but urges more restrained assertions of mission and righteousness, a sobering restraint furthered by other writers who contemplated Norumbega.

For example, William Cullen Bryant mocked the quest for a primordial Norse past in his *Popular History of the United States* (1874). It is clear from his initial comment on the specious nature of primordialism as a whole that Bryant means to probe the telling hubris at the core of colonialist civilization and history: "What were these great Western continents stretching from pole to pole unknown till 1492 to the nations who had made the world's history? The pride of human knowledge has for four centuries resented such imputation. If facts were wanting, ingenious suppositions of more or less probability were made to take the place of facts" (35). This opens a two-chapter sequence on, first, the Norse, and, next, the other proposed primordial whites, both ones discussed here and ones that remain "fantastic archaeology."[18] Of the Norse—whose time in North America he cannot deny—Bryant notes: "They made indeed no permanent settlement, and if it may be held as an argument against the probability of their having made the discovery at all that if it is hard to find a continent, it may, with quite as much force, be urged that it is harder still to lose one, when found" (36). Bryant then reads the sagas' description of the Viking settlement as catering to the most base elements of the settler population: "Not less conclusive is the simplicity, sometimes even childishness, of the narratives, . . . characteristic of all unlettered people who, like children, delight in marvels and are captured by novelty" (63). While the rest of the *Popular History* betrays the same colonialist sentiments of his Mound-Builder poem "The Prairies," Bryant here excoriates Americans who sought in the Vikings role models in their quest for identity in Norse adventure just because they shared white skin.

Nonetheless, in the 1880s, Horsford became Norumbega's staunchest champion. Horsford begins his 1889 pamphlet, *The Discovery of the Ancient City of Norumbega*, with a note from Judge George Daly, president of the National Geographic Society, who proclaims "the primitive home of the Aryans—the central point of departure or migration of that great civilizing race . . . was not, as has hitherto been supposed, the country lying of the mountains of the Hindoo Kush . . . but was someplace in the southeastern part of Scandinavia; which would make the Northmen the progenitors of the Greeks, the Romans, and . . . of all the nations of modern Europe"

(7). The inclusion of this and similar sentiments raises Horsford's project beyond antiquarianism and into the realm of racial destinarianism. To commemorate this, Horsford commissioned the building of a tower in Watertown, Massachusetts, and erected a statue of Leif Ericson, Norumbega's presumptive founder, for which Whittier composed the skeptical "Norumbega Hall," whose irony was lost on Horsford. The poet would not attend the unveiling or read his poem.

Horsford's protracted "proof" of Norumbega's location very closely resembles the wishful earlier "proofs" that the protoindustrial, commercial farming, and earth-moving engineering Mound Builders had been white: Horsford's Norsemen built gristmills for grain produced by their farms, harvested "mosur" wood for shipment to the Old World, and constructed dams and levees to harness the tides and protect themselves from snowmelt in the spring. At the end, he appends a selection of poems by primordialist Norse poems by Whittier, Emerson, and Bayard Taylor.[19] Finally, he adds his own. "Vinland Rune" imagines the discovery of a rune on the banks of the Charles, firing the primordialist imagination, now linked to democratic politics:

> Sing, We, then, a ragged tune
> In Emerson's and Whittier's tune,—
> Verse for honest spoken folk,
> Compact as stuff as egg of yoke,
> Simple, blunt, but yet not course;
> Native, and still something Norse,
> As is meet for kindred race
> Dwelling in the very place
> Where Norsemen moored their ships
> And left their names of savage lips. (50)

Despite a wholesale lack of evidence, and despite his abandonment by Whittier, Horsford performs the rituals of primordialism: ignoring Indian history to find "a kindred race" "in the very place" of the new white nation. Moreover, at the moment, New England was coming to perceive itself as no longer the nation's cultural center—best signified perhaps by William Dean Howells's shift from the *Atlantic* in Boston to *Harper's* in New York—and Horsford's region-specific hope for primordial ascendance was an anachronism by 1890.[20]

Almost immediately, Horsford's claims were debunked. A local historian, James Waldo Colby, responded in verse:

But Viking fresh from roving flight,
Freebooter, monk, and mailed knight,
   From Alpha to Omega
Reached not the goal for which they pressed;
For some sailed east and some sailed west,
But never a man when put to test,
   Had seen far Norumbega!
Twas sixteen hundred, so they say,
When fabled city passed away,
   Not razed by armed beleaguer;
More like the leaves before the wind,
Or dreams that vanish from the mind,
Till nought was left so one can find
   Where stood fair Norumbega! (3)

As to Horsford himself, Colby notes, "A perusal of the dear, old Professor's published works, and particularly his book on phrenology, will convince most readers that he is sometimes a little wild in his theories" (18). Likewise, writing in the *New England Magazine,* Alice C. Clarke conducted a far more professional examination of Horsford's assertions but finds, "Indications of the whereabouts of the lost Norumbega are such stuff as dreams are made of" (266). Clarke's analysis, however, remains wholly local, as does Colby's. Harvard librarian and historian Justin Winsor in the 1889 edition of his magisterial *Narrative and Critical History of the United States* offered a more sustained critique. Winsor begins by quoting his mentor George Bancroft, whose own voluminous national histories always dismissed any primordial conjectures: "'Though Scandinavians may have reached the shores of Labrador, the soil of the United States has not one vestige of their presence.' This is as true now as when first written. Nothing could be slenderer than the alleged correspondence of languages as we see in Horsford's *Discovery of America by the Northmen,* to what a fanciful extent a confident enthusiasm can carry it" (1:98). Winsor, better known for his iconoclastic biography of Columbus, critiqued the settler colonialism as initiated by Columbus as it had shaped the nation's history from the primordial past to his imperial present.[21] For Winsor, when Columbus sailed, "Vinland was practically forgotten. . . . Madoc was as unknown as Elidocthon. While the New Indies were not in their turn to be forgotten, their discoverer was soon lost in a world of conjecture. . . . It is by no means sure, with all our boast of benevolent progress, that atrocities not much short of those which we ascribe to Columbus and his compeers may not at any time disgrace the coming [century] as they have blackened the past years of the nineteenth century"

(*Christopher Columbus*, 499–500). Winsor exposes the propaganda of Columbian hagiography as providing cover for "atrocities" in nationalist historiography, even into the 1890s, as he links them to the slaughter of the Sioux at Wounded Knee. While critiques such as Winsor's undermined Columbus's legacy and attached it to the sins of settler colonialism—anticipating more successful late twentieth-century efforts to do the same—they were ultimately unsuccessful, as Bjornsdottir notes. Ericson still exists as a foil to Columbus, a wishful means of disavowing Columbus's sins that conveniently exploits the primordial obscurity of Ericson.

Nonetheless, of these responses to the nation's search for Norumbega, Bryant's identification of primordialism with adolescent credulity resonated. On both sides of the Atlantic, stories set there targeted the emergent genre of "boys" literature in late nineteenth-century print culture, a genre entangled with the rhetoric of empire. In the introduction to her versified, child-friendly translation of Norse legends, *Valhalla: The Myths of Norseland* (1878), Julia Clinton Jones opened a new market for primordialist exposition: "The broad Atlantic proved no bar to their progress, and the first European who trod American soil was a Norseman. . . . Planting wherever they trod, the germs of a glorious freedom, they were the revolutionists of that age, and all succeeding ages owe them a lasting debt of gratitude for the noble harvest that has sprung up from the seeds of liberty and truth by them sown" (11). As archaeology and anthropology increasingly eliminated or trivialized any white presence in North America before 1492, the primordialist imagination shifted more to the realm of the fantastic. More particularly, it found a home in "boy's" literature, a niche of turn-of-the-century print culture where allegory, imagination, and propaganda often intermingle. Three decades after Jones established the link, Ottilie Adelina Liljencrantz's Norumbega trilogy (1902–1906) transformed nearly every aspect of eighty years of Norumbegan narratives into "ripping yarns" aimed at white adolescent males. In her re-creation of Norumbega, she allegorizes the risks and rewards of the adventure of settlement, while still advocating for empire based on the innate superiority of the Teutonic male, entangling the corrective ambivalence of Longfellow, Whittier, and Winsor with the Teutonic triumphalism of Simms, Emerson, and Horsford. Her Norumbega offers atonement for Viking brutality but leaves settler colonialism in place, albeit with a kinder, gentler face, in ways implying a transformative reflective of the culturally genocidal Dawes Act and its innate replication of the white man's burden.[22]

She begins well: Liljencrantz identifies a dangerous moral absence as she describes the founding of her fictional Norumbega in ways her readers who recognize as re-creating how the settler nation founded itself by expanding into a so-called wilderness. In an essay not included in *In Search of First Contact*, Kolodny identifies Cooper as having the most direct influence on Liljencrantz, especially *Randvar the Songsmith* (1906), the trilogy's concluding volume: "What makes these novels of interest is not merely the borrowings from Cooper but, more importantly, Liljencrantz's successful grafting of the frontier adventure stories onto the substratum of a heroic Viking past. Liljencrantz and other writers like her thereby forever implanted the Norse as essential precursors in the nation's increasingly mythologized frontier heritage" ("When East Was West," 73). The authentication of a "mythologized frontier heritage" characterizes primordialism as a component of settler colonialism. In two ways, Kolodny's reading repositions the frontier as the leading edge of colonization. First, *Randvar* is set in Norumbega—a settler colony—not Vinland, an exploitative colony. At the end of Liljencrantz's trilogy's second volume, *The Vinland Champions* (1904), her Vikings abandon Vinland for lack of profitability. Second, while Randvar begins as a Norse Natty, by novel's end he marries the daughter of the departed ruler and assumes leadership, more like Cooper's educated Oliver Edwards from *The Pioneers* than the gruff, unlettered frontiersman.

Cooper's relationship to settler colonialism—and thus to the nation's "frontier heritage"—entangles complicity and condemnation in the crimes of colonialism. Most recently, Oana Godeanu-Kenworthy, citing Wayne Franklin and Sandra Gustafson, has noted, "Cooper . . . undermines the jingoistic and nationalistic rhetoric of westward expansion" (753), as he would more concisely in *Oak Openings* in reference to lost tribe theory.[23] Like Cooper, Liljencrantz stands at a critical distance from any triumphalist version of that heritage. To embody this, like Oliver, Randvar displaces a corrupt and selfish white dominion with a more benevolent, paternalistic means of community building. While the old regime was antagonistic toward the Skraelings, Randvar claims his will be based in cohabitation, though they comply with decisions throughout. Thus while Liljencrantz's references to Cooper share his disparaging of the methods of settler colonialism, neither offers a systemic or comprehensive critique or hints at decolonization. While Liljencrantz worked overtly in "boy's stories," Cooper himself had been rebranded to that genre before the end of the century, leaving his biting social invective defanged in its repackaging as puerile propaganda.[24]

The late Victorian/Edwardian "boy's story" genre has been implicated in the rhetoric of empire. Jeffrey Richards traces the genre to Daniel Defoe, as it "provided the means by which the mercantile exploration-colonization tradition, epitomized by Robinson Crusoe, was reconciled with the chi-valric aristo-military" (3). Martin Green labels such tales "Robinsonades," after Defoe's 1719 *Robinson Crusoe*. In them, white males—alone or in groups—are isolated in the savage wilderness. Victims, but also settlers, they encounter "savages" and establish the rudiments of the "home" or im-perial culture. Boy's stories also incorporated a British/Norse primordial-ism: R. M. Ballantyne's *Norsemen in the West* (1872) recounted the Ericson legend from a British-Canadian perspective. Addressing Ballantyne in par-ticular, Stuart Hannabuss explains: "Throughout these accounts, we can see the tacit assumption of the white man's right to roam and appropriate ter-ritory, and persistent contrasts, redounding to European (and particularly Christian) life, are made between pre-colonial savagery and post-colonial civilization. This type of free community typified the Gladstonian senti-ment of 'Liberty for ourselves, Empire for the rest of mankind'" (66). British Robinsonades advocated empire, especially settler colonialism, uncritically. Ballantyne, Frederick Marryat, and H. Rider Haggard sold well throughout the dominions, reflecting, again, the imitative nature of settler affiliation.[25]

As a second-generation Norse immigrant, Liljencrantz subtly departed from the conventions of the genre in ways that reflect insecurities intrin-sic to settler subjectivity. In many important ways, the "boy's" novel was transformed in the context of a settler nation, reflecting the complexities that characterize an aspirant ex-coloniality. In his study of Australian boy's stories, Robert Dixon makes a key distinction. While for British writers and readers, "no other literary form was more revealing of the anxieties which attended the end of empire and the beginnings of modernity," by contrast, in the settler nation's adventure novel, "one is struck by the clamour of compet-ing discourses and the sheer impossibility of their realization in a coherent 'well-made' narrative. . . . They stage a construction of the national culture whose conflicted and endlessly proliferating identities are, in a word, im-plausible" (8–9). Accordingly, neither Cooper's nor Liljencrantz's narratives are plausible or "well-made." Dixon recognizes such stories as attempts to ac-knowledge the paradoxes, and even some of the crimes, of settler history, not merely for purposes of exculpation and redemption. Liljencrantz challenges her young readers to improve on the badly tarnished legacy of white colo-nization. Along with Cooper, she implicitly reconceptualizes colonialism as humane and liberal-minded: the next generation must move beyond the vio-lence of conquest, the materialism of settlement, and the corruptions of the power to restart a better and more tolerant nation. In brief, Liljencrantz tasks her boy readers to transform the settler project's core values from power and profit to patience and paternalism—to bear the white man's burden.

Throughout the trilogy, Liljencrantz merges the Cooperian ethos and Whittier-based Norumbegan traditions both to advocate for colonialism and to warn of its dangers.[26] Despite this paradox, her books were popular. She died in 1910, at thirty-four, and never saw the first volume, *The Thrall of Leif the Lucky* (1902) twice filmed: in 1928 (silent) and 1931 (sound) as *The Viking*. The trilogy as a whole synthesizes seventy years of Norse primordialism. For example, to merge Anglo-Saxon and Norse into a singular Teuton, *The Thrall* begins with the arrival in Norway of Alwin, an enslaved—enthralled—young Anglo-Saxon nobleman. He soon easily learns Norse—implying the proximity of Norse and Anglo-Saxon languages—and proves himself by defeating and then befriending the most accomplished Vikings. Because of his literacy and Christianity, Alwin serves the newly converted Ericson himself. After many convolutions the Anglo-Saxon marries a Norsewoman in America, implying a New World reunification of Teuton and the Anglo-Saxon. In *The Thrall*, Christianity, literacy, racial consolidation, physical strength, and due process make telling appearances: the ideals of the imperial American republic mixed together in a tale of danger, deprivation, disguise, and discovery.

By contrast, *Randvar* allegorizes larger issues involving the ethics of settlement by centering much more directly on Norumbega. Set in 1066, three generations after settlement, "In the Old World over the Ocean the storm of the Norman Conquest was raging." As *Randvar* begins, Norumbega is an established city with a corrupt ruling jarl family installed as the local aristocracy, making Norumbega a stand-in for America on the eve of Revolution. A day's travel away is the small beach settlement of the descendants of the couple from Longfellow's "The Skeleton in Armor," which is reprinted in the front matter. However, Liljencrantz embellishes Longfellow's narrative: the berserker, now named Rolf, had escaped with not only the princess but also a crew of fellow, now aging, Vikings. Randvar is their creole child. In the opening scene, some Norumbegans are searching for the jarl's "freakish son" (1), Helvin. A courtier, the Norman Olaf, the novel's degenerate antagonist, leads the search incompetently, representing an inferior strain of Norse. They cross paths with "two figures just emerging into the open from a brush-hidden trail," in a scene reminiscent of Cooper: "One was a savage of the new-world race which the early Norse explorers called Skraelings, with hair as black as freshly turned leaf-mould, and a shining naked body the hue of an oak leaf in November; and the other in the deerskin garb of a forester, with uncovered locks reflecting the son was a descendant of the Vikings themselves and showed untamed blood in his handsome face as he raised it to look ahead at the horsemen" (5). A long dialogue follows between Randvar and his unnamed companion in which Skraeling and Norseman refer to each other as "brother" and, consistent with Cooperian intimacy, share the same drinking skin. First, they discuss Randvar's relation to Norumbega, as opposed to Rolf's encampment. Randvar's rejection of transplanted Old World courtly life in the city identifies him as uncorrupted and apart, the stereotypical American Adam: "The young forester shrugged his broad shoulders. 'No gifts would I buy at the price Starkad Jarl asks, . . . I know the lot of those who follow him. When he gives the sign they go to roost, whether they are sleepy or not. When his priest rings a bell they say their prayers, even though it breaks in at a time when cursing would come more easily to them'" (8). Rejecting the arbitrary power of both nobility and church, Randvar expresses a de facto antinomian Protestantism. Then they discuss Helvin, the jarl's son, bound by birth to a domestic existence. Randvar notes: "It is said that he was born with the wanderlust upon him, so that every breath is a panting to take ship and travel the sea-king's road wheresoever the wolf of the sail might choose to drive him. But because the sons that came before him are dead and the only other heir is a maiden, his sister, he is not allowed to risk his life" (10). Helvin represents the enclosed white man that the young reader might become if he misses out on the adventure of empire, emasculated by domesticity.

Finally, Randvar describes the already-decaying town, "which is now in danger of becoming more lifeless than a bone-heap" (11). The jarl's extravagance, complacency, hubris, and racism risk Norumbega, and thus the future of white settlement in North America. The Skraeling complains: "Truth to say, the young braves of my race do not feel much love for the white man. He comes among us as one who comes among animals—driving them out to possess himself of their feeding ground—dealing with them only when he wants profit out of their hides" (12). By this logic, Norumbega, and hence America, is doomed to fail, vacating the Doctrine of Discovery, as the materialism intrinsic to settlement had not been subordinated to a nobler calling. By valuing the Skraelings only for their furs, the Norse colony exists only for material ends, abjuring their racial obligation to civilize the savages. Randvar responds:

> Judge not, brother, all of the white race from the behavior of one overbearing old man. It seems to me that your people and my people should dwell together like sons of one father. Our hands are equally open to a friend, and no less hard clinched against a foe; and you do not surpass us much in freedom

and fearing nothing. When it has befallen the other white men to see the wonder of your woodcraft as I have seen it, and to be sheltered and fed by your hospitality as I have been, there will be much awanting if they do not hold you as high in honor as I do. (12–13)

A well-governed settler nation practicing restraint and equality, by implication, benefits both races, but only in acquiescing to "one father," who turns out to be Randvar himself, prefiguring Randvar's forthcoming reformation of Norumbega when he becomes, first, the jarl's second in command, and, second, by novel's end, its elected leader, a gesture toward democracy that echoes the ideals of the settler nation. By juxtaposing these ideals with the actual practices of the corrupt Norse regime, Liljencrantz would demand better behavior from her young readers in their own empire and in the new century.

In the meantime, adventures retain young readers' attention. Before the chapter ends, Randvar witnesses the ruling Jarl Starkad attacked by a giant dog that turns out to be his son Helvin in werewolf form, the physical manifestation of suppressed Teuton masculinity.[27] More important, this incident reveals Randvar's control over the berserker rage that plagued his father: "With his first forward motion, he was seized by a sudden madness as though he had stepped within the ring of whirlpool and was being sucked into a black abyss of horror. It lasted but an instant. Battling against it, his fingers clutched instinctively at his knife-hilt, missed it and closed instead upon the blade, and the smart of cut flesh brought him to himself" (115). Learning to withstand impulsive violence, yet never losing his transcendent and superior racial atavism, Randvar embodies the Teutonic masculine ideal: in the terms of Roy Harvey Pearce, like all white heroes on the American frontier, he can "out-savage the savage" (29) but chooses not to. Randvar heads home singing a song he has written about the early settlers, only to be accosted by the Norman, Olaf, sent by Brynhild, Starkad's daughter, who overheard his singing. When Randvar resists, Olaf attacks with a sword while Randvar defends himself with only a knife. Yet Randvar, intimate with the American landscape—"As a trout knows the rapids, his feet knew the snares" (21)—maneuvers Olaf into tripping over roots. He is about to strike when Brynhild intervenes. Dismissing the duel, they discuss songwriting. Randvar confesses: "In the unsettled places where I love, one hears only verses which the old people brought over the ocean under the hatches of memory. . . . My foster-father, who had worked at a forge in his youth, said that the skalds he had met with were like traders, who do no more than pass on what other men had made; but that a singer who melts scraps together and hammers them out in new shapes is a songsmith" (30). As the settler-artist, Randvar hybridizes Old World materials in the New. Subsequently, when he concedes he is the son of a commoner but the grandson of royalty, like Cooper's Oliver, Byrnhild questions his "deerskin husk and his untrimmed hair." His answer reveals Cooperian values: "If my King's blood cannot show itself through a layer of deerskin, daughter of Jarls, I hold it for a spring that has run dry" (32). By novel's end, like Cooper's Oliver and Elizabeth Temple, likewise the daughter of the similarly unfit leader, they are wed in the wilderness by a "forest priest." Plastic Viking and natural aristocrat, Randvar embodies the Teutonic settler who acts on democratic sympathy and civility rather than aristocratic pretense or violence: he retains his whiteness in the woods, befriends indigenes, chastens corrupt whites, controls his inner berserker, becomes a husband (and implicitly a father), and writes new songs for the New World.

As the novel climaxes, Randvar and Brynhild flee Norumbega to Rolf's beachhead. When they are still twenty miles from home, they hear hoofbeats, and Randvar conceals his bride. However, it is Helvin in werewolf form: "Hurling the song-maker from him upon the earth, he was gone on a bound to some dearer prey beyond" (301). That prey is Olaf, and, once Olaf is dead, Helvin commits suicide, cleansing the settler nation of the degenerate vestiges of both British aristocracy and Norman degeneracy—standins for British (and Confederate—see below) efforts to corrupt the national mission. On the beach, they find other white men who had been expelled from the jarl's degenerate city. The Skraelings also wait, unbidden, to defend Randvar: "Say to the white chief that the men of the stone-ax race have set up their houses around him. Say to him that they turn their weapons whither he points. Say to him that they will bring him the white sachem's scalp whenever he gives the sign" (301). Moreover, the Skraelings' inferior technology—"the stone-ax people"—establishes their need of his righteous guidance. Next, Randvar rejects escape to Norway: a creole, he belongs in the New World. When the Norumbegans approach, Randvar is suspicious, and all the outcasts bare their weapons, ready to fight and die for him. However, a courtier reports Randvar's absolution, bowing to Brynhild: "We have come to offer to you, Starkad's daughter, who are the next of kin—To you and to your husband, who is of all men the most beloved by the folk of the new lands" (312–14), the leadership of Norumbega. Popular acclamation by "the folk of the new lands" imports republican politics to Liljencrantz's primordial settler nation.

After Liljencrantz's novels, fortunately, Norumbega vanished from the American imagination. The frontier closed, the Vikings tamed, and

Norumbega in the right hands, Indians should have no more to fear from settlers, or so the story went. With the Randvars of the world in charge, assimilation can begin, as benevolent creole patriarchs rather than degenerate Europeans would conduct their transformation. As such, Liljencrantz's was a primordialist fantasy suited to the Gilded Age. After 1890, the white man's burden, as reproduced in progressive reform after 1890, assumed the stabilization and completion of white colonialism in North America. As trustworthy and enlightened progressives, elite whites could impose their culture on peoples and places badly in need of their paternal governance. Hence, boarding schools, forced severalty, and neglected reservations became the final stage of continental conquest, deliberately seeking to complete and therefore end settler colonization by both erasing Indian culture and atoning for past sins through confessions of contrition and atonement. Of course, the Dawes Act mostly just allowed whites to congratulate themselves for sacrificing moments of material comfort to work among the poor Indians. Liljencrantz's reformed settler colonialism, like Cooper's, stops short of systemic critique, and so only contributes to newer and more insidious forms of dominion. While the Dawes Act domesticated the white man's burden, its more usual guise was global imperialism, although as Carman noted in the epigraph to this chapter, they are two sides of the same coin.

To that end, starting around 1850, the Norse were repurposed to participate in debates over the nation's colonization of noncontiguous territories: the Norse would be redeployed first as filibusters and finally as administrators of an exploitative, overseas empire, though this was always cloaked in the dissimulation of the burden. As early as the 1850s, as these efforts began, Vinland was reimagined as an outpost of a global empire, accompanying Norumbega's fantasy of continental inhabitation. Yet the exportation of a national identity first required excising its exogenous elements, most prominently the economically, politically, and racially divergent South. As Simms's regionalism, a component of which was the Irish White Man's Land, morphed into secessionist nationalism, southern sectionalism hardened. As a settler nation itself, the Confederacy conjectured a blood-based fantasy of regional cultural descent from primordial Normandy, a Viking settler colony started in the ninth century. Just as Liljencrantz's *Norseman* Randvar had to overcome the *Norman* Olaf, the contestation of two Norse-based primordialisms was allegorized even in anticipation of the Civil War. In the end, the Norse and Northern victory accomplished two goals, each of which enabled the settler nation to pursue noncontinental imperialist endeavors: first, national identity would coalesce around of a Northern (and

Norse) model, and, second, the primordial impulse morphed from geography to biology.

Interlude: The Competing Primordialisms of the Civil War

If nothing else should come out of this war, it would have affected enough in my mind in this, that a vast amount of sickening folly and disgusting mock romances, like this precious Norman blood, will have been ridiculed out of sight.

—"Mace Sloper," *Knickerbocker Magazine*, 1861

As a collection of diverse former colonies, like all settler nations, the United States faced the problem of internal consolidation. As rehearsed in the two Irish primordialisms, binding a settler nation required testing the boundaries of divergence of its foundational norms. Chris Prentice defines expansionism by settler colonies as beginning with internal singularization, even purgation: these enunciations "stand for the delimitation of legitimate cultural activity. In order to assert its own security of identity, threats to that identity had to be defined as external" (48). In the young nation, implicit threats became explicit as the Civil War approached: sectionalism and slavery had to be marked beyond the "delimitation of legitimate cultural activity," and the Norse, operating from a northern home base, were invoked to discipline such divergence.

Likewise, and to serve the same function in the South, Confederate nationalism seized a subcategory of the primordial Norse legacy to claim its own unifying and legitimizing roots in an archaic past: the aristocratic Norman. However, this conjecture had no purchase in a pre-Columbian territorial presence: operating on a fiction of regionally shared primordial bloodlines, the Confederacy claimed French Huguenots to gain access to a medieval Norman culture of courtliness, feudalism, and chivalry. These, it was asserted, distinguished the South from the Norse-based North, now degenerated to a dull Anglo-Saxon mediocrity. As the conflict approached, each side identified the other as an exogenous other. More specifically, each assumed different aspects of the primordial Norse legend and its baseline in Teutonic genetics to define distinct notions of "legitimate cultural activity," thereby delegitimizing their opponents' claim to the same.[28] If the North's Anglo-Saxons derived from an earlier splinter of the ascendant Teutonic culture, contemporary historians saw the Saxons supposedly splitting off from the Teutons in the fourth century CE. By contrast, the South claimed descent from a group whose superiority was based in having split more recently, and from a more fully articulated and refined Teutonic culture. An ex-Viking, Rollo, settler-colonized Normandy with the blessing of the Franks in the late ninth century. His descendants, in turn, settler-colonized Saxon England in 1066.[29] Neither history was accurate in terms of genetics or demographics, but neither set of Americans cared. Ritchie Devon Watson Jr. claims: "The leaders of Dixie's political and journalistic establishment would begin feverishly concocting the myth of the South's aristocratic and chivalric racial inheritance, and it would imagine the newly minted Norman race to be in a fight for survival with an implacable foe: a northern Saxon race descended from the middling commercial and yeoman classes of England and imbibed with deeply implanted racial qualities of Puritan self-righteousness and intolerance" (34). Watson further claims that, after reading Sir Walter Scott's romances, "Southrons" embraced the Norman strain of the ever-plastic Norse identity as its own distinct primordial inheritance. Even Simms ceased discussing the Irish and joined the Norman bandwagon.[30] Southern Norman primordialism was enunciated in the medievalist texts of Simms, Henry Timrod, and others, as the *Knickerbocker's* correspondent complained.[31] In the *Southern Quarterly Review* (1858), the editor bragged: "A Warrior race will found an empire, illustrious in arms, as renowned in art, and will show the cavalier blood to be still worthy of its Norman origin" (qtd. in William Taylor, 204). Confederate war poetry perhaps best expressed this primordialist historiography. In "A Poem Which Needs No Dedication," from *War Songs of the South* (1862), James Barrow Hope begins a recruiting pitch bathed in rhetoric of ethnic reawakening intrinsic to romantic nationalism:

> When you hold yourselves as freemen
> Tyrants love just such as ye!
> Go! Abate your lofty manner!
> Write upon the Old State's Banner,
>   *A furore Normanorum*
>   *Libera nos, Domine!* (22)

These last two lines—translated as "From the wrath of the Normans / Free us, Lord!"—stand as chorus, repeated fifteen times as the verses chart Norman history from the Vikings through William the Conqueror and finally to the purported Huguenot migration to the Carolinas. In so doing, Hope performs the essential southern embrace of primordial Norman valor and violence.

Such historical revision was not received well in the North. Charles Loring Brace responded by defining Normans as poor colonizers: "Though holding an important French province for several centuries, they left behind them no language, no literature, no mythology or architecture" (134). The Normans, that is, became French, rather than forcing the French to become Norse. In *English Traits,* Emerson defined this as the reverse of Teutonic dominion: "When they live with other races, they do not take their language, but bestow their own. . . . They assimilate other races to themselves and are not assimilated" (459). In Normandy, these erstwhile Vikings had accommodated rather than dominated, exchanging the Teutonic cultural imperative to dominate for material comfort and continental sophistication. The editors of *Knickerbocker* were having none of it. They began the "Editor's Table" in their August 1861 issue with a commentary from a "Mace Sloper," part of which serves as the epigraph for this section, rejecting the idolatry of the South's manufactured Norman mythology. After a thorough examination of actual immigration and census records that revealed how precious little Huguenot blood there was among the slaveholders, "Sloper" attacks the South's fascination with its fabricated Norman primordialism: "All this must change. For instance, we are to hear no more nonsensical comparison between Norman gentlemen of the South and the Saxon churls of the North." (9). Nonetheless, the South embraced the Normans for their purported chivalric gentility and hierarchy. As a conflict between secondhand Anglo-Saxon Norse and secondhand Norman Norse, the war matched battling primordialisms.

In their war poetry, northern writers exploited this divergence to expand their own prior imaginative investment in the primordial Norse. Ada Thomas's 1862 poem "On to the Southward" most directly calls forth Norse berserker skills to eliminate the corrupted Norman southerners and cleanse the nation in preparation for its transition to empire. Thomas, writing in *The Ladies' Repository,* equated Union soldiers and Viking warriors.[32] Yet the Norse legacy she has in mind is not random Viking violence but rather their reluctant yet inevitable righteousness, a duty reluctantly taken up to cleanse the nation of the corruptions of southern degeneration. Thus the poem encapsulates a post–Mexican War continental nation rising to the national virtue mandated by having fulfilled its Manifest Destiny. The Confederacy's rupturing of that continental nation, and doing so in the name of the moral evil of slavery, raises the stakes to that of racial mission and, implicitly, an early version of the white man's burden.[33] She envisions the Norse North saving the nation not just from the degenerate Normanism of the Confederacy but also the otherwise unbroken Teutonic trajectory toward global dominion:

> Hail to the Norsemen! The men of the morning!
> Hail to the ruddy cheeked men of the snow!
> Thor hath awakened, he giveth his warning!
> Hail to the land where the evergreens grow!
> Where are the Norsemen, these men of the morning?
> Show us the strong-sinewed men of the North! (31)

She follows with a continental range, venturing from the St. Lawrence valley to San Francisco, including the Great Lakes, the wild Missouri, and Iowa's plains, avoiding all southern geography. Her nineteenth-century Norsemen are "From the bays of the East to the mighty Pacific, / From fair Illinois to the lakes banked with snow / . . . Gentlest in love, but in anger pacific." The rhyming of "pacific" with "Pacific" merges the settler's disavowal of interracial violence with the rhetoric of Manifest Destiny. The sleeping Norsemen within every Union soldier embodies a racial teleology of progress and expansion:

> Hail to the Norsemen as Southward they pass!
> Press to the Southward, and level the borders,
> Nations amazed, view the war that ye wage
> Cures from the North, for the World's disorders!
> Hail to the Norsemen! The first in the age! (31)

While Thomas's immediate end is to "Cure" the nation of effeminizing slavery, her geography hints at global ambitions: "Cures from the North, for the World's disorders!" Invigorated by defeating the South with "northern" energies, the North, both geographically and figuratively, was poised to continue the civilizing mission begun by their ancestors from Scandinavia: wherever the Americans were to go, their Norse blood enabled their dominion, not a privilege based in an obscure legend of tenth-century sojourners who had left the Western Hemisphere as soon as they could. Once the Norseman had ridden South, Thomas implies, they would ride across the globe, their racial mission transcending any local obligation.

The competing primordialisms of the Civil War catalyzed some paradigmatic shifts as primordialism was adopted to postbellum circumstances.

As Thomas suggests, although the actual Norse raided only in the North Atlantic and Europe, their ancestors endeavored to attain global dominion. Lands far beyond the contiguous nation had come within the latter-day Norse ambit, as blood-based authentication added international adventurism to its repertoire of techniques for colonizing peoples and places it believed it was destined to dominate. By this logic, Vinland was reimagined not as a settler colony but rather as a potential exploitive colony: not a new home, but an imperial outpost from which colonizers returned.

Vinland

We come, the children of thy Vinland,
The youngest of the World's high peers,
O land of steel, and song, and saga
To greet thy glorious thousand years.
Hail! Motherland of skalds and heroes
By love of freedom hither hurled;
For in thy hearts as in thy mountains,
And strength like them to shake the world. . . .
What though thy native hearts be silent?
The chord they struck shall ours prolong
We claim thee kindred, call thee mother
O land of sagas, steel, and song!

—Bayard Taylor, "America to Iceland," 1874

Approximately a millennium after its discovery by the Viking Floki, Iceland celebrated its founding. Bayard Taylor's 1874 poem "America to Iceland" commemorated the event as a brief poem soaked in the ideology of primordialism.[34] Taylor refers to "Iceland" as America's "mother," "claims" her as "kindred," and announces Americans as "the children of thy Vinland." At the same time, he raises anxieties typical of the settler colonial. For example, America's usual "mother"—Great Britain—is absent, as such a powerful parent would cast its child into shadows, reminding it of its subordinate status as offspring. Iceland offered less of a threat. Moreover, though its overseas adventurism was fairly recent, Taylor speaks for an America that is "the youngest of the world's high peers." His America, because of its Icelandic heritage, has become one of the "conquering nations." Finally, as Icelandic poets seem missing, Taylor assumes the continuation of "the chord they struck." The many subtexts of Taylor's poem exemplify

Kolodny's assertion that "the image of the Norse in the postwar decades helped provide Americans with both historical precedent and a racially-inherited legitimacy for their latest dreams of empire" (*In Search of First Contact*, 207).

However, both the efforts and the imagery started sooner, even before the war. The postwar overseas mission implied by Thomas was already underway. The US Navy "opened" Japan in 1854, and, while the government and the public were slow to accede to "empire," nongovernmental white entrepreneurial filibusters initiated an informal, nongovernmental imperialist process. Private invasions of other countries, starting with Mexico in the early 1830s, were not officially sanctioned but were, nonetheless, celebrated as enacting national ambitions and racial destinies and were often legitimized and disputed through textual linkages with the primordial Norse imagery: Vinland became, in a sense, a filibuster settlement itself. Primordial imagery based in Vinland pervaded American efforts—official and unofficial—to put into practice the "racially-inherited legitimacy" that would create overseas colonies that would enrich the settler postcolony, now imperial nation, under the guise of the burden of its whiteness.

Robert E. May defines filibusters as "American adventurers who raised or participated in private military forces that either invaded or planned to invade foreign countries with which the United States was formally at peace. . . . Often damned at home and abroad as pirates, the filibusters were also worshipped as heroes by masses of people" (xii–xiii). While May downplays the racial aspects of filibustering, the targeted territories were always occupied and governed by nonwhite populations. More direct, Amy Greenburg describes how "faith in the racial superiority of the Anglo-Saxon and in the inferiority of the 'mixed race' peoples of Latin America" (45) empowered the filibusters. In most filibustering efforts, to recruit mercenaries and operatives, stock shares against future profits were often offered in lieu of cash, broadening its economic appeal to a nation of speculators. Once again, the plastic Viking was reinvented to reflect this ambition even before the Civil War in Charles Loring Brace's *The Norse-Folk* (1857) and William Dowe's essay "The Ericcsons" (1853). Each reimagined the Vinland Vikings as filibusters to validate a white imperialism that transcended republican principles, transposing American and Norse, rather than Norman, legacies.

At the same time, moral and legal challenges to filibustering were likewise based in the legacy of the Vikings. In a review of the decidedly primordialist and historically inaccurate Benjamin De Costa's *The Pre-Columbian Discovery of America by the Northmen* (1868), Charles Harberman wrote: "Our friends the Vikings were more pirates than colonists. . . . Let us take the Northmen as we have it; that excludes any settlements that were of long duration. The argument *ex silencio* of course is in itself not conclusive. But where there are no monuments, relics, or other indicators to contradict or modify our direct testimony, it is sadly better to accept it as it stands, and not to construct any history from our own sense of what we would have done under the same circumstances" (493–94). Harberman here, like Belknap and others before him, challenges both the fact and the need for a primordial past. De Costa's book itself, an unapologetic attempt to supplant Columbus with Ericson, provoked Harberman's recognition that primordialism mostly reflects the settler's blinding need for a justifying, archaic tradition: the former colonials growing so obsessed with finding a usable past that they ignore any contradictory evidence. Nonetheless, beginning at midcentury a blood-based fantasy of racial hierarchy and global adventurism pervaded American print culture to justify offshore colonization.

Brace is best known as the founder of the Children's Aid Society and the inventor of the Orphan Trains that placed abandoned white children from the eastern cities in western homes, addressing a problem he experienced firsthand while serving as a minister in the notorious Five Points section of New York City, despite his genteel New England upbringing.[35] As a young man as well, he traveled covertly with his friend Frederick Law Olmsted as the latter collected materials for his abolitionist exposé *The Cotton Kingdom* (1854). Brace framed these missions as racial and moral obligations to administer to the "lower races" from his position as a superior Anglo-Saxon. He showed his Teutonism in his travel book about Baltic regions, *The Norse-Folk*: "To the American, a visit to the home of the Old Norsemen is a visit back to his forefather's house. A thousand signs tell him he is in the cradle of the race that leads the modern enterprise, and whose Viking power on both hemispheres has not yet ceased to be felt" (n.p., preface). Later, betraying sentiments that would attract him to social Darwinism, Brace links the landscape to its peoples, describing it as "a natural home for that daring race of pirates and filibusters who scourged Europe for so many centuries, and who finally infused their savage vigor into its effeminated and superstitious people" (124). Like Thomas, Brace positions the Norse as a "cure" for the tendency of other nations to fall into the effeminizing sloth and ignorance.[36] Brace's use of "effeminated" as a pejorative reiterates the masculinist core the Teutonic colonization of all the northern Europeans and identifies them as the patriarch to all European cultures. As racial filibusters, they transcended artificial borders to improve not only themselves but also the peoples and places they conquered.

Moreover, Brace's idea of Norse ideology presages political and economic modernity in which the profit motive inspires individual participation that generates salutary progress: "Feudalism could do little against the fierce democracy of the Vikings. With the Northern robbers, every private soldier was a landholder, and an independent man. . . . They united a boundless ambition and enterprise with the most firm animal courage, and a reckless contempt for death" (128). Brace's Norseman, embodying Wawn's and Kolodny's ever-shifting imperial man, glory in their Emersonian contradictions, their ends justifying their means. Alfred the Great's defeats of the Vikings notwithstanding, the Saxons—without Norse intervention and oversight—had lost their Teutonic energy: "The English Saxons, even as the other Christian peoples of the continent, had felt the depressing and unmanning influence of monkish superstitions. They had become a weak, almost effete race. Industrious on the soil, potent with mechanical labor, they had no taste for the sea-faring life, or the dangers and the toils of warfare. They fell an easy prey to the vigorous, relentless Northmen. Henceforth England had stamped on her native character the morals of the Norwegian sea-kings; and their American progeny yet bears them even more distinctly" (132). Brace's Norsemen, as democratic coinvestors, had cleansed northern Europe a thousand years ago, anticipating by centuries the values of capitalism and Protestantism. In the nineteenth century, Americans awaited their opportunity to distill that essence into global dominion. Brace finally links racial and Protestant destinies through his primordial Norse avatar: "The Scandinavians were among the first to accept Protestant reform because it left them more freely to an isolated individualism, and releases them from the trammels of authority to the contemplation of the sublime abstractions in which they delight. . . . The stronghold of Christianity is the Northern Mind—it will eventually work its way to the uprooting of all traditional bondage—democracy must look to the North for its only hope" (191). That is, only the Protestantism of northern Europe counts as genuinely Christian and thus genuinely democratic. For Brace and others like him, filibustering then becomes, through the Norse model, a model of economic, political, and Christian racial and capitalist evangelism. For Brace, the Norse forefathers of America embodied a crucial shift from place- to a race-based primordialism, and as such well suited to global exportation once the settler nation had unified behind the Norse, not the Norman or the Anglo-Saxon, primordial legacy.

Dowe's essay in *Graham's American Monthly Magazine* more directly defines the coming of American globalism as rooted in its filibustering Teutonic primordialism. "The Ericcsons: An Old Story and a New One" combines Ericson's colonization of North America and Emerson's, Simms's, and Brace's Teutonism to celebrate American John Ericcson's invention of a caloric engine. For Dowe, this symbolizes a transcendent racial trajectory from Norse filibustering to American imperialism, specifically in the soon to be "opened" Japan.[37] However, the lack of a comprehensive diplomatic policy in the 1850s left Japan and other western Pacific regions open to filibusters, and Dowe meant to embolden American efforts by reminding them of their Norse inheritance.[38] An Irish immigrant, a friend of Longfellow, and a regular contributor to *Graham's,* Dowe begins by invoking Coleridge's "Rhyme of the Ancient Mariner," whose popularity assured familiarity and an implied congratulation to the "discursive" reader: "Nothing like giving literary matter an attractive heading, as most writers are very well aware. This takes the discursive reader captive, at the first setting out, and conciliates his partialities—holding him, in fact, as the Ancient Mariner holds the Wedding Guest by his glittering eye, til he comes to the end of his story" (385). Citing Ericsson's invention as "rank[ing] him with [Robert] Fulton in the peerage of American science—above him in the opinion of a great many," Dowe asserts: "He is, in fact, only one of our famous Ericcsons. The historic reader will remember, though the general reader has perhaps forgotten, that an Ericcson was the first discoverer of America, and that by right of priority and precedence, we ought to be Ericcsonians! . . . Before speaking of the achievement of the modern Ericcson, then, we may just glance at those of his old Norse name sakes—perhaps ancestors—who knows?" (385). Dowe synthesizes a number of primordialisms here: place-based precedents interact with genetic inheritance to create a double bond of Norse-American continuity.

These linkages are enabled by Coleridgean mysticism: a familial lineage that states directly what most Teutonists and primordialists only implied. Next, Dowe summarizes the stories that had fascinated American readers since Rafn's publication. By defining Vikings raids as "filibustering," he invokes the recently annexed Texas:[39] "Stream after stream, the Varinger or Vikingr came down in arms, pushing all weaker races before them. And filling their brave dragon-barks with every thing portable that fell in their way; a vigorous race, with a rich, restless blood in their veins, such as feeds the growth of the most splendid and valuable civilization" (385–86). Dowe then records a brief chronology of Viking filibustering in the Old World, before they head west to Iceland, Greenland, and Vinland. Like Emerson, he equates the sagas and the Greco-Roman classics, "as faithfully preserved as the classics were by their brethren of the south" (387). Dowe next shifts from continental to global scales: the Norse inhere not because they stayed in North America, but because they operated on a hemispheric scale suited to the transportation technology available to them. Vinland was just the western node of a global ambit. To illustrate the primordial inheritance of modern industrialism, Dowe shifts to Ericcson's engine: "The performance of our cotemporary, the captain, is far greater than that of the ancient pilot, his namesake, and, indeed, with reason; for the modern promises to be of far greater benefit to the world than the ancient." Like Simms, Dowe warns that primordial glory is a dead letter if it remains antiquarian. Primordial ideology must serve a forward-looking nation: obsessing over the past for its own sake signifies degeneration.[40] As to the engine, Dowe describes at length its use in oceangoing ships: "Caloric ships will traverse the ocean at one-fifth the present expense; a state of things which ensures the five-fold increase of commerce and general intercourse. . . . All these things, reacting upon one another, and thus multiplied, may well justify us in anticipating a beneficent success from the achievement of this scientific Norseman" (388). Dowe's conclusion directly invokes how these inventions bolstered the global American presence. Noting that the United States' interest in open-ing Japan as a coal-refueling station for transpacific vessels, Dowe unites the racial, the technological, and the imperial: "We have been grounding our Japan expedition—or rather floating it on—the necessity of getting coals; and now Ericcson almost knocks the plea down—showing that coal depots will not be much needed under the caloric regime. However—that Japanese oyster ought to be opened; and we hope there are pretexts enough left for that purpose" (389). A brief essay that begins with the "filibustering Scan-dinavians" ends with a demand that the United States "open" Japan, regard-less of need or pretext. For Dowe, and for most northerners whose gaze was turning global even before the Civil War, the nation's Norse-derived technology and genetics would enable it to pry open any oyster—any un-exploited site of colonial adventure—to enrich themselves with the pearl within, and, incidentally, to cleanse the world of its shortcomings.

At the same time, race-based filibustering—as well as globalization—was also and already challenged for its primordialist self-justification, under-mining its insistence on both Norse heroism and blood-based racial virtues. For example, William Ellery Channing condemned filibustering in Mexico in his 1837 pamphlet, *Letter to Hon. Henry Clay, On the Annexation of Texas* as a component of his broader rejection of Anglo-Saxonism more generally and filibustering specifically. As to the Norse, he identifies the filibuster-ing Texans as anything but the innocent victims of Mexican colonialism they claimed to be. He compares their invasion of Mexico as re-creating acts of unredeemed Viking savagery: "The colonists and their coadjutors can satisfy themselves with nothing short of an empire. They have left their Anglo-Saxon ancestors behind them. Those barbarians conformed to the maxim of their age, to the rude code of nations in the time of thickest heathen darkness. They invaded England under their sovereigns and with the gloomy religion of the North" (20–21). To Channing, filibustering vacated modern claims to Anglo-Saxonism's link to moral righteousness. Channing, breaking from his friend Emerson, claims that these virtues had always been misrepresented, coming, as they did, from the "thickest heathen darkness." Channing's recognition that the invasion of Mexico signaled a desire for "nothing short of empire" was exceptionally perceptive, even noting the use of misdirection (and self-deception) intrinsic to settler colonialism in their identifying themselves "colonists." Charles T. Porter in his *Review of the Mexican War* (1849) likewise saw through the corrupt self-justifications of the Texans and their American backers: "Let us not attempt to deceive ourselves. The lust of conquest has begun to rage among us. It is called 'making room for the Anglo-Saxon race,' 'working out our Manifest Destiny,' and 'enlarging the area of freedom.' It has assumed the noblest garb of humanity and covered its face with a mask of wonderful virtue. But it is the spirit of conquest still" (164). Like Channing, Porter identifies Anglo-Saxonism as a cover for violence and greed. That race-based primordialism disingenuously validated conquest in the name of freedom is revealed as mere propaganda. Senator James Shields was most direct: "If anything was wanting to prove that this age is an age of imbecility and false philosophy, it is furnished in this drivel about races. The Anglo-Saxon race and the Celtic race, and this race and that race, seem to be the latest discovery of the present time to account for all moral, social, and political phenomena. This new theory is founded in neither Christianity nor Philosophy" (qtd. in Horsman, 249). Along the same lines, Senator Thomas Corwin imagines a patriotic Mexican saying, "There I bled for liberty! And shall I now surrender that consecrated home of my affections to the Anglo-Saxon invaders?" (349). In other words, the Teutonization of America was specifically refuted by preachers, historians, and politicians as re-creating the worst, not the best, of western civilization, striking at the core of primordialism's entanglements of race, nation, and destiny.

Nonetheless, the same arguments over American adventurism—both filibustering and official—would be repeated after the War and would be, again, set against a Vinland-based primordialist backdrop. By century's end, in the Spanish- and Philippine-American Wars, the government's role would be more direct, making the nation officially imperial. This began with the purchase of Alaska from Russia: "I can conceive no greater boon to our

Pacific states, and I cannot suppose that the Atlantic senators will deny to
the people of those states the fisheries depending upon Russian America
now within their grasp. We need such a nursery of seaman, such a commerce, as these fisheries will produce. They will feed the coasts and islands
of the Pacific and the vigorous climate will breed a race of hardy adventurers to repeat on the Pacific, softened by Christian civilization, the deeds
of the old Norse Sea-Kings on the Atlantic" (31), wrote General Benjamin
Meigs in 1867 to encourage Secretary of State William Seward to purchase
Alaska for its exploitable resources and as a site for training young men to
replicate the deeds of their (supposed) Viking forebears.[41] Though the Civil
War had ended just two years before, Meigs voices a creeping fear that white
American men were increasingly out of touch with the race-based strengths
and skills of their Norse legacy. In an 1899 letter, Theodore Roosevelt expresses the same fear: "Over-sentimentality, over-softness, in fact washiness
and mushiness are the great dangers of this age and these people. Unless we
keep the barbarian virtues, gaining the civilized ones will be of little avail"
(qtd. in Jacobson, *Barbarian*, 3). These barbaric virtues represent an intrinsic blood-based primordialism: the dormant Viking lurking within every
Anglo-Saxon male must be awakened to expand empire and to globalize
white civilization, a transcendent linkage of the archaic past and the global
future.

Simultaneous efforts to build both a domestic nation and a transoceanic
empire required white men, "hardy adventurers," reconnected with their
Norse-based "barbarian virtues." John Carlos Rowe has spoken to the role
of literature in imperial adventurism: "With their reliance on an aesthetics of pleasure and their address to relatively stable middle-class audiences,
novels tend to reinforce the notion that culture contributes to imperialism
primarily by mystifying the otherwise ugly practices of the military conquest of foreign lands" (15). Liljencrantz certainly engaged this in her trilogy.
Yet novels can also *demystify* imperial enterprises. As far back as Aphra
Behn's *Orinooko* (1688), popular fiction has brought those "ugly practices"
to light and demanded that imperial men conduct themselves in ways more
aligned with civilization's ideals. After the Spanish-American War, Americans had, for the first time, an obvious, undisavowable empire, subordinate
peoples of color under their dominion, and a print culture broad enough
both to propagate and expose its practices. Initially, however, to instruct
white Americans on their role in their governing the world, Norse primordialist fantasies contributed to the nation- and empire-making conversations. Yet the war also generated explicitly "anti-imperialist" publications
and movements.[42] Before 1898, challenges to American imperialism had

been framed as reactionary, as Albert Carman noted in this chapter's epigraph, demonstrating that most white Americans were in denial that their progressive republic could also be an exploitative empire. Progressive legislation like the Dawes Act was intended to mitigate damages left by centuries of colonization and conquest yet failed badly to account for Indian resistance to forced acculturation of a "white" social and cultural norm. As such, Helen Hunt Jackson's books from the 1880s compelled the liberal paternalism of the Dawes Act yet failed to account for the extent of the white racism that had created the Indians' misery in the first place. Only a critique that met the racist rhetoric of empire on its own terms, that broached the blood-based primordial sources of white nationalism—Anglo-Saxonism and its parent Teutonism—communicated the real stakes. This challenge was undertaken by, among others, Jack London, James Weldon Johnson, and Mark Twain, all of whom refer to blood-based primordial conjectures such as "Anglo-Saxonism" and "Teutonism" as models of American racial self-fashioning that concealed the ongoing agendas of settler colonialism and white nationalism.

Unfortunately, they had a plethora of imperialist texts to which they could respond. A popular fiction based in a blood-based primordialist fantasy, Frank Norris's *Moran of the Lady Letty* (1898), merges Viking and imperialist narratives. Norris began his career by writing boy's stories, albeit without the self-deprecating critical perspective of Cooper or Liljencrantz.[43] Like his British models Ballantyne and Marryat, Norris combined genetic Teutonism, filibustering empire building, and blood-curdling adventures to reinforce the nation's broader racial and imperial ambitions and to recruit young men raised in the era of Roosevelt to the imperial cause. His hero is Ross Wilbur, a bored San Francisco gentleman caught up in the effeminizing whirlwind of teas, tennis, yachting parties, and debutante balls with his Ivy League comrades. Understanding that American boys cared little for such scenes (or at least that they shouldn't), Norris asks his readers' patience: "This is to be a story of a battle, at least one murder, and several sudden deaths" (3). Fortunately, Wilbur is soon "shang-hai'd" on a small fishing boat operated by a corrupt white captain and a crew of deceitful Chinese.

Once beyond the Golden Gate, Wilbur embraces life at sea: "I don't know when I've been—when I've had—I've been happier than these last few weeks" (60). Leading Roosevelt's "strenuous life," having recovered those barbarian virtues, he is finally free and finally himself. Norris wastes little time establishing conflict between the noble Norse and the inferior Chinese. The heroine—the eponymous Moran—is a beauty "of the fine, hardy Norse type" (28) whose ship they find after it had been raided by Chinese pirates and left adrift. Within Wilbur, the latent Teutonic berserker awaits: "Somewhere deep down in the heart of every Anglo-Saxon lies the predatory instinct of his Viking ancestors—an instinct that a thousand years of respectability and taxpaying have not quite succeeded in eliminating" (29). Soon Wilbur comes to love Moran: "She seemed to him some Bradamente, some mythical Brunhilde, some Valkyrie of legend, born out of season, lost and unfamiliar in this end-of-century time" (61). In the climactic fight on a deserted Baja beach, Wilbur kills his first man, and, as opposed to Liljencrantz's Randvar, glories in unleashing his latent berserker: "Then suddenly, at the sight of his smitten enemy, rolling on the ground at his feet, the primitive man, the half-brute of the stone age, leaped to life in Wilbur's breast—he felt muscles thrilling with a strength they had not known before. . . . Never had he conceived such savage exultation as that which mastered him at that moment" (79). So aroused, Wilbur and Moran take out their sexual tension in a subsequent sexual battle with each other, in a problematic scene that glorifies rape and disregards a woman's stated consent, enacting the ultimate expression of racial as well as sexual dominance. Worse yet, his victory refeminizes her: "Her Berserker rage had worked itself clear" (80). This, however, makes her vulnerable, at novel's end, to betrayal and murder by the supposedly trusted "coolie" Hoang upon their return to San Francisco.[44] While the Viking could be aroused to serve the empire, the shield maiden could not. Building the empire was man's work.

Before that, though, sailing north from Baja with his hard-won riches and his newly submissive woman, during a brief stop in San Diego, Wilbur finds his astonished old Yale friends. When they try to update him on the latest gossip, he responds: "Do you think there's any fun in that for me now? Why, man, I've fought—fought with a naked dirk, fought with a coolie who snapped at me like an ape—and you talk to me of dancing and functions and german favors! It wouldn't do some of you people a bit of harm if you were shanghaied yourselves. That sort of life, if you don't do anything else, knocks a big bit of seriousness into you. You fellows make me sick" (94). Following that, he announces plans to "filibuster" in Cuba. When Hoang murders Moran, steals the booty, and sets the ship to sail into the Pacific with only her corpse as crew, Wilbur is bereft. Nonetheless, reawakened, he will not return to the "small things" of his previous existence. Moran— "sea rover and daughter of a thousand Vikings" (98)—was sacrificed to revive the Norseman sleeping within Wilbur and, by extension, the young reader. Published on the eve of war, Norris's novella soon found many imitators who now had the advantages of both specific sites for the adventure

of empire and the government's sanction and participation. In the decade
to follow, many of these imitators featured Vikings implicitly, like Norris,
or explicitly, like Liljencrantz. Either way, Teutonic adventurism met with
broad popularity in sensational fictions before, during, after the Spanish-
and Philippine-American Wars, whether the war brought colonies to settle,
such as Hawaii, or colonies to exploit, such as the Philippines or Cuba.

However, the genre and its primordial subtexts were also ripe for critique. These depicted the Norse as creating a legacy of savagery and deceit
rather than glory and virtue. For example, in a review of pseudonymous
British novelist "Du Chaillu's" *Ivar the Viking* (1891), an anonymous critic in
Boston's *Catholic World* responded: "To the unfortunate inhabitants of the
Scottish, the English, and the Irish coasts, they never appeared in any other
light than a race of unmitigated savages, cruel, barbarous, and inimicable
to progress beyond any scourges which ever made piracy and brigandage
their usual means of livelihood. . . . Their inroads were the means of retard-
ing civilization by many centuries in the countries in which they made their
hunting grounds" (Anon., "Talk about New Books," 441–42). Like all primordialists, Du Chaillu (like Ballantyne, he was primordializing British imperialism) celebrated Ivar's conquest of Ireland as the inevitable unfolding
of racial destiny. By contrast, this reviewer also rejects the sanitized Vikings
presented in stories such as Jones's or Liljencrantz's. Ironically, of course,
imperial soldiers behaved very much like Vikings as described by the
reviewers, a sentiment further elaborated in other texts.

To that end, the purported altruism of imperialism was likewise undermined by its claim that noble Vikings rehearsed the "altruism" of the imperial adventure. More reflective of resisting values are the stories of Miriam
Michaelson. Instead of celebrating the bloody cruelty of Teutonic tradition, she saw through Norse adventurism to identify its more perfidious
sources.[45] In particular, her story "The Cradle" features the repeated rape
and sale of an enslaved female Viking, a victim of masculine abuse denied
the freedoms embodied by the shield maidens of Liljencrantz or Norris. In
addition, Michaelson's "Fayal, the Unforgiving" focuses on the politics of
representation and reputation. Though feared as a berserker, Fayal is mild-
mannered, very forgiving, but he has been designated to serve the figure-
head for hidden men who "kill, torture, punish—relentless, unangered,
unfeeling" (85). This darker, covert cabal turns Viking violence on itself as
a means of imposing tyranny and greed, hardly the democratic values primordialists projected on the Norse. In other words, the fierce Viking is a ve-
neer, a mask hiding a deeper evil, one hidden even from common Vikings

themselves. Michaelson understood such inventions of tradition as rhetori-cal sleight of hand: by distracting readers in the romance of a mystical past, primordialism disguised exploitation as adventure.

Transcending direct reference to Vikings, the racialization of the white American male as heir to world-conquering Norseman confronted the racial politics of empire more directly. Although most missed Rudyard Kipling's irony, "The White Man's Burden"—both the poem and the slogan—branded the Anglo-Saxon empire a scaffolding of solipsistic martyrdom beneath which resource-based profits were gathered.[46] Yet as Gretchen Murphy has argued, Kipling's poem had a more complex relationship with impe-rialism for its settler nations: "Rather than supporting the linkage between whiteness and American empire, the poem exacerbated anxieties about the meaning and importance of whiteness for a U.S. global mission" (16–17). For instance, in 1899 Morrison L. Swift looked back on a century of continental appropriation:

> This state of things does not suggest that [Anglo-Saxons] are gifted to raise inferior peoples. It would be a delicate question to ask if we shall prepare the Cubans and the Filipinos for self-government. . . . Our rule of [the Indians] has bloomed in robbery and progressive extermination, and behind the swindling officials has stood the moral and military forces of the nation. We may say that it is for the good of the world that the breath of civilization exterminates such races—some assent to this—but it shakes the argument of philanthropy. Is it good for *them* to be exterminated? (2–3; emphasis in original)

Swift perceived that overseas imperialism continued the genocidal trajec-tory of continental settler colonialism, subverting its claim to the benevo-lent stewardship of newly colonized populations. Such patterns reflected the settlers' lingering colonial subordination: by claiming the "burden," Ameri-cans imitated their British elders, so betraying their unwillingness to ex-plore their own peculiar space between "Briton and Indian," as suggested by Philip Deloria, to explore other options or, better yet, disengaging the pro-cess altogether. Instead, they reinscribe their own colonial status by embrac-ing a secondhand Anglo-Saxonism and its analog in literary Teutonism. In the embrace of racial primordialism, the settler denies he was ever colonial, that his identity transcends history and is based in biology.

Raymond L. Bridgeman's anti–Philippine War novel *Loyal Traitors* (1903) demonstrates both the destructive outcomes of such hubris and the limits of self-critique within settler discourse. While his white American heroes sacrifice themselves for the cause of anti-imperialism, their adventure in the

Philippine War is still immersed in Anglo-Saxon superiority: the heroes are New England white men who view the war as directly opposed to the republic's stated goals. At the same time, they are better fighters and leaders than the Filipinos themselves. They die by the hands of their own countrymen, perhaps the truest means bearing the burden. Bridgeman, that is, affirms racial hierarchy while undermining its national and imperial applications. Like Swift, Bridgeman sees this as a continuation of older forms of colonialist racial violence, not a leap into a new adventure. *Loyal Traitors* also enacts an emergent white awareness of the romantic problem of equating race and nation. One of Bridgeman's secondary heroes—the first to die, of course—is a former slave who takes up the Filipino cause by noting, "I am ashamed to say that there are two regiments of Negroes in the US Army who have gone over to help white men conquer these brown men" (97). Like Swift, Bridgeman sees a subordinate population—ex-slaves—exploited not to expand the freedom of people of color but rather, ironically, to expand and replicate the same patterns of racial hierarchies abroad as Jim Crow did at home.

Yet Bridgeman was a white writer whose novel cannot coherently contain the paradoxes of his efforts at anti-imperialist critique. Emergent writers of color offered more comprehensive diatribes that identified the core issue Bridgeman obliviously affirmed: the primordialist myth of Anglo-Saxon superiority rooted in Teutonic origins.[47] African American writer James Weldon Johnson would offer more trenchant reflections on the use of primordial imagery to define and enforce American racial hierarchies.[48] First, his unproduced and unpublished lyric opera *Tolosa* (1901) scathingly satirized the annexation of Hawaii. Furthermore, after depicting a brutal lynching in his *Autobiography of an Ex-Coloured Man* (1912), Johnson linked the literature of Teutonic righteousness to the subordination of racial minorities: "So can an ordinary peace-loving citizen sit by a comfortable fire and read with enjoyment of the bloody deeds of pirates and the fierce brutality of Vikings. This is the way in which we gratify the old, underlying animal instincts and passions; but we shudder with horror at the mere idea of such practices being realities in this day of enlightened and humanitarianized thought" (138). Johnson identified the gratuitous uses to which the purported racial past of American whites was exploited to establish and justify the exercise of dominion over nonwhite populations and how primordialism packaged that mission as both traditional and heroic. In a later essay, Johnson elaborated more fully: "The mythical Anglo-Saxon, and his culture as well, never existed. . . . The 'Anglo-Saxon' acts as if he had something to fear. He behaves like a coward. . . . He had better stop twaddling about democracy, liberty, and what-not. Let him come out and boldly say: this is a country who consider themselves Anglo-Saxon without knowing what they mean; people who intend to make America their own private cozy little club where everyone else can exist on suffrance only" ("On the Anglo-Saxon Race," 69–70). Johnson identifies white claims to "Anglo-Saxonism" as not only historically ignorant but also an aspiration based on fear and self-loathing rather than faith and confidence—a cringing colonial consciousness made so by its internalization of imitativeness and mimicry. More authoritatively than white skeptics, Johnson calls out primordialists for appropriating the archaic past as a front for material exploitation and antidemocratic violence. He begins with wholesale rejection of the primordial core of biological definitions of race that strike at the heart of the issue: the very idea of identifiable racial purity at the heart of raced and romantic nationalisms. Gareth Griffiths has noted that racism assumes primordial "zones of racial purity" existing in long ago and far away, moments when each race's essential essence was crystallized.[49] Decades ahead of his time in his conceptualization and practice of what amounts to a postcolonial critique, Johnson saw through the sophistry of Anglo-Saxonism in general, and Viking worship more specifically, to identify each as revealing a profound racial anxiety.

Jack London's short story "When the World Was Young" (1913) synthesizes these doubts to reimagine the Teutonic ideal as a danger to itself and to the world. In the story, the myth of biological atavism links white men not only to their inner Teuton but also to their inner savage, regressing past the Nordic superman to arrive at the prehuman. London has been grouped with Norris as a naturalist, a group of writers who applied social Darwinism to contemporary cultural politics, and so found in Darwin scientific confirmation of the superiority of the momentarily ascendant Anglo-Saxons.[50] For the first half of his career, London's prejudices nearly matched Norris's. Yet John Eperjesi has noted a lurking ambivalence: "London channels doctrines of Anglo-Saxon masculinist supremacy one minute and exposes the horrors of such a worldview the next" (106). For example, in *The Daughter of the Snows* (1902), while the characters wait out an Arctic storm, the "flaxen-haired, typically Saxon" heroine celebrates her lineage: "We are a race of doers and fighters, of globe-encirclers and zone-conquerors. . . . Will the Indian, the Negro, or the Mongol ever conquer the Teuton? Surely not. . . . All that the other races are not, the Anglo-Saxon, or Teuton, if you please, is. All that the other races have not, the Teuton has." In response, the hero offers a longer perspective, noting that the Jews and the Romans in the past, and the Slavs in the future, either had or would enjoy moments of dominion:

"It's a common characteristic of all peoples to consider themselves superior races,—a naïve, natural egotism, very healthy and very good, but none the less manifestly untrue" (37). Despite the eventual union of these characters, this conversation betrays London's early ambivalence that whiteness itself was the ultimate primordial fantasy.

More important, London, in Eperjesi's terms, "became Hawaiian" during his voyage through Pacifica at midcareer.[51] Subsequently, his sympathy with peoples of color was refracted through his reconsideration of white claims to Anglo-Saxon superiority. In the three-part narrative of "When the World Was Young" London tells the story of a wealthy San Francisco businessman, James Ward, who, like Liljencrantz's Jarl Helvin, has suppressed his inner berserker to maintain a facade of civility. The first section is told from the perspective of a thief breaking onto Ward's Mill Valley estate. Fearing he is being stalked, the thief tries his flashlight:

> In that instant, his tiny searchlight, sharp and white, had shown him what a thousand years would not allow him to forget,—a man huge and blond, yellow haired and yellow bearded, naked except for soft skinned moccasins and what seemed like goatskin around his middle, arms and legs were bare, as were his shoulders and most of his chest. . . . Still this alone was not what made the man scream out. What caused his terror was the unspeakable ferocity of the face, the wild animal glare of the blue eyes scarcely dazzled by the light, . . . the whole formidable body crouched and in the act of springing at him. (67–68)

The thief, Dave, flees, and the warrior undertakes superhuman efforts to chase him, limited only by the strong fences surrounding the estate and the thief's bicycle. The flashlight and the bicycle empower the modern man through technology, suggesting that the animalism of Teutonism had become itself archaic. As the second part of the story opens, Dave visits Ward in his downtown office the next day to warn him of the insane man running loose on his estate. In their conversation, Ward divulges himself as the wild man and narrates his backstory. Born to wealth, his regressive episodes began when he was a child. Sent to the family ranch in Wyoming, he is sent home for destroying cattle. His parents take him to a doctor, who observes: "Inside himself there were two men, and these men were several thousand years or so apart. His one self was that of a man whose rearing and education were modern and who had lived through the latter part of the nineteenth century and well into the first decade of the twentieth. His other half he had located as a savage and a barbarian living under the primitive conditions of several thousand years before" (80). Dr. Wertz, a "language" expert, identifies a savage side that emerges only at night and chants in "early Teuton." Unlike Norris's hero, whose Teutonic awakening is salutary, the revelation of the inner savage within paralyzes London's Ward. Subsequently, he becomes obsessed with containing it, indulging it only within his well-fenced estate. Nonetheless, he bullies the well-intended Dave by grabbing his arm: "'You were lucky,' Mr. Ward was saying, and Dave noticed that his face and eyes were cruel and gloating and proud. 'You were lucky. Had I wanted I could have torn your muscles out of your arms and thrown them into the waste-basket over there'" (87). Dave had come to warn Ward of a danger on his estate. Rather than providing the calm moral leadership expected of the Anglo-Saxon elite, Ward's bullying protects only himself, rejecting any public responsibility other than narrow self-interest: he is "gloating and proud" that the primordial warrior inhabits him.

London's plot turns on a combination of concurrent theories of schizophrenia and past life regression, a pseudo-scientific notion in which former identities persist in an individual's cellular makeup. London explored this theme more extensively in his 1915 novel *Star Rover*, in which a prisoner confined to a straitjacket regresses to a prehuman condition.[52] The strictures of modernity have triggered the same regression in Ward, manifesting in the surfacing of an ancient Teutonic ancestor. While Meigs, Roosevelt, and Norris sought to free this beast, London recognized it as just that—a beast. For London, a pure Teuton like Ward cannot contain his inner berserker and so presents a danger to himself and others. The primordial "half" of Ward is not a positive force or a marker of any kind of innate superiority other than bestial—it contributes nothing to the progress of the man or his civilization and can bear no burden. To expose the danger posed by the regressed Teuton in the modern world, London sexualizes the suppressed white man's de facto lycanthropy in ways Liljencrantz could not, given her adolescent readers. Ward responds to pressure to wed, an act necessary for the perpetuation of the breed. Conventionally courting in the evening, he reverts to "the uncouth wife-stealing bane of the dark German forests" (87). Another courtship ends in an implied attempted rape, the woman fleeing, "bruised and bleeding" (89). A little at a time, Ward learns to contain his inner Teuton, pushing his transformation later into the evening through brutal physical training, and soon he becomes engaged. At the engagement party, Ward hears a grizzly bear—a domesticated escapee from a local circus, as it turns out—in the woods being attacked by his dogs. Unable to restrain himself, and before the cream of Bay Area society, he reverts to the "crude savage who, by some freak of chance, lived again after thrice a thousand years" (93). After a long fight, Ward clubs the bear to death in full view of his guests, singing, in his triumph, "a song so ancient that Professor Wertz would have given ten years of his life for it" (94). London ironizes this regression, and thus the purity of his savagery, by having him brutalize a domesticated bear rather than a wild one. Teutonic wildness requires wilderness, and there is no more, thanks to the success of the settler project. With no wilderness, the berserker is an embarrassing anachronism. Like the bear, Ward is more a sensational oddity than a manifestation of transcendent racial superiority.

Other writers likewise dismissed Norse-based Anglo-Saxon primordialism to demonstrate a more general waning of the romantic nationalism that called it into being a century before. For example, in 1906, Mark Twain attended a meeting of the Ends of the Earth Club, an enclave for elite white men. There, Twain hears "a retired Army officer proclaim, 'We are of the Anglo-Saxon race, and when an Anglo-Saxon wants a thing *he just takes it*'" (181; emphasis in original). Twain later explains: "The soldier man's utterance, interpreted by the expression which he put into it, meant, in plain English, 'The English and the Americans are thieves, highwaymen, pirates, and we are proud of that combination'" (182). While Twain's view during Roosevelt's administration was apostasy, a generation later, in the enormously popular *The Great Gatsby* (1925), F. Scott Fitzgerald has the oafish and cruel Tom Buchanan ventriloquize the standard cant: "'This idea is that we're Nordics. I am and you are and—' After an infinitesimal hesitation he included Daisy with a slight nod, and she winked at me again. '—And we've produced all the things that go to make civilization—oh, science and art, and all that'" (14). Daisy's wink represents her indulgence of Tom's banal repetition of Rooseveltian propaganda. She does not take him seriously, and, in Tom's mouth, primordialism becomes a punch line.[53]

The Call of the Blood

> We Americans are always going some place. Our Norse ancestry still persists in the blood and the love of achievement lingers. Civilization develops both the powers and restlessness of initiative, and the call of the blood is so elemental, so profoundly native, that its actions and retroactions, being the true disclosures, form a basis for literature.
>
> —Anonymous, *American Reviews of Reviewers*, 1908

Echoing Simms's evocation from sixty years before, this call for Nordic Americanism fell on deaf ears: the moment had passed. Although Viking

fantasies persist, they do so in a minor key, as have those of the other proposed pre-Columbian populations. The few recent reconstructions have
lost their "problem orientation" and occupy the margins of the sensational
and the antiquarian. Every now and then, the old issues arise: every October, as Columbus Day approaches, varying versions of two internet memes
debate who "discovered" America. On one, Columbus is depicted on a
"wanted" poster, accused of centuries of genocidal violence. Its text bears
out the accusations: "Wanted: Christopher Columbus: Grand Theft, Genocide, Racism, Initiating the Destruction of a Culture, Rape, Torture and
Maiming of Indigenous People, and Instigation of the Big Lie: Five Hundred Years of Tourism." Even now, settler colonials strive to disavow for
the sins of colonization by foisting them off on Columbus, as the nation
claims to have reconciled the crimes of its past.[54] Currently, Columbus is,
ironically, *un*wanted in an age when apology is the newest iteration of settler
self-acquittal.

By contrast, Ericson's meme stands as a counternarrative. Around a pho-
toshopped version of his ennobled visage from Horsford's statue in Massachusetts, the text absolves the Viking: "Leif Ericson: Discovers North
America Nearly Five Hundred Years Before Columbus. Doesn't Rape, Pi-
lage [sic] & Commit Genocide on the Indigenous Peoples." Given that the
Icelandic sagas record only a meager and temporary settlement in Vinland
and that Norway supported no further expeditions, any opportunity for
Ericson or other Vikings to realize their settler colonialist ambitions—
as Liljencrantz conjectured—never materialized. On the contrary, the sagas
tell of an unprovoked massacre of nine Skraelings sleeping under their boats
by Ericson's brother's men. The implicit potential for violence seems clear,
but, for the land in question, for the Vikings, it was not worth the trouble.[55]
North America offered little they wanted: the Skraelings had nothing the Vikings considered worth stealing. Nonetheless, Ericson's meme conjectures a
sanitized primordiality, a new and improved white prehistory, yet one that
still erases Indian history.

Most visible has been *Pathfinder,* a series of graphic novels, video games,
and finally a movie in 2007. In its backstory, a Viking boy survives shipwreck in Newfoundland. Adopted by the local Skraeling tribe, he lives as
an Indian until the next Viking crossing. Once they arrive in all their evil
darkness, using an old Norse sword, the Pathfinder—his name, a reference
to Cooper's Natty Bumppo, as was Liljencrantz's hero—fights off what turns
out to be his uncle's crew and saves the otherwise doomed Skraelings. At
story's end, Pathfinder travels south to warn other tribes against the inevitable Viking invasions to come, leaving his Indian lover carrying his child,

implying a multiracial genetic lineage in pre-Columbian America. Implicit, of course, is that Indians, children of the forest, would have been exterminated by bad white men had not their own good white man defended them, using white technology—metallurgy—beyond Indian abilities. For all its multicultural revisionism, *Pathfinder*—the opening of the New World, the end of its prehistory—is the fantasy of a white man who is no longer an invader but a protector, a repositioning that only affirms Indian emasculation, anachronization, and subordination.

Reflecting this lingering self-deception, during the quincentenary of Columbus's landing, a minor Norse revival occurred. In her preface to the book of an enormous Smithsonian exhibit dedicated to Norse prehistory, then–First Lady Hillary Clinton comments: "I've been interested to learn, for example, that within Viking society women had a good deal of freedom to engage in trade and to become active participants in the political and religious lives of their communities. . . . This Viking exhibition will remind us that there are places on our own continent where you can see traces of human exploration and settlement that date back one thousand years" (9). Like all primordialists, Clinton grasps for a primordial white presence. Of course, other humans had left evidence of "exploration and settlement" in "our own continent" and had done so for many thousands of years. Moreover, in many indigenous tribes, women had far more power than did Viking shield maidens Gudrid or Freya in the sagas. Lost in primordial romance, Clinton shares the first-person possessive pronoun favored by all settler colonialists—"our"—and supplants millennia of Indian history with a few shacks on a Newfoundland beach.

NOTES

Introduction

1. See Gellner, Renan, Benedict Anderson, Hobsbawm, and During. My thoughts on nationalism and primordialism have been most influenced by Anthony Smith and James Drake. As to the imitative nature of American settler nationalism, see Tennenhouse and Yokota. See Godeanu-Kenworthy, St. George, and Warner.

2. See Hunter; Mann; Stephen Williams; Kennedy; Kehoe; and Barnhart, *American Antiquities*. All of these describe the emergence of the professionalization of the social sciences from esotericism.

3. See in particular Murray on Irving. See also Watts, *Writing and Postcolonialism*, chapter 6.

4. In his introduction to *The Routledge Handbook of the History of Settler Colonialism*, Lorenzo Veracini offers this definition: "As a system defined by unequal relationships (like colonialism) where an exogenous collective aims to locally and permanently replace indigenous ones (unlike colonialism), settler colonialism has no geographical, cultural, or chronological bounds. . . . Settler colonialism is in many ways an exercise in the deliberate alteration of time and space. Triumphant settler colonialism is, after all, a violent act against geography: settler colonialism turns someone else's place into space and then into place again" (4–5).

5. See in particular Hunter and Barnhart, *American Antiquities*. These sources recur to the same set of nineteenth-century texts. I have limited myself to texts that were available to American readers on the national scale, those that circulated broadly in the emergent print cultures of the long nineteenth century. While certain sections of Kolodny's *In Search of First Contact* (119–42) in particular approach an integrative analysis of more than one group, only Dahl's essays address more than two of these groups. Otherwise, there has been no prior scholarly attempt to draw together the literature of pre-Columbian whites as a distinct body of texts united by their narrative commonality. Moreover, only about one-third of *In Search of First Contact* addresses nineteenth-century texts. Other sections address their origins in Icelandic sagas and the historical presence of Vinland itself, especially as it lingered in Mik-maq culture. Works by Gustafson ("Nations of Israelites"), Hurt, Dahl ("Mound Builders"), and others study different episodes in isolation from the others.

6. See Martin and Hedges on the hagiography of Columbus before Irving. See Rubin-Dorsky on Irving's Columbus. On Irving's earlier career, see Hedges. On the Black Legend of the Spanish conquest, see the essays in Greer, Mignolo, and Quilligan. See also Gibson. On efforts to erase the Indian, see Conn, Deloria, Carr, and Hunter. Rifkin's *Manifesting America* has been particularly useful.

7. "White," as both cultural construct and purported biological category, shifted greatly over the century this book addresses. My use of it is often repositioned every chapter, as early anxieties about the loss of whiteness are displaced later by efforts to police the boundaries of whiteness. See Ignatiev, Roediger, Dain, and Brodkin. On the history of "race" more generally, see Gossett, Horsman, Bieder, Wheeler, Saxton, and Painter. See especially Nelson, *National Manhood,* 29–60, and Chiles, 1–28.

8. On romantic nationalism in America, see Kerrigan, Marlon B. Ross, and Kramer. On a more global scale, see Hobsbawm and Gellner.

9. On the effect of the discovery of America on European modernity, see Enterline and the essays in Kupperman's *America in European Consciousness,* especially Burke and Elliot. More recently, see Rifkin, *Beyond Settler Time*: "The emergence and recognition of modernity as a specific sort of temporal experience appears intimately connected to the decimation of Native peoples, but more than simply providing a period marker (with modern serving as a name for what comes in the wake of Allotment, for example)" (8–9).

10. For the best overviews of specific purported inhabitants, see Gwyn Williams (*Madoc*) on the Welsh, Shalev on the lost tribes, Kolodny's *In Search of First Contact* and "When the East was West" on the Norse, and Kehoe, Barnhart's *American Antiquities,* Sayre's "The Mound Builders," Kennedy, and Silverberg on the Mound Builders. Kolodny and Gwyn Williams set the standard for scholarly address of specific episodes. This is not to say that each group has not been addressed at great length throughout myriad centuries and media. However, these texts I have excluded because of their sensational premise and amateurish methods. Their objective is more often simply anti-Columbian, so they imagine a New World to which virtually everyone with access to oceanic exploration sailed in the premodern era. This began with sensational texts in the 1830s and extends to the early twenty-first century in fan fiction and internet-based arenas. Extensive archaeological materials exist regarding each of the groups addressed in this book.

11. The vast majority of other texts addressed the Mound Builders, albeit from an archaeological or historical perspective. See Hunter, Kennedy, Mann, Barnhart's *American Antiquities,* and Gwyn Williams's *Madoc.* The Mound Builders featured prominently in development of American social sciences, as has been studied at length by these scholars. Moreover, the Welsh, the lost Jews, and the Vikings were all at one point, among many others, suggested as the Mound Builders. See Stephen Williams and McNiven, Russell, and Schaffer. See Kennedy and Michaelsen on the reduction of antiquarianism to mere curatorship. In this iteration, the past is mere curiosity and sensation—esoteric academic study—especially in the case of the Mound Builders. Kehoe addresses how this reduction further annihilated Indian cultures.

12. Australian critic A. A. Philips coined "Cultural Cringe" in 1950. See Yokota, Tennenhouse, and Belich for the best studies of this sense of cultural cringe.

13. See Belich for the most comprehensive study of "the setter diaspora." As to its cultural politics, see Crow, Robert Young, Veracini's *Settler Colonialism*, Prentice, and Tiffin and Lawson on the sense of the cultural subordination imposed on the colonies—even the settler colonies—as a means of inculcating dependence and marginality. While the work of each makes important and large cultural claims, the role of the literary in these phenomena has gone largely unexplored, with few close readings being endeavored. Dixon, Stafford and Williams, and Carter, all in their work on settler texts, provide an alternative model for settler reading strategies. Decolonization is a problematic term in settler postcolonial studies. While Veracini remains adamantly political, he notes, "Settler colonialism has been resistant to decolonisation" (*Settler Colonialism*, 95) in that genuine decolonization would be full reinvestment of political sovereignty to indigenous peoples. However, he also concedes the necessity of gradualism based in "discontinuing settler forms" that will require "conceptual frames and supporting narratives of reconciliation that have yet to be fully developed and narrated" (115).

14. On clothes, see Yokota. As to the popularity of American books, John Neal's *American Writers* series appeared in London in the early 1820s to address that complaint. Child's introduction to *Hobomok* (1824) satirizes the American taste for British novels. Both refer to the refusal of American readers to buy American books.

15. On histories of racial theory, see Horsman, Wheeler, Painter, and Dain. On their literary uses, see Chiles.

16. See Kramer, Warner, Kammen, Gustafson's "Nations of Israelites," Nelson's *National Manhood*, and Howe on early republic versions of Enlightenment-based civic nationalism's entanglement with romanticism's less contained ideologies.

17. On telos and nation, see Anthony Smith's *National Identity*, particularly 99–118. On the relation of these ideas to romantic nationalism, see Marlon Ross and Kerrigan. Benjamin Park has more recently documented the erosion of these categories: "Nationalism was never a set of static self-dependent principles that were agreed upon by a majority of the citizens. . . . American nationalisms should therefore be understood as plural" (6). Moreover, as the controversies studied in this book reveal, those movements were simultaneous and interactive.

18. On the reception of *The Aeneid* in the early republic, see McWilliams, 18–26.

19. Gidal offers the best overview of the Ossian controversies, primarily linking them to issues of nationalism, industrialism, and modernity: "Mapping Ossian onto the Glenn Etive Hills registers a longevity to the land and the witness of its peoples have borne to its terrain over many generations. But the standard of authenticity in such a gesture lies in a capacity for translation among the poetry, the land, and an ever-hastening modern age" (81). On Scottish culture and postcolonialism, see the essays in Gardiner, MacDonald, and O'Gallagher's collection.

20. See Chiles, 111–20, for Crèvecoeur on race. In particular, the concept of whites transforming to Indians—"Indianization"—informs her reading, as well as my own.

21. On the post-Revolutionary nationalism quest for "beginnings," see in particular Martin, 3–44. Dowling's work on the "Connecticut Wits" in *Poetry and Ideology* establishes their role in the articulation of classically nationalist literary goals. However, their

application was mostly regional in New England, and so they failed to find a national audience or following. See Kramer, 29–56, and Anthony Smith, *Nationalism and Modernism*, 121–32. See McWilliams on epic formats and nationalism in early American writing.

22. On Simms's evolving nationalism, see Jeffery Rogers, 17–44. See also Quigley, 50–86, and Watson, 19–46.

23. For general background on settler colonialism, see Veracini, *Settler Colonialism*; Hixson; Wolfe; Ford; and Bush. Most recently, Cavanaugh and Veracini's *The Routledge Handbook of the History of Settler Colonialism* (2016) provides a comprehensive overview of the subject. On traditions of ambivalence and resistance among settlers, see Farred.

24. On "colonial nationalism" in settler colonies, see Jebb and essays collected by Eddy and Schreuder. On the imitative nature of these nations, see Morgan. On their cultures of mimicry, see Bhabha's "Of Mimicry and Man" in *The Location of Culture*: "The discourse of mimicry is construed around an ambivalence; in order to be effective mimicry must continually produce its slippage, its excess, its difference. The authority of that mode of colonial discourse that I have called mimicry is therefore stricken by an indeterminacy: mimicry emerges as the representation of a difference that is itself a process of disavowal. Mimicry is, thus the sign of a double articulation; a complex strategy of reform, regulation and discipline, which 'appropriates' the Other as it visualizes power. Mimicry is also a sign of the inappropriate, however, a difference or recalcitrance which coherers the dominant strategic function of colonial power, intensifies surveillance, and poses an imminent threat to both 'normalized' knowledges and disciplinary powers" (86). As acts of mimicry, primordialist texts engage these complexities while maintaining an implicit articulation of self-doubt and inauthenticity.

25. See Kaplan's "Introduction: The Absence of Empire in American Studies." On settler nationalism as a disavowal of "empire" in America, see Watts, "Settler Postcolonialism," but also Lawson, Ford, Tennenhouse, and Yokota. See in particular Pearson and Coombes. Pearson writes, "In settler societies myths of origin and destiny are drawn upon to create, sustain, and recapture a unity of present identity and experience" (9). I refer not so much to Benedict Anderson's much-cited title but rather to his reference to "that remarkable confidence of community in anonymity which is the hallmark of modern nations" (36) as generated by the common reading across a nation afforded by modern print culture. Loughran instead suggests that exposure of the diversity of print cultures performed an antithetical function in the United States by exposing readers to their differences more than their similarities. Such paradoxes reveal the facade beneath all forms of settler nations as each is an amalgam of former colonies sharing only geographic contiguity.

26. Literary studies that presuppose the imperial aspect of American literary culture include Schueller, Doolen's *Fugitive Empire*, Kazanjian, Byrd, and Rowe, all filling the void identified by Kaplan. Rowe suggests that empire had always pervaded American culture: "the national myths and political rhetoric justifying such [late nineteenth-century overseas empires] were also developed in the colonization of peoples and their folkways living within the United States prior to or apart from these acquisitions" (6). On the role of literature in this process, see in particular Brennen and Bhabha's "DissemiNation."

27. Bulmer-Thomas has recently framed the many shapes empire has taken in American history, many of which are cultural or commercial rather than political or military. See Madsen in the context of imperial studies; for a more recent treatment, see Kessler. On the complexities of nineteenth-century print culture that generated exceptionalist discourse, see Reynolds and Gross. Wilentz, Howe, Wiebe, Kammen, Burstein, and Waldstreicher elaborate extensively on the print- and nonprint-based rituals and rhetoric of nationalism. At the same time, the tradition of dissent has more recently been elaborated upon in the essays in Tyrell and Sexton's *Empire's Twin*.

28. Recent work by Belich, Veracini ("Introduction: Settler Colonialism"), Yokota, and Hixson, as well as Kazanjian, Byrd, Pearson, Doolen, Buell, and many others, makes a powerful argument to put American culture studies—especially for the period in question—in conversation with work from Australia, New Zealand, Canada, and South Africa. Scholars from settler communities have been doing so for decades. A lingering myth of exceptionalism has deterred Americanists from joining these important conversations. Initial theorizing in this area was done by A. A. Philips and Lipset.

29. The mythography of the "pioneer" was developed very early in the development of American studies and was based on a line of thinking running back through Jefferson, Emerson, Lincoln, Roosevelt, and others. These scholars included R. W. B. Lewis, Roy Harvey Pearce, Henry Nash Smith, and Richard Slotkin.

30. Aside from Bercovitch's *American Jeremiad,* Gorski offers a more recent and comprehensive history of the concept of covenant and its linkages to concepts such as the Puritan "City on a Hill" and O'Sullivan's "Manifest Destiny." From the religious history perspective, see Hatch, Tuveson, and Abzug. For its Old Testament origins, see Shalev. Rifkin's *Manifesting America* speaks most directly to the effect of this ideology of Indian relations.

31. See Veracini, *Settler Colonialism,* 89. John Hay has recently crafted a larger argument about apocalyptic fears in antebellum American culture, as has Jason Phillips.

32. Lawson's foundational observation, nearly thirty years ago, that the settler is both "colonized and colonizing" has informed debates over the nature of settler identity. The term "settler" emerged in the mid-1990s growing out of Lawson's work. Stasiulis and Yuval-Davis's *Unsettling Settler Societies* (1995) brought the term to bear in a comparative sense. Only since 2002 has the term been in wide use to describe white American ex-colonials.

33. As to the transfer of the concept of covenant to the concept of nation, I refer to Benedict Anderson's noting "that remarkable confidence of community in anonymity which is the hall mark of modern nations" (36) as generated by the common reading across a nation afforded by modern print culture. However, the diversity of print cultures performed an antithetical function in the United States by exposing readers to their differences more than their similarities, according to Loughran, thus creating a troubling multiplicity of covenants. Moreover, Veracini notes, "Settler colonial theory locates the consolidating settler collective in history's latter days, hence a stubborn, recurring, and inherent anxiety at the prospect of defeat or compromise" (*Settler Colonialism,* 99).

34. These failures are cataloged in Howe, Hietala, Wilentz, and Wiebe. On the particular failure of the Mexican War, see Foos and Johannsen. Moreover, my comments on genocide and imperialism draw on the essays in Moses's *Empire, Colony, Genocide*, especially Moses's introduction and Docker's contribution. Tricia Logan's essay "Memory, Erasure, and National Myth" signifies an important continuation of this conversation. On postbellum imperialism, Jacobson, Eperjesi, and Love in particular have influenced my thinking. See Nelson, *National Manhood*, 176–202.

35. As to settler colonialism as an adjunct to other fields, see Ford, Mackey, and Pateman on, for example, legal systems and treaty policies in Australia, New Zealand, Canada, and the United States. Along the same lines, Gary Anderson's use of "ethnic cleansing" rightly links the process to the study of genocide as global phenomenon.

36. In *Settler Colonialism*, Veracini writes, settler stress could adapt seemingly liberal policies as a means of atonement, but this had unforeseen consequences: "Even if it is devised as an exercise in settler nation building, even well-meaning processes of indigenous and national reconciliation . . . ultimately contribute to the erasure of variously defined indigenous sovereignties and therefore to the reproduction of settling colonizing practices" (109). However, the gesture toward inclusion relieves settler stresses over their project's inevitable unilateralism.

37. The greatest "trauma" facing settlers was interracial encounter, followed quickly by the specter of multiraced populations. Chiles builds her argument from the theories of Horsman, Hannaford, Tawil, and Wheeler. For a settler theory perspective, Veracini notes that settlers bear "paranoid fears about degenerative aspects in the settler social body . . . and concerns about the possibility that the land will turn against them" (*Settler Colonialism*, 81) and reassign their race and thus their entitlement to the land. As to the literal transformation to nonhuman status as a settler fear and on the notion of literally howling wilderness and the settler imagination, see Robisch. On the more common figurative usage, see Nash, Regis, and Lawson-Peebles.

38. In his contribution to the *Routledge Handbook*, Mathew Crow writes, "Settler colonialism matters to any understanding of the history of the United States simply because, in the American context, settler colonialism has worked by allowing the predominant settler population not to recognize itself as one" (95). What has happened to the settler prior to his arrival in the colonial space, that is, is only indirectly relevant to the process of colonization enacted upon arrival. Victim status in the Old World does not justify invasion and violence in the New, but it has allowed settlers to assume that it does.

39. Gwyn Williams (*Madoc*), O'Donoghue, and Kolodny ("When the East Was West") trace the role of primordial nationalism in these prospective nations. Finland's Elias Lonnrot's *Kalevala* (1835) explicitly served such a function. Because this project centers on the entanglement of primordialism and nationalism, I am omitting simultaneous European texts on many of these groups throughout the period in question, save when overlaps occur, such as when Southey's epic *Madoc* was published to fund a Welsh settlement in America. Likewise, other conversations will be omitted if not connected to the public aspects of primordialism as conducted (mostly) by Americans: scholarly exchanges concerning the lost tribes among and between Jewish and Gentile scholars shaped debates

surrounding anti-Semitism in Europe; the Mound Builders fascinated early European as well as American archaeologists, as Silverberg an Kennedy have noted; Irish and Catholic hagiographies of Saint Branden have inspired two stand-alone bibliographies; and, obviously, Norse pride in the generation of Ericson is extensive, but not directly pertinent here. In certain cases as well, especially with the Welsh, the Irish, and the Norse, the same figures were invoked to establish a primordial past in their home countries as well, as they all—latecomers to the field—nervously sought to stabilize their own national identities and cultures in the age of romantic nationalism.

1. Welsh Indians in the Early Republic

An earlier version of this chapter was published as "'To Plant Himself in with Soveranity': Welsh Indians and the Early Republic" in *Mapping Region in Early American Writing*, ed. Edward Watts, Keri Holt, and John Funchion (Athens: University of Georgia Press, 2015), 25–44. Reprinted with permission.

1. On the *Port-Folio* and its publisher, Joseph Dennie, see Slawinski, chapter 1, or Dowling's *Literary Federalism*.

2. Throughout, much of my knowledge of the legend and its sources in British culture is based in Gwyn Williams's *Madoc*.

3. On Federalist values and the uses of the Columbus legend in the Federalist era, see Martin; Nelson, *National Manhood*; and, in particular, Larkin. Ferguson breaks down this issue to the level of metaphor and diction (124–49). See Jebb, Mathews, and Ford on linkages between settler nationalism and political republicanism.

4. On links between sectarianism and the national imagination, see Horsman (117–33). More recently, Wilsey and Kessler have linked Manifest Destiny to its roots in Puritan eschatology. See also Madsen and Howe. On the linkage of Manifest Destiny and evangelical Christianity, see Hietala, Hatch, Howe, Bloch, Nelson (*National Manhood*), and Greenburg.

5. On alcoholism in early America and it links to colonialism, see Mancall, *Hakluyt's Promise*.

6. See Bjornsdottir on the early uses of Ericson to displace Columbus. See also Sale and Bartosik-Velez more specifically on the Black Legend. See Martin on the rise of Columbus.

7. Eaton addresses these reviews (75–78). As to Federalist attempts to nationalize Columbus, see Meister, especially chapter 4. Crow, Lawson, and Tennenhouse all elaborate on this point in settler culture more specifically.

8. These represent the standard account and its most popular variants as summarized in Stoddard, Bowen, Burder, Traxel, Dana Olson, Armstrong, Deacon, and Gwyn Williams (*Madoc*). For analyses of the development of colonialist propaganda in the 1590s, see Mancall's *Hakluyt's Promise*, 34–53; for the 1790s, see Smith-Rosenberg, 47–55; Rowe, 24–53; and Griffin, 240–71. James Drake, 260–316, has been most influential to my thinking as to the concept of continentalism.

9. Discussions of environmental theories of race such as Blumenbach's can be found in Chiles, Dain, Painter, and Wheeler.

10. European perspectives on the Black Legend are addressed in essays by Burke and Armitage. See also Bauer, 77–117.

11. On the ideology and ambivalence of early republic expansionism, see Watts's *An American Colony*, but in particular Elkins and McKitrick, 401–38. Doolen and Gunn have most recently excavated its imperialist underpinnings.

12. See Locke's *Second Treatise of Government* (originally 1689; rpt. 1768), section 16. See Miller and Ford for the application of his ideas in settler land issues.

13. On the British reconciliation of moral paradoxes of imperialism, see Mancall's *Envisioning America*, Green, and Burke.

14. See Pateman, 35–78. On the instability of the West in the post-Revolutionary decades, see Slaughter, Hoagland, Dowd, and Griffin. On the distrust of the frontiersman, see Buss and Smith-Rosenberg as well as Chiles on the instability of their whiteness.

15. See Gwyn Williams, *Madoc*, 9–30.

16. Ibid., 187.

17. See Davies, 125–64, who traces major linguistic changes to the Unification Act of 1586, part of which included the translation of the Bible.

18. See Crèvecoeur, 224–27. Farmer James worries his children will become "Indianized" in his new western home at the end of *Letters*. See Chiles, 111–20.

19. See John Williams, Burder, and Bowen for comprehensive bibliographies of accounts of Welsh Indians. Williams in particular notes the links made between the Welsh and the Aztecs by Southey and others (189–95). Eighteenth-century French accounts are also listed in Burder's *The Welch Indians* (1797). Benjamin Bowen's 1876 *America Discovered by the Welsh in 1170* reprinted a great number of accounts of Welsh Indians.

20. While Mackey reads Locke comparatively across a range of settler/indigenous land conflicts, Miller focuses more precisely on the invocation and history of the Doctrine of Discovery in early nineteenth-century America.

21. Miller's discussion tracks the Doctrine's origins to the First Crusade, linking Euro-American expansionism more generally to broader patterns of global space acquisition rather than as an exception divergent from established patterns.

22. Traxel and Gwyn Williams (*Madoc*) provide the best reviews of the politics of Hakluyt's and Powell's late sixteenth-century versions of the story. Mancall's *Hakluyt's Promise* has provided the Elizabethan background needed here.

23. See Newcomb in particular on the Doctrine's linkage of virtue and proselytization, 4–23. See Peyer on the Indian use of the missionary system and its methods for articulating resistance.

24. On Indian haters and white savagery, see Barnett, 121–45. See also Pearce, Sullivan, and Watts, introduction to Hall's *The Indian Hater and Other Stories*. See Slaughter, James Drake, and Szatmary on western uprisings as embodiments of deracination. See also Nichols, Slotkin, and Silver for discussions of savage frontiersmen.

25. See Wheeler, 49–89, on transatlantic fears of race slippage.

26. See Axtell for a discussion of how early republic spokesmen from Crèvecoeur to Franklin struggled with the pattern of returned white captives returning to their captor's tribes and lifeways (165–72). On the Shawnee in particular, see Edmunds. On the fear of racial slippage on the settler frontier see Chiles, Dain, and Shoemaker. Nichols discusses these anxieties extensively. On race in early republic writing, see in particular Nelson's *The Word in Black and White.* Berkhofer surveys the field more completely.

27. On the emergence of a binary paradigm for defining race in the post–early republic moment, leading to removal, see Gary Anderson, Miller, Payne, Dain, Howe, and many others.

28. These definitions of the linkage of race and nation are drawn from Anthony Smith, Gellner, and James Drake. See the introduction.

29. On shifts in Indian and treaty policy after 1815, see Wilkinson, Robertson, and Banner. Banner delineates the process most completely (112–49).

30. See Truett for an especially insightful reading of Filson and the Welsh Indians. On speculation and early land companies, see Kulikoff, 280–338. Bowen's and Burder's overviews list Carver, Webster, Croghan, and many other testimonials to Welsh presence. None were ever materially or genetically substantiated.

31. Southey's *Madoc* is a sprawling and incoherent account of Madoc leading the Welsh against the armies of the Aztecs in Florida. Encouraged by Samuel Taylor Coleridge, Southey hoped that profits from the verse epic would fund the founding of a pantisocratic community somewhere in America. The book sold poorly, and the community was never founded. Catherine Franklin and David Craig relate the poem to romantic nationalism. By contrast, W.P.'s brevity and emphasis on reason reflect the Federalist values usually endorsed by Dennie in the *Port-Folio.* See Dowling's *Literary Federalism.*

32. Juliet Shields in particular studies the links to the Aztecs. See also Wertheimer's *Imagined Empires* on the Aztecs in early American print culture.

33. See Gwyn Williams's *The Search for Beulah Land,* chapters 3 and 4. See also Fulford and Kitson.

34. I have used Aron for information on Stoddard. Stoddard embodied the republican idea of the literate gentleman. Sandweiss presents a brief biography in her headnote to Stoddard's 1804 speech welcoming Missouri to the Union (35–40).

35. In *A Summary View,* Jefferson reminds his readers in England of primordial Saxon roots for their own legal system: "That their Saxon ancestors had under this universal law, in like manner, left their native wilds and woods in the North of Europe, had possessed themselves of the island of Britain, then less charged with inhabitants, and established there that system of Laws which has so long been the glory and protection of that country" (*Portable Thomas Jefferson,* 4). Jefferson envies and, as a colonial, wants access to British nationalism's roots in primordial fictions. On Jefferson sending Lewis to search for Welsh Indians, see Gwyn Williams, *Madoc,* 84. See Sheehan and Wood as well.

36. See chapter 2 for an extensive discussion of the lost tribe theory. See Chiles, 3–34; Wheeler, 281–303; and Bauer, 200–240, on New World race shifting.

37. On linkages to the Aztec coat of arms, see Juliet Shields, 98–112.

38. On Evans's life and exploration see Deacon, 137–50, John Williams, and David Williams, 179–93. More recently, see Wood. Belich's "hypercolonization" refers to the explosive growth of settler colonies (1820–60).

39. Gould links Belknap and Federalist policies concerning expansion. My comments on romantic nationalism are based in Anthony D. Smith's *Nationalism and Modernism*, 63–79.

40. See Keller for biographical information on Henry Marie Brackenridge.

41. On the emergent reformulation of racial theory along scientific lines, see Chiles, 201–10. See also Robert Young's *White Mythologies*, Gary Anderson, Nelson's *National Manhood*, and Dain. Dain writes, "Self-evident, visible, perceptible truths would not be able to capture this thing called race. Race itself was a monster if ever Americans conceived one, but a monster hidden in their minds, not, as many of them came to think, in the reality of a nature behind the appearances" (vii).

42. Clark's introduction to Toulmin's collection, *A Description of Kentucky*, is the best source of biographical information on Toulmin. I use that edition here. See Venable, 13.

43. On Decalves and Trumbull, see Watts, "Exploration."

44. The rereading of Crèvecoeur as ironic began in the 1980s. See Arch, Winston, and Dennis Moore for representative arguments.

45. See the introduction. In *Playing Indian*, Deloria's focus is on efforts to combine the indigeneity of the continent's aboriginal inhabitants with the unavoidably European basis of their culture. Such efforts represent a paradoxical "unassemblability." In *In This Remote Country*, Watts explores the deracination of the colonial French in Anglo-American writing.

46. See Ford's delineation of Marshall's ambivalence (34–56). See in particular Pateman, 35–78, and Rifkin, *Manifesting America*, 75–108, on the use of the Doctrine in America and other settler colonies.

47. Marshall, majority opinion in *Johnson and Graham's Lessee v. William M'Intosh*, 36.

48. Marshall, majority opinion in *Cherokee Nation v. Georgia*, 59.

49. Wilkinson reviews Marshall's evolving opinion in the Cherokee cases (25–53). See Robertson, 75–116, as well. See Ford, 30–54, and Pateman, 26–38. See Sayre, *The Indian Chief as Tragic Hero*: "Colonizers recognized, at some semiconscious level, their responsibility for these deaths but summoned up complex responses to assuage or dismiss this responsibility" (4), including the catharsis of tragedy.

50. See Robertson, 92–142, and Banner, 172–222.

51. See Inskeep, 256, for a discussion of this semiapocryphal quotation.

52. On the transition to empire, see Kaplan's "The Anarchy of Empire," Kazanjian, and particularly Rowe.

53. Most recently, Armstrong (1950), Deacon (1966), Gwyn Williams (*Madoc*, 1987), Dana Olson (1987), and Traxel (2004) demonstrate this pattern.

54. Recent information on Madoc's plaque can be found at https://americymru.net /alabama-welsh-society/blog/4387/prince-madoc-plaque-information-alabama-welsh -society.

2. The Lost Tribes and the Found Nation

Throughout this chapter, my comments on lost tribe theory and Jewish history in America come from Shalev, 118–50, and Goldman's *God's Sacred Tongue*, 7–30. See also Grant Underwood. The role of conversion in American millennial or biblical self-definitions is studied by Goldman, *God's Sacred Tongue*, 89–136; Dalin; Shalev, 50–83; and Abzug, 40–53. On the covenant in America, see Bercovitch, *American Jeremiad* 72–108; and Howe, 285–327. Ideas about the millennial or "chosen" nature of Americans, or at least New England orthodoxy, see Fliegelman, 155–83; Gould, 172–209; and Gary Anderson, 36–51. See Nordholt for covenantal prefigurations of Manifest Destiny.

1. See Hatch and Abzug, but particularly see Lee, 53–110.

2. On Roger Williams, land, and conversion, see Richter, Robertson, and Ford.

3. See Baltzell for an overview of the relations between the groups.

4. See Hatch, 162–90, and Abzug, 105–24, on leveling in the Second Great Awakening.

5. On the covenantal nature of early American thought, see Bloch, 3–21, 187–201, and Bercovitch's *Puritan Origins*, 136–86, and *American Jeremiad*, 132. Of the Second Great Awakening's preoccupation with "futurity," Bercovitch writes, "To modernize the Chosen People and God's Country meant opening those concepts to precisely the uncertainty of things to come which the Bible precludes" (*Rites*, 179). See Bercovitch's *American Jeremiad*. For a broader historical view, see in particular Howe, 164–87. Noll and Harlow's collection has also influenced my thinking. Murphy's *Prodigal Nation* provides a longer overview.

6. Here, I use Eric Wolf's term "people without history" to define people whose history has been taken from them as void of moral meaning: "History is thus converted to a tale about the furtherance of virtue, about how the virtuous win out over the bad guys. Frequently, this turns into a story of how the winners prove that they are virtuous and good at winning" (5). As to Jews in colonial America, see Pencak, David Shields, and Shalev.

7. See Wyss and Peyer for overviews of the relationship of conversion and millennialism. Butler writes, "The Revolution was an event whose character and outcome seemed to have signaled the beginning of Christ's thousand-year reign, thus making the apocalypse either history or irrelevant. Millennialism also had important political implications. Millennialist rhetoric secured an unwilling and often perplexed society to the Christian plow with the harness of Christian time" (217). See Bloch, 3–27; Tuveson, 91–136; and Butler, 216–18.

8. On progressive reform in the Second Great Awakening, see Bloch, Hatch, and Abzug, but especially see Hankins, 43–75. As to the whiteness of the Jews in early America, aside from Brodkin, see especially Pencak, as well as Dalin and David Shields. Nineteenth-century essays by Nicholas Street and Samuel Langdon have also informed my ideas of Jewish modeling in the early republic.

9. Barnhart (*American Antiquities*), Kehoe, and Kennedy especially observe Adair's unbiased methodology.

10. See Tuveson and Hatch, but also see Marsden.

11. On the biblical morphology of non-Europeans, see Robert Young, 32–53. For the link to other social reformist textualities, Loughran studies the distribution networks within antebellum print culture, especially with regard to abolitionist texts (303–62).

12. See Goldman on pre-1840s versions of continental destinarianism and apocalyptic thought. On the entanglement of removal and colonization, see Burin and Krauthammer.

13. Many scholars have addressed the simultaneity of genocidal violence and religious fervor. See Smith-Rosenberg, 207–49; Bellin, 71–97; Gary Anderson, 98–125; and Hixson, 38–43.

14. For a succinct biography of Elias Boudinot (née Buck Watie), see Perdue, 3–38.

15. For the name borrowing and other details of the white Boudinot's life, see Boyd's biography. Den Hartog provides a concise and useful overview of Boudinot's life and career.

16. See Hedges on Irving's early work. While first published in the *Analectic Magazine* in 1814 (the version used by Boudinot), Irving collected "Traits" into *The Sketch Book of Geoffrey Crayon* (1818). On "Traits" more generally, see Slotkin, Drinnon, and Berkhofer.

17. See Hogan's "A Parallel." In order to preempt challenges these texts pose to Joseph Smith's *Book of Mormon*, the Mormon Press has kept of Ethan Smith's *Views* and Spaulding's *Manuscript* (see chapter three) available for the last century. See Shalev, 128–45, on the reception of the Christian press to Boudinot and Ethan Smith (see below). The debate was whether or not Jewish Indians fell within the Awakening's opening of the orthodoxy.

18. See chapter 3 below for discussions of similar narratives of the Mound Builders by Solomon Spaulding and William Cullen Bryant. For both, as for Smith, a more savage population destroys the Mound Builders, as would be the case in *The Book of Mormon*. These multiple versions of the same tradition suggest a trope wherein the facts of the narrative matters less than the author's use of those facts to draw moral and historiographic inferences, intertextual borrowings notwithstanding.

19. My reading of Mormon history and the history of *The Book of Mormon* is based on Hogan; Grant Underwood, 1–24; Southerton, 3–46, 117–32; Shalev, 84–114; Bushman, 54–70; Hatch, 113–35; Maffly-Kipp, vii–xxviii; and Dahl, "Mound Builders." On evangelical fiction, see Tricomi. See Bushman's critical biography of Joseph Smith for a more extensive discussion of the text's production.

20. See Southerton, 47–57. Nearly identical versions of the same narratives were reproduced and rearranged ad infinitum in postrepublican print culture—Henry Nash Smith and Richard Slotkin have established the pattern of multiple retellings of the same story as integral to the process whereby legends become printed material. McGill has discussed this as having little to do with definition of authorial creativity and originality (93–102). However, few of these aspired to adding another testament to the Bible. Debates over the gold plates and the story Joseph Smith purportedly found etched on the plates have long plagued Mormon adherents. Like all legends of pre-Columbian whites, in the absence of material evidence, primordialists fabricated their narratives. See Riskas.

21. See Maffly-Kipp and Colvin and Brooks on the Mormon presence in the Pacific.

22. See Eperjesi and Igler on the American transpacific imagination during this era.

23. See Van Wagoner's biography of Rigdon for a discussion of Mormon leadership, as well as Rigdon's importation of Baptist practices to Mormon liturgy. As to the relation of Mormonism to Campbellism and Millerism, see Grant Underwood, 58–76.

24. See Farmer, 53–72, on Mormons and Indian removal. See Southerton and Grant Underwood for the limited impacts of Mormonism. For a more complete critical analysis, see Riskas.

25. On Mormons, race, and Indian reservations, see Farmer, but especially see Garrett's introduction for a thorough background.

26. Livermore's life and career figure prominently in Brekus. See in particular the bibliographic footnote, 347.

27. On how the Second Great Awakening birthed liberal reform movements, see Butler, 257–87; Hatch, 193–209; Tuveson, 136–54; Abzug, 56–74; and Howe, 243–84. See especially Lears. As to the racial aspects of this process, later in the period, the Friends of the Indians, an organization similar to the NAACP, stated: "While the Dawes Bill will change the Indian's legal and political status, it will not change his character. The child must become a man, the Indian must become an American; the pagan must be new created a Christian. His irrational and superstitious dread of imaginary gods must be transformed into a love for the All-Father; his natural and traditional hatred for the pale-face into a faith in Christian brotherhood; his unreasoning adherence to the dead past into an inspiring hope in a great and glad future" (qtd. in King, 130).

28. For biographical information on Sigourney and her long career as a literacy advocate, see Haight's biography and Kelly's extensive introduction to her *Selected Poetry and Prose.*

29. On biblical monogenism, see Bieder, 88–90, as well as Kennedy, Hietala, and Conn; on Indian extinction, see Dippie; on Tekakwitha, see Greer's biography.

30. On women in the Second Great Awakening, see in particular Cott, 126–37.

31. See "Biographical Sketches" (1:293–334) of *The Payne-Butrick Papers,* as well as the editors' introduction to the same (1:xiii–xxiv). Payne described his experience among the Cherokee in "Indian Justice" and "The Captivity of John Howard Payne."

32. On Payne helping to draft the Cherokee Memorials, see Moulton, 67–74. See Konkle, 87–93.

33. See Shalev, 151–84; Brodkin, 103–37; and Goldman, *God's Sacred Tongue,* 112–35. Each argues that frontier settings create apertures for accommodation and inclusion that close once a community stabilizes, especially in settler colonies, for Gilman.

34. Payne penned dozens of plays, most of them lost. In 1815, an anonymous American reviewer noted, "Mr. Payne is, we believe, the only native American to whom [the British] have ever given celebrity" (Anon., *Memoirs* ii). Payne wrote "The Uses of Adversity" upon his return to New York.

35. See Bartlett for an account of the Edomites that belies the fanciful nature of Payne's account.

36. Lost tribe theory thrived for centuries in Britain. Mordecai Noah was an English rabbi who sought to establish a Jewish homeland—not unlike the efforts of the Welsh

Baptist leader Morgan Rhys—in eastern New York, citing the Jewish Indians as forerunners. See Shalev, 76–82, 139–43, and Popkin, 79–85.

37. On the Panic of 1837, see Lepler. Also see Howe and Wilentz.

38. On the growth of antebellum anti-Semitism, see Dinnerstein, 13–34.

39. Maddox comments, "If contemporary circumstances made it possible for [Lydia] Child and [Catherine] Sedgwick to begin rewriting the history of women in America, however, they made it very difficult to rewrite, in any significant way, the history of Indians in America" (96).

40. My source here is Frantz Fanon's definition of "native intellectual." Warrior has complicated this role by demanding that it "does not collapse into an uncritical and, I believe unhelpful nativism . . . [by] requiring much more than championing native culture" (85). Apess's and Warren's embrace of lost tribe theory must be understood then abrogating the era's racial absolutism to expose its practical impossibility. See Lis on lost tribe theory and Igbo heritage.

41. On the role of native intellectuals, Vizenor observes, "They create their stories with a new sense of survivance. The Warriors bear the simulations of their time and counter the manifest narratives of domination. . . . The natural reasons of the tribes anteceded by thousands of years the invention of the Indian. The [native intellectual] ousts the inventions with humor, new stories, and simulations of survivance" (5). Fanon describes this process at length. More recently, Byrd has studied how the responses of colonized people have updated Fanon's models (185–220). As to "Native," I refer to Patrick Wolfe's unwillingness to use the term "indigenous" or "aboriginal," as each is rooted in the colonial ideology of prehistorical meaninglessness. "Rather, in its contestedness, the category 'Native' takes on transformed historical modalities that bear the imprint of anticolonial practice, flexibly registering the ever-shifting hegemonic balance between those with a will to colonize and those with a will to be free" (9–10).

42. See Peterson for a comparative reading. From indigenous perspectives, see Weaver, Womack, and Warrior, 19–37; David Moore, 3–27; and Krupat, 1–24.

43. See Lopenzina. In addition, see O'Connell's introduction to Apess's autobiography, *On Our Own Ground* (xiii–lxxvii). My reading of Apess is informed by Konkle, 101–46; Peyer, 117–65; Warrior, 1–48; and David Moore, 261–68.

44. Griffiths and many others have discussed how a transgression of imperial discourse through such acts of transgression constructs a paradigm of horizontal cohabitation rather than vertical hierarchy. In a sense, Griffiths recognizes that the concepts of "race" and "ethnicity" themselves represent fantasies of primordial racial isolation that model contemporary insistence on difference and hierarchy. See Allen, 143–92.

45. See Schenck for biographical information on Warren. On his religious upbringing, see 11–19, and Buffalohead. See Konkle, 191–203, for readings of Warren's Christianity and historiography. As to the falling away from literal readings of the Bible, see Hatch, 210–19; Butler, 225–56; Shalev, 151–84; and Tuveson, 187–214. J. Fletcher Williams's "Memoir" provides essential insight as well.

46. On the debate between monogenesis and polygenesis, see Chiles, 91–106; Painter, 114–18; Kehoe, 46–51; and Horsman, 132–46, as well as Dain, Bieder, and Conn.

47. Schenck's biography describes the Metis presence in northern Minnesota in the early 1850s very well. As to the Metis themselves, see Watts, *In This Remote Country*, 129–79, and Richard White, 518–25. On Metis experience, see Peterson and Brown, *New Peoples*.

48. On Schoolcraft, see Watts, *In This Remote Country*, 140–57.

49. See Hatch, 193–209, and Howe, 462–84.

50. See Michaelsen, 122–25, and Tricomi, 41–63, for readings of *Oak-Openings*. On Cooper as an ambivalent settler, see Godeanu-Kenworthy. On the rise of anti-Semitism more generally, see Dinnerstein, 13–34.

51. Willis writes, "When Cooper is read in the context of the Federalists that he was surrounded by in his youth, the environmental concerns in his texts, which can otherwise seem extremely problematic, become quite apparent and wholly legitimate" (43). Willis also explores Cooper's rejection of the colonial tropes of tabula rasa and the vanishing Indian (46–53).

3. White Mound Builders and the Lessons of Prehistory

1. For information on Henry Marie Brackenridge, see Keller's biography. See chapter 1 of the present volume for more on his political career.

2. For information on Gallatin, see Adams's and Dungen's biographies. See Slaughter on the Whiskey Rebellion, although Hoagland provides a larger national context. Kennedy focuses on Gallatin and the mounds (23–39). See Silverberg, 9–50; Mann, 51–105; and Kennedy, 218–88, for a fuller historiography of the various contributors to the debates concerning the mounds. See Bieder, 16–54, and Lewis, 34–57, as well.

3. On internal improvements and republicanism, see Larson and Seelye. Larson has especially influenced my thinking on improvements, nationalism, and collectivism. Phillips, Malone, and Fair have especially informed my thinking on the relationship of internal improvement and the asymmetrical developments that contributed to the source of the Civil War.

4. Between 1800 and 1840 there were hundreds of publications addressing the mounds. I have tried to focus mostly on those that identify the mounds with nineteenth-century concepts of race and nation. See Kennedy, Silverberg, Stephen Williams, Kehoe, and Barnhart, *American Antiquities*, for far more comprehensive histories of how study of the mounds was foundational to the field of American archaeology. Livermore provides a comprehensive history of the role of canals and federal funding in the West. Hietala, however, most comprehensively links terraforming to destinarian narratives.

5. See Sayre's "The Mound Builders" on tourism in 1820s. Hunter provides a comprehensive history of the many ways in which the mounds were present in the national consciousness during the nineteenth century. His emphasis in terms of textuality is their role in the evolution of the professions of history, anthropology, antiquarianism, and archaeology.

6. Aside from Gallatin, Atwater, and their contributors, those who observed and mourned the "ploughing over" of the southern mounds in particular include William

Bartram, Samuel Gardner Drake, and Catlin. See Kennedy, 23–39, for how the Mound Builders were understood as the ancestors of contemporary Indians during the early republic. See also Barnhart (*American Antiquities*), Kehoe, and Mann. See Cronon, 71–98, for ideas about Anglo-Americans and the idea of terraforming. Terraforming is a concept borrowed from science fiction, in which the colonization of celestial bodies is preceded by efforts to make them safe for human habitation. Its application to the study of more earthly colonized spaces has been addressed by Laurie Brown and Oberg, 23–55. Nye discusses the subject most comprehensively.

7. See chapter 3 above for William Warren's 1852 observations concerning the invisibility of Indians in the American imagination. A generation later Helen Hunt Jackson's *A Century of Dishonor* began from the same premise.

8. Aside from Slaughter, see Hoagland for the rebellion's impact on other national debates. See Silverberg, 9–29, and Kennedy, 125–51. Both provide insightful and useful accounts of the debates concerning the mounds in the cultural politics of the antebellum decades. Barnhart, *American Antiquities*, 94–151, most comprehensively links mounds research to the politics of expansion.

9. While Larson, Howe, and many others describe the transformative power of steam, Seelye's *Beautiful Machine* remains the most impressive analysis of the entanglement of steam power, internal improvement, sectional fissures, and the colonization of the West. See Larson on collectivity and internal improvements. On the resistance to collectivity, see Shain and Lewis; on frontier identity, see Slotkin.

10. See Sword on those losses and the failure of state and local militias.

11. See Buss and Bergmann on the overlooked but broad effects of the subsequent Treaty of Greenville. See Winkler, 24–63, for a fuller discussion of the implications of this battle. Watts, *In This Remote Country,* works within how White's concept of the Middle Ground reflected the doubts of many white skeptics regarding race and expansion in the new nation.

12. See Slaughter and Hoagland on the resolution of the rebellion.

13. See Robertson, Banner, and Newcomb on how Indian collectivism was the target of the Dawes Act's insistence on "severalty." See also Atkinson and Miller for legal analysis.

14. See Larson, Hietala, Ha, and Seelye on the growing role of sectionalism in national debates. My ideas about evolving trends in nationalism and regionalism, and how they made the Civil War inevitable, are drawn from many sources. Phillips, 1–35, and Grant, 37–80, have been most useful. See also Wiebe, 145–89, and Wilentz, 141–217.

15. On republicanism and the social and moral politics of restraint, see the essays in Klein, Brown, and Hench. See also Kramer, 74–89, on "civic nationalism" and Nelson, 29–60, on republican brotherhood. Howe and Wilentz discuss the demise of the republican paradigm after 1815, thus representing a scholarly consensus, though some date it to the election of Jackson in 1828. As to its role in the funding of internal improvements, see Ha, Nye, Malone, and Bergmann. See Larson, Seelye, Hietala, Ha, and Bergmann for overviews of the relationship of these plans to capitalism, industrialism, nationalism, and expansion. On hypercolonization, see Belich, 335. This term represents Belich's notion that transportation and other technologies in the early nineteenth century allowed

settler colonies to develop ten times faster than they had before, outstripping the cultural and social apparatus that had stabilized older colonies.

16. See Dungen, 67–82, on Gallatin's efforts to galvanize corroboration while secretary of the Treasury.

17. Gallatin's linkage of language and national unity is outlined by Seelye and Kuppenheimer. See also Dungen, 153–67 and Gallatin's own "Synopsis."

18. While a few texts circulated prior to 1820—such as Barton (1797) or McCulloh (1816)—Atwater marks the beginning of the primordialist Mound Builder episode. See Silverberg, 57–60, and Kennedy, 239.

19. Webster's study was based strictly on the shape of the mounds and their use in Celtic burial rituals.

20. In *American Antiquities,* Barnhart notes both the lack of southern studies and that "archaeology in the service of the state is hardly an exceptional or uniquely American story, but it most certainly is an American story" (6). Throughout this section, I am indebted to Barnhart, Kehoe, and Mann.

21. See Venable for the most thorough account of antebellum Cincinnati. See also Watts, *An American Colony,* 140–61. On Atwater, see Weisenburg's biography.

22. See Mann on Atwater and Bering Strait theory. See Conn, 122–31, for an integrated discussion of Atwater and Squier and Davis.

23. On modernity and the Enlightenment and their rhetoric of scientific progressivism as applied to race theory, see Hietala and especially Friedman.

24. On the evolution of professional methodologies in archaeology, see Barnhart's comprehensive biography of Squier. See also Harvey, chapter 4.

25. See especially Bieder. See also Mann, 28–38, and Painter, 190–200. Jordan's *White over Black* first brought many of these conversation to maturation.

26. See William H. Young, 375–410, on the influence of Mill and Bentham on American institutions. See O'Brien on their rejection in the South. See also Larson, 16–49, and Seelye, 78–122. Dearborn provides a long-term and first-hand history of the issue. See in particular Ha and Robertson.

27. See Barnhart, *American Antiquities,* 220–27. Squier subsequently traveled southeast to conduct his own survey of southern mounds. On Squier, Bieder, 104–45; Kehoe, 150–71; and Barnhart, *Ephraim George Squier,* 152–204, give the best histories of the role of the mounds in the development of American archaeology.

28. On Mathews's life and career, see Stein's critical biography. Aside from Giles's and Sundquist's brief analyses, Dahl's "Moby Dick's Cousin Behemoth" offers the only other sustained reading. On Mathew's membership in a republican revivalist group, the Young America Movement, see Lause and Eyal. See also Stein, 32–65.

29. See Lewis on the mythic American male who must encounter the land itself in the nude and stripped of technology to be reborn with the aboriginal intimacy that had been missing prior to that moment.

30. Benedict Anderson defines that feeling thus: "It is imagined because the members of even the smallest nation will never know most of their fellow members, meet them, or even hear of them, yet in the minds of each lives the image of that communion" (6).

31. William Henry Harrison imagined "a feeble band, remnants of mighty battles fought in vain to make a last effort for the country of their birth" (35), only to be slaughtered by invading Indian savages. As sensational texts, these might be placed in the context of the popular "western" format. See Henry Nash Smith and Slotkin. On the textuality of western violence, see Slotkin, Henry Nash Smith, Griffin, and Smith-Rosenberg. Smith-Rosenburg in particular studies the crossover between the violence of frontier life and sensationally bloody popular culture texts.

32. Hunter asserts, "A final question of belonging asks: Who belongs in history? Historians of the nineteenth century were confident that Indigenous people lay outside of it, both in their own pasts and in their present experiences. . . . Indigenous culture lay beyond the interests of academic history because it did not meet the profession's objective of describing humanity's ascent to civilization" (17).

33. This history, as well as that of the text itself, is established by Jackson and Reeve in their introduction. See also Grant Underwood, Southerton, Maffly-Kipp, and Riskas. The contention is that Joseph Smith plagiarized elements of the text for *The Book of Mormon.* Jackson and Reeve provide a comprehensive history of the text's odd history. As a Mormon historian, Jackson finds that Smith could not have seen Spaulding's text. However, many other texts about the Mound Builders may have influenced his composition. The mound building of the Nephilites in *The Book of Mormon* is incidental, and so not discussed here. However, as displaced Jews in the New World, they are discussed in chapter 2.

34. Hale was consciously writing to find a profitable market. As a young widow, she had been lent money to support herself and her children while trying to earn a living as a writer. She published the first canto to exploit the market established by Atwater, and once she was hired to edit the *Ladies Home Journal,* she abandoned the project. Nonetheless, this proves the popularity of primordial fantasies as early as the 1820s. See Sherbrooke Rogers's biography of Hale and Gail Underwood.

35. Gibbon's book went through over twenty American editions. See Boorstin and O'Brien.

36. See Ed White's essay for a foregrounding of my use of Jenks. Both Jenks and Spaulding attest to interregional tension well before the War of 1812.

37. Lobaska is thought to correspond with the Mormon belief in Christ's bodily appearance in America after his crucifixion and resurrection. However, Lobaska's reforms are thoroughly republican, and he leaves his community in the hands of his children.

38. See Bickham. Rossignol marks how the war enabled romantic nationalism's ascendance over its civic counterpart: "By 1812, American nationalism was undergoing a change in its very nature. . . . The nation's patriotic feeling no longer had to be stirred up by deft political maneuvers. . . . It spontaneously expressed itself on the street and in the newspapers. The point was no longer to create but merely to consolidate national feeling. . . . The War of 1812 was the endpoint of this nationalist process" (196).

39. In all the texts of the Norse revival, Viking penetration of the continent is limited to the Atlantic watersheds. Only late nineteenth-century fantasies linked them to sites of later Scandinavian settlements in Minnesota and Wisconsin. Beach was most likely

working from legends and material drawn from Mallett, as had been Jeremy Belknap. See Kolodny's *In Search of First Contact*, Thurin, Barnes, and chapter 5 of the present volume more generally.

40. This speech is also known as "Reply to Cram," as it occurred during a larger council. Published separately, it garnered national attention: "Brother, listen to what we say. There was a time when our forefathers owned this great island. Their seats extended from the rising to the setting sun. The Great Spirit had made it for the use of Indians. He had created the buffalo, the deer, and other animals for food. He made the bear and the beaver, and their skins served us for clothing. He had scattered them over the country, and taught us how to take them. He had caused the earth to produce corn for bread. All this he had done for his red children because he loved them. If we had any disputes about hunting grounds, they were generally settled without the shedding of much blood. But an evil day came upon us; your forefathers crossed the great waters, and landed on this island. Their numbers were small; they found friends, and not enemies; they told us they had fled from their own country for fear of wicked men, and come here to enjoy their religion. They asked for a small seat; we took pity on them, granted their request, and they sat down amongst us; we gave them corn and meat; they gave us poison in return. The white people had now found our country; tidings were carried back, and more came amongst us; yet we did not fear them, we took them to be friends; they called us brothers; we believed them, and gave them a larger seat. At length, their numbers had greatly increased; they wanted more land; they wanted our country. Our eyes were opened, and our minds became uneasy. Wars took place; Indians were hired to fight against Indians, and many of our people were destroyed. They also brought strong liquor among us; it was strong and powerful, and has slain thousands." See Ganter's introduction to *Collected Speeches*.

41. See Watts and Rachels for the most recent reprinting of Crawford's account. Various pamphlets describing the attack were in print for decades from 1784 through 1860.

42. See Richard White. I have explored this pattern in Anglo-American writing at length in *In This Remote Country*. See also Buss and James Drake.

43. See Steven Olson, 3–24, on Bryant's time in the West.

44. On the Black Hawk War, see Jung. For a condemnation of the war and its militarization of the northwestern frontier, see Benjamin Drake, *The Life and Adventures of Black Hawk* (1840). See Wilkinson, Miller, Wilentz, Conn, and Howe for discussions of the legal and racial machinations of removal. Horsman, 190–203, addresses the racial thinking at its roots. See Drinnon, 154–80, but, more generally, Berkhofer, Scheckel, Conn, and Dippie concerning the culture wars over removal in the 1820s and 1830s.

45. Thompson was a prolific dime novelist. Biographical information can be found on Wikipedia: https://en.wikipedia.org/wiki/Daniel_Pierce_Thompson.

46. See Emmet Field Horine's new study of Daniel Drake. For a biographical sketch and useful collection of Drake's writings, see Shapiro.

47. Coggeshall was a prolific editor, novelist, advocate, and diplomat. Best known for throwing a bomb from Abraham Lincoln's inaugural train, his 1860 essay "On the Protective

Policy in Literature" called for Americans to write and read locally, foreshadowing the re-gionalist movement later in the century. See Watts, *An American Colony*, and Venable.

48. On Micah and Timothy Flint, see Doolen, *Territories of Empire*, 163–64. See Ven-able, 345–50, and Folsom's critical biography of Timothy.

49. Coggeshall's headnote for Jones offers very little in the way of biographical infor-mation. His poems are also published in Gallagher's *Selections of the Poetical Literature of the West*. In "Tecumseh," Jones eulogizes the Shawnee leader:

> And he whose ashes slumber here,
> Though man in form was god in mind.
> What matter he was not like thee,
> In race and color; . . .
> All that a man can give he gave;
> His life; the country of his sires
> From the oppressor's grasp to save. (Coggeshall, 208)

50. Biographical information on Tyng can be found in Coggeshall's headnote, but mostly here: https://en.wikipedia.org/wiki/Hattie_Tyng_Griswold.

51. For information on Hall, see Randall's biography; Venable, 361–86; and Watts, *In This Remote Country*. "Three Hundred Years Hence" is reprinted in Watts and Rachels, 497–502, and its authorship attributed to Hall. Apap questions that attribution (145). Hall's review of Beecher's *The Catholic Question* is reprinted in Watts and Rachels, 502–19. See Watts, *In This Remote Country*, on Hall and nativism.

52. Biographical information on Benjamin Drake can be found in the biographies of his brother Danial Drake (Horine and Shapiro) and Hall (Randall).

53. Hay's *Postapocalyptic Fantasies in Antebellum American Literature* appeared after the completion of this manuscript. His reading of mounds literature (113–31) generally dovetails with mine. Bluffton/Hall's use of class foreshadows a shift in apocalyptic visions that occurred more generally after the Civil War.

4. Dwarf Epics and the Ancient Irish

1. See Phillips, 30–34, for a description of this event. Phillips's project in general docu-ments how Americans perceived the coming conflict from the moment of independence.

2. See Stuart Henry's 1973 biography of Beecher for the details of his mission to the West. See also Watts, *In This Remote Country*, 181–218, on Beecher. See also Franchot.

3. See Loughran, Gunn, and Hsu for how expansion and the subsequent emergence of regional difference destabilized antebellum America.

4. On a global scale, Eddy and Schreuder identify internal consolidation as central to all settler nations. As to the status of Ireland as a "colony," Horning writes, "Ireland, with its longstanding continental cultural and religious connections, was an unlikely practice ground for the colonization of the Americas, yet its history became intertwined with

that of colonial America. Ireland sat both within a Virginian Sea, and, at the same time, firmly within Europe" (26).

5. Lawson refers to the settler as both "colonizer and colonized" simultaneously. In the thirty years since he made the distinction, more recent settler theorists have preferred, to paraphrase, that the settler is both colonizing and colonial. See Veracini, *Settler Colonialism*; Wolfe; and Mackey.

6. See the introduction's discussion of Deloria.

7. Snydor's linkage of the Missouri Compromise and the rise of southern sectionalism has informed more recent scholars such as Grant and Quinlan.

8. See Nellis's *An Empire of Regions* and Gimpel and Schuknecht on the cultural politics of sectionalism.

9. See Greeson and O'Brien for readings of southern sectionalism of a phenomenon indicative of a settler colony. Quigley studies the evolution of southern nationalism more generally. See Quinlan and McWhiney for deeper linkage of southern and Irish cultures.

10. Kolodny's *In Search of First Contact* explores this subject comprehensively. See William R. Taylor and Watson for discussions of the role of medievalism in this imagery.

11. For general biographical a bibliographical information and insight on Simms, the work of Guilds, Busick, and Jeffrey Rogers informs my comments. See also Quigley, 50–86.

12. Page references for both the essay in which Simms attacks Cooper and his review of *Northern Antiquities* are from the more available *Views and Reviews in American Literature* (1845), in which he collected recent criticism. Busick's critical reading of Simms's historiography has been essential to my understanding of Simms's regionalism and nationalism.

13. See Jeffrey Rogers, 45–74, and Grant, 45–70. On southern views of western territory, see also Howe, Wilentz, and Calore, 153–66.

14. As evidenced by its exploration of the concept of the "Southron," Simms's *Southward Ho!* (1854) marks his transition from his earlier nationalist texts to a virulent identification with the South rather than the nation. See Quigley, 115–20. As to other southern nationalists who pushed Simms's radicalization, I refer to Tucker's *The Partisan Leader*, an 1836 publication that saw renewed and redoubled readership in the 1850s South. See Quigley, 85.

15. I will be using the version of the essay Simms republished in the second volume of *Views and Reviews in American Literature* (1845). The Norse revival is discussed in chapter 5, below. Wawn, Kolodny, Thurin, and Barnes document its textual and cultural history. Kolodny, *In Search of First Contact*, 125–29, identifies Beamish as Irish.

16. See Hagstette on the rivalry between Cooper and Simms. On Columbian mythography more generally, see Martin. See Sale and Bartosik-Velez, as well as Bjornsdottir for commentary on the shifting Columbian "legacy."

17. See chapter 3 above. Simms's knowledge of the Mound Builders seems derived almost entirely from Atwater's collection.

18. Like most southerners, however, Simms was unwilling to examine the radically different mounds all around the South. On Simms's sympathetic yet paternalistic views on Indians, see Hudson.

19. See Downham on the centuries-long Viking occupation and transformation of Ireland.

20. See Jeffrey Rogers, 1–15, on Simms in 1830s Charleston. Simms here signals his discontent with the normal primordial linkage of Norse and Puritanical culture. Instead, this signals what would become a southern embrace of the purportedly more festive Norman branch of the Norse legacy, a legacy more openly embraced by southern nationalists in the 1850s. See Watson.

21. See Horsman, 29, on due process as a contrived Teutonic invention. In the early nineteenth century, Henry Wheaton and Sharon Turner credit the Saxons with its origins, in their larger separation of Gothic and Teutonic cultures. See Kolodny, *In Search of First Contact*, 125–27. See also Emerson's *English Traits*, discussed chapter 5, below.

22. Tucker's *Partisan Leader* (1836) forecast the coming Civil War and celebrated the prospect of southern independence.

23. This passage is from "Americanism in Literature," reprinted in *Views and Reviews in American Literature*, 1:1–25.

24. *Southward Ho!* represents more a critique of northern claims on the nation, a sign of Simms's developing alienation. As to Simms's sectionalism and eventual secessionism, see Quigley, 24–50. Jeffrey Rogers, 17–45, provides the most recent elaboration.

25. On post–Civil War erasure, see Jacobson's *Whiteness*, 126–87, and Painter, 201–12.

26. On the need for the Irish and other exogenous whites, see Painter and Jacobson, *Whiteness*. New Zealand historian James Belich defines this era of American colonialism as "hyper-colonization": "Explosive colonizations . . . triggered by particular settler transitions and mass transfers, and then powered more by a boom mentality than rational choice" (314).

27. On the affinity of Irish and aboriginal characters in aboriginal writing, see Watts, "In Your Head You Are Not Defeated."

28. For the political origins of "Scots-Irish" as a term designed to mitigate the otherness of the Irish, see McWhiney, Ignatiev, and Quinlan. For a general overview, see Doyle.

29. See Dowd and Giemza for the most recent scholarly commentary on the Irish in early American culture and literature.

30. See Ignatiev, 3–24, on the whitening of the Irish in the Mexican War. For a differing view, see Rodriguez, 17–28. See also Jacobson, *Whiteness*, 41–55, for a general overview of the blight and its relation to immigration and the destabilization of American ideas of whiteness. See Horsman, 30–32; Painter, 98–150; Dain, 180–84; and Dunne on Irish whiteness. See especially Knobel and Rees, 47–50. Even as Painter begins her discussion of virulent nativism, she observes, "So while an aversion to Catholics and Catholicism was hardly a trivial fact of America life and could flare up in deadly violence, it never defined American identity in the long haul" (146), thus creating a context for the partial expansion of American whiteness to include the Irish. See Ignatiev, 6–34. As to the need for more whites in the ongoing project of settler colonialism, see Juliet Shields, Belich, and Painter.

31. See Campbell, 144–56, on the Brendan vogue in Irish culture.

32. O'Donoghue provides the most comprehensive history of the legend and the variant manuscripts. See O'Donoghue, 1–31, and O'Meara's introduction to his translation. These, as well as Burgess and Strijbosch's book-length critical bibliography, have informed my account of the text's history.

33. As to the production of negative stereotypes of the Irish, see Quinlan in particular. See McWhiney more generally.

34. *Brendaniana* collected dozens of appropriations of Brendan's voyage in America, including the naming of schools and parishes. It also tracks variant versions of the legend. Aside from Cahill, see Dowd, 5–27. See especially Mulrooney's introduction, xiii–xx. Many of Brendan's fellow monks were canonized. See O'Donoghue, 270–305, and Walsh.

35. See Spurr and Said on feminization as a form of colonization. See Douglas, 17–24, on immigrants compromising American masculinity, especially Catholics. See also Dana Nelson, *National Manhood*, 102–35, and Greenburg, 75–101. On gender and southern medievalism, see Pugh and Ignatiev.

36. Josiah Priest and C. S. Rafinesque (*Ancient History*), for example, both argued that there were Irish crossings prior to the current era (over two thousand years ago). However, as their accounts are presented as merely antiquarian curiosities, lacking Barnhart's "problem orientation," they cannot be considered as primordial. Neither was linked to any contemporary literary or cultural contexts.

37. Nativists suspected celibate priests of various perversions. As an example of suspicions of Catholicism and republican domesticity, George Lippard's *The Quaker City* (1847) epitomized sensational and voyeuristic nativist rhetoric about clerical corruption and depravity.

38. On colonialist aspects of the concept of tabula rasa, see Veracini, *Settler Colonialism*, 80. See McNiven, Russell, and Schaffer, 4, on the implication of Rousseau in the culture of settler colonialism. Miller et al.'s discussion of the Doctrine of Discovery (see Miller's introduction, 1–64, in particular) has especially informed my thinking on the subject.

39. On Longfellow, see Kolodny's *In Search of First Contact*. See also O'Donoghue, 298–305. See Freitag for a scholarly review of the subject.

40. See Gunn and Doolen's *Territories of Empire* for linkages of western travel to imperial ambitions. See also Watts, "Exploration," and the essays in Hamilton and Hilliard for the many ways colonial Europeans considered western prospects, especially essays by Miles and Lush. Armitage and Burke identify the same strains in continental European thought.

41. See Horsman, 257, and Hietala, 255–63, on the origins and application of "Manifest Destiny."

42. On the persistence of Irish otherness, see Brundage, 127–46, as well as Painter, Hoganson, and Saxton. On traditions of Irish resistance, see Webb. On the Irish on both sides of the Civil War, see Ural, "Ye Sons of Erin Green Assemble," and Gleeson.

5. The Norse Forefathers of the American Empire

1. On anti-imperialism, see Tyrell and Sexton, Beisner, and Cullinane. See Jacobson (*Barbarian Virtues*) and Twain as well. On the colonialism of the Progressive Age, see Hixson, 125.

2. Following Carman, and more recent observers of the continuity he establishes, such as Kaplan, "The Absence of Empire," and Rowe, this chapter traces the transfer of the primordialist impulse from territorial to overseas forms of colonialism. The link to specific acts of settlement was replaced by fantasies of conquest related more to race than place, especially in latter sections.

3. On the switch from environmental to biological theorizations of race, see Chiles, Painter, Dain, and Wheeler. As we have seen in millennialist and Mound Builders primordialisms, however, the popular imagination often lagged behind the cutting edge of "scientific" theory.

4. Spellings of Leif's name varies greatly, through Norse, Icelandic, English, and other appropriations. Because most of the nineteenth-century writers studied here employ the Americanized "Leif Ericson," I am retaining that spelling to signal his role as a domesticated construction of American culture, a persona not to be confused with the actual historical figure, though the original has been retained in quoted materials.

5. Irving's 1828 biography was most responsible for Columbus's hagiography. Martin traces Joel Barlow's *Columbiad* and *Visions of Columbus* as attempts to fit his life into epic poetry. My thinking of Columbus more generally is based in Rivera, 34–67. On the rivalry, also see Kolodny, *In Search of First Contact*, 213–55; see also Rivera, 20–34; Bjornsdottir; and DeGuzmán.

6. Volume 1 of Rowson's *Reuben and Rachel* fictionalizes the intermarriage of Columbus's descendants with Incan and Algonquian Indians. However, in volume 2 the family is recognized and behaves as if wholly white.

7. Throughout, I am indebted to Kolodny, Wawn, Thurin, and Barnes for background and analytical grounding. See Kolodny, *In Search of First Contact*, 151–213, for an overview of the Norse revival. Thurin and Barnes address more directly its American and transnational literary aspects.

8. Wawn, Enterline, Barnes, and Bjornsdottir document Rafn's publication as an event that catalyzed the consolidation of racial hierarchy throughout Europe and North America, as different groups sought the primordial grandeur they describe.

9. See Seitler. This also defines notions of racial transformation and degeneration in Chiles and Dain. Kolodny, *In Search of First Contact*, 67–71, recounts the conflicts; see also Barnes, 14–20, and *Sagas of the Icelanders*, 1:25. Jakobsson best contextualizes the violent nature of the Vinland settlements. My reading of Emerson's *English Traits* is indebted to Painter, 165–83. As to the gendered nature of Emerson's language, see Douglas, 26–42. On Emerson and race, see particularly Powell, 122–51, and Jack Turner, 66–87. Daniel Kock links Emerson's feelings on race to his time in Europe with Carlyle and others. See Painter.

10. On Anglo-Saxonism, see Horsman, Painter, Bieder, and Dain. Sharon Turner, 341–52, and Wheaton, 94–110, distinguish Gothic and Teutonic as distinct cultures. Wheaton and Longfellow were close friends and Harvard classmates.

11. See Horsman, 29–39, for a historiography of this intraracial distinction. My thinking here is informed by the history of race in America, especially as written by Saxton, Painter, and Horsman. Painter even refers to "Teutomania" (245–50) to describe the postbellum national obsession. Below, see in particular, Emerson's and Norris's direct evocation of the poetic and romantic Teutonic Norse as literary analogs to the more mundane Anglo-Saxon tradition. On literary Teutonism in the Norse revival, aside from Kolodny, see Thurin, 13–32, and Barnes, 37–59. On American historiography, see Luczak and Gossett, 84–122.

12. By "natural nation," I refer to the romantic notion that nation evolves from a long intimacy of people and place. See Anthony Smith's writings for a theoretical explanation; see James Drake and Tom Hallock for its location in America. Simms's ideas about southern nationalism and primordialism are addressed above in chapter 4. Paul Carter theorizes the concept for Australia and other settler colonies.

13. The myth of Norumbega is most comprehensively addressed in Emerson Baker et al. See D'Abate's essay in particular.

14. See Kolodny, *In Search of First Contact*, 151–70. See Trumpener on the relation of the linkage of bardic revivalism and empire building. For other readings of "Skeleton," see Barnes, 120–27, and Higgins, "Longfellow's Conversations."

15. See Foos and Johannsen on the propaganda surrounding the war.

16. D'Abate and all of Baker's contributors omit reference to the Norse in their studies of Norumbega. D'Abate instead comments: "Beginning with the voyage of Verrazano in 1524, the European concept of a place or a region known as Norumbega took about fifty years to elaborate. . . . It was the product of a limited number of actual explorations, a great deal of speculation and mythical projection, and an admirably developed cartographical record" (67).

17. Kribbs's collection on Whittier discusses his work more generally. See Thurin and Barnes in particular. Whittier's "Norembega" poems are studied by Kolodny in *In Search of First Contact*, 173–77.

18. Stephen Williams coined the term "fantastic archaeology" to describe purported discoveries and legends that were geared toward attracting paying audiences—tourists, readers, audiences—rather than advancing the actual study of the distant past.

19. Horsford wrote five books on his discovery of Norumbega. I focus on *Discovery* as it drew the most critical attention and made the most literary references. Kolodny briefly addresses this issue (*In Search of First Contact*, 250–55). Norumbega, though unfound, was central to late nineteenth-century debates concerning the possibility that Vikings had been not only in the New World but more precisely in New England. Rasmus Anderson, De Costa, and Horsford led public campaigns to displace Columbus and for funding to search for Norumbega. See Kammen, 242–51, for the celebrations surrounding the erection of the Ericson statue in 1887 in Boston.

20. See Sale, Bartosik-Velez, and Bjornsdottir for histories of Columbus's reputation. In Winsor's day, De Costa's defense of Ericson was directly rooted in a rejection of Columbus on racial, religious, and ethnic grounds.

21. In reference to the self-congratulatory tone of Progressivism, Jason Black writes, "[Progressives] reinforced the US government's ideology of republican fatherhood, and efforts to assimilate Native communities through yeoman farming, American domestic life, Christianity, the English language, and capitalism. Clearly the progressive movement to 'kill the Indian but not the man' . . . reconfirmed and fed into the US government's construction of dependent American Indians and a colonially powerful US nation" (73).

22. Godeanu-Kenworthy reads Cooper as a colonialist against the Canadian Odawa writer John Richardson to explore the range of ambivalences available in adventure fiction.

23. See Baker and Sabin's extensive study of the repackaging of Cooper and the many convolutions of Cooper's The Last of the Mohicans (16–39).

24. See Brantlinger, 47–72, on the interplay of colonial boys and imperial values in the late Victorian era. See also Wawn, 190–95. For links to empire building and masculinity, see Hixson, 23–34; Belkin, 5–22; and Greenburg, 171–208. Horsman traces out the evolution of this view most specifically (25–42).

25. See Wayne Franklin's critical biography and Gustafson, Imagining Deliberative Democracy, 181–89. On Cooper and "frontier patriarchy," see Motley. Most information about Liljencrantz's life can be found at https://en.wikipedia.org/wiki/Ottilie_A._Liljencrantz. As to Liljencrantz's invocation of multiracial cohabitation, I refer to the larger goals of the Dawes Severalty Act of 1887, as inspired by Helen Hunt Jackson's two books, A Century of Dishonor (1881) and Ramona (1884). See Berkhofer, 153–75; Rosenthal, 143–48; and Conn, 198–230.

26. Since this chapter was completed, Kolodny briefly addressed Randvar and its links to imperialism in "When the East Was West." Henry Nash Smith's Virgin Land brought dime novels and youth-oriented literature into the study of race and class in America. Slotkin, Denning, and others built upon his model of the linkage of masculinist myth-making and nationalist racial fantasy. On the relation of frontier narratives to American empire building, see Streeby, 139–59. See Barnett.

27. See Robisch on the werewolf myth and its interplay with American masculinity. This refers to white men who, when needed, had the latent race-based atavistic ability to "out-savage the savage" if "awakened" to his potential. See Pearce, 228. Line 30 of "The Skeleton in Armor" mentions Rolf's hearing the "werewolf's cry" while still in Scandinavia. Like other Old World corruptions, such as aristocracy, Randvar purges the New World of such taints by linking it to the republic's cleansing the colony of the degenerate aristocracy. See Seitler, 94–128.

28. Watson and William Taylor inform my comments throughout this section. On Simms and Normanism, see Farmer, 11–16, and Cantrell, 235–39.

29. See Jewett and Wheaton on the history of the Normans.

30. On southern medievalism, see Lears, 98–113, and Pugh, 32–47. On Simms's, see Jeffrey Rogers and Guilds.

31. On the basis of southern Normanism in the historical romances in the school of Sir Walter Scott more generally see Pugh and, more precisely, Chibnall, 55–60.

32. The *Ladies Repository and Gatherings of the West* was published in Cincinnati, 1841–76. However, there is no evidence that Thomas herself was from Cincinnati, as there is no mention of her in either Coggeshall's nor Gallagher's collections of poetry from the region.

33. See Jordan, *White Man's Burden*, and Gretchen Murphy for critical readings of both the poem and the ideology.

34. See Hjaltalín's account. See also Wheaton, Mallett, and Rafn.

35. See O'Connor for biographical information on Brace.

36. See Spurr, 170–83, and Said, 31–48.

37. On Dowe, see Hanlon, 125–32. On caloric engines, see Thulesius. Ericcson built ironclad ships for the Union and developed submarine technology. See Feifer on the "opening" of Japan and its links to American imperialism.

38. On filibustering and its literary celebration, see May, 59–80, and Greenburg, 47–53. See Belich, 244–50, and Wilentz, 162–66, on the issue of private colonization in both British and American empires.

39. On filibustering in Texas, see Greenburg, 23–30.

40. Barnhart writes that romantic historians perceived antiquarians as "narrow, non-analytical, and lack[ing] a problem orientation, thus rendering them anathema to the scholarship valued by professional historians and archaeologists" (*American Antiquities*, 30). Within that context, primordialism sought to assume the "problem orientation" of genuine disciplines while still evoking the license to fabricate assumed by romantic authorship.

41. See Farrow, 53–71, on Alaska and its entanglement with Manifest Destiny and other imperialist discourses.

42. On anti-imperialism, see Beisner in particular. See Jacobson, *Barbarian Virtues*, 106–20, and the essays in Tyrell and Sexton's collection. Love, Greenburg, and Eperjesi have influenced my thinking as well. Moreover, a wealth of boy's stories set in each site of imperial expansion soon proliferated.

43. See McElrath and Crisler, 30–33, 260–79, for information on Norris in general and this story's racial politics. See also Seitler, 199–226. Norris's own essay "Child Stories for Adults" perhaps introduced the interlinkages of race, empire, and the rhetoric of recruitment in juvenile literature.

44. See Wu for a reading from a Chinese American critical perspective.

45. On Michaelson, see Harrison-Kahan.

46. Gretchen Murphy concludes, "Beyond the catchy phrase, Kipling's poem called to mind discrepancies in racial narratives of empire and the tenuousness of whiteness as empire's justification and goal. As familiar and recognizable verse, the poem became a powerful conduit for chanelling and broadcasting those discrepancies" (57). See O'Brien as well.

47. See Rowe, 195–216. More particularly, Rowe comments about Johnson's friend and colleague W. E. B. Du Bois: "US Imperialism originates in slavery and depends on racism

to legitimate colonial practices of territorial acquisition, economic domination, and psychological subjugation. . . . Given the tendency of even America's most vigorous modern critics to localize its imperialism in such specific ventures as the Spanish-American War and the general myopia of Americans until quite recently in regard to the imbrication of US racism and imperialism, Du Bois is a forerunner of contemporary cultural and postcolonial criticisms of the role culture has played in disguising the imperialist practices of the United States" (196).

48. The most extended treatment of Johnson's work on race are the essays in part 2 of Price and Oliver's collection.

49. Griffiths suggests that colonial and racial discourse depends upon concepts of "home" and "white" that are—and have always been—undiluted, the primordial sources of each nation and, in turn, race.

50. See Reesman for a fuller discussion of London's career-long obsession's with race and his (mis-)placement among the naturalists. See Furer for a useful reading of London and race.

51. Eperjesi writes, "While in Hawai'i, London de-naturalizes white skin (but not the privilege that went with it) while hyper-naturalizing brown skin . . . thus separating pigmentation from power relations" (127).

52. See Newton, 250–54, for an overview of London's use of past life regression and racial memory in both stories.

53. See Fussell's monumental text on how the disillusionment caused by the First World War led to the general questioning of all romantic constructs, including Anglo-Saxonism, and, by implication, primordialism.

54. Recently, a number of states and communities have shifted the second Monday of October from Columbus Day to Indigenous Peoples Day. See Sale and Bartosik-Velez.

55. See "The Greenlander's Saga," 61–62, in *The Sagas of the Icelanders*. See Kolodny, *In Search of First Contact*, 57–60, and Barnes, 17.

BIBLIOGRAPHY

Abzug, Robert. *Cosmos Crumbling: Reform and the Religious Imagination.* New York: Oxford University Press, 1994.

Adair, James. *The History of the American Indians.* London: Dilly, 1775.

Adams, Henry. *A Life of Albert Gallatin.* Philadelphia: Lippincott, 1880.

Allen, Chadwick. *Trans-Indigenous: Methodologies for Global Native Literary Studies.* Minneapolis: University of Minnesota Press, 2012.

Anderson, Benedict. *Imagined Communities: Reflections on the Origins and Spread of Nationalism.* Rev. ed. London: Verso, 1983.

Anderson, Gary Clayton. *Ethnic Cleansing and the Indian: The Crime That Should Haunt America.* Norman: University of Oklahoma Press, 2014.

Anderson, William L., Jane L. Brown, and Anne F. Rogers. Introduction. xiii–xxiv in *The Payne-Butrick Papers,* edited and annotated by Anderson, Brown, and Rogers. Lincoln: University of Nebraska Press, 2010.

Anon. *Memoirs of John Howard Payne: The American Roscius.* London: Miller, 1815.

Anon. "Review of *The Norse-Folk; Or a Visit to the Homes of Norway and Sweden* by Charles Loring Brace." *Emerson's US Magazine* 5.2 (1857): 190–91.

Anon. *Sagas of the Icelanders,* ed. Jane Smiley. London: Penguin, 2005.

Anon. "Talk about New Books." *Catholic World* 58.1 (December 1894): 441–42.

Anzaldua, Gloria. *Borderlands / La Frontera.* San Francisco: Aunt Lute Books, 2007.

Apap, Christopher C. *The Genius of Place: The Geographic Imagination in the Early Republic.* Lebanon, NH: University Press of New England, 2016.

Apess, William. *On Our Own Ground: The Complete Writings of William Apess, A Pequot.* Edited by Barry O'Connell. Amherst: University of Massachusetts Press, 1992.

Arch, Steven Carl. "The 'Progressive Steps' of the Narrator in Crèvecoeur's *Letters from an American Farmer.*" *Studies in American Fiction* 18 (1990): 145–58.

Armitage, David. "The New World and British Historical Thought: From Richard Hakluyt to William Robertson." 52–77 in Kupperman.

Armstrong, Zella. *Who Discovered America? The Amazing Story of Madoc.* Chattanooga, TN: Lookout, 1950.

Aron, Stephen. *American Confluence: The Missouri Frontier from Borderland to Border State.* Bloomington: Indiana University Press, 2006.

Atkinson, George Wesley. *History of Kanawha County from Its Organization to the Present Time.* Charleston, 1876.

Atwater, Caleb. *A Description of the Antiquities Discovered in the Western Country, Originally Communicated to the American Antiquarian Society. 1818. 6–170* in *The Writings of Caleb Atwater.* Columbus, OH, 1833.

Axtell, James. *The Invasion Within: The Contest of Cultures in Colonial North America.* New York: Oxford University Press, 1985.

Baker, Emerson W., et al., eds. *American Beginnings: Exploration, Culture, and Cartography in the Land of Norumbega.* Lincoln: University of Nebraska Press, 1994.

Baker, Martin, and Roger Sabin. *The Lasting of the Mohicans: The History of an American Myth.* Oxford: University of Mississippi Press, 2004.

Ballantyne, Robert Michael. *The Norsemen in the West; Or America before Columbus.* London: Nisbet, 1872.

Baltzell, T. Digby. *Puritan Boston and Quaker Philadelphia.* Philadelphia: Transaction, 2007.

Banner, Stuart. *How the Indians Lost Their Land: Law and Power on the Frontier.* Cambridge, MA: Harvard University Press, 2005.

Barnes, Geraldine. *Viking America: The First Millennium.* Cambridge: Brewer, 2001.

Barnett, Louise. *The Ignoble Savage: American Literary Racism, 1790–1890.* Westport, CT: Greenwood, 1975.

Barnhart, Terry A. *American Antiquities: Revisiting the Origins of American Archaeology.* Lincoln: University of Nebraska Press, 2015.

———. *Ephraim George Squier and the Development of American Anthropology.* Lincoln: University of Nebraska Press, 2005.

Barone, Robert W. "Madoc and John Dee: Welsh Myth and Elizabethan Imperialism." *Elizabethan Review,* http://www.ramtops.co.uk/madocdee.html. Accessed 23 October 2012.

Bartlett, John Raymond. *Edom and the Edomites.* New York: JSOT, 1989.

Barton, Benjamin Smith. *New Views of the Origin of the Tribes and Nations of America.* Philadelphia, 1797.

Bartosik-Velez, Elise. *The Legacy of Christopher Columbus in the Americas: New Nations and a Transatlantic Discourse of Empire.* Nashville: Vanderbilt University Press, 2014.

Bauer, Ralph. *The Cultural Geography of Colonial American Literatures: Empire, Travel, Modernity.* New York: Cambridge University Press, 2003.

Beach, Samuel Bellamy. *Escalala: An American Tale.* Utica, NY: Williams, 1824.

Beamish, North Ludlow, and Carl Christian Rafn. *The Discovery of America by the Northmen in the Tenth Century.* London: Boone, 1841.

Beatty, Charles. *A Journal of Two Months Tour to the Westward of the Alle-Gheny Mountains.* London, 1768.

Beecher, Lyman. *A Plea for the West.* Cincinnati: Leavitt, 1835.

Beede, Benjamin. *The War of 1898 and US Interventions, 1898–1934.* New York: Taylor and Francis, 1994.

Beisner, Robert L. *Twelve against Empire: The Anti-Imperialists, 1898–1900.* 3rd ed. Chicago: University of Chicago Press, 1985.

Belich, James. *Replenishing the Earth: The Settler Revolution and the Rise of the Anglo-World, 1783–1939*. New York: Oxford University Press, 2011.

Belkin, Aaron. *Bring Me Men: Military Masculinity and the Benign Façade of American Empire, 1898–2001*. New York: Oxford University Press, 2012.

Belknap, Jeremy. *American Biography; Or, An Historical Account of Those People Who Have Been Distinguished in America*. 1794–98. 2 vols. Boston: Thomas and Andrews, 1847.

Bellin, Joshua David. *The Demon of the Continent: Indians and the Shaping of American Literature*. Philadelphia: University of Pennsylvania Press, 2001.

Bercovitch, Sacvan. *The American Jeremiad*. Madison: University of Wisconsin Press, 1978.

———. *The Puritan Origins of the American Self*. New Haven, CT: Yale University Press, 1975.

———. *Rites of Assent: Transformations in the Symbolic Construction of America*. New York: Routledge, 1990.

Bergmann, William H. *The American National State and the Early West*. New York: Cambridge University Press, 2012.

Berkhofer, Robert F., Jr. *The White Man's Indian: Images of the American Indian from Columbus to the Present*. New York: Vintage, 1978.

Bhabha, Homi K. "DissemiNation: Time, Narrative, and the Margins of the Modern Nation." 241–322 in Bhabha, *Nation and Narration*.

———. *The Location of Culture*. New York: Routledge, 1994.

———, ed. *Nation and Narration*. New York: Routledge, 1991.

Bickham, Troy. *The Weight of Vengeance: The United States, the British Empire, and the War of 1812*. New York: Oxford University Press, 2012.

Bieder, Robert E. *Science Encounters the Indian, 1820–1860: The Early Years of American Anthropology*. Norman: University of Oklahoma Press, 1986.

Bjornsdottir, Inga Dora. "Leifr Eiriksson versus Christopher Columbus: The Use of Leifr Eiriksson in American Political and Cultural Discourse." 220–28 in Wawn and Sigurðardóttir.

Black, Jason Edward. *American Indians and the Rhetoric of Removal and Allotment*. Jackson: University Press of Mississippi, 2015.

Bloch, Ruth. *Visionary Republic: Visionary Themes in American Thought, 1756–1800*. New York: Cambridge University Press, 1985.

Blumenbach, Johann Fredrich. *On the Natural Varieties of Mankind*. Translated by Karl Marx. 1775. London: Bergman, 1865.

Bonivanua-Mar, Tracey. *Decolonisation and the Pacific: Indigenous Globalization and the Ends of Empire*. New York: Cambridge University Press, 2016.

Boorstin, Daniel J. *The Creators: A History of Heroes of the Imagination*. New York: Knopf, 2012.

Boudinot, Elias. *A Star in the West*. Trenton, NJ: Fenton, 1816.

Bowen, Rev. Benjamin F. *America Discovered by the Welsh in 1170 AD*. 1873. Philadelphia: Lippincott, 1876.

Boyd, George Adams. *Elias Boudinot: Patriot and Statesman.* New York: Greenwood, 1969.

Brace, Charles Loring. *The Norse-Folk: Or a Visit to the Homes of Norway and Sweden.* New York: Bentley, 1857.

Brackenridge, Henry Marie. *Views of Louisiana, Together with a Journal of a Voyage Up the Missouri River in 1811.* Pittsburgh: Cramer, 1814.

Bradford, Alexander Warfield. *American Antiquities and Researches into the Origin of the Red Race.* New York: Wiley and Putnam, 1843.

Brantlinger, Patrick. *Rule of Darkness: British Literature and Imperialism, 1830–1914.* Ithaca, NY: Cornell University Press, 1988.

Brekus, Catherine A. *Strangers and Pilgrims: Female Preaching in America, 1740–1845.* Chapel Hill: University of North Carolina Press, 1998.

Brennen, Timothy. "The National Longing for Form." 44–71 in Bhaba, *Nation and Narration.*

Bridgeman, Raymond L. *Loyal Traitors: A Story of Friendship for the Filipinos.* Boston: West, 1903.

Brodkin, Karen. *How Jews Became White Folks and What That Says About Race in America.* New Brunswick, NJ: Rutgers University Press, 1998.

Brooks, Moses. "An Apostrophe on the Mounds." 115 in Coggeshall.

Brown, Charles Brockden. "For the Literary Magazine. Southey's *Madoc.*" *Literary Magazine* 4.26 (Nov. 1805): 342–43.

Brown, Laurie. *Terraforming the American West.* Baltimore: Johns Hopkins University Press, 2000.

Bruyneel, Kevin. *The Third Space of Sovereignty: The Postcolonial Politics of US/Indigenous Relations.* Minneapolis: University of Minnesota Press, 2007.

Bryant, William Cullen. *A Popular History of the United States: From the Discovery of the Hemisphere by the Norsemen until the End of the Civil War.* New York: Scribner's, 1883.

———. "The Prairies." 298–302 in *Early American Poetry,* edited by Jane Donohue Eberwein. Madison: University of Wisconsin Press, 1978.

Buell, Lawrence. "American Literary Emergence as a Postcolonial Phenomenon." *American Literary History* 4.3 (1992): 411–42.

Buffalohead, W. Roger. Introduction. ix–xvii in *History of the Ojibway People,* by William Warren (1885). Minneapolis: Minnesota Historical Society Press, 1984. (Collected from essays first published in 1852.)

Bullock, Steven C. *Revolutionary Brotherhood: Freemasonry and the Transformation of American Social Order, 1730–1840.* Chapel Hill: University of North Carolina Press, 1996.

Bulmer-Thomas, Victor. *Empire in Retreat: The Past, Present, and Future of the United States.* New Haven, CT: Yale University Press, 2018.

Burder, George. *The Welch Indians: Or A Collection of Papers Respecting a People Whose Ancestors Emigrated from Wales to America, In the Year 1170, With Prince Madoc.* London, 1797.

Burgess, Glyn S., and Clara Strijbosch. *The Legend of St. Brendan: A Critical Bibliography.* Dublin: Royal Irish Academy, 2002.

Burin, Eric. *Slavery and the Peculiar Solution: A History of the American Colonization Society.* Gainesville: University Press of Florida, 2008.

Burke, Peter. "America and the Rewriting of World History." 33–51 in Kupperman.

Burstein, Andrew. *Sentimental Democracy: The Evolution of America's Romantic Self-Image.* New York: Hill and Wang, 1999.

Bush, Barbara. *Imperialism and Postcolonialism.* New York: Routledge, 2014.

Bushman, Richard Lyman. *Joseph Smith: Rough Stone Rolling.* New York: Vintage, 2007.

Busick, Sean. *A Sober Desire for History: William Gilmore Simms as Historian.* Columbia: University of South Carolina Press, 2005.

Buss, James Joseph. *Winning the West with Words: Language and Conquest in the Lower Great Lakes.* Norman: University of Oklahoma Press, 2011.

Butler, Jon. *Awash in a Sea of Faith: Christianizing the American People.* Cambridge, MA: Harvard University Press, 1990.

Byrd, Jodi A. *The Transit of Empire: Indigenous Critiques of Colonialism.* Minneapolis: University of Minnesota Press, 2011.

Cahill, Thomas. *How the Irish Saved Civilization.* New York: Doubleday, 1995.

Calore, Paul. *The Causes of the Civil War: The Political, Cultural, Economic, and Territorial Disputes between North and South.* New York: McFarland, 2014.

Campbell, Matthew. *Irish Poetry under the Union, 1801–1924.* New York: Cambridge University Press, 2013.

Cantrell, James P. *How Celtic Culture Invented Southern Literature.* New York: Pelican, 2005.

Carman, Albert Richardson. *The Ethics of Imperialism: An Enquiry Whether Christian Ethics and Imperialism Are Antagonistic.* Boston: Turner, 1905.

Carr, Helen. *Inventing the American Primitive: Politics, Gender, and the Representation of Native American Literary Traditions, 1789–1936.* Cork, Ireland: University of Cork Press, 1996.

Carter, Paul. *The Road to Botany Bay: An Exploration of Landscape and History.* New York: Knopf, 1987.

Catlin, George. *The Manners, Customs, and Conditions of the North American Indians.* Philadelphia: Lippincott, 1841.

Cavanaugh, Edward, and Lorenzo Veracini, eds. *The Routledge Handbook of the History of Settler Colonialism.* New York: Routledge, 2016.

Channing, William Ellery. *Letter to the Hon. Henry Clay, On the Annexation of Texas.* Boston: Munroe, 1837.

Cherry, Conrad, ed. *God's New Israel: Religious Interpretations of American History.* Chapel Hill: University of North Carolina Press, 1998.

Chibnall, Marjorie. *The Debate on the Norman Conquest.* Manchester: Manchester University Press, 1999.

Child, Lydia Marie. *Hobomok: A Tale of the Early Times.* Boston: Cummings, 1824.

Chiles, Katy L. *Transformable Race: Surprising Metamorphoses in the Literature of Early America*. New York: Oxford University Press, 2014.

Clark, Beverly Lynn. *The Cultural Construction of Children's Literature in America*. Baltimore: Johns Hopkins University Press, 2004.

Clark, Thomas. Introduction. iv–xix in Toulmin.

Clarke, Alice C. "Where Are Vinland and Norumbega?" *New England Magazine* 4.2 (April 1891): 261–66.

Clinton, Hilary Rodham. Preface, 8–10 in Fitzhugh and Ward.

Coggeshall, William T., ed. *The Poets and Poetry of the West*. Columbus, OH: Foster, 1860.

Colby, James Waldo. *Norumbega, the Ancient City on the Charles*. Waltham, MA: Adams, 1890.

Colvin, Gina, and Joanna Brooks. *Decolonizing Mormonism: Approaching a Postcolonial Zion*. Salt Lake City: University of Utah Press, 2018.

Conn, Steven. *History's Shadow: Native Americans and Historical Consciousness in the Nineteenth Century*. Chicago: University of Chicago Press, 2004.

Coombes, Anne E., ed. *Rethinking Settler Colonialism: History and Memory in Australia, Aotearoa New Zealand, and South Africa*. Manchester: Manchester University Press, 2006.

Cooper, James Fenimore. *Lionel Lincoln; Or, The Leaguer of Boston*. 1833. Preface to revised edition, v–xvii. London: Bentley, 1932.

———. *Oak Openings, or The Bee Hunter*. London: Bentley, 1848.

Corwin, Thomas. *Speeches of Thomas Corwin with a Sketch of His Life*. Edited by Isaac Strohm. Dayton, OH: Comly, 1859.

Cott, Nancy F. *The Bonds of Womanhood: Women's Sphere in New England, 1780–1835*. New Haven, CT: Yale University Press, 1997.

Craig, David Marcellus. *Robert Southey and Romantic Apostasy: Political Argument in Britain, 1780–1840*. London: Royal Historical Society, 2007.

Cramer, Zadok. *The Navigator*. Pittsburgh, 1807.

Crèvecoeur, J. Hector St. John. *Letters From an American Farmer*. 1782. Edited by Ludwig Lewisohn. New York: Fox, Duffield, 1904.

Cronon, William. *Changes in the Land: Indians, Colonists, and the Ecology of New England*. New York: Hill and Wang, 1983.

Crow, Matthew. "Atlantic North America from Contact to the Late Nineteenth Century." 95–108 in Cavanaugh and Veracini.

Cullinane, Michael Patrick. *Liberty and Anti-Imperialism, 1898–1909*. New York: Palgrave, 2012.

Cushman, Robert. "Reasons and Considerations Touching the Lawfulness of Removing Out of England into the Parts of America." 1626. 88–96 in *Mourt's Relation: A Journal of the Pilgrims at Plymouth*, edited by Dwight B. Heath. Plymouth: Applewood Books, 1963.

D'Abate, Richard. "'On the Meaning of a Name': 'Norumbega' and the Representation of North America." 61–88 in Baker et al.

Dahl, Curtis. "Moby Dick's Cousin Behemoth." *American Literature* 31.1 (1959): 21–29.

———. "Mound Builders, Mormons, and William Cullen Bryant." *New England Quarterly* 34.2 (1961): 178–90.

Dain, Bruce. *A Hideous Monster of the Mind: American Race Theory in the Early Republic.* Cambridge, MA: Harvard University Press, 2002.

Dalin, David G. "Jews, Judaism, and the Founders." 63–83 in Dreisbach and Hall.

Davies, Janet. *The Welsh Language.* Cardiff: University of Wales Press, 2012.

Deacon, Richard. *Madoc and the Discovery of America: Some New Light on an Old Controversy.* London: Muller, 1966.

Dearborn, Henry A. *Letters on Internal Improvement and the Commerce of the West.* Boston: Wentworth, 1839.

Debus, Allen A. *Prehistoric Monsters: The Real and Imagined Creatures of the Past That We Love to Fear.* New York: McFarland, 2009.

De Calves, Don Alonso (John Trumbull). *The Narratives of Don Alonso de Calves, John Van Deleure, and Captain James Van Leason: Apocryphal Accounts of Travels, Voyages, and Adventures.* 1786. Fairfield, WA: Galleon, 1996.

De Costa, Benjamin Franklin. *The Pre-Columbian Discovery of America by the Northmen.* 1868. 2nd ed. Albany, NY: Munsell, 1890.

———. Review of *The Lost City of Norumbega* by Eben Horsford. *Magazine of American History* 23 (1890): 173–74.

DeGuzmán, María. *Spain's Long Shadow: The Black Legend, Off-Whiteness, and Anglo-American Empire.* Minneapolis: University of Minnesota Press, 2005.

Deloria, Philip J. *Playing Indian.* New Haven, CT: Yale University Press, 1998.

Den Hartog, Jonathan. "Elias Boudinot, Presbyterians, and the Quest for a Righteous Republic." 253–76 in Dreisbach and Hall.

Dinnerstein, Leonard. *Anti-Semitism in America.* New York: Oxford University Press, 1994.

Dippie, Brian. *The Vanishing American: White Attitudes and United States Indian Policy.* Middletown, CT: Wesleyan University Press, 1985.

Dixon, Robert. *Writing the Colonial Adventure: Race, Gender, and Nation in Anglo-Australian Popular Fiction, 1875–1914.* New York: Cambridge University Press, 1995.

Docker, John. "Are Settler Colonial Inherently Genocidal? Re-Reading Lemkin." 81–101 in Moses.

Doolen, Andy. *Fugitive Empire: Locating Early American Imperialism.* Minneapolis: University of Minnesota Press, 2005.

———. *Territories of Empire: US Writing from the Louisiana Purchase to Mexican Independence.* New York: Oxford University Press, 2014.

Douglas, Ann. *The Feminization of American Culture.* Rev. ed. New York: Noonday, 1998.

Dowd, Christopher. *The Construction of the Irish in American Literature.* New York: Routledge, 2010.

Dowe, William. "The Ericcsons: An Old Story and a New One." *Graham's American Monthly Magazine of Literature, Art, and Fashion* 42.4 (1853): 385–90.

Dowling, William C. *Literary Federalism in the Age of Jefferson: Joseph Dennie and The Port Folio.* Columbia: University of South Carolina Press, 1999.

———. *Poetry and Ideology in Revolutionary Connecticut.* Athens: University of Georgia Press, 1990.

Downham, Clare. *Viking Kings in Britain and Ireland: The Dynasty of Ivarr to A.D. 1014.* Edinburgh: Dunedin, 2010.

Doyle, David S. "The Irish in North America, 1776–1845." 43–67 in *Making the Irish Americans: History and Heritage of the Irish in the United States,* edited by J. J. Lee and Marion Casey. New York: New York University Press, 2006.

Drake, Benjamin. *The Life and Adventures of Black Hawk.* Cincinnati: James, 1841.

Drake, Daniel. *Natural and Statistical View, Or Picture of Cincinnati and Miami County.* Cincinnati: Hooker and Wallace, 1815.

———. "Remarks on the Importance of Promoting Literary and Social Concert in the Mississippi Valley." Cincinnati: Clarke, 1833.

Drake, James D. *The Nation's Nature: How Continental Presumptions Gave Rise to the United States of America.* Charlottesville: University of Virginia Press, 2011.

Drake, Samuel Gardner. *Biography and History of the Indians of North America: From Its First Discovery.* Boston: Perkins, 1834.

Dreisbach, Daniel L., and Mark David Hall, eds. *Faith and the Founders of the American Republic.* New York: Oxford University Press, 2014.

Drinnon, Brian. *Facing West: The Metaphysics of Indian Hating and Empire Building.* Minneapolis: University of Minnesota Press, 1980.

Dumont, Julia. "The Tumulus." 51–52 in Coggeshall.

Dungen, Nicholas. *Gallatin: America's Swiss Founding Father.* New York: New York University Press, 2010.

Dunne, Robert. *Antebellum Irish Immigration and the Emerging Ideologies of Race: A Protestant Backlash.* New York: Mellen, 2002.

During, Simon. "Literature—Nation's Other? The Case for Revision." 138–53 in Bhabha, *Nation and Narration.*

Eaton, Joseph. *The Anglo-American Paper War: Debates over the New Republic, 1800–1825.* London: Palgrave, 2012.

Eddy, John, and Deryck Schreuder, eds. *The Rise of Colonial Nationalism: Australia, New Zealand, Canada, and South Africa First Assert Their Nationalities, 1880–1914.* Sydney: Allen and Unwin, 1988.

Edmunds, R. David. *The Shawnee Prophet.* Lincoln: University of Nebraska Press, 1995.

Elkins, Stanley, and Eric McKitrick. *The Age of Federalism: The Early American Republic.* New York: Oxford University Press, 1995.

Emerson, Ralph Waldo. *The Portable Ralph Waldo Emerson.* Edited by Carl Bode and Malcolm Cowley. New York: Penguin, 1957.

Enterline, James Robert. *Erikson, Eskimos, and Columbus: Medieval European Knowledge of America.* Baltimore: Johns Hopkins University Press, 2002.

Eperjesi, John R. *The Imperialist Imaginary: Visions of Asia and the Pacific in American Culture.* Hanover, NH: Dartmouth University Press, 2005.

Eyal, Yonatan. *The Young America Movement and the Transformation of the Democratic Party, 1828–1861.* New York: Cambridge University Press, 2007.

Fair, Clinton Mahan. *Internal Improvements and the Sectional Controversy.* Madison: University of Wisconsin Press, 1937.

Fanon, Frantz. *Black Skin, White Masks.* 1952. Translated by Richard Philcox. New York: Grove, 2008.

Faragher, John Mack. *Daniel Boone: The Life and Legend of an American Pioneer.* New York: Holt, 1993.

Farmer, Jarrad. *On Zion's Mount: Mormons, Indians, and the American Landscape.* Cambridge, MA: Harvard University Press, 2009.

Farred, Grant. "The Unsettler." *South Atlantic Quarterly* 107.4 (2008): 791–808.

Farrow, Lee A. *Seward's Folly: A New Look at the Alaska Purchase.* Fairbanks: University of Alaska Press, 2016.

Feifer, George. *Breaking Open Japan: Commodore Perry, Lord Abe, and American Imperialism in 1853.* Washington, DC: Smithsonian Books, 2006.

Ferguson, Robert A. *The American Enlightenment.* New York: Cambridge University Press, 1994.

Filson, John. *The Discovery, Settlement, and Present State of Kentucky.* Wilmington, NC, 1784.

Fitzgerald, F. Scott. *The Great Gatsby.* New York: Scribner's, 1925.

Fitzhugh, William W., and Elisabeth I. Ward, eds. *Vikings: The North American Saga.* Washington and New York: Smithsonian Institution Press in association with the National Museum of Natural History, 2000.

Fliegelman, Jay. *Prodigals and Pilgrims: The American Revolution against Patriarchal Authority, 1750–1800.* New York: Cambridge University Press, 1982.

Flint, Micah. "The Hunter." 57–58 in Coggeshall. (Originally 1–21 in *The Hunter, and Other Poems* by Micah Flint. Boston: Cummings, 1826).

Flint, Timothy. *Recollections of the Past Ten Years Passed in Occasional Residences in the Valley of the Mississippi.* Boston: Cummings, 1826.

Folsom, James K. *Timothy Flint.* New York: Twayne, 1965.

Foos, Paul. *A Short, Offhand Killing Affair: Soldiers and Social Conflict in the Mexican-American War.* Chapel Hill: University of North Carolina Press, 2002.

Ford, Lisa. *Settler Sovereignty: Jurisdiction and Indigenous People in America and Australia, 1788–1836.* Cambridge, MA: Harvard University Press, 2010.

Franchot, Jenny. *Roads to Rome: The Antebellum Protestant Encounter with Catholicism.* Berkeley: University of California Press, 1994.

Franklin, Benjamin. "An Edict by the King of Prussia." 1773. 302–6 in *Franklin: The Autobiography and Other Writings on Politics, Economics, and Virtue,* edited by Alan Houston. New York: Cambridge University Press, 2004.

Franklin, Catherine. "The Welsh American Dream: Iolo Morganwg, Robert Southey, and the Madoc Legend." 69–84 in *English Romanticism and the Celtic World,* edited by Gerard Carruthers and Allen Rawes. New York: Cambridge University Press, 2003.

Franklin, Wayne. *James Fenimore Cooper: The Early Years*. New Haven, CT: Yale University Press, 2007.

Freedman, Carl. *The Incomplete Projects: Marxism, Modernity, and the Politics of Culture*. Middleton, CT: Wesleyan University Press, 2002.

Freitag, Barbara. *Hy Brasil: The Metamorphosis of an Island from Cartographic Error to Celtic Elysium*. Amsterdam: Rodopi, 2013.

Friedman, John Black. *The Monstrous Races in Medieval Art and Thought*. Cambridge, MA: Harvard University Press, 1981.

Fulford, Tim, and Peter J. Kitson, eds. *Romanticism and Colonialism: Writing and Empire, 1780–1830*. New York: Cambridge University Press, 1998.

Fussell, Paul. *The Great War and Modern Memory*. New York: Oxford University Press, 2013.

Gallagher, William Davis, ed. *Selections of the Poetical Literature of the West*. Cincinnati: James, 1841.

Gallatin, Albert. *Report of the Secretary of the Treasury on the Subject of Public Roads and Canals*. Washington, DC, 1807.

——. "A Synopsis of the Indian Tribes of North America." *Transactions of the American Antiquarian Society* 2 (1836): 1–422.

——. *A Treatise on Internal Navigation*. New York: Doubleday, 1808.

Gardiner, Michael, Graeme MacDonald, and Niall O'Gallagher, eds. *Scottish Literature and Postcolonial Literature*. Edinburgh: Edinburgh University Press, 2011.

Garrett, Matthew. *Making Lamanites: Mormons, Native Americans, and the Indian Student Placement Program, 1947–2000*. Salt Lake City: University of Utah Press, 2016.

Gellner, Ernst. *Nations and Nationalism*. 2nd ed. Ithaca, NY: Cornell University Press, 2008.

Gibbon, Edward. *The History of the Decline and Fall of the Roman Empire*. 6 vols. London: Strahan, 1776–88.

Gibson, Charles. *The Black Legend: Anti-Spanish Attitudes in the Old World and the New*. New York: Knopf, 1971.

Gidal, Eric. *Ossianic Unconformities: Bardic Poetry in the Industrial Age*. Charlottesville: University of Virginia Press, 2015.

Giemza, Bryan A. *Irish Catholic Writers and the Invention of the American South*. Baton Rouge: Louisiana State University Press, 2013.

Giles, Paul. *The Global Remapping of American Literature*. Princeton, NJ: Princeton University Press, 2011.

Gimpel, James, and Jason E. Schuknecht. *Patchwork Nation: Sectionalism and Political Change in American Politics*. Ann Arbor: University of Michigan Press, 2009.

Gleeson, David T. "Irish Rebels, Southern Rebels: The Irish Confederates." 133–56 in Ural.

Godeanu-Kenworthy, Oana. "Creole Frontiers: Imperial Ambiguities in John Richardson's and Jams Fenimore Cooper's Fiction." *Early American Literature* 49.3 (2014): 741–70.

Goldman, Shalom. *God's Sacred Tongue: Hebrew and the American Imagination*. Chapel Hill: University of North Carolina Press, 2004.

———, ed. *Hebrew and the Bible in America: The First Two Centuries*. Hanover, NH: University Press of New England, 1993.

Goldstein, Alyosha, ed. *Formation of United States Colonialism*. Durham, NC: Duke University Press, 2014.

Gorski, Philip. *American Covenant: A History of Civil Religion from the Puritans to the Present*. Princeton, NJ: Princeton University Press, 2017.

Gossett, Thomas F. *Race: The History of an Idea in America*. New York: Oxford University Press, 1997.

Gould, Philip. "Representative Men: Jeremy Belknap's *American Biography* and the Political Culture of the Early Republic." *Auto/biography* 9/10 (1994): 83–97.

Grant, Susan-Mary. *North over South: Northern Nationalism and American Identity in the Antebellum Era*. Lawrence: University of Kansas Press, 2000.

Green, Martin. *Dreams of Adventure, Deeds of Empire*. New York: Basic Books, 1979.

Greenburg, Amy S. *Manifest Manhood and the Antebellum American Empire*. New York: Cambridge University Press, 2005.

Greer, Allen. *Mohawk Saint: Catherine Tekakwitha and the Jesuits*. New York: Oxford University Press, 2005.

Greer, Margaret R., Walter Mignolo, and Maureen Quilligan, eds. *Rereading the Black Legend: The Discourses of Religious and Racial Difference in Renaissance Empires*. Chicago: University of Chicago Press, 2008.

Greeson, Jennifer Rae. *"Our South": Geographic Fantasy and the Rise of National Literature*. Cambridge, MA: Harvard University Press, 2010.

Griffin, Patrick. *American Leviathan: Empire, Nation, and Revolutionary Frontier*. New York: Hill and Wang, 2007.

Griffith, John T., ed. *Rev. Morgan John Rhys, "The Welsh Baptist Hero of Civil and Religious Liberty of the Eighteenth Century."* Lansford, PA: published by the author, 1899.

Griffiths, Gareth. "The Myth of Authenticity." 235–41 in *The Post-Colonial Studies Reader*, edited by Griffiths, Helen Tiffin, and Bill Ashcroft. New York: Routledge, 1995.

Gross, Robert. "Introduction." 1–51 in *A History of the Book in America*. Vol. 2, *An Extensive Republic: Print Culture and Society in the New Nation, 1790–1840*, ed. Robert Gross and Mary Kelley. Chapel Hill: University of North Carolina Press, 2010.

Guilds, John Caldwell. *Long Years of Neglect: The Work and Reputation of William Gilmore Simms*. Fayetteville: University of Arkansas Press, 1988.

Gunn, Robert Lawrence. *Ethnography and Empire: Languages, Literature, and the Making of the North American Borderlands*. New York: New York University Press, 2015.

Gustafson, Sandra. *Imagining Deliberative Democracy in the Early American Republic*. Chicago: University of Chicago Press, 2011.

———. "Nations of Israelites: Prophecy and Cultural Autonomy in the Writings of William Apess." *Religion and Literature* 26.1 (Spring 1994): 31–53.

Ha, Songho. *The Rise and Fall of the American System: Nationalism and the Development of the American Economy, 1790–1837*. New York: Routledge, 2015.

Hagstette, Todd, ed. *Reading William Gilmore Simms: Essays of Introduction to the Author's Canon*. Columbia: University of South Carolina Press, 2017.

Haight, Gordon. *Mrs. Sigourney: The Sweet Singer of Hartford.* New Haven, CT: Yale University Press, 1911.

Hakluyt, Richard. *The Principal Navigations, Voyages, Traffics, and Discoveries of the English Nation.* London, 1589.

———. *The Voyages, Navigation, Traffiques, and Discoveries of the English Nation.* London, 1582.

Hale, Sarah Josepha Buell. *The Genius of Oblivion and Other Original Poems.* Concord, NH: Moore, 1823.

Hall, James. "Three Hundred Years Hence" (attrib.). 497–502 in Watts and Rachels. (Published originally under pseudonym "Bluffton" in *Illinois Monthly Magazine* 3.2 [1833]: 1–7.)

Hallock, Thomas. *From the Fallen Tree: Frontier Narratives, Environmental Politics, and the Roots a National Pastoral, 1749–1826.* Chapel Hill: University of North Carolina Press, 2004.

Hamilton, Amy T., and Tom J. Hilliard, eds. *Before the West Was West: Critical Essays on Pre-1800 Literature of the American Frontiers.* Lincoln: University of Nebraska Press, 2014.

Hanlon, Christopher: *America's England: Antebellum Literature and Atlantic Sectionalism.* New York: Oxford University Press, 2013.

Hannaford, Ivan. *Race: The History of an Idea in the West.* Washington, DC: Woodrow Wilson Center Press, 1996.

Hankins, Barry. *The Second Great Awakening and the Transcendentalists.* New York: Greenwood, 2004.

Hannabuss, Stuart. "Ballantyne's Message of Empire." 53–71 in Richards.

Harberman, Charles G. "Review of De Costa's *History of America Before Columbus.*" In *Historical Records and Studies for the Washington Catholic Historical Society.* Philadelphia: Lippincott, 1900.

Harrison-Kahan, Lori. "Introduction: Miriam Michaelson, Frontier Feminist." 3–31 in *The Superwoman and Other Writings by Miriam Michelson,* edited by Harrison-Kahan. Detroit: Wayne State University Press, 2019.

Harrison, William Henry. *Discourse on the Aborigines of the Valley of the Ohio.* Cincinnati, 1834.

Harvey, Bruce Allen. *American Geographics: U.S. National Narratives and the Representation of the Non-European World, 1830–1865.* Palo Alto, CA: Stanford University Press, 2001.

Hatch, Nathan O. *The Democratization of American Christianity.* New Haven, CT: Yale University Press, 1989.

Hawthorne, Nathaniel. *The Whole History of Grandfather's Chair.* Boston: Tappen, 1841.

Hay, John. *Postapocalyptic Fantasies in Antebellum American Writing.* New York: Cambridge University Press, 2017.

Hedges, William L. *Washington Irving: An American Study, 1802–1832.* Baltimore: Johns Hopkins University Press, 1965.

Henry, Stuart Clark. *Unvanquished Puritan: A Portrait of Lyman Beecher.* Grand Rapids, MI: Eerdmans, 1973.

Hietala, Thomas. *Manifest Design: Anxious Aggrandizement in Late Jacksonian America.* Ithaca, NY: Cornell University Press, 2003.

Higgins, Andrew. "Evangeline's Mission: Anti-Catholicism, Nativism, and Unitarianism in Longfellow's *Evangeline.*" *Religion and the Arts* 13.4 (1999): 542–560.

Hine, Edward. *Forty-Seven Identifications of Anglo-Saxons with the Lost Tribes of Israel.* New York: Huggins, 1878.

Hixson, Walter L. *American Settler Colonialism: A History.* New York: Palgrave, 2013.

Hjaltalín, Jón Andrésson. *The One Thousandth Anniversary of the Norwegian Settlement of Iceland.* Reykjavik, 1874.

Hoagland, William. *The Whiskey Rebellion: George Washington, Alexander Hamilton, and the Frontier Rebels Who Challenged America's Newfound Sovereignty.* New York: Simon and Schuster, 2010.

Hobsbawm, Eric. "Introduction: Inventing Tradition." 1–14 in *The Invention of Tradition,* edited by Hobsbawm and Terence Ranger. New York: Cambridge University Press, 1983.

Hogan, Mervin B. "A Parallel: A Matter of Chance versus Coincidence." 17–30 in Ethan Smith, *View of the Hebrews* (1823, 1825). Salt Lake City: Utah Lighthouse Ministry, 2008.

Hoganson, Kirsten. *Fighting for American Manhood: How Gender Politics Provoked the Spanish-American War.* New Haven, CT: Yale University Press, 1998.

Hope, James Barrow. "A Poem Which Needs No Dedication." 22–25 in *War Songs of the South,* edited by William G. Shepperson. Richmond: West, 1862.

Horine, Emmet Field. *Daniel Drake: Pioneer Physician of the Midwest.* Philadelphia: University of Pennsylvania Press, 2017.

Horning, Audrey. *Ireland in the Virginian Sea: Colonialism in the British Atlantic.* Chapel Hill: University of North Carolina Pres, 2013.

Horsford, Eben Norton. *The Defenses of Norumbega.* Boston: Houghton Mifflin, 1891.

———. *The Discovery of the Ancient City of Norumbega.* Boston: Houghton Mifflin, 1889.

———. *The Landfall of Leif Ericson, AD 1000 and the Site of His Houses in Vineland.* Boston: Darnell and Upham, 1892.

Horsman, Reginald. *Race and Manifest Destiny: The Origins of American Racial Anglo-Saxonism.* Cambridge, MA: Harvard University Press, 1981.

Howe, Daniel Walker. *What God Hath Wrought: The Transformation of America, 1815–1848.* New York: Oxford University Press, 2007.

Hsu, Hsuan. *Geography and the Production of Space in Nineteenth-Century American Literature.* New York: Cambridge University Press, 2010.

Hudson, Charles. "An Ethnohistorical View." xxxiv–liv in *An Early and Strong Sympathy: The Indian Writings of William Gilmore Simms,* edited by John Caldwell Guilds and Hudson. Columbia: University of South Carolina Press, 2003.

Hunter, Douglas. *The Place of Stone: Dighton Rock and the Erasure of America's Indigenous Past.* Chapel Hill: University of North Carolina Press, 2017.

Hurt, James. *Writing Illinois: The Prairie, Lincoln, and Chicago.* Urbana: University of Illinois Press, 1992.

Igler, David. *The Great Ocean: Pacific Worlds from Captain Cook to the Gold Rush*. New York: Oxford University Press, 2013.

Ignatiev, Noel. *How the Irish Became White*. New York: Routledge, 1995.

Inskeep, Steve. *Jacksonland: President Andrew Jackson, Cherokee Chief John Ross, and a Great American Land Grab*. New York: Penguin, 2015.

Irving, Washington. *The Collected Works of Washington Irving*. 30 vols. Edited by Henry A. Pochmann et al. Madison: University of Wisconsin Press, 1969–86.

Jackson, Helen Hunt. *A Century of Dishonor: A Sketch of the United States Government's Dealing with Some of the Indian Tribes*. New York: Harper Brothers, 1881.

———. *Ramona: A Story*. 2 vols. Boston: Little Brown, 1884.

Jackson, Kent P., and Rex Reeve. Introduction. vii–xxxii in Spaulding.

Jacobson, Matthew. *Barbarian Virtues: The United States Encounters Foreign Peoples at Home and Abroad, 1876–1917*. New York: Hill and Wang, 2000.

———. *Whiteness of a Different Color: European Immigrants and the Alchemy of Race*. Cambridge, MA: Harvard University Press, 1998.

Jebb, Richard. *Studies in Colonial Nationalism*. London: Arnold, 1905.

Jefferson, Thomas. *The Portable Thomas Jefferson*. Edited by Merrill Peterson. New York: Penguin, 1975.

Jenks, William. *A Memoir of the Northern Kingdom*. Boston: Fernand and Malloy, 1808.

Jewett, Sarah Orne. *The Story of the Normans*. 1886. New York: Putnam's, 1905.

Johannsen, Robert Walter. *To the Halls of Montezuma: The Mexican War in the American Imagination*. New York: Oxford University Press, 1985.

Johnson, James Weldon. *The Autobiography of an Ex-Coloured Man*. 1912. New York: Penguin, 1990.

———. "On the Anglo-Saxon Race." 68–74 in *The Selected Writings of James Weldon Johnson*, edited by Sondra Kathryn Wilson, vol. 2, *Social, Political, and Literary Essays*. New York: Oxford University Press, 1995.

Jones, Charles. "The Old Mound" and "Tecumseh." 205–7 in Coggeshall.

Jones, Julia Clinton. *Valhalla: The Myths of Norseland*. San Francisco: Bosqui, 1878.

Jordan, Winthrop. *The White Man's Burden: The Historical Origins of Racism in the United States*. New York: Oxford University Press, 1974.

———. *White over Black: American Attitudes towards the Negro*. Chapel Hill: University of North Carolina Press, 1968.

Jortner, Adam. "Solomon Spaulding's Indians, Or, What the *Manuscript Found* Really Tells Us." *Journal of Mormon History* 38.4 (Fall 2012): 226–47.

Jung, Patrick J. *The Black Hawk War of 1932*. Norman: University of Oklahoma Press, 2007.

Kammen, Michael. *The Mystic Chords of Memory: The Transformation of Tradition in American Culture*. New York: Knopf, 1991.

Kaplan, Amy. "Introduction: The Absence of Empire in American Studies." 2–34 in *Cultures of US Imperialism,* edited by Kaplan and Donald Pease. Durham, NC: Duke University Press, 1993.

Kazanjian, David. *The Colonizing Trick: National Culture and Imperial Citizenship in Early America*. Minneapolis: University of Minnesota Press, 2001.

Kehoe, Alice Beck. *The Land of Prehistory: A Critical History of American Archaeology*. London: Routledge, 1998.

Keller, William F. *The Nation's Advocate: Henry Marie Brackenridge and Young America*. Pittsburgh: University of Pittsburgh Press, 1956.

Kelly, Gary. Introduction. iii–xxvi in *The Selected Poetry and Prose of Lydia Sigourney*, edited by Kelly. Peterborough, ON: Broadview, 2008.

Kennedy, Roger G. *Hidden Cities: The Discovery and Loss of Ancient North American Civilizations*. New York: Macmillan, 1994.

Kerkering, John. *The Poetics of National and Racial Identity in Nineteenth-Century American Literature*. New York: Cambridge University Press, 2003.

Kerrigan, William Thomas. *"Young America": Romantic Nationalism in Literature and Politics, 1843–1861*. Ann Arbor: University of Michigan Press, 1997.

Kessler, Amelia. *Inventing American Exceptionalism*. New Haven, CT: Yale University Press, 2017.

King, Thomas. *The Inconvenient Indian: A Curious Account of Native People in North America*. Minneapolis: University of Minnesota Press, 2012.

Klein, Milton, Richard D. Brown, and John B. Hench, eds. *The Republican Synthesis Revisited*. Worcester, MA: American Antiquarian Society Press, 1992.

Knobel, Dale T. "Celtic Exodus: The Famine, Irish Ethnic Stereotypes, and the Cultivation of American Racial Nationalism." 79–97 in Mulrooney.

Kock, Daniel. *Ralph Waldo Emerson in Europe: Race and Consciousness in the Making of an American Thinker*. London: Tauris, 2012.

Kolodny, Annette. *In Search of First Contact: The Vikings of Vinland, the Peoples of the Dawnland, and the Anglo-American Anxiety of Discovery*. Durham, NC: Duke University Press, 2012.

———. "When the East Was West: Vinland in the American Imaginary." 53–79 in Hamilton and Hilliard.

Konkle, Maureen. *Writing Indian Nations: Native Intellectuals and the Politics of Historiography, 1827–1863*. Chapel Hill: University of North Carolina Press, 2004.

Kramer, Lloyd. *Nationalism in Europe and America: Politics, Cultures, and Identities since 1775*. Chapel Hill: University of North Carolina Press, 2011.

Krauthammer, Barbara. *Black Slaves, Indian Masters: Slavery, Emancipation, and Citizenship*. Chapel Hill: University of North Carolina Press, 2013.

Kribbs, Jayne K., ed. *Critical Essays on John Greenleaf Whittier*. Boston: Hall, 1980.

Krupat, Arnold. *All That Remains: Varieties of Indigenous Expression*. Lincoln: University of Nebraska Press, 2009.

Kulikoff, Allen. *From British Peasants to Colonial American Farmers*. Chapel Hill: University of North Carolina Press, 2014.

Kuppenheimer, C. B. *Albert Gallatin's Vision of Democratic Stability: An Interpretive Profile*. New York: Praeger, 1996.

Kupperman, Karen Ordahl, ed. *America in European Consciousness, 1493–1750*. Chapel Hill: University of North Carolina Press, 1995.

Kutzer, M. Daphne. *Empire's Children: Imperialism in Classic British Children's Books*. London: Routledge, 2010.

Langdon, Samuel. "The Republic of Israelites an Example to the American State." 93–105 in Cherry.

Larkin, Ed. *The American School for Empire*. New York: Cambridge University Press, 2016.

Larson, John Lauritz. *Internal Improvement: National Public Works and the Promise of Popular Government in the Early United States*. Chapel Hill: University of North Carolina Press, 2001.

Lause, Mark A. *Young America: Land, Labor, and Republican Community*. Urbana: University of Illinois, 2005.

Lawson, Alan. "Comparative Studies and Postcolonial Settler Cultures." *Australian/Canadian Studies* 10.2 (1992): 153–59.

Lawson-Peebles, Robert. *Landscape and Written Expression in Revolutionary America*. New York: Cambridge University Press, 1988.

Lears, T. J. Jackson. *No Place of Grace: Antimodernism and the Transformation of American Culture*. Chicago: University of Chicago Press, 1981.

Lee, Michael J. *The Erosion of Biblical Certainty: Battles over Authority and Interpretation*. New York: Springer, 2013.

Lepler, Jessica. *The Many Panics of 1837: People, Politics, and the Creation of a Trans-Atlantic Financial Crisis*. New York: Cambridge University Press, 2013.

Lewis, R. W. B. *The American Adam: Innocence, Tragedy, and Tradition in the Nineteenth Century*. Chicago: University of Chicago Press, 1955.

Liljencrantz, Ottilie Adelina. *Randvar the Songsmith; A Romance of Norumbega*. New York: Harpers Brothers, 1906.

———. *The Thrall of Leif the Lucky, a Story of Viking Days*. Chicago: McClure, 1902.

———. *The Vinland Champions*. New York: Appleton, 1904.

Lippard, George. *The Quaker City: Or, the Monks of Monk Hall*. Philadelphia: Lippard, 1847.

Lipset, Seymour Martin. *The First New Nation: The United States in a Historical and Comparative Perspective*. New York: Norton, 1963.

Lis, Daniel. *Jewish Identity among the Igbo of Nigeria: Israel's Lost Tribe and the Question of Belonging to the Jewish State*. Lagos: Africa World Press, 2015.

Livermore, Harriet. *The Harp of Israel: To Meet the Loud Echo in the Wilds of America*. Philadelphia, 1835.

Livermore, Shaw. *Early American Land Companies: Their Influence on Corporate Development*. Washington, DC: Beard Books, 2000.

Locke, John. *Two Treatises on Government*. 1688. London, 1768.

Logan, Tricia. "Memory, Erasure, and National Myth." 161–209 in *Colonial Genocide in Indigenous North America*, edited by Alexander Hinton, Andrew Woolford, and Jeff Benevenuto. Durham, NC: Duke University Press, 2014.

London, Jack. *A Daughter of the Snows*. New York: Grosset and Dunlap, 1902.

——. "When the World Was Young." 65–91 in *The Night-Born*. New York: Grosset and Dunlap, 1913.

Longfellow, Henry Wadsworth. "The Skeleton in Armor." 89–95 in *Poems*, vol. 1. Boston: Ticknor and Fields, 1842.

Lonnrot, Ernst. *The Kalevala: The Epic Poem of Finland*. Helsinki, 1835.

Lopenzina, Drew. *Through an Indian's Looking Glass: A Cultural Biography of William Apess*. Amherst: University of Massachusetts Press, 2017.

Loughran, Trish. *The Republic in Print: Print Culture in the Age of U.S. Nation Building, 1770–1870*. New York: Columbia University Press, 2007.

Love, Eric. *Race over Empire: Racism and US Imperialism, 1865–1900*. Chapel Hill: University of North Carolina Press, 2004.

Luczak, Ewa Barbara. *Breeding and Eugenics in the American Literary Imagination: Heredity Rules in the Twentieth Century*. London: Palgrave, 2015.

Lush, Rebecca. "The Royal Frontier: Colonist and Native Relations in Aphra Behn's Virginia." 130–60 in Hamilton and Hilliard.

Lyons, Scott Richard. *X-Marks: Native Signatures of Assent*. Minneapolis: University of Minnesota Press, 2010.

MacCarthy, Denis. "The Voyage of St. Brendan." 71–109 in *Ballads, Poems, and Lyrics Original and Translated*. Dublin: McGlashon, 1850.

Mackey, Eva. *Unsettled Expectations: Uncertainty and Settler Decolonization*. Toronto: Fernwood, 2016.

MacLean, John Patterson. *The Mound Builders*. Cincinnati: Clarke, 1876.

Macoun, Alissa, and Elizabeth Strakosch. "The Ethical Demands of Settler Colonial Theory." *Settler Colonial Studies* 3.3–4 (2013): 426–43.

Maddox, Lucy. *Citizen Indians: Native American Intellectuals, Race, and Reform*. Ithaca, NY: Cornell University Press, 2005.

Madsen, Deborah. *American Exceptionalism*. Edinburgh: Edinburgh University Press, 1998.

Maffly-Kipp, Laurie F. Introduction. vii–xxviii in Joseph Smith.

Mallett, Paul Henri. *Northern Antiquities; Or, A Description of the Manners, Customs, Religion, and Laws of the Ancient Danes*. Translated by Thomas Percy. 2 vols. London: Carnan, 1770.

Malone, Lawrence J. *Opening the West: Federal Improvements before 1860*. Westport, CT: Greenwood, 1998.

Mancall, Peter C. *Envisioning America: English Plans for the Colonization of America*. New York: Macmillan, 2016.

——. *Hakluyt's Promise: An Elizabethan's Obsession for an English America*. New Haven, CT: Yale University Press, 2007.

Mann, Barbara. *Native Americans, Archaeologists, and the Mounds*. New York: Lang, 2003.

Marsden, George M. *Fundamentalism in American Culture*. New York: Oxford University Press, 2006.

Marshall, John. Majority opinion in *Cherokee Nation v. Georgia* (1831). 57–60 in *Documents in US Indian Policy*, edited by Francis Paul Prucha. Lincoln: University of Nebraska Press, 2000.

———. Majority opinion in *Johnson and Graham's Lessee v. William McIntosh* (1823). 35–37 in *Documents in US Indian Policy*, edited by Francis Paul Prucha. Lincoln: University of Nebraska Press, 2000.

Martin, Terence. *Parables of Possibilities: The American Need for Beginnings.* New York: Columbia University Press, 1992.

Mathews, Cornelius. *Behemoth: A Legend of the Mound Builders.* New York: Langley, 1839.

May, Robert E. *Manifest Destiny's Underworld: Filibustering in Antebellum America.* Chapel Hill: University of North Carolina Press, 2002.

McCulloh, James H. *Researches in America.* Baltimore, 1816.

McElrath, Joseph, and Jesse S. Crisler. *Frank Norris: A Life.* Urbana: University of Illinois Press, 2006.

McGill, Meredith. *American Literature and the Culture of Reprinting, 1834–1853.* Philadelphia: University of Pennsylvania Press, 2007.

McNiven, Ian S., Lynette Russell, and Kay Schaffer, eds. *Constructions of Colonialism: Perspectives on Eliza Fraser's Shipwreck.* London: University of Leicester Press, 1998.

McWhiney, Grady. *Cracker Culture: Celtic Ways in the Old South.* Tuscaloosa: University of Alabama Press, 1980.

McWilliams, John C., Jr. *The American Epic: Transforming a Genre, 1770–1860.* New York: Cambridge University Press, 1990.

Meigs, General M. C. "Letter to William Seward, 4 April 1867." 31 in *Russian America: A Message from the President of the United States, Andrew Johnson.* Washington, DC, 1868.

Meister, Robert. *After Evil: A Politics of Human Rights.* New York: Columbia University Press, 2012.

Michael, Robert. *A Concise History of American Anti-Semitism.* Lanham, MD: Rowman, 2005.

Michaelsen, Scott. *The Limits of Multiculturalism: Interrogating the Origins of American Anthropology.* Minneapolis: University of Minnesota Press, 1999.

Michaelson, Miriam. "The Cradle." 79–126 in *The Awakening of Zojas.* New York: Doubleday, 1910.

———. "Fayal, the Unforgiving." *The Smart Set: A Magazine of Cleverness* 10.3 (1903): 83–87.

Miles, John David. "Captured by Genre: Mary Rowlandson's Western Imagination on the Nineteenth-Century Frontier." 107–29 in Hamilton and Hilliard.

Miller, Robert J. *Native America, Discovered and Conquered: Thomas Jefferson, Lewis & Clark, and Manifest Destiny.* Westport, CT: Praeger, 2006.

Miller, Robert J., et al., eds. *Discovering Indigenous Lands: The Doctrine of Discovery in the English Colonies.* New York: Oxford University Press, 2010.

Mitchell, Samuel L. "Communication." *Transactions of the American Antiquarian Society* 1 (1820): 313–55.

Moore, David L. *That Dream Shall Have a Name: Native Americans Rewriting History.* Lincoln: University of Nebraska Press, 2013.

Moore, Dennis. "Introduction: Like the Various Pieces of a Mosaik Work Properly Reunited." ix–lxxxvii in *More Letters from the American Farmer*, by J. Hector St. John Crèvecoeur, edited by Moore. Athens: University of Georgia Press, 1995.

Moreton-Robinson, Aileen. *The White Possessive: Property, Power, and Indigenous Sovereignty.* Minneapolis: University of Minnesota Press, 2015.

Morgan, Cecelia. *Building Better Britains? Settler Societies in the British World, 1783–1920.* Toronto: University of Toronto Press, 2017.

Morrison, Toni. *Playing in the Dark: Whiteness and the Literary Imagination.* New York: Vintage, 1993.

Morse, Jedediah. *The History of America in Two Books.* Philadelphia: Dobson, 1795.

———. *Universal Geography.* Philadelphia: Dobson, 1792.

Moses, A. Dirk, ed. *Empire, Colony, Genocide: Conquest, Occupation, and Subaltern Resistance in World History.* London: Berghahn, 2010.

Motley, Warren. *American Abraham: James Fenimore Cooper and the Frontier Patriarch.* New York: Cambridge University Press, 1987.

Mulrooney, Margaret M., ed. *Fleeing in the Famine: North America and Irish Refugees, 1845–1851.* Westport, CT: Greenwood, 2003.

Murphy, Andrew R. *Prodigal Nation: Moral Decline and Divine Punishment from New England to 9/11.* New York: Oxford University Press, 2011.

Murphy, Gretchen. *Shadowing the White Man's Burden: US Imperialism and the Problem of the Color Line.* New York: New York University Press, 2009.

Murray, Laura. "The Aesthetics of Dispossession: Washington Irving and Ideologies of (De-)Colonization in the Early Republic." *American Literary History* 8 (1996): 209–31.

Nash, Roderick. *Wilderness and the American Mind.* New Haven, CT: Yale University Press, 1983.

Neal, John. *American Writers: A Series of Papers Contributed to Blackwoods Magazine (1824–1825).* Edited by Fred Lewis Pattee. Durham, NC: Duke University Press, 1937.

Nellis, Eric. *An Empire of Regions: A Brief History of Colonial British America.* Toronto: Toronto University Press, 2010.

Nelson, Dana D. *National Manhood: Capitalist Citizenship and the Imagined Fraternity of White Men.* Durham, NC: Duke University Press, 1998.

———. *The Word in Black and White.* New York: Oxford University Press, 1989.

Newcomb, Steven. *Pagans in the Promised Land: Decoding the Doctrine of Christian Discovery.* New York: Fulcrum, 2008.

Newman, John B. *The Early Peopling of America and Its Discovery before the Time of Columbus.* Boston: Husted, 1848.

Newton, Michael. "The Atavistic Nightmare: Memory and Recapitulation in Jack London's Ghost and Fantasy Stories." 239–59 in *The Oxford Handbook of Jack London*, edited by Jay Williams. New York: Oxford University Press, 2017.

Nichols, David Andrew. *Red Gentlemen and White Savages: Indians, Federalists, and the Search for Order on the American Frontier.* Charlottesville: University of Virginia Press, 2008.

Nispel, Marcus, dir. *Pathfinder.* 20th-Century Fox, 2007.

Noll, Mark, and Luke E. Harlow, eds. *Religion and American Politics from the Colonial Period to the Present.* 2nd ed. New York: Oxford University Press, 2007.

Nordholt, J. W. Schulte. *The Myth of the West: America as Last Empire.* Grand Rapids, MI.: Eerdmans, 1993.

Norris, Frank. *Moran of the Lady Letty.* New York: Doubleday, 1898.

———. *The Responsibility of the Novelist and Other Literary Essays.* New York: Doubleday, 1903.

Nye, David G. *America as Second Creation: Technology and Narratives of New Beginnings.* Cambridge, MA: MIT Press, 2004.

Oberg, James Edward. *New Earths: Restructuring Earth and Other Planets.* Harrisburg, PA: Stackpole Books, 1981.

O'Brien, Anne. *Philanthropy and Settler Colonialism.* New York: Springer, 2014.

O'Connell, Barry. Introduction. xiii–lxxiii in *On Our Own Ground: The Complete Writings of William Apess, A Pequot,* edited by O'Connell. Amherst: University of Massachusetts Press, 1992.

O'Connor, Stephen. *Orphan Trains: The Story of Charles Loring Brace and the Children He Saved and Failed.* Chicago: University of Chicago Press, 2003.

O'Donoghue, Denis. *Brendaniana: Brendan the Voyager in Story and Legend.* 2nd ed. Dublin: Browne and Nolan, 1895.

Olson, Dana. *The Legend of Prince Madoc and the White Indians.* Jeffersonville, IN: Olson Enterprises, 1987.

Olson, Steven. *The Prairie in Nineteenth-Century American Poetry.* Norman: University of Oklahoma Press, 1995.

O'Meara, John J. *The Voyage of St. Brendan: Journey to the Promised Land.* Gerrard's Cross, England: Smythe, 1991.

Painter, Nell Irvin. *The History of White People.* New York: Norton, 2010.

Park, Benjamin E. *American Nationalisms: Imagining Union in the Age of Revolutions, 1783–1833.* New York: Cambridge University Press, 2018.

Pateman, Carole. "The Settler Contract." 64–91 in *Contract and Domination,* edited by Pateman and Charles W. Mills. Cambridge: Polity Press, 2007.

Paulding, James Kirke. *Letters from the South.* New York: Harper, 1835.

Payne, John Howard. "The Captivity of John Howard Payne." *North American Quarterly Magazine* 7.33 (January 1836): 107–24.

Payne, John Howard, and Sabin Buttrick. *The Payne-Butrick Papers.* Edited and annotated by William L. Anderson, Jane L. Brown, and Anne F. Rogers. 2 vols. Lincoln: University of Nebraska Press, 2010.

———. "The Uses of Adversity." *Ladies Home Companion* 7 (1837): 165–99.

Pearce, Roy Harvey. *Savagism and Civilization: A Study of the Indian and the Idea of Civilization.* 1953. Rev. ed. Berkeley: University of California Press, 1988.

Pearson, David. *The Politics of Ethnicity in Settler Societies: States of Unease.* New York: Springer, 2001.

Pencak, William. *Jews and Gentiles in Early America, 1654–1800.* Ann Arbor: University of Michigan Press, 2005.

Pencak, William, and Daniel Richter. *Friends and Enemies in Penn's Wood: Colonists, Indians, and the Racial Construction of Pennsylvania.* University Park: Pennsylvania State University Press, 2010.

Penn, William. *The Political Writings.* 5 vols. Philadelphia: University of Pennsylvania Press, 1986.

Perdue, Theda. "Introduction." 3–38 in *Cherokee Editor: The Writings of Elias Boudinot,* ed. Perdue. Athens: University of Georgia Press, 1996.

Peterson, Charles F. *DuBois, Fanon, Cabral: The Margins of Elite Anti-Colonial Leadership.* New York: Lexington, 2007.

Peterson, Jacqueline, and Jennifer S. H. Brown. *The New Peoples: Being and Becoming Metis in North America.* Winnipeg: University of Manitoba Press, 1985.

Peyer, Bernd C. *The Tutor'd Mind: Indian Missionary-Writers in Antebellum America.* Amherst: University of Massachusetts Press, 1997.

Philips, A. A. *The Cultural Cringe.* Melbourne: Melbourne University Press, 1950.

Phillips, Jason. *Looming Civil War: How Nineteenth-Century Americans Imagined the Future.* New York: Oxford University Press, 2018.

Pigeon, William. *Traditions of De-Coo-Dah, and Antiquarian Researches.* New York: Thayer, 1858.

Poole, William Henry. *Anglo-Israel: Or the British Nation, the Lost Tribes of Israel.* London: Bengough, 1879.

———. *Fifty Reasons Why the Anglo-Saxons Are the Lost Tribes of Israel.* London: Bengough, 1882.

Popkin, Richard H. "The Rise and Fall of the Jewish Indian Theory." 70–90 in Goldman, *Hebrew and the Bible.*

Powell, Thomas. *The Persistence of Racism in America.* Lanham, MD: Rowman Littlefield, 1993.

Prentice, Chris. "Some Problems of Response to Empire in Settler Postcolonial Societies." 45–59 in *De-Scribing Empire: Post-Colonialism and Textuality,* edited by Chris Tiffin and Alan Lawson. New York: Routledge, 2002.

Price, Kenneth, and Lawrence J. Oliver. *Critical Essays on James Weldon Johnson.* Boston: Hall, 1997.

Priest, Josiah. *American Antiquities and Discoveries in the West.* Albany, NY: Hoffman and White, 1834.

Pugh, Tison. *Queer Chivalry: Medievalism and the Myth of White Masculinity in Southern Literature.* Baton Rouge: Louisiana State University Press, 2013.

Quigley, Paul. *Shifting Grounds: Nationalism and the American South, 1848–1865.* New York: Oxford University Press, 2012.

Quinlan, Kieran. *Strange Kin: Ireland and the American South.* Baton Rouge: Louisiana State University Press, 2005.

Rafinesque, C. S. "The American Nations and Tribes Are Not Jews." *Atlantic Journal and Friend of Knowledge* 1 (1833): 98–101.

———. *Ancient History; or the Annals of Kentucky*. Frankfort, KY, 1824.

Rafn, Carl Christian, ed. *Antiquitates Americanae, sive Scriptores Septentrionales Rerum Ante-Columbianarum, in America*. Copenhagen: Royal Society of Northern Antiquities, 1837.

Rakove, Jack. "Ambiguous Achievement: The Northwest Ordinance." 13–27 in *The Northwest Ordinance: Essays on Its Formulation, Provisions, and Legacy*, edited by Fletcher Williams. East Lansing: Michigan State University Press, 1988.

Randall, Randolph C. *James Hall: Spokesman for the New West*. Columbus: Ohio State University Press, 1964.

Red Jacket (Seneca). "Reply to Cram." 141–45 in *The Collected Speeches of Sagoyewatha, or Red Jacket*, edited by Granville Ganter. Syracuse, NY: Syracuse University Press, 2006.

Regis, Pamela. *Describing Early America: Bartram, Jefferson, Crèvecoeur, and the Influence of Natural History*. Philadelphia: University of Pennsylvania Press, 1999.

Renan, Ernest. "What Is a Nation?" 8–22 in Bhabha, *Nation and Narration*.

Rees, Elizabeth. *Celtic Saints of Ireland*. New York: History Press, 2013.

Reesman, Janet Campbell. *Jack London's Racial Lives: A Critical Biography*. Athens: University of Georgia Press, 2009.

Reynolds, David. *Beneath the American Renaissance: The Subversive Imagination in the Age of Emerson and Melville*. New York: Oxford University Press, 1988.

Richards, Jeffrey, ed. *Imperialism and Juvenile Literature*. New York: Manchester University Press, 1989.

Richter, Daniel K. *Trade, Land, and Power: The Struggle for East North America*. Philadelphia: University of Pennsylvania Press, 2013.

Rifkin, Mark. *Beyond Settler Time: Temporal Sovereignty and Indigenous Self-Determination*. Durham, NC: Duke University Press, 2017.

———. *Manifesting America: The Imperial Construction of U.S. National Space*. New York: Oxford University Press, 2009.

Riskas, Thomas. *Deconstructing Mormonism: An Analysis and Assessment of the Mormon Faith*. Edited by Frank M. Zinder. New York: Atheist, 2011.

Rivera, Luis N. *A Violent Evangelism: The Political and Religious Conquest of the Americas*. Louisville: Westminster / John Knox, 1992.

Robertson, Lindsay. *Conquest by Law: How the Discovery of America Dispossessed Indigenous Peoples of Their Lands*. New York: Oxford University Press, 2005.

Robisch, S. K. *Wolves and the Wolf Myth in American Culture*. Reno: University of Nevada Press, 2009.

Rodriguez, Jaime Javier. *The Literatures of the US-Mexico War: Narrative, Time, Identity*. Austin: University of Texas Press, 2010.

Roediger, David. *The Wages of Whiteness: Race and the Making of the American Middle Class*. New York: Verso, 1991.

Rogers, Jeffrey J. *A Southern Writer and the Civil War: The Confederate Imagination of William Gilmore Simms*. Lewisburg, PA: Bucknell University Press, 2015.

Rogers, Sherbrooke. *Sarah Josepha Hale: A New England Pioneer, 1788–1879.* Boston: Thompson and Rutter, 1985.

Rosaldo, Renato. *Culture and Truth: The Making of Social Analysis.* New York: Beacon, 2001.

Ross, Dorothy. *The Origins of American Social Science.* New York: Cambridge University Press, 1991.

Ross, Marlon B. "Romancing the Nation: The Poetics of Romantic Nationalism." 56–85 in *The Macropolitics of Nineteenth-Century Literature,* edited by Jonathan Arac. Durham, NC: Duke University Press, 1995.

Rossignol, Marie-Jeanine. *The Nationalist Ferment: The Origins of US Foreign Policy, 1789–1812.* Columbus: Ohio State University Press, 2004.

Rowe, John Carlos. *Literary Culture and US Imperialism from the Revolution to the Civil War.* New York: Oxford University Press, 2000.

Rowson, Susanna Haswell. *Reuben and Rachel: A Family History.* 2 vols. New York, 1799.

Rubin-Dorsky, Jeffrey. *Adrift in the Old World: The Psychological Pilgrimage of Washington Irving.* Chicago: University of Chicago Press, 1988.

Russell, Lynette. "Mere Trifles and Faint Representation: The Representations of Savage Life Offered by Eliza Frazier." 51–62 in McNiven, Russell, and Schaffer. et al.

Said, Edward. *Orientalism.* New York: Vintage, 1979.

Sale, Kirkpatrick. *The Conquest of Paradise: Christopher Columbus and the Columbian Legacy.* New York: Hodden and Staughton, 1992.

Sandweiss, Lee Ann. *Seeking St. Louis: Voices from a River City.* St. Louis: Missouri Historical Museum, 2000.

Saxton, Alexander. *The Rise and Fall of the White Republic: Class Politics and Mass Culture in Nineteenth-Century America.* London: Verso, 1990.

Sayre, Gordon. *The Indian Chief as Tragic Hero: Native Resistance and the Literatures of the Americas from Moctezuma to Tecumseh.* Chapel Hill: University of North Carolina Press, 2006.

———. "The Mound Builders and the Imagination of American Antiquity in Jefferson, Bartram, and Chateaubriand." *Early American Literature* 33.3 (Fall 1998), 225–49.

Scheckel, Susan. *The Insistence of the Indian: Race and Nationalism in Nineteenth-Century American Culture.* Princeton, NJ: Princeton University Press, 1998.

Schenck, Theresa. *William W. Warren: The Life, Letters, and Times of an Ojibwe Leader.* Lincoln: University of Nebraska Press, 2007.

Schueller, Malini Johar. *U.S. Orientalisms: Race, Nation, and Gender in Literature, 1790–1890.* Ann Arbor: University of Michigan Press, 1997.

Seelye, John. *Beautiful Machine: Rivers and the Republican Plan, 1755–1825.* New York: Oxford University Press, 1991.

Seitler, Dana. *Atavistic Tendencies: The Culture of Science in American Modernity.* Minneapolis: University of Minnesota Press, 2008.

Shain, Barry Allen. *The Myth of American Individualism: The Protestant Origins of American Political Thought.* Princeton, NJ: Princeton University Press, 1996.

Shalev, Eran. *American Zion: The Old Testament as a Political Text from the Revolution to the Civil War.* New Haven, CT: Yale University Press, 2013.

Shapiro, Henry B., ed. *Physician to the West: Selected Writings of Daniel Drake on Science and Society.* Lexington: University Press of Kentucky, 1970.

Sheehan, Bernard. *Seeds of Extinction: Jeffersonian Philanthropy and the American Indian.* Chapel Hill: University of North Carolina Press, 1973.

Shields, David S. "Cosmopolitanism and the Anglo-Jewish Elite in British America." 143–62 in Shuffelton.

Shields, Juliet. *Nation and Migration: The Making of British Atlantic Literature, 1765–1835.* New York: Oxford University Press, 2016.

Shoemaker, Nancy. *A Strange Likeness: Becoming Red and White in Eighteenth-Century North America.* New York: Oxford University Press, 2004.

Shreve, Thomas H. "To an Indian Mound." 181–82 in Coggeshall.

Shuffelton, Frank, ed. *A Mixed Race: Ethnicity in Early America.* New York: Oxford University Press, 1993.

Sigourney, Lydia. *The Poetical Works.* London: Routledge, 1857.

Silver, Peter. *Our Savage Neighbors: How Indian War Transformed Early America.* New York: Norton, 2009.

Silverberg, Robert. *The Mound Builders.* Athens: Ohio University Press, 1986.

Simms, William Gilmore. *Southward Ho! A Spell of Sunshine.* 2 vols. New York: Redfield, 1854.

———. *Views and Reviews in American Literature, History and Fiction.* 2nd series. 2 vols. New York: Wiley and Putnam, 1845.

Slaughter, Thomas P. *The Whiskey Rebellion: Frontier Epilogue to the American Revolution.* New York: Oxford University Press, 1988.

Slawinski, Scott. *Validating Bachelorhood: Audience, Patriarchy, and Charles Brockden Brown.* New York: Routledge, 2005.

"Sloper, Mace." "Editor's Table." *Knickerbocker Magazine* 58.2 (August 1861): 1–9.

Slotkin, Richard. *Regeneration through Violence: The Mythology of the American Frontier, 1600–1800.* Norman: University of Oklahoma Press, 1973.

Smith, Anthony D. *National Identity.* New York: Penguin, 1991.

———. *Nationalism and Modernism.* London: Routledge, 1998.

Smith, Ethan. *View of the Hebrews; or the Tribes of Israel in America.* 1823, 1825. Salt Lake City: Utah Lighthouse Ministry, 2008.

Smith, Henry Nash. *Virgin Land: The American West as Symbol and Myth.* Cambridge, MA: Harvard University Press, 1950.

Smith, Joseph, trans. *The Book of Mormon* (1830). New York: Penguin, 2008.

Smith, Joshua Toulmin. *The Northmen in New England in the Tenth Century.* Boston: Grey, 1839.

Smith-Rosenberg, Carroll. *This Violent Empire: The Birth of American National Identity.* Chapel Hill: University of North Carolina Press, 2010.

Snydor, Charles S. *The Development of Southern Sectionalism, 1819–1848.* Baton Rouge: Louisiana State University Press, 1966.

Southerton, Simon. *Losing a Lost Tribe: Native Americans, DNA, and the Mormon Church*. Salt Lake City: Signature Books, 2004.

Southey, Robert. *Madoc: A Poem*. Boston: Monroe, 1805.

Spaulding, Solomon. *Manuscript Found: The Complete Original "Spaulding Manuscript."* Edited by Kent P. Jackson. Provo, UT: Brigham Young University Press, 1996.

Spurr, David. *The Rhetoric of Empire: Colonial Discourse in Journalism, Travel Writing, and Imperial Administration*. Durham, NC: Duke University Press, 1993.

Squier, Ephraim G., and Edwin H. Davis. *Ancient Monuments of the Mississippi Valley*. Washington, DC: Smithsonian Institution Press, 1848.

Stafford, Jane, and Mark Williams. *Maoriland: New Zealand Literature, 1872–1914*. Wellington: Victoria University Press, 2006.

Stasiulis, Daiva, and Nira Yuval-Davis, eds. *Unsettling Settler Societies: Articulating Gender, Race, Ethnicity, and Class*. New York: Sage, 1995.

State of New York. *Documents of the Assembly of the State*. 5.243 (10 March 1838): 1–14.

Stein, Allen F. *Cornelius Mathews*. New York: Twayne, 1974.

Stephanson, Anders. *Manifest Destiny: American Expansion and the Empire of Right*. New York: Hill and Wang, 1995.

St. George, Robert. Introduction. 3–29 in *Possible Pasts: Becoming Colonial in Early America*, edited by St. George. Ithaca, NY: Cornell University Press, 2000.

Stoddard, Amos. *Sketches Historical and Descriptive of Louisiana*. Philadelphia: Carey, 1812.

Stone, William. "*Grave of the Indian King*." 203–21 in *Tales and Sketches, Such As They Are*. Boston: Harper and Brothers, 1834.

Streeby, Shelley. *American Sensations: Class, Empire, and the Production of Popular Culture*. Berkeley: University of California Press, 2002.

Street, Nicholas. "The American States Acting over the Part of the Children of Israel in the Wilderness." 67–81 in Cherry.

Sugirtharajah, R. S. *The Bible and the Third World: Precolonial, Colonial, and Postcolonial Encounters*. New York: Cambridge University Press, 2001.

Sullivan, Alexander. "The American Republic and the Irish League of America." *American Catholic Quarterly Review* 9 (1884): 35–45.

Sullivan, Sherry. "The Debate over 'The Indian' in the Nineteenth Century." *American Indian Culture and Research Journal* 9.1 (1985): 13–31.

Sundquist, Eric J. *Empire and Slavery in American Literature, 1820–1865*. New York: Cambridge University Press, 1995.

Swift, Morrison L. *Imperialism and Liberty*. Los Angeles: Rombroke, 1899.

Sword, Wiley. *George Washington's Indian Wars: The Struggle for the Old Northwest*. Norman: University of Oklahoma Press, 1993.

Szatmary, David. *Shays' Rebellion: The Making of an Agrarian Insurrection*. Amherst: University of Massachusetts Press, 1980.

Tawil, Ezra. *The Making of Racial Sentiment: Slavery and the Birth of the Frontier Romance*. New York: Cambridge University Pres, 2006.

Taylor, Bayard. *The Poetical Works*. Household ed. 1880. Boston: Houghton Mifflin, 1907.

———. "America to Iceland." 161–62 in *Poems and Places: Scotland, Denmark, Iceland, Norway, and Sweden*, edited by Henry Wadsworth Longfellow. Boston: Osgood, 1876.

Taylor, William R. *Cavalier and Yankee: The Old South and American National Character.* 1961. New York: Oxford University Press, 1993.

Tennenhouse, Leonard. *The Importance of Feeling English: American Literature and the British Diaspora, 1750–1850.* Princeton, NJ: Princeton University Press, 2007.

Thomas, Ada H. "On to the Southward." *Ladies Repository* 31.3 (1862): 28–29.

Thompson, Daniel P. *Centeola and Other Tales.* New York: Carleton, 1864.

Thulesius, Olav. *The Man Who Made the Monitor: Naval Engineer John Ericcson.* New York: McFarland, 2007.

Thurin, Erik Ingvar. *The American Discovery of the Norse: An Episode in Nineteenth-Century American Literature.* Lewisburg, PA: Bucknell University Press, 1999.

Tiffin, Chris, and Alan Lawson. "Reading Difference." 236–49 in *De-Scribing Empire: Post-Coloniality and Textuality*, edited by Tiffin and Lawson. New York: Routledge, 2002.

Toulmin, Harry. *A Description of Kentucky in North America.* 1793. Edited by Thomas Clark. Lexington: University Press of Kentucky, 1945.

Traxel, William L. *Footprints of the Welsh Indians.* New York: Algora, 2004.

Truett, Samuel. "The Borderlands and Lost Worlds of Early America." 300–324 in *Contested Spaces of Early America*, edited by Juliana Barr and Edward Countryman. Philadelphia: University of Pennsylvania Press, 2014.

Tricomi, Albert H. *Missionary Positions: Evangelism and Empire in American Fiction.* Gainesville: University Press of Florida, 2011.

[Trumbull, John]. *New Travels to the Westward by Alonso Decalves.* New Haven, CT: Springer, 1786.

Trumpener, Katie. *Bardic Nationalism: The Romantic Novel and the British Empire.* Princeton, NJ: Princeton University Press, 1997.

Tucker, Beverley. *The Partisan Leader: A Novel.* Washington, 1836.

Turner, Frederick Jackson. *The Frontier in American History.* New York: Henry Holt, 1921.

Turner, Jack. *Awakening to Race: Individualism and Social Consciousness in America.* Chicago: University of Chicago Press, 2012.

Turner, Sharon. *The History of the Anglo-Saxons.* 3 vols. London: Longman, 1807.

Tuveson, Ernst. *The Redeemer Nation: The Idea of America's Millennial Role.* Chicago: University of Chicago Press, 1968.

Twain, Mark. *Mark Twain's Weapons of Satire: Anti-Imperialist Writings on the Philippine-American War.* Edited by Jim Zwick. Syracuse, NY: Syracuse University Press, 1992.

Tyng, Hattie. "Ruins." 686 in Coggeshall.

Tyrell, Ian, and Jay Sexton. *Empire's Twin: US Anti-Imperialism from the Founding Era to the Age of Terrorism.* Ithaca, NY: Cornell University Press, 2015.

Underwood, Gail Parker. *More Than Petticoats: Remarkable Women of New Hampshire.* Guildford, CT: Globe, 2009.

Underwood, Grant. *The Millennial World of Early Mormonism.* Urbana: University of Illinois Press, 1999.

United States and Democratic Review. "Book Reviews." 30 (1852): 156.

Ural, Susannah, ed. *Civil War Citizens: Race, Ethnicity, and Identity in America's Bloodiest Conflict.* New York: New York University Press, 2010.

———. "Ye Sons of Erin Green Assemble." 99–132 in Ural.

Van Wagoner, Richard. *Sidney Rigdon: A Portrait in Religious Excess.* New York: Signature, 2005.

Venable, William H. *The Beginnings of Literary Culture in the Ohio Valley: Historical and Biographical Sketches.* Cincinnati: Clarke, 1891.

Veracini, Lorenzo. "Introduction: Settler Colonialism as a Distinct Mode of Domination." 1–8 in Cavanaugh and Veracini.

———. *Settler Colonialism: A Theoretical Overview.* London: Palgrave, 2010.

Vizenor, Gerald. *Manifest Manners: Narratives of Post-Indian Survivance.* Lincoln: University of Nebraska Press, 1994.

Waldstreicher, David. *In the Midst of Perpetual Fetes: The Making of American Nationalism, 1776–1820.* Chapel Hill: University of North Carolina Press, 1997.

Walsh, Thom. *History of the Irish Hierarchy.* New York: Sadler, 1854.

Warner, Michael. "What's Colonial about Colonial America?" 49–70 in *Possible Pasts: Becoming Colonial in Early America,* edited by Robert St. George. Ithaca, NY: Cornell University Press, 2000.

Warren, William W. *History of the Ojibway People.* 1885. Minneapolis: Minnesota Historical Society, 1984.

Warrior, Robert. *The People and the Word: Reading Native Nonfiction.* Minneapolis: University of Minnesota Press, 2005.

Watson, Ritchie Devon, Jr. *Normans and Saxons: Southern Race Mythology and the Intellectual History of the American Civil War.* Baton Rouge: Louisiana State University Press, 2008.

Watts, Edward. *An American Colony: Regionalism and the Roots of Midwestern Culture.* Athens: Ohio University Press, 2002.

———. "Exploration, Trading, Trapping, Travel, and Early Fiction, 1780–1850." 9–22 in *A Companion to the Literature and Culture of the American West,* edited by Nicolas Witschi. New York: Blackwell-Wiley, 2012.

———. *In This Remote Country: French Colonial Culture in the Anglo-American Imagination, 1780–1860.* Chapel Hill: University of North Carolina Press, 2006.

———. "In Your Head You Are Not Defeated: The Irish in Aboriginal Literature." *Journal of Commonwealth Literature* 26.1 (1991): 16–33.

———. "Introduction: James Hall and Writing the American Frontier." 2–21 in *The Indian Hater and Other Stories by James Hall,* ed. Edward Watts. Kent, OH: Kent State University Press, 2009.

———. "Settler Postcolonialism as a Reading Strategy." *American Literary History* 22.2 (2010): 459–70.

———. *Writing and Postcolonialism in the Early Republic.* Charlottesville: University Press of Virginia, 1998.

Watts, Edward, and David Rachels, eds. *The First West: Writing from the American Frontier, 1776–1860.* New York: Oxford University Press, 2002.

Bibliography

Wawn, Andrew. *The Vikings and the Victorians: Inventing the Old North in 19th-Century Britain*. Cambridge: Brewer, 2000.

Wawn, Andrew, and Þórunn Sigurðardóttir, eds. *Approaches to Vinland*. Reykjavik: Nordal, 2001.

Weaver, Jace, Craig S. Womack, and Robert Warrior. *American Indian Literary Nationalism*. Albuquerque: University of New Mexico Press, 2005.

Webb, Jim. *Born Fighting: How the Scots-Irish Shaped America*. New York: Broadway, 2004.

Webster, Noah. *A Collection of Essays and Fugitive Writings on Moral, Historical, Political, and Literary Subjects*. Boston: Andrews, 1790.

Weisenburg, Francis Phelps. *Caleb Atwater: Pioneer Politician and Historian*. Cincinnati, 1959.

Wertheimer, Eric. *Imagined Empires: Incas, Aztecs, and the New World of American Literature*. Chicago: University of Chicago Pres, 1999.

Wheaton, Henry. *History of the Northmen, or Danes and Normans, from the Earliest Times to the Conquest of England by William of Normandy*. London: Murray, 1831.

Wheeler, Roxann. *The Complexion of Race: Categories of Difference in Eighteenth-Century England*. Philadelphia: University of Pennsylvania Press, 2000.

White, Ed. "The Ends of Republicanism." *Journal of the Early Republic* 30 (2010): 179–99.

White, Richard. *The Middle Ground: Indians, Empires, and Republics in the Great Lakes Region, 1650–1815*. New York: Cambridge University Press, 1991.

Whittier, John Greenleaf. *The Complete Poetical Works*. Edited by Horace E. Scudder. Cambridge ed. Boston: Houghton Mifflin, 1894.

Wiebe, Robert. *The Opening of the American Mind: From the Adoption of the Constitution to the Eve of Disunion*. New York: Knopf, 1984.

Wilentz, Sean. *The Rise of American Democracy: Jefferson to Lincoln*. New York: Norton, 2005.

Wilkinson, Charles F. *American Indians, Time, and the Law: Native Societies in a Modern Constitutional Democracy*. New Haven, CT: Yale University Press, 1988.

Williams, David. "John Evans: The Welsh Indians." *American Historical Review* 54.2 (January 1949): 277–95.

Williams, Gwyn A. *Madoc: The Legend of the Welsh Discovery of America*. New York: Oxford University Press, 1987.

———. *The Search for Beulah Land*. London: Croom, 1980.

Williams, J. Fletcher. "Memoir of William W. Warren." 9–22 in Warren.

Williams, John. *Further Observations on the Discovery of America by Prince Madog ab Owen Gwynedd About the Year 1170*. London: Brown 1797.

Williams, Stephen. *Fantastic Archaeology: The Wild Side of American Prehistory*. Philadelphia: University of Pennsylvania Press, 1991.

Willis, Lloyd. *Environmental Erosion: The Literary, Critical, and Cultural Politics of "Nature's Nation."* Albany: SUNY Press, 2012.

Wilsey, John D. *American Exceptionalism and Civil Religion: Reassessing the History of an Idea*. Downer's Grove, IL: Intervarsity, 2015.

Winkler, John F. *Fallen Timbers, 1794: The US Army's First Victory.* New York: Osprey, 2013.

Winsor, Justin. *Christopher Columbus: And How He Received and Imparted the Spirit of Discovery.* New York: Houghton Mifflin, 1891.

———. *Narrative and Critical History of the United States.* 8 vols. New York: Houghton, 1889.

Winston, Robert. "Strange Order of Things: The Journey to Chaos in *Letters from an American Farmer.*" *Early American Literature* 19.3 (1984–85): 249–67.

Wolf, Eric. *Europe and the People without History.* Berkeley: University of California Press, 1982.

Wolfe, Patrick. "Settler Colonialism and the Elimination of the Native." *Journal of Genocide Research* 8.4 (2006): 387–409.

Wood, W. Raymond. *Prologue to Lewis and Clark: The Mackey and Evans Expedition.* Norman: University of Oklahoma Press, 2003.

W.P. "Original Poetry: Madoc." *Portfolio* 2 (1806): 123.

Wu, William. *The Yellow Peril: Chinese Americans in American Fiction, 1850–1940.* New York: Archon, 1982.

Wyss, Hilary E. *Writing Indians: Literacy, Christianity, and Native Community in Early America.* Amherst: University of Massachusetts Press, 2000.

Yokota, Kariann Akemi. *Unbecoming British: How Revolutionary America Became a Postcolonial Nation.* New York: Oxford, 2011.

Young, Robert. *White Mythologies: Writing History and the West.* New York: Routledge, 1990.

Young, William H. *Ordering America: Fulfilling the Ideals of Western Civilization.* New York: Xlibris, 2010.

Zuck, Rochelle Raineri. "William Apess and Indigenous Survivance." *Studies in American Indian Literature* 25.1 (Spring 2013): 1–26.

INDEX

Printed in the USA
CPSIA information can be obtained
at www.ICGtesting.com
LVHW102344080823
754630LV00003B/170